Antiquities Smuggling in the Real and Virtual World

This book examines the illicit trade in antiquities, a trade which has increased massively since the destruction and looting of ancient Near Eastern sites in the Middle East. Focusing on the distribution networks for looted antiquities, especially the routes to the West, the book considers the dealers and facilitators who are key in getting the objects to market, explores the methods used that include online marketplaces and social media sites, analyses demand and buyers, revealing that objects are often available at very affordable prices. It outlines the efforts of law enforcement agencies, including the military, and legal systems to contain the trade. Throughout, the book highlights the difficulties of putting a stop to this illicit trade, particularly in a conflict region.

Layla Hashemi is a Postdoctoral Researcher at the Terrorism, Transnational Crime, and Corruption Center at George Mason University, Washington, DC.

Louise Shelley is the Hirst Chair, Professor at the Schar School of Policy and Government and Director of the Terrorism, Transnational Crime, and Corruption Center at George Mason University, Washington, DC.

Routledge Transnational Crime and Corruption

Published in association with the Terrorism, Transnational Crime and Corruption Center, Schar School of Policy and Government, George Mason University, USA

Organized Crime and Corruption in Georgia
Edited by Louise Shelley, Erik Scott and Anthony Latta

Russia's Battle with Crime, Corruption and Terrorism
Edited by Robert W. Orttung and Anthony Latta

Human Trafficking and Human Security
Edited by Anna Jonsson

Irregular Migration from the Former Soviet Union to the United States
Saltanat Liebert

Human Security, Transnational Crime and Human Trafficking
Asian and Western perspectives
Edited by Shiro Okubo and Louise Shelley

Labour Migration, Human Trafficking and Multinational Corporations
The commodification of illicit flows
Edited by Ato Quayson and Antonela Arhin

Environmental Crime and Corruption in Russia
Federal and regional perspectives
Edited by Sally Stoecker and Ramziyá Shakirova

Disengaging from Terrorism – Lessons from the Turkish Penitents
Kamil Yilmaz

The Political Economy of Corporate Raiding in Russia
Ararat Osipian

Corruption and the Russian Economy
How Administrative Corruption Undermines Entrepreneurship and Economic Opportunities
Yulia Krylova

Antiquities Smuggling in the Real and Virtual World
Edited by Layla Hashemi and Louise Shelley

Antiquities Smuggling in the Real and Virtual World

Edited by
Layla Hashemi and Louise Shelley

LONDON AND NEW YORK

First published 2022
by Routledge
2 Park Square, Milton Park, Abingdon, Oxon OX14 4RN

and by Routledge
605 Third Avenue, New York, NY 10158

Routledge is an imprint of the Taylor & Francis Group, an informa business

© 2022 selection and editorial matter, Layla Hashemi and Louise Shelley; individual chapters, the contributors

The right of Layla Hashemi and Louise Shelley to be identified as the authors of the editorial material, and of the authors for their individual chapters, has been asserted in accordance with sections 77 and 78 of the Copyright, Designs and Patents Act 1988.

All rights reserved. No part of this book may be reprinted or reproduced or utilised in any form or by any electronic, mechanical, or other means, now known or hereafter invented, including photocopying and recording, or in any information storage or retrieval system, without permission in writing from the publishers.

Trademark notice: Product or corporate names may be trademarks or registered trademarks, and are used only for identification and explanation without intent to infringe.

British Library Cataloguing in Publication Data
A catalogue record for this book is available from the British Library

Library of Congress Cataloging-in-Publication Data
A catalog record has been requested for this book

ISBN: 978-0-367-90201-8 (hbk)
ISBN: 978-1-032-17128-9 (pbk)
ISBN: 978-1-003-02304-3 (ebk)

DOI: 10.4324/9781003023043

Typeset in Times New Roman
by Taylor & Francis Books

Contents

List of figures		vii
List of tables		ix
List of contributors		x

PART I
Setting the Context | 1

Introduction | 3
LAYLA HASHEMI AND LOUISE SHELLEY

1 The Looting and Trafficking of Syrian Antiquities Since 2011 | 21
NEIL BRODIE

2 Hobby Lobby, the Museum of the Bible and the Law: A Case
Study of the Looting of Archaeological Artifacts from Iraq | 59
PATTY GERSTENBLITH

3 The Hearing Hand: Scribes and Seal Cutters in the Ancient
Near East | 96
IRA SPAR AND ANTONIETTA CATANZARITI

PART II
The Illicit Antiquities Trade | 135

4 Antiquities Trafficking from Syria Along the Northern Route | 137
MAHMUT CENGIZ

5 The Value of Financial Investigations in the Battle Against
Artifact Smuggling | 158
MICHAEL LOUGHNANE

vi *Contents*

6 Working a Case on Looted and Smuggled Ancient Coins as an
  Expert Witness 178
  NATHAN T. ELKINS

PART III
Antiquities Trade in the Cyberworld 191

7 Plenitudinous: An Analysis of Ancient Coin Sales on eBay 193
  UTE WARTENBERG AND BARBORA DMITRIČENKO

8 Investigating the Online Trade of Illicit Antiquities 218
  LAYLA HASHEMI AND ABI WADDELL

Index 240

Figures

1.1	Map of Syria, showing places mentioned in the text	22
1.2	The changing shape of the antiquities trade since 1970, showing how Internet and social media trading have increased the importance of metal detectors and created more opportunities for marketing fakes.	34
2.1	Cuneiform tablet, acquired by Hobby Lobby in 2010–11, returned to Iraq in May 2018	61
2.2	Cuneiform bulla, acquired by Hobby Lobby in 2010–11, returned to Iraq in May 2018	62
2.3	"Gilgamesh Dream Tablet" Museum of the Bible	66
2.4	Empty stand of the "Gilgamesh Dream Tablet" Museum of the Bible	67
2.5	The Phiale of Achyris. Hellenistic, Gold, 23 cm × 4 cm	73
2.6	Cuneiform tablets seized by British authorities for declaration as ceramic tiles in 2011, originated from Umma, Larsa and Irisagrig, and probably looted in 2003 or soon after; returned to Iraq August 2019	73
3.1	Photo of tablets of various shapes. First row (left) from the top: Ur III Sumerian account of expenditures; below an Old Assyrian letter. Second row from the top: Neo-Babylonian record of expenditures of silver; Ur III receipt for a goat; Early Dynstic III (meaning unknown); Old Babylonian loan of silver. Row three from the top: Old Babylonian Private Letter; Achaemenid period field ease. Fourth row from the top: 3 Neo-Babylonian economic tablets: Agreement regarding disposition of slaves; Proxy contract for purchase of a slave; Promisory note for silver	100
3.2	Sumerian, eleven column register of field yields. The tablet is almost a perfect square measuring ca. 12 × 12 inches in size.	101
3.3	Proto-cuneiform tablet with seal impressions: administrative account of barley distribution	102
3.4	Ten joins from tablet fragments. Letter of King Sin-sharra-ishkun to King Nabopolassar	103

viii *List of figures*

3.5	Assyrian ivory and wax writing board found in a well at Nimrud	105
3.5a	A funerary stela of Tarhunpiyas	106
3.6	Detail from a gypsum neo-Assyrian sculptured relief depicting two scribes recording booty(?) from one of Tiglath-Pileser III campaigns into southern Babylonia.	107
3.7	Private letter regarding slaves and the management of a trading company. Tablet with envelope and small "second page" found inside of the case	109
3.8	Lenticular school exercise tablet with a god name Urash	111
3.9	Clay model of a sheep's liver	112
3.10	Gypsum alabaster neo-Assyrian relief, the king with his chief official	113
3.11	Black limestone kudurru reign of Marduk-nadin-ahhe	114
3.12	Clay votive cone of Lipit-Eshtar	116
3.13	Stamped Sumerian brick	117
3.14	Neo-Assyrian eight-sided clay prism (bottom)	118
3.15	Kidney-shaped stamp seal and modern impression with animal motifs	122
3.16	Cylinder seal with three panels showing figures engaging in work activities	122
3.17	Cylinder seal and modern impression with contest scene	124
3.18	Inscribed cylinder seal and modern seal impression with a royal figure and suppliant	125
4.1	Top 20 Turkish provinces with the most antiquities trafficking investigations (ASOD 2018: 49)	144
4.2	Top 20 Turkish provinces with the most antiquities seized from traffickers (ASOD 2018: 50)	145
4.3	Flowchart of small-scale trafficking of Syrian antiquities	148
4.4	Flowchart of large-scale trafficking of Syrian antiquities	149
4.5	Flowchart of antiquities trafficking by Hay'at Tahrir al-Sham (HTS) and the Syrian National Army (SNA) and FSA (Free Syrian Army)	152
5.1	Illicit artifact flow	165
5.2	Windsor antiquities false provenance document	170
5.3	Windsor antiquities false provenance document	171
7.1	Sale of uncleaned ancient coin on Amazon.com	203
7.2	Uncleaned ancient coins from Israel on eBay	204
7.3	Export license accompanying uncleaned ancient coins	205

Tables

3.1	Layout of main differences between genuine seals and forgeries	127
6.1	Legible late Roman bronze coins from the seizure	184
6.2	Legible Byzantine coins from the seizure	184
6.3	Legible Greek coins from the seizure	186
6.4	Legible Roman provincial coins from the seizure	187
6.5	Legible medieval and modern coins from the seizure	187
7.1	Overall coins and lots[22]	201
7.2	Republican coins by metal	202
7.3	Roman imperial coins by metal	202
7.4	Greek coins by metals	202
7.5	Uncleaned ancient coins and lots	203
7.6	Number of ancient coins per series and per price category (March 2016)	206
7.7	Dollar amount of ancient coins per series and price category (March 2016)	206
7.8	Estimate of number of Greek and Roman coins sold on eBay (March 2016)	208
7.9	Number of ancient coins, with subdivisions provided by eBay, accessed on 30 July 2020	209
7.10	Estimate of number of ancient coins sold on eBay (based on figures accessed on 30 July 2020)	209
7.11	Based on Dataset 2: July 2020	210
8.1	Monitoring overview	219
8.2	Online sales monitoring list	220
8.3	Marketplace countries	227

Contributors

Louise Shelley, Ph.D. *Founder and Director, Terrorism, Transnational Crime, and Corruption Center.* Dr. Louise Shelley is the Omer L. and Nancy Hirst Endowed Chair and a University Professor at George Mason University. She is in the Schar School of Policy and Government and directs the Terrorism, Transnational Crime and Corruption Center (TraCCC) that she founded. She is a leading expert on the relationships between terrorism, organized crime and corruption, as well as human trafficking, transnational crime and terrorism, with a particular focus on the former Soviet Union. She also specializes in illicit financial flows and money laundering. She was an inaugural Andrew Carnegie Fellowship, and her newest book, *Dark Commerce*, on illicit trade and sustainability was released this year by Princeton University Press.

Neil Brodie, Ph.D. *Senior Research Fellow, School of Archaeology, University of Oxford.* Dr. Brodie is based at the Endangered Archaeology of the Middle East and North Africa project at the University of Oxford. Over the past twenty years, he has written some of the most important works on the illicit antiquities trade, including studies of the trafficking of Iraqi and Syrian antiquities and the operation of the Internet and auction markets in selling smuggled antiquities. Dr. Brodie is networked to the major stakeholder communities involved in this issue.

Patty Gerstenblith, J.D., Ph.D. *Distinguished Research Professor at DePaul University College of Law.* Dr. Gerstenblith is a respected expert on antiquities and the law, as well as Director of DePaul's Center in Art, Museum and Cultural Heritage Law and member of the Steering Group of the American Bar Association's International Art and Cultural Heritage Law Committee. She is the founding president of the Lawyers' Committee for Cultural Heritage Preservation. In 2011 she was appointed by President Barack Obama to chair the U.S. State Department's Cultural Property Advisory Committee to which she had previously been appointed by President Bill Clinton. The fourth edition of her casebook, *Art, Cultural Heritage and the Law*, was published in 2019. She received her J. D. from Northwestern University and Ph.D. from Harvard University.

Before joining DePaul, she served as a clerk to the Honorable Richard D. Cudahy of the Seventh Circuit Court of Appeals.

Ira Spar, Ph.D. *Professor of Ancient Studies, Ramapo College of New Jersey.* Dr. Spar is an ancient historian and Assyriologist, an expert on the reading and interpretation of Babylonian and Sumerian cuneiform texts. For many years he was the Research Assyriologist in the Department of Ancient Near Eastern Art at The Metropolitan Museum of Art in New York City where he edited and published the Museum's complete collection of cuneiform texts.

Antonietta Catanzariti, Ph.D. *Scholar and Assistant Curator for Ancient and Near Eastern Art, Freer Sackler Galleries.* Dr. Catanzariti is the Robert and Arlene Kogod Secretarial Scholar and Assistant Curator for the ancient Near East, at the Freer Gallery of Art and Arthur M. Sackler Gallery, the Smithsonian's National Museum of Asian Art. She is a specialist in the archaeology and art of the ancient Near East and has performed extensive archaeological field work in the region, including Jordan, Syria, Lebanon, and most recently, in Iraqi Kurdistan where she is currently running an excavation project in the Qara Dagh district. She writes and lectures on topics related to her research in the field and on the study of ancient forms of interactions and trade.

Mahmut Cengiz, Ph.D. *Research Scholar, TraCCC.* Dr. Mahmut Cengiz is Assistant Professor and Research Faculty with Terrorism, Transnational Crime and Corruption Center (TraCCC) and the Schar School of Policy and Government at George Mason University. Dr. Cengiz has international field experience where he has delivered capacity building and training assistance to international partners in the Middle East, Asia and Europe. He also has been involved in the research projects for the Brookings Institute, the European Union, and various U.S. agencies. Dr. Cengiz regularly publishes books, articles and Op-eds on Syrian conflict, terrorism, transnational crime and corruption issues in the Middle East. His recent 2019 book, *The Illicit Economy in Turkey: How Criminals, Terrorists, and the Syrian Conflict Fuel Underground Economies*, analyzes the role of criminals, money launderers and corrupt politicians, and discusses the involvement of ISIS and al-Qaida-affiliated groups in the illicit economy. He is teaching Terrorism and American Security Policy courses at George Mason University, USA.

Michael Loughnane, CFE, CAMS *Founder and President, Loughnane Associates, LLC.* Mr. Loughnane is a former special agent and senior manager who has led complex procurement fraud, public integrity, cybercrime and information security investigations in several departments of the US Government. For the past six years he has developed and led counter terror finance training programs for the Department of Defense, including US law enforcement agencies and military/intelligence community

xii *List of contributors*

members. Mike presents internationally about financial investigations to law enforcement and the professional community and brings extensive knowledge in the design and delivery of training programs.

Nathan T. Elkins, Ph.D. *Associate Professor and Director of the Allbritton Art Institute, Baylor University.* Dr. Elkins' research areas and expertise include Roman art, coinage and coin iconography, topography and architecture, sport and spectacle, and the illicit antiquities trade. He is a Fellow of the Society of Antiquaries of London, the Royal Numismatic Society and the American Numismatic Society. He has published and lectured broadly and participated in fieldwork in the Middle East.

Ute Wartenberg, D.Phil., FSA *Research Curator, The American Numismatic Society; Adjunct Member, Department of Classics, Columbia University.* Dr. Wartenberg is a specialist in ancient Greek numismatics and history. She is Research Curator at the American Numismatic Society after having served for two decades as its Executive Director. Her scholarly interests focus on ancient Greek coins, in particular of the Archaic and Classical period, cultural property and provenance issues, and the history of collecting antiquities and ancient coins. Dr. Wartenberg was a Rhodes Scholar at Oxford University and worked at the British Museum as a curator of Greek coins. She serves on the Committee of the International Numismatic Council and is Chairperson of ICOM's International Committee for Money and Banking Museums.

Barbora Dmitričenko *Archaeologist & Researcher.* Barbora Dmitričenko's first contribution to the field of antiquities trafficking was an award-winning dissertation for the University of Reading, in which she analyzed the looting of archaeological sites and museums during recent conflicts in Iraq and Egypt. She later received an Academic Excellence Scholarship for the International Cultural Heritage Law course in Geneva and collaborated with academics based in the UK and the US. In the course of research, she began to develop a methodology for the online investigation of the illicit trade of antiquities, which she continues to refine to this day. Barbora's work puts a strong emphasis on the impact of the destruction of cultural sites on modern identities and wellbeing, as well as on the social and economic benefits that an ethical and sustainable consumption of heritage can have. She joined the CLASI team as a Research Advisor at the beginning of 2018.

Layla M. Hashemi, Ph.D. *Researcher and Data Analyst, Terrorism, Transnational Crime, and Corruption Center.* Dr. Hashemi is a research assistant at George Mason University's Terrorism, Transnational Crime and Corruption Center (TraCCC). Ms. Hashemi received her Ph.D. from George Mason University in Public Policy and her M.A. from New York University in International Relations and Middle Eastern and Islamic Studies. Ms. Hashemi has worked for various organizations including Forum 2000 and *The Journal of Civil Society*. She is currently Adjunct Professor of Political Science at Montgomery College where she teaches a variety of courses including Comparative Politics, International Conflict Resolution and a course she helped develop on Global Human Rights. Her current research focuses on illicit trade, human trafficking and corruption in the Middle East and North Africa (MENA).

Abi Waddell *Security and Research Specialist.* Ms. Waddell is an experienced information consultant and researcher, with an extensive background in both the ancient history of the Middle East and information security and law enforcement fields, particularly in data gathering, security reviews and testing, threat assessment and open source investigations. Ms. Waddell has experience obtaining information using advanced non-invasive techniques, including data leakage of sensitive information from public sources, in addition to conducting research of online antiquities markets. She holds degrees in Cuneiform and Ancient Near Eastern Studies with foci on Akkadian and Sumerian grammar and literature, ancient Near Eastern history and cuneiform tablet autopsy from the University of Birmingham, UK, and Egyptology from the University of Liverpool, UK.

Part I
Setting the Context

Introduction

Layla Hashemi and Louise Shelley

With the recent intensive destruction and looting of ancient Near Eastern sites in the Middle East, the illicit trafficking of artifacts deriving from countries such as Syria and Iraq have flooded onto the illegal art market and online auction platforms. This has caused irreparable damage and loss to the cultural heritage of the people of these countries and the international community. Therefore, our ability to advance our understanding of history in this region, often referred to as the cradle of civilization, represents a future loss to the shared history of mankind. The accelerated destruction of recent years is a manmade act whose consequences will only be understood in coming decades as we fully appreciate the loss of ancient material culture to our understanding of history.

There are clear patterns to this destruction and trade. Illicit trade in antiquities grows at times of conflict. This is not exclusively a problem of the Middle East, the focus of this collection. The problem of the illegal trade of antiquities is also underway in North and West Africa, regions also affected by terrorism, conflict and instability (Stanyard and Dhaouadi 2020).

The illicit antiquities trade, as will be discussed in the book's chapters, involves diverse actors along the supply chain ranging from amateurs, criminals and terrorists who are involved in the massive looting that have left the region pockmarked by the hasty digging and excavation of coins, tablets, jewelry and household items of antiquity. Dealers and facilitators are key in delivering objects to market. At certain periods, these actors operate as individuals or networks of illicit entrepreneurs, at other points they have functioned under license from ISIS and other terrorist groups (Sargent et al. 2020;15; Westcott 2020). This volume examines diverse actors, routes and methods of sales as well as the means that military, law enforcement and legal systems use to address and investigate and disrupt this trade. It addresses the networks behind this illicit trade and the convergence of illicit trade with the legitimate economy as recognized art sellers market these looted goods and online marketplaces facilitate their sale.

The antiquities market is a small share of the global illicit economy. But there are some illicit items traded for which the value of the object does not reflect the loss. These priceless items are non-renewable and irreplaceable.

DOI: 10.4324/9781003023043-2

4   *Louise Shelley and Layla Hashemi*

For example, in the wildlife trade, the tusks of a rhino may be sold for several hundred thousand dollars, a significant sum but nothing compared to the extinction of a species which is advanced by the killing of the animal. A similar analogy may be made for the antiquities trade. The sale of looted ancient coins on a website may yield considerably less profit than a rhino tusk but the loss to our historical understanding is great. The looting of ancient sites and the sale and dispersion of objects such as coins undermines our ability to understand history, the nature of trade and the interactions among peoples since antiquity. The money derived from this loss is inconsequential compared to the shared loss of our understanding of history and culture.

This volume on illicit antiquities trade is unique. Its authors come from a variety of fields providing a truly multi-disciplinary perspective. Yet it is also distinctive in its historical scope in that it spans over four millennia from the illicit trade in antiquities to the modern cyber-enabled trade in antique art and coins that has vastly increased in recent decades, particularly the last ten years. The ancient coin market is an integral part of the antiquities trade and is indeed the largest part of it in terms of volume (Elkins 2008, 2012).

Experts of ancient history reveal that the history of crime in the ancient Middle East has remarkable similarities to the present. We find that human beings since antiquity have engaged in smuggling and illicit trade. School children learn about the raiders of tombs in ancient Egypt who stole valuable items from the burial sites of previous civilizations. Neither is counterfeiting a new phenomenon as even in ancient times commodities were counterfeited to enhance profits and increase market share. As historians Ira Spar and Antonietta Catanzariti write in their chapter,

> During the Neo-Babylonian period (6th century B.C.E.), priests of the temple of the Sun god in the ancient city of Sippar, forged a stone monument purported to be from the time of Manishtushu, king of Akkad (23rd century B.C.E.) granting the priests the rights to certain lands and privileges. The text ended with the statement, "this is not a lie."[1]

Forgeries also date back millennia. Spar and Catanzariti point out with lively quotes from ancient documents that illicit traders have historically evaded law enforcement personnel and trade regulators to enhance profits and engage in forbidden sales.

Smuggling and tax evasion were common in ancient times. Merchant letters reveal that smugglers bribed guards, deceived customs officials by making false import declarations, and mixed cleared goods with non-taxed merchandise to avoid additional import payments. Houses were raided by government officials to find smuggled goods and smugglers' penalties ranged from a fine to house arrest or even possible incarceration.

The chapters of this book reveal that with present day antiquities smuggling we are dealing with a problem of transnational crime. As in many other

Introduction 5

forms of illicit trade, antiquities smugglers and sellers rely on false documents and forgeries. They falsify the provenance of the objects and many have perfected the art of copying faithfully from the originals. Free-trade zones are often key elements of the supply chain to obscure the origins and the goods. Sometimes, the objects are stored in free trade zones or warehouses for extended periods, the sellers hoping that the stolen object recedes from the memory of the source country or law enforcement that has pursued it.

Looted antiquities may also be laundered as they are combined with the goods sold by licensed dealers. Dr. Gerstenblith discusses the central role played by Israeli dealers in the sale of antiquities in the famous Hobby Lobby case (Department of Justice 2017). After a recent discovery of many stolen antiquities in Israel, Amir Ganor, head of the theft prevention unit at the Israel Antiquities Authority, commented on Israel that

> It is one of the only countries around the Mediterranean basin where the law enables antiquities merchants to obtain a license to sell. At the moment, there are 47 licensed antiquities dealers. So, if one has illegal antiquities and slips them into the inventory of a licensed trader, they're effectively whitewashed.
>
> (Schuster 2021)

Like many other illicit commodities, the illicit antiquities trade involves cross-border networks that blend elements of the legal and illegal commercial world. These networks may smuggle much more than antiquities. While working against nuclear smuggling in Turkey in the early 2000s, one contributor to this collection had his counter-proliferation unit uncover an antique object moved along with nuclear materials. Although this convergence of crimes is rarely so lethal, antiquities can easily pass through borders when the wheels have already been greased and border and customs officials will turn a blind eye to the passage of contraband. Therefore, corruption is absolutely key to the movement of looted and smuggled antiquities.

Yet the antiquities trade is distinctive from other forms of illicit trade with which it may intersect. Many of the buyers in this world of high-end illegal antiquities are powerful and wealthy individuals, as Patty Gerstenblith's chapter reveals. Moreover, high end items can be purchased from high-end dealers who differ dramatically from the transnational criminals who control the drug and human trafficking trade. Much of the analysis focuses on the supply chains flowing to western countries but successful examples of countering the trade reveal a broader range of destinations. In case studies reported to a recent G20 meeting hosted by Italy on the protection of cultural heritage and illicit trafficking, speakers reported on successful investigations involving the Middle East and Far East Asia which are different from the analyses presented in this book.

6 *Louise Shelley and Layla Hashemi*

International cooperation also involves the return of cultural objects to their country of origin. For example in 2019, the Kingdom of Saudi Arabi, represented by the Saudi Commission for Tourism and National Heritage (SCTH) the country returned historical Iraqi documents in implementation of the 1970 UNESCO Convention on the Means of Prohibiting and Preventing the Illicit Import, Export and Transport of Ownership of Cultural Property which was ratified by Saudi Arabia in 1976 (*Saudi Gazette* 2019; Almalaq 2021).

A very complex transnational case was successfully investigated by French authorities as antiquities trafficked from the Middle East transited through a major French airport. In a joint investigation by French police and customs in cooperation with customs and law enforcement in Lebanon and Thailand, investigators were able to identify individuals involved in the supply chain trafficking Syrian stones from Lebanon to Thailand through France. The stones were identified by experts at the Louvre Museum as likely coming from a Christian church in Syria, though the particular church was unknown, with a destination of a gallery in Thailand. Cooperation between French judicial investigators and police specializing in cultural property and counterfeits revealed suppliers in the Middle East and the recipients in Thailand. Using Lebanon customs information, investigators identified the sender of the stones as a Syrian citizen based in Lebanon and Turkey who had recently sent stones from Lebanon to Thailand. With Thai police information, investigators identified associates of a Bangkok art gallery affiliated with Afghanistan, Pakistan and Iran. In France, investigators also identified a French man with connections to Thailand who likely facilitated the trafficking of the stones (Payraud 2021). This complex network reveals the truly international cooperation needed to address the antiquities trade that can follow circuitous routes to its destination.

The cyber environment has democratized the antiquities trade. Previously, the trade consisted of niche networks of those associated with galleries and auction houses. While the trade was transnational, there were high barriers to entry preventing the average person from becoming involved. Today's antiquities market has been democratized by the internet and online platforms that allow for the free and often open sale of cultural property and the availability of ancient goods, particularly coins, often at affordable prices. Therefore, what was once a high-end and exclusive commodity is now available to a wide-ranging customer base. This is discussed in Chapter 8 "Investigating the Online Trade of Illicit Antiquities" and is a particular focus of the Hashemi and Waddell.

Despite the expansion of buyers and sellers, illegal antiquities sales have not been prioritized by law enforcement in the United States or Europe, the intended markets for these ancient goods, as Michael Loughnane's chapter and several other authors reveal. This has encouraged the looting of historical sites in the Middle East as there are almost no consequences for anyone participating in this activity along the entire supply chain. In fact, in some locales in the Middle East, as will be discussed by Loughnane in this book, there is literally "looting on order" as looters fill orders for high end items. Looting to order is much rarer because it is focused on valuable antiquities rather than mass markets. This contradicts the RAND report which claims that there is no evidence of looting to order transactions being fulfilled (Sargent et al. 2020; 60).

The victims of the antiquities trade are very different from those of other forms of transnational crime. Individuals who trade in antiquities or buy them often do not suffer personal physical harm as they do from the illicit drug trade in human trafficking or the online market of counterfeit pharmaceuticals where substandard diabetic or oncological drugs may cause substantial harm. Apart from the absence of risk, those who participate in this trade may even derive substantial pleasure and profit from their transactions. There is, however, a major victim of antiquities trade. It is the human collective that loses its history, its ability to learn about and appreciate the past. Its victims are like that of environmental crime, illegal logging, fishing and wildlife poaching – all of humanity. This volume seeks to reach the many who are concerned with the mass destruction of our common heritage.

The Market for Antiquities

The antiquities market is what is known as a grey market where licit and illicit goods are mixed, making it difficult to detect the difference. There is a long international history of policy makers and law enforcement ignoring the conflict-driven trafficking of antiquities from Syria and other countries, laying the groundwork for post-2011 looting. The trade in looted or illicit antiquities takes place transnationally with objects moving from source through transit and ultimately onto destination markets. While in transit, freeports are often used to launder artifacts and falsify their provenance and accompanying documents. Neil Brodie's Chapter 1 discusses this in regard to the Geneva freeport (Koltrowitz and Arnold, 2016). While some research has been conducted on source and transit countries, little attention has been paid to destination markets.

There is not one country or group of citizens who are especially associated with the purchase of antiquities. But Americans, with their fascination with the Bible and religion, are particularly associated with the purchase of antiquities from the Middle East. Many Americans are also passionately interested in antique coins as Nathan Elkins, Ute Wartenberg and Barbora Dmitričenko discuss in their chapters. More niche markets also exist in ancient tablets as Spar and Catanzariti discuss in Chapter 3. These two areas of antiquities are special foci of several of our contributors, and American interest in these elements of ancient material culture results in a very lively virtual market in these items.

American's role in the antiquities market is just part of their significant involvement in the global arts market. "The U.S. remains the world's largest

8   *Louise Shelley and Layla Hashemi*

art market, valued at $26.6 billion and accounting for 42 percent of the global total in 2017. The European art and antiquities market, a close second, accounts for nearly $23 billion annually" (Antiquities Coalition 2018). American interest in art and antiquities continues to rise, with the U.S. comprising 44 percent of the global art market in 2019 (Portman and Carper 2020; 2). Although there is demand for antiquities in the Middle East and Asia (Sargent et al. 2020; 90), this market is smaller, and less understood. The western and online markets, as our contributors show, are key to the current proliferation of illicit trade in antiquities (Al-Azm and Paul 2018). Thus, educating western buyers as to the perils of the antiquities market is key.

Marketing of many detected looted antiquities has occurred through elaborate supply chains that bring the items to western purchasers as well as Middle Eastern markets. The supply chains for these antiquities are examined in several chapters. Neil Brodie focuses on the looting of Syrian antiquities since 2011. Mahmut Cengiz (Chapter 4) focuses on the role of Turkey as a transit state along transnational trade routes. Michael Loughnane (Chapter 5) focuses on the characteristics of the supply chain from source to point of sale. Patty Gerstenblith's (Chapter 2) discussion of the Hobby Lobby case reveals the international supply chain behind this trade.

Wartenberg, Dmitričenko, Waddell and Hashemi pay special attention to the role of online marketplaces in this trade. The anonymity of online marketplaces and the use of online payment methods and platforms has allowed new purchasers to access and buy antiquities on an unprecedented scale. Dr. Layla Hashemi and Abi Waddell (Chapter 8) analyze the online trade and the use of social media to sell antiquities. They also examine the extent to which the dark web is used in this trade, concluding that the dark web plays a limited role as there is no reason to go to this less accessible platform as there is little effort to curtail online sales on the open web. The trade has clearly democratized as coins have entered the online market in enormous numbers as Ute Wartenberg and Barbora Dmitričenko explain. Ancient coins, cylinder seals and cuneiform objects are now available for sale often at very affordable prices online because of a significant increase in supply as millions of coins have been dug up in recent years from ancient Middle Eastern sites.

Many online buyers who are not sophisticated and knowledgeable have been defrauded. Therefore, the democratization of the market allows for many more potential purchases of fake merchandises. As Chapters 7 and 8 reveal, counterfeits have proliferated in online markets along with genuine coins and other antiquities.

Buyers are often ready purchasers of these ancient items sold by seemingly legitimate online sellers. The ease with which individuals can now purchase antique coins and other cultural artifacts online divorces them from the destruction that is associated with their acquisition. An online platform desensitizes the purchaser from the illicit networks (criminal, terrorist and insurgent) that are often associated with the looting, transport and profit from this trade. Much emphasis is placed within the cultural property

Introduction 9

community on repatriating objects instead of focusing on eliminating this illicit trade and the terrorist financing associated with it as mentioned by Hashemi and Waddell in Chapter 8.

Buyers who are new to the antiquities market need to understand the questionable provenance of many goods they acquire and who may be profiting from this grey and illicit trade. Regardless of location, many buyers have minimal interest in provenance and have a relaxed attitude towards policies and standards that prohibit and prevent the sale of illicit antiquities. The problem of provenance cannot be overstated. The lack or falsification of documents outlining ownership history and place of origin is one of the single biggest challenges in tracking antiquities supply chains. With artifacts misrepresented in often fraudulent or falsified customs and sales documents, these trafficked and illicit objects are traded with impunity as buyers often fail to understand the negative consequences of their purchases.

The Origins of this Volume

In 2017, the Terrorism, Transnational Crime and Corruption Center (TraCCC) at George Mason University was awarded a grant by the U.S. State Department to examine the looting and trade of antiquities from Iraq and Syria. The project brought together a diverse international and multidisciplinary team that has continued to work together even after the project ended in 2019. This volume combines not only the expertise of specialists in antiquities but also that of those who have experience in combating this illicit trade either on the ground in the Middle East or as experts in courtrooms in the West. Their multidisciplinary expertise (antiquities, crime, cyber, legal, law enforcement and military) sets this volume apart from other studies on the illicit antiquities trade in using a much broader range of expertise. The chapters provide careful technical analysis of the marketplace and cover topics and insights not available elsewhere in the academic literature (Brodie and Walker Tubb 2002; Brodie 2006; Green and Mackenzie 2009; Charney 2016; Chappell and Hufnagel 2017; Anderson 2017; Hufnagel and Chappell 2019). It incorporates cutting edge research methods applied to the new technology that has greatly enhanced the illicit and grey antiquities trade. The book provides important insights on the use of information technology, online platforms and social media to perpetuate the global trade of illicit antiquities. Therefore, the research that is presented here reflects up to date analyses of trends in the illicit antiquities trade as well the legal response to the problem.

The project was referred to as CLASI (Countering the Looting of Antiquities from Syria and Iraq). Significant attention was given, and is reflected in this volume, to illicit trade in ancient coins and cuneiform as these (small objects) are heavily represented in the online trade and the ongoing looting and smuggling. This research is distinguished from recent works which did not include coins as we place great emphasis on the trade in coins, a very significant element of the antiquities trade. The commercial dominance of ancient coins, especially in online marketplaces, also represents a particular challenge as it often represents the convergence of the licit and illicit trade.

Interdisciplinary analysis and a wide range of skills are needed to unravel the routes, commodities and participants in illicit antiquities markets. The CLASI project examined how the market has changed in recent decades with the development of online platforms that facilitate communications and sales. The difficulties in countering the sale of these products is complicated not only by the scale of the phenomenon online, but also by the absence of legal authority in the conflict region where these antiquities have originated. This work focused on Iraq and Syria but conflict regions in Africa and Asia which are also sources for illicit antiquities (Stanyard and Dhaouadi 2020).

Various online sales platforms provide novice enthusiasts with easy access to the trade, often with low barriers to entry. Platforms such as Facebook allow traffickers to reach a large audience with a casual interest in antiquities, thus normalizing the idea of looting for profit (Sargent et al. 2020). These online venues range from private Facebook groups as reported by the Antiquities Trafficking and Anthropology Research Project (ATHAR) to fora used to discuss the authenticity and value of specific items. While Facebook recently announced a ban of the sale of historical artifacts, ATHAR, the Alliance to Counter Crime Online (ACCO), the Terrorism, Transnational Crime and Corruption Center (TraCCC) and others have shown that antiquities traffic on Facebook still occurs, and in some instances are part of a crime–terror nexus, funding terrorist activity through the revenues earned through the sale of looted and trafficked artifacts (Al-Azm and Paul 2019; Brodie et al. 2019).

The research conducted by the CLASI team found no evidence of antiquities trafficking on the dark web despite searches in multiple languages including Arabic, Farsi, Kurdish and Turkish. But the research team did find extensive use of open source technology throughout the supply chain. Buyers and sellers use marketplaces on the open web to conduct their trade with impunity. For example, online marketplaces allow for convenient and often anonymous transfer of goods. We also found that despite the lack of antiquities trade on the dark web, encrypted communication technology (WhatsApp, Telegram, Signal) were critically important not only for supporting the supply chain but also for conducting investigations, confirming previous findings of antiquities activity on encrypted channels (Sargent et al. 2020). Discussion of online marketplaces and monitoring methodologies can be found in Chapters 7 and 8 of this volume. Several of the chapters mention the use of person-to-person encrypted messaging by dealers as well as for a member of our research team to conduct interviews with actors involved in the trade.

Explaining a Lack of Dark Web Trade

While there are many explanations for why antiquities trafficking does not take place on the dark web, the simple answer is that it does not need to.

The dark web is often thought of as the dangerous underbelly of the internet. While much of the activity and content on the dark web is not illegal, the sales that take place through darknet marketplaces are over-whelmingly comprised of drugs, weapons and images of child abuse and exploitation. In 2017, approximately 80 percent of annual darknet sales revenues came from drugs (Denton 2017). An earlier study examining the content of nearly 3,000 dark web sites found that 57 percent hosted illicit content such as drugs or child pornography (Whitwam 2016). These transactions are facilitated by bullet proof payment processes that tailor their services to protect merchants and prevent detection of their illicit activity (Tian et al. 2018).

The dark web is popular with criminals because it allows for increased anonymity and privacy to conduct illicit trade, permitting them to avoid detection by law enforcement and other regulators. Because the illicit sale of antiquities can take place on open and often publicly available platforms with little risk to vendors or buyers, there is simply no need for antiquities sellers to advertize on the dark web when they can reach a larger market on social media platforms and online fora. As Neil Brodie explains, there is no need to sell on the dark web because trafficked antiquities can be sold openly on publicly accessible websites with seemingly little risk to vendors (Brodie 2017; 5; Sargent et al. 2020; 43). Dark web transactions are based on trust, which takes time to build. An additional obstacle of dark web trade is the high level of technical skill needed to access and enter these closed communities where illicit trade occurs (Shelley 2018; 141–142).

The trade in antiquities remains a relatively niche market and is often based on personal connections. Despite the high level of discretion in the trade, buyers often want to know who they are purchasing from, something anonymous dark web transactions do not permit. Major measures were adopted by the US Congress in late 2020, including introducing financial transparency measures into the arts and antiquities market. These new leg-islations adopted as part of the National Defense Authorization Act expan-ded the US's Bank Secrecy Act (BSA) to apply to the antiquities market (Small 2021). There was significant impetus for this legislation as the U.S. Senate Permanent Subcommittee on Investigations released a report in July 2020 showing how Kremlin-associated oligarchs utilized art to move large amounts of money through the US financial system. The Senate Sub-committee report called for Congress to amend the Bank Secrecy Act to add businesses handling high-value art to ensure that wealthy bad actors cannot use valuable works of art to evade US sanctions (Portman and Carper, 2020; 14). The legislation effecting this change occurred within six months. With greater scrutiny of the antiquities market, trade on open platforms may be disrupted and sellers may shift the trade into more private channels that protect the practices and payment processes of illicit transactions.

Contents of the Volume: Antiquities Edited Volume Chapter Summaries

The volume combines eight chapters divided into three parts: Setting the Context, The Illicit Antiquities Trade and Antiquities Trade in the Cyberworld. The initial section is set by archaeologists and historians who have insight into the structure of markets, the history of illicit trade in antiquities and recent developments. This analysis is brought to life by lively cases and examples that show not only the absence of novelty of the problem but also its recent acceleration in the contemporary period of serious conflict in the Middle East.

The volume begins with Dr. Neil Brodie's "The Looting and Trafficking of Syrian Antiquities since 2011" (Chapter 1) which explains how over the past thirty years, technological and political developments have increased the trade's commercial reach and destructive potential, radically altering the nature of material being traded. Syria's 4,500 documented archaeological sites make the country one of the largest source countries for antiquities in the world (Shelley and Metz 2017; 79). The looting of antiquities has been a scourge throughout history, especially in times of war. But over the past decade there have been changes in technology – especially in excavation, transport and marketing via social media and the internet – that have expanded and globalized the trade, making it easier for non-experts to reap the profits.

The opening chapter by Dr. Brodie looks at the current state of the trade in looted antiquities from Iraq and Syria, the role of new technologies that make it easier for terrorists and criminal groups to profit and new ways to track and disrupt terrorist involvement in the trade. Looting and trafficking of antiquities has occurred on a notable scale since the 1980s, but minimal attention was given to the issue until 2011 with the rising interest in links to terrorist funding. The illicit trade of antiquities is facilitated by a broad range of participants and like most criminal activity, corruption is essential to maintaining supply chains. Given the transnational nature of the trade, participants include a range of actors from smuggling networks to high ranking political and customs officials who facilitate the transport of materials across borders. Corruption is thus key to this trade. In many instances, linguistic and cultural ties facilitate smuggling across borders. Diverse skill sets, authorities, language and cultural capacities are needed to counter this trade that has become an important source of revenue for corrupt dealers, facilitators and non-state actors.

In Chapter 2 "Hobby Lobby, the Museum of the Bible and the Law: A Case Study of the Looting of Archaeological Artifacts from Iraq" Dr. Patty Gerstenblith discusses both the importance of legal expertise in advising potential purchasers on avoidance of the purchase of potentially trafficked antiquities as well as the role of lawyers in advising the preparation of cases for the courts of antiquities smuggling. Dr. Gerstenblith's chapter combines her training in art history and law, providing concrete analyses of how this

Introduction 13

trade operates. She points out that an auction house that has questions about the legitimacy of an artifact does not necessarily refuse to sell the object. Instead, as Dr. Gerstenblith explains, "it may choose to sell the artifact privately in order to avoid public scrutiny. In other words, questionable background may influence the business model chosen by an auction house rather than the decision whether to sell" (Chapter 2).

The chapter provides an expert and detailed account of legal violations typically involved in the illegal import of cultural artifacts, including imports in violation of restrictions imposed under the Convention on Cultural Property Implementation Act (19 U.S.C. §§ 2601–13), the domestic legislation implementing the US's ratification of the 1970 UNESCO Convention on the Means of Prohibiting and Preventing the Illicit Import, Export and Transfer of Ownership of Cultural Property. Dr. Gerstenblith uses the Hobby Lobby case and the purchase of thousands of items of illicitly excavated cuneiform tablets and fragments of the Dead Sea scrolls for display in the Museum of the Bible in Washington, D.C. On March 13, 2020 it was revealed that all of the Dead Sea Scroll manuscripts in the Museum's collections are forgeries, demonstrating the serious problems of illicit trade in antiquities and the failure of eager buyers to properly vet their acquisitions.

In Chapter 3 "The Hearing Hand: Scribes and Seal Cutters in the Ancient Near East" Drs. Spar and Catanzariti provide an overview of the historical relevance of ancient Near Eastern material culture, helping the reader understand the types of material that are presently for sale to buyers after excavation from ancient sites. The second section of the chapter discusses important steps to be taken for the correct documentation and preservation of ancient Near Eastern material culture. Information on methods to distinguish original from fake artifacts are provided including instructions on correct handling techniques that should be utilized during transportation and establishing a record of the object. Particular attention is given to cuneiform tablets and seals in this chapter.

Drs. Spar and Catanzariti write that ever since the 19th century cuneiform forgeries have flooded the antiquities market and fakes have entered into private and museum collections, libraries and monasteries. It became, and still is, a common dealer ruse to offer for sale a small group of illicitly excavated cuneiform tablets, combined with a much larger collection of freshly crafted forgeries. Few museums, dealers or collectors have the necessary expertise to detect forgeries. The untrained eye may not be able to detect small imprecisions in the composition of the seals or note inaccuracies in the writing, which sometimes may be illegible or senseless. Key signs of forgeries are improper weight, thickness and color of a forged tablet as well as inaccurately written tablets where the language is written in the wrong direction. The chapter also echoes Brodie's chapter by pointing out that the appearance of illicitly excavated cuneiform texts on the market attests to the desperate need for income for those caught in the Near Eastern war, corruption and civil strife.

14 *Louise Shelley and Layla Hashemi*

Part II takes a closer look at supply chains from the perspective of law enforcement, financial investigators and subject matter experts working as experts in the legal and law enforcement fields. These unique accounts provide both fascinating anecdotes of the trade while also offering valuable recommendations on how to combat this transnational trade.

Chapter 4 by Dr. Mahmut Cengiz, "Antiquities Trafficking from Syria Along the Northern Route" was written by a scholar and practitioner who lived in Turkey close to the Syrian and Iraqi border for years, an area where he investigated smuggling and illicit trade. Ongoing conflict in the region has created security vacuums filled by criminal and terrorist organizations. The terrorist organization has used the northern route, often collaborating with Turkish antiquities traffickers. The chapter investigates how antiquities in Iraq and Syria have been looted by criminal and terrorist groups and how they have been trafficked across Turkey, confirming insights from other scholars (Westcott 2020; Brodie and Sabrine 2018).

Dr. Cengiz identifies the diverse participants in this trade including criminals, terrorists, corrupt government officials and facilitators who help move and sell the items. Interviews by the author with three Syrian and four Turkish antiquities traffickers operating in borderland areas revealed two complicated networks: one small-scale network linked to a local trafficker or refugees and another large-scale network consisting of high-end buyers. Dr. Cengiz explains the strategic shift by traffickers in 2011 from using Southern trade routes through Lebanon to using Northern routes traversing Turkey to transport Syrian artefacts to Western European destination countries.

The chapter outlines the development of antiquities trafficking in Turkey across two distinct periods, the earlier period from the 1990s to 2000 and the more recent period spanning from 2000 to the present. The second period is marked by the involvement of organized crime groups and their collaboration with local smugglers. As Cengiz explains, After the fall of ISIS from power, al Qaeda-affiliated groups such as Hay'at Tahrir al-Sham (HTS) and Turkish-backed insurgent groups such as the Syrian National Army (SNA) stepped in to fill the void. Cengiz's thorough analysis of the involvement of HTS and SNA's (formerly FSA's) in the trafficking of Syrian antiquities reveals how despite the defeat of ISIS in Syria, the involvement of terrorist groups in antiquities trafficking remains and ongoing danger.

Chapter 5, "The Value of Financial Investigations in the Battle Against Artifact Smuggling" by Michael Loughnane explains the antiquities trade from the perspective of a financial investigator and offers solutions for how law enforcement and other actors can detect and disrupt illicit supply chains. Efforts to stem the flow of illicit artifacts and stolen antiquities, often concern themselves with more direct efforts such as attempting to protect historical sites to deter theft rather than following money flows. Often overlooked in investigations are the illicit networks that support the movement of stolen antiquities from their point of origin to their eventual point of sale. Loughnane's chapter explains why identifying the support structures

Introduction   15

that acquire, transport and sell illicit artifacts, and the international financial structures that support these transactions is essential. The use of financial investigations can deter or deny tools used by criminal and terror organizations as well as impede their ability to use artifact smuggling as a source of revenue.

Loughnane and Cengiz's chapters both demonstrate the convergence between the antiquities trade and other forms of transnational crime. Organized criminals often use the same trade routes, tactics and networks. Thus, financial and criminal investigations of the antiquities trade may reveal important information about other forms of transnational crime and illicit trade.

In Chapter 6, Dr. Nathan Elkins draws on his broad experience working on cases of smuggling and illicit trade in coins where he has advised investigators and served as an expert witness. He discusses the innovative ways that deep knowledge of coins can help us unravel patterns and participants in the trade of ancient coins. The chapter examines the methodology used by the author to determine the country of origin of trafficked ancient coins, a method necessary for legal cases seeking to bring smugglers to justice. Elkins also indicates that smugglers often use the antiquities trade to launder money from other illicit activities in which they are involved, a concern also raised by Brodie and other contributors.

Dr. Elkins explains that even some numismatic scholars who work comfortably with traders in coins recognize the growing and unregulated trade in ancient coins creates problems for the study of archaeology and history. Therefore, based on his knowledge of numismatic material and the realities of their circulation, Elkins developed his own methodology for identifying the countries of origin of looted and smuggled coins that he clearly explains in his chapter. These techniques have aided federal investigators from Customs and Border Protection, Homeland Security Investigations, and the Federal Bureau to understand the questionable trade in ancient coins.

Part III of the volume turns to an increasingly important topic, antiquities trafficking in the cyberworld. In Chapter 7, "Plenitudinous: An Analysis of Ancient Coin Sales on eBay" Wartenberg and Dmitričenko explain that ancient coins are often found in large numbers all over the world and, over the last two decades, are being increasingly sold in an expanding online marketplace allowing for no-questions-asked sales and nearly unlimited global reach. Coins dug up from archaeological objects sites have become one of the most plentiful categories of antiquities traded through online channels, representing opportunities but also challenges in the study of the illicit antiquities trade. In this chapter, the authors focus on trends in eBay sales of ancient Greek and Roman coins. The authors of the RAND report did not fully integrate all types of antique coins into their analysis. They only focused on the sale of Roman antiquities on eBay whereas other periods were neglected. Therefore, their numbers differ to some extent from the findings of

16 *Louise Shelley and Layla Hashemi*

the contributors of this volume. The RAND report provides two different estimates for the market of antiquities in their study: they value the total illicit antiquities market at tens of millions of dollars a year (Sargent et al. 2020; 88) but provide a much larger estimate of a few hundred million dollars for both the licit and illicit antiquities market (Chapter 7, Sargent et al. 2020; 84–88). This volume's focus is only on the illicit market.

Wartenberg and Dmitričenko note that their analysis comes up with similar numbers for the value of coins with an estimated $300–500 million dollars in annual profits. The online antiquities and collectibles market is quite active, with over 2.5 million coins offered on eBay. While capturing the sellers' and buyers' attitudes to the transactions, the authors also illustrate the scope, nature and dynamics of sales that raise questions regarding their legitimacy but, at the same time, reveal difficulties with distinguishing legal and illegal practices amongst them. In the course of the authors' research, it became rapidly clear that coins were undoubtedly among the most popular archaeological items looted in Syria and Iraq.

In Chapter 8, "Investigating the Online Sale of Illicit Antiquities" Dr. Layla Hashemi and Abi Waddell address how the rise of online antiquities marketplaces democratized the trade of cultural artifacts and what this means for future investigations of this illicit trade. Focusing on open source intelligence (OSINT), the chapter explores what sources, methods and tools are most effective for combating the transnational illicit trade of antiquities in the 21st century. By evaluating data collection methods from marketplace listing and social media data, the authors examine various technology and tools that can not only detect and disrupt antiquities trafficking but also promote the responsible consumption of cultural property. The chapter illustrates the importance of open source intelligence in detecting, analysing and mapping illicit antiquities networks and explains the authors' development of software tailored to achieve the CLASI team's research objectives.

Hashemi and Waddell's chapter presents a generalizable methodology for monitoring antiquities marketplaces and activity on both the open and dark web. The authors provide an analysis of how developments in communication technology have facilitated information sharing and increased connectivity among transnational criminal networks, allowing looters in source countries quick and easy access to interested buyers in destination countries despite long distances. As the authors explain, despite the final transaction occurring through private person to person encrypted messaging, information available on Facebook, eBay and various online antiquities marketplaces provide valuable insights into the trade and its networks.

Conclusion

The democratization of the antiquities trade occurred since the 2000s due to the rise of the internet and other digital technology. A greater number of antiquities became available as individuals in conflict zones became desperate

Introduction   17

for income especially after the tumult that followed the so-called Arab Spring. Failed and weak states in the Middle East led by corrupt leaders lack the capability and resources to prevent these kinds of crime and, therefore, they continue on a large scale. In some contexts (esp. conflict zones), the antiquities trade may be a key source of revenue for leaders and a source of financial survival for those engaged in the actual digging and looting.

The democratization of the market has occurred as Facebook and other social media platforms allow antiquities traffickers to reach a large audience with a casual interest in antiquities, thus normalizing the idea of looting for profit. Reports by ATHAR, TraCCC, ACCO, RAND and others provide ample evidence of the high level of transnational antiquities trafficking facilitated by Facebook and other open web technology (Al-Azm and Paul 2019; Sargent et al. 2020, Brodie 2019). Facebook's 2020 ban on historical artifacts as well as the recent legislation trying to prevent illicit financial flows through antiquities purchases could result in a shift of activity to the dark web as individuals seek to evade monitoring and detection.

The pernicious effects of this democratization of the market must also be addressed in order to detect and disrupt illicit supply chains. Further research must focus on preventing the destruction and trafficking of artifacts rather than returning looted material. This book presents research based on the Middle East but its recommendations for investigating the illicit trade have applicability outside of the region.

There is a need for a multimethod and multidisciplinary approach to investigating the antiquities trade. This requires including experts from diverse sectors and backgrounds, as was the case with the CLASI project. They must be equipped not only with traditional investigative and research techniques but also with the skills to conduct large scale data analytics. They need to understand the whole supply chain for the trade.

Only with an experienced and multi-disciplinary team could such comprehensive and innovative research have been conducted. Efforts to detect and disrupt the illicit antiquities trade must include law enforcement, academia, financial investigators, art galleries, archaeologists and subject matter experts to promote transnational and cross-organizational collaboration. Future efforts should also partner with technology and other private companies to gain access to critical data on these platforms on which the trade is taking place (Facebook, WhatsApp, etc.), providing important investigative evidence.

To match the innovation and flexibility of criminals, researchers must develop new and innovative tools and software to track and disrupt these dynamic global networks. Building upon previously successful investigative methods, these new tools must consider the tactical developments accompanying the democratization of the antiquities market, including the use of social media, encrypted messaging and electronic payment processing. Similar to the tool proposed in Chapter 8 of this volume, customized investigative software and methods need to be developed in order to detect and disrupt the illicit supply chains of antiquities that are destroying our collective cultural property and funding violence and corruption in many locales around the world in which the remnants of ancient civilizations remain.

Law enforcement and the legal system must give higher priority to the illicit antiquities trade. It has become increasingly popular as a revenue generator and means to launder money for pernicious non-state actors as well as oligarchs seeking to mask their ill-gotten gains (Portman and Carper 2020). Therefore, corruption is key to this trade as it not only facilitates the looting of historical sites and their movement across international supply chains but also the purchase of looted objects as purchasers seek to hide their wealth resulting from large-scale corruption.

Finally, there is a need to educate buyers and promote responsible consumption of historical artifacts. Efforts must be made to increase public awareness of the reasons for the lack of documentation or the common phenomenon of faked documentation provided by sellers. Then individuals who purchase antiquities may seek to ensure that the items are accompanied with proper provenance and documentation. Such greater diligence can be achieved by making potential buyers aware of the historical losses that result from looting and plundering of ancient sites.

The looting and trafficking of cultural property causes the loss of heritage for the source country and is an irreplaceable loss of history for archaeologists. When artefacts are taken from the ground without scientific documentation, we lose much about the object's use and destroy the object's rich history and our possibility of understanding more of its historical context. Once an item is looted, almost all of the information about what the artifact is and when and why it was made will be instantly lost. Only with greater consciousness of the costs of this trade can the trafficking of cultural artefacts be stemmed. Fortunately, enhanced measures to follow the money and efforts to police the internet may yield some reduction in this destructive trade.

Note

1 See https://www.britishmuseum.org/collection/object/W_1881-0428-118-b. Compare the similar Donations of Constantine, a 8th century C.E. forgery of a Roman imperial decree of the Emperor Constantine the Great granting Pope Sylvester I (314–335) and his successors vast territory, spiritual authority and temporal power over Rome. For the text of the forgery and a short commentary see, https://sourcebooks.fordham.edu/source/donatconst.asp.

References

Al-Azm, A., and K.A. Paul. 2019. Facebook's Black Market in Antiquities: Trafficking, Terrorism, and War Crimes. Athar Project. http://atharproject.org/report2019.

Al-Azm, A., and K.A. Paul, 2018. How Facebook Made It Easier Than Ever to Traffic Middle Eastern Antiquities. https://www.worldpoliticsreview.com/insights/25532/how-facebook-made-it-easier-than-ever-to-traffic-middle-eastern-antiquities.

Almalaq, Bandar. 2021. G20 Culture Ministerial Protection of Cultural Heritage and Illicit Trafficking: The World Heritage Commission, A view of Saudi Arabia's efforts in combating illicit trade in cultural goods, Multi-Stakeholder Webinar, April 9, 2021. https://youtu.be/rMUCZIA7PDc.

Anderson, Maxwell Lincoln. 2017. *Antiquities: What Everyone Needs to Know.* Oxford: Oxford University Press.

Antiquities Coalition. 2018. "Looting and Laundering Art, Antiquities, and Financial Crimes." https://theantiquitiescoalition.org/looting-and-laundering-art-antiquities-a nd-financial-crimes.

Brodie, Neil, ed. 2006. *Archaeology, Cultural Heritage, and the Antiquities Trade.* Cultural Heritage Studies. Gainesville, FL: University Press of Florida.

Brodie, Neil. 2017. "How to Control the Internet Market in Antiquities? The Need for Regulation and Monitoring," *Antiquities Coalition*, Policy Brief No. 3.

Brodie, Neil. 2019. "Final Report: Countering Looting of Antiquities in Syria and Iraq." https://traccc.gmu.edu/sites/default/files/Final-TraCCC-CTP-CTAQM-17-006-Report-J an-7-2019.pdf.

Brodie, N., and I. Sabrine. 2018. The Illegal Excavation and Trade of Syrian Cultural Objects: A View from the Ground, *Journal of Field Archaeology*, 43:1, 74–84, doi:10.1080/00934690.2017.1410919.

Brodie, Neil, and Kathryn Walker Tubb, eds. 2002. *Illicit Antiquities: The Theft of Culture and the Extinction of Archaeology.* One World Archaeology42. London: Routledge.

Chappell, Duncan, and Saskia Hufnagel. 2017. *Contemporary Perspectives on the Detection, Investigation, and Prosecution of Art Crime: Australasian, European, and North American Perspectives.* http://www.vlebooks.com/vleweb/product/openrea der?id=none&isbn=9781317160571.

Charney, Noah, ed. 2016. *Art Crime: Terrorists, Tomb Raiders, Forgers and Thieves.* London: Palgrave Macmillan.

Denton, David L. 2017. "Annual Sales Estimation of a Darknet Market." May 25, 2017. https://rstudio-pubs-static.s3.amazonaws.com/279562_48fcbe87ec814596944fb8bb59b1 0ae3.html.

Department of Justice. 2017. *"United States Files Civil Action to Forfeit Thousands of Ancient Iraqi Artifacts Imported by Hobby Lobby."* July 5, 2017. https://www.jus tice.gov/usao-edny/pr/united-states-files-civil-action-forfeit-thousands-ancient-iraqi-artifacts-imported.

Elkins, Nathan T. 2008. A Survey of the Material and Intellectual Consequences of Trading in Undocumented Ancient Coins: A Case Study on the North American Trade. *Frankfurter elektronische Rundschau zur Altertumskunde* 7: 1–13. Electronic document, http://www.fera-journal.eu.

Elkins, Nathan. 2012. "The Trade in Fresh Supplies of Ancient Coins: Scale, Organization, and Politics." In *All the King's Horses: Essays on the Impact of Looting and the Illicit Antiquities Trade on Our Knowledge of the Past*, edited by Paula Kay Lazrus and Alex W. Barker, 91–107. Washington, D.C.: SAA Press, Society for American Archaeology.

Green, Penny, and S. R. M. Mackenzie, eds. 2009. *Criminology and Archaeology: Studies in Looted Antiquities.* Oñati International Series in Law and Society. Oxford: Hart Publishing.

Hufnagel, Saskia, and Duncan Chappell. 2019. *The Palgrave Handbook on Art Crime.* Basingstoke: Palgrave Macmillan.

Koltrowitz, Silke, and Paul Arnold. 2016. "Freeports Boom Highlights Risks of Shady Activities." *Reuters*, September 22, 2016. https://www.reuters.com/article/us-swiss-freeports-idUSKCN11S1OL.

Payraud, Valentin. 2021. G20 Culture Ministerial Protection of Cultural Heritage and Illicit Trafficking: Finances Judicial Investigation Service – Investigator, A joint investigation on cultural goods trafficking by the French Customs and Police, Multi-Stakeholder Webinar, April 9, 2021. https://youtu.be/rMUCZIA7PDc.

Portman, Rob, and Carper, Tom. 2020. "The Art Industry and U.S. Policies That Undermine Sanctions," 150 pp. http://www.hsgac.senate.gov/download/majority-and-minority-staff-report_-the-art-industry-and-us-policies-that-undermine-sanctions.

Sargent, Matthew *et al.* 2020. Tracking and Disrupting the Illicit Antiquities Trade with Open Source Data. RAND Corporation. https://www.rand.org/pubs/research_reports/RR2706.html.

Saudi Gazette. 2019. "Saudi Arabia Returns Stolen Historical Documents to Iraq." Saudigazette. November 6, 2019. http://saudigazette.com.sa/article/581932.

Schuster, Ruth. 2021. "Vast Cache of Stolen Antiquities Found in Huge Raid in Central Israel", *Archaeology*. Haaretz.Com. January 5, 2021. https://www.haaretz.com/archaeology/.premium-vast-cache-of-stolen-antiquities-found-in-central-israel-1.9424209.

Shelley, Louise I. 2018. *Dark Commerce: How a New Illicit Economy Is Threatening Our Future.* Princeton, NJ: Princeton University Press.

Shelley, Fred M., and Reagan Metz. 2017. *Geography of Trafficking: From Drug Smuggling to Modern-Day Slavery.* 1st Edition. Santa Barbara, CA: ABC-CLIO, an imprint of ABC-CLIO, LLC.

Small, Zachary. 2021. "Congress Poised to Apply Banking Regulations to Antiquities Market." *The New York Times*, January 1, 2021, sec. Arts. https://www.nytimes.com/2021/01/01/arts/design/antiquities-market-regulation.html.

Stanyard, Julia, and Rim Dhaouadi. 2020. "Culture in Ruins: The Illegal Trade in Cultural Property across North and West Africa." https://enact-africa.s3.amazonaws.com/site/uploads/2020-11-12-culture-in-ruins-main-paper-01.pdf.

Tian, Hongwei, Stephen M. Gaffigan, D. Sean West, and Damon McCoy. 2018. "Bullet-Proof Payment Processors." In *2018 APWG Symposium on Electronic Crime Research (ECrime)*, San Diego, CA: IEEE, 1–11. https://ieeexplore.ieee.org/document/8376208/ (September 29, 2020).

Westcott, T. 2020. *Destruction or Theft: Islamic State, Iraqi antiquities and organized crime.* https://globalinitiative.net/wp-content/uploads/2020/03/Destruction-or-theft-Islamic-State-Iraqi-antiquities-and-organized-crime.pdf.

Whitwam, Ryan. 2016. "Researchers Index Dark Web, Find Most of It Contains Illegal Material – ExtremeTech," *Extreme Tech.*, February 1, 2016. https://www.extremetech.com/internet/222245-researchers-index-dark-web-find-most-of-it-contains-illegal-material.

1 The Looting and Trafficking of Syrian Antiquities Since 2011[1]

Neil Brodie

Introduction

Proceeds from antiquities trafficking have long been used to support armed violence in conflict zones (Hardy 2015a). In the early 1970s, North Vietnamese and Cambodian government troops engaged directly in the plunder and sale of Cambodian antiquities, joined in the late 1980s by the Khmer Rouge and other paramilitaries (Davis and Mackenzie 2015). In August 1981, members of a Lebanese Christian militia stole hundreds of antiquities from a storage facility at JBeil (ancient Byblos) (USA 2017a: 7). By 2018, 13 of the stolen pieces had been recovered from the possession of dealers and collectors in Europe and North America (Afeiche 2018). In 1990s Afghanistan, various militia groups were engaged in looting (Dupree 1996), and by 1998 the authorities in at least one Taliban-controlled province were exacting a 20 per cent tax on all antiquities sales (Dupree 1998). In Iraq, during the aftermath of the 2003 Iraq War, insurgency groups were reportedly involved in antiquities trading (Bogdanos 2005).

Yet although it was known that antiquities trafficking could be used to finance terrorists, insurgents and other armed non-state actors (ANSAs), it was not generally recognized by the international community until the emergence of the Islamic State of Iraq and Syria (ISIS) in 2014 with its brutal and very public human rights violations. Before then, policy-makers were still very much focused upon the damage antiquities looting and trafficking causes to cultural heritage, not its financial support of armed violence. But the large (and probably exaggerated) sums of money ISIS was said to be extracting from antiquities trading in support of its campaign of terror were seen to threaten international security and caused widespread public concern. Political action followed, with new laws drafted to control antiquities trafficking specifically citing terrorist financing.

This chapter presents an evidence-based overview and synthesis of what is known about the looting and trafficking of Syrian antiquities since the onset of civil conflict in 2011 (Figure 1.1). There is a special emphasis on the involvement of terrorist and other ANSA groups, particularly the Salafist-jihadist groups ISIS, Jabhat al-Nusra (JAN) and its successor organization

DOI: 10.4324/9781003023043-3

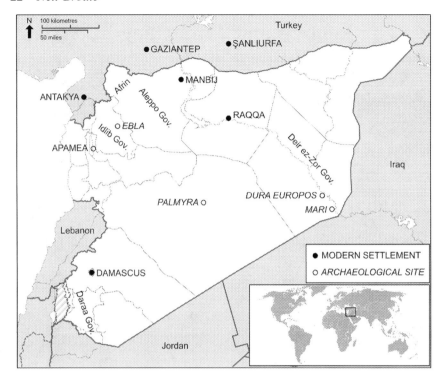

Figure 1.1 Map of Syria, showing places mentioned in the text

Hayat Tahrir as-Sham (HTS)[2], and the potential profitability of the trade for such groups. The first section provides a necessarily brief introductory account of archaeological looting in Syria. The following two sections then describe the structure and operation of the antiquities trade, both generally and specifically for the case of Syria. The next two sections present a diachronic perspective on the trade, showing how over the past thirty years technological and political developments have increased its commercial reach and destructive potential, and radically altered the nature of material being traded. These observations are fundamental to the following four sections which consider the criminal organization of the antiquities trade, its financial structure and its likely profitability for terrorists and other ANSAs. In the final section, some thought is given to the problem of policy failure – why public policy has very obviously failed to suppress or obstruct antiquities trafficking out of Syria.

The Recent History of Looting in Syria

Syrian antiquities have been looted and trafficked since at least the 1980s, sometimes with the facilitation or active involvement of government officials, police, Mukhabarat or army personnel (Brodie 2015a: 323–326; Clark 2016; Moos 2020: 28). Official involvement or corruption grew worse when some government agents became involved in general organized crime after Syria's 1976 occupation of Lebanon, which secured for them control of Lebanese roads and ports and provided opportunities for extracting bribes and illegal taxes from smuggling and other illegal enterprises (Herbert 2014). Shabiha criminal gangs were also implicated (Al-Haj Salih 2015). Membership of the Shabiha is largely Alawite, and after 2011 it morphed into a pro-Assad militia (BBC 2012). The looting and trafficking continued through the 1990s and 2000s and prompted new Syrian legislation in 1999 (Abdulrahman 2001). Pre-2011 satellite imagery of archaeological sites documents widespread evidence of looting, sometimes on a large scale (Cunliffe 2012: 18–20; Casana and Panahipour 2014: 148, table 1). In 2017, 450 out of a sample of 2,641 archaeological sites (17 per cent) showed evidence of pre-March 2011 looting (Casana and Laugier 2017: 14, table 2). For the Hellenistic–Roman site of Dura Europos, for example, "hundreds or possibly thousands of looting holes" were counted on an image dating to 2007 (Casana and Panahipour 2014: 143).

Since the start of the conflict in Syria in March 2011, in one way or another all combatant factions have tolerated or participated in antiquities looting.[3] In 2012, the Syrian army or its Shabiha paramilitaries were reported to be engaged in looting at the Roman-period site of Palmyra (AFP 2012; Zablit 2012; AGI 2012; Barnard 2014), and by 2013 material looted from Palmyra had been recovered in Syria and Lebanon (Ali 2015: 49–53) while more was on sale in Lebanon and Turkey (Jaba and Arbuthnott 2013; Soguel 2014; Kadi 2015). The looting of the Hellenistic–Roman site of Apamea was reported as proceeding with the knowledge and connivance of local Syrian army commanders (ASOR 2014: 11–12; ASOR 2016a: 63; Harkin 2014). Through 2013, the Syrian Directorate-General of Antiquities and Museums (DGAM) reported hundreds of people digging at the Bronze Age site of Mari and at Dura Europos, where they were said to be employed by "mafia" from Turkey, Iraq and Lebanon (Cockburn 2014; DGAM 2014). Satellite imagery subsequently identified thousands of recently-dug looters' pits at Dura Europos (AAAS 2014: 5–9), though fewer at Mari (AAAS 2014: 19–21). Both sites are located in Deir ez-Zor Governorate, on territory that was at the time contested between different opposition groups, including the Free Syrian Army (FSA), JAN and ISIS. Further to the west in Idlib Governorate, looting was ongoing at the Bronze Age site of Ebla between 2012 and 2013 while it was under FSA control (AAAS 2014: 10–16; Kaercher et al. 2018), though there was some evidence of official intolerance (Chivers 2013).

But it has been the involvement in antiquities looting and trafficking of Salafist groups such as ISIS and JAN, designated terror groups by the United States (USA n.d.), which has focused international attention. ISIS emerged as a military force in 2013 when it began to occupy territory in northern Syria and western Iraq. In March 2013, it seized control of Raqqa,

24 *Neil Brodie*

proclaiming the Syrian city to be its new "capital", where it plundered the museum and associated storehouses and started looting archaeological sites (Lamb 2014a). Then, in June 2014, it burst into media prominence with the rout of the Iraqi army at Mosul and the occupation of a major part of western Iraq. By the end of 2014, ISIS occupied large areas of Syria and Iraq, controlling a population of seven or eight million adult people (Burke 2017; CNN 2019). Mari fell under ISIS control in June 2014 and looting intensified thereafter with hundreds of looters' pits identified on satellite imagery (AAAS 2014: 19–21; Butterlin and Mura 2019: 211–213). By February 2015, when Dura Europos was firmly under the control of ISIS, looting was ongoing (DGAM 2015). Looting also continued at Palmyra which was occupied by ISIS in May 2015 and not finally liberated until March 2017 (Cuneo et al. 2016). From 2015 onwards, concerted military action by a range of oppositional forces slowly recovered ground from ISIS, with Mosul liberated in July 2017 and Raqqa in October 2017 (Burke 2017).

Jabhat al-Nusra (JAN) was formed in 2012 and in January 2017 merged with four other Salafist groups to form Hayat Tahrir al-Sham (HTS) (Ali 2020). HTS acted to consolidate its control over Idlib Governorate (which in early 2020 was still resisting Syrian government and Turkish offensives) and established the civil authority Salvation Government (Al-Azm and Paul 2019: 41; Moos 2020: 5, 18). The Salvation Government was charged with protecting cultural heritage, but illegal excavations throughout Idlib continued (Nassar and Atieh 2020; Darke 2020; Moos 2020: 19–23) and increased at Ebla (Kaercher et al. 2018).

With the defeat of ISIS, media attention wandered away from Syria and reports and investigations of archaeological looting have been harder to come by. In territories once more under government control it looks like business as usual with ongoing looting assisted by corrupt government officials and army personnel (Limoges et al. 2018). As well as in areas of HTS or government control, there have been reports of looting by opposition militias in the Afrin district of Aleppo Governorate, which has been under Turkish occupation since January 2018 (Abdulkareem 2020).

Satellite imagery allows quantitative evaluation of post-2011 archaeological site looting, providing information about chronological trends and the types of material targeted. By 2017, 355 out of a sample of 2,641 archaeological sites (13 per cent) showed evidence of post-March 2011 looting (Casana and Laugier 2017: 14, Table 2). Of those 355 sites, 276 exhibited a minor amount of damage, 52 a moderate amount of damage and 27 a severe amount of damage. There were looted sites in areas controlled by all combatant factions, including the Syrian army, with 50 per cent of looted sites in areas never occupied by ISIS, though some of the most severely looted sites were in areas that had been or were subject to ISIS control (Casana and Laugier 2017: 12). The most severe looting had been of Bronze Age sites (sources of cuneiform inscribed objects, cylinder seals, statuary, bronze objects and jewelry), and Roman and Late Roman (or Byzantine) sites (sources of mosaics, mortuary statuary, jewelry, glass and coins) (Casana and Laugier 2017: 26).

The Transnational Structure and Operation of the Antiquities Trade

The antiquities trade comprises three stages or markets: source, transit and destination (Mackenzie et al. 2020). Antiquities are stolen or looted in source countries (such as Syria), smuggled out and transported through one or more transit countries (such as Turkey and Lebanon), before arriving for sale on the destination market. Destination market countries such as the United States and others in Europe and Asia possess the cultural and commercial institutions necessary to support and validate antiquities collecting. The destination market is legal in that antiquities trading and collecting are not subject to any specific or targeted regulation, though it might still be illegal to trade in antiquities stolen from other countries or otherwise illegally imported. Antiquities circulating on the destination market may have arrived there by legal or illegal means, days, decades or even centuries ago. No matter how long they have been in circulation, antiquities are usually sold with only minimum indications of provenance (previous ownership history), so that it is difficult for a discriminating collector to separate stolen or otherwise illegally-traded antiquities from legitimate material. This mixing of black and white has caused the antiquities trade to be characterized as a "grey" trade, neither demonstrably legal nor illegal (Mackenzie and Yates 2016). Recently looted and smuggled antiquities (and fakes) can be "laundered" passing through the transit market for entry on to the destination market by the provision of legal export documents from transit countries, falsified customs declarations and invented accounts of provenance. As the boundaries of ancient cultures often spread across the borders of several modern countries and jurisdictions, it is difficult to pinpoint the country of origin for any one specific object, to establish the date of export from its country of origin or to determine whether the export was legal or not.

There are several methods used by antiquities smugglers for evading customs inspections and securing entry into a destination market country (USA 2011, 2017b: 4–6). They include:

- False declaration of the value of a shipment (lower than market value).
- False declaration of the country of origin of a shipment (a transit rather than source country).
- Vague and misleading descriptions of a shipment's contents.
- Splitting a single large object into several smaller pieces for separate deliveries, allowing informal entry and later reassembly after receipt.
- Addressing a shipment to a third party, falsely stated to be the addressee or purchaser, for subsequent transfer to the actual purchaser.
- Failure to complete appropriate customs paperwork.

26   *Neil Brodie*

- Concealing antiquities in shipments of similar, legitimate commercial goods.
- Addressing shipments to several different addresses for receipt by a single purchaser.

Military and diplomatic personnel are exempt from customs inspections and can carry material across borders. Contents descriptions matching categories in Chapters 68–70 (stone, ceramic and glass objects) and 97 (artworks and antiques) of the Harmonized Tariff Schedule (Harm.TS) are often used to hide or disguise antiquities on entry documentation. It is difficult for an untrained eye to distinguish between similar-appearing ancient and modern products. In August 2015, for example, California dealer Mohamad Yassin Alcharihi imported a Byzantine mosaic, alleged by the FBI to have been exported illegally from Syria, along with 83 other objects, mainly pottery. The objects were described on the US Customs entry form as 82 pieces of "Ornamental Art Oth. Material" (Harm.TS 6913.90.500), valued at $1,808, with the mosaic described as "Ceramic, Unglazed Tiles, Hub" (Harm.TS 6907.10.000), valued at $391 (USA 2018). When interviewed, Alcharihi admitted paying $12,000 for the material and declaring a lower value to reduce customs duties. The practice of including stolen or looted antiquities in shipments of ostensibly similar legitimate material has been termed "piggybacking" (St Hilaire 2014). The practice must be more common than is occasionally revealed by customs seizures.

Once inside a destination country, invented provenances ease the passage of looted and trafficked antiquities onto the open market. Invented provenances are intended to reassure a good faith or naïve collector that an object is on the market legally. They also provide a bad faith collector with plausible deniability of incriminating knowledge and thus limit any potential criminal liability. It is difficult to prove criminal intent on the part of any possessor of an antiquity that is stolen. During the 2016 FBI raid on Alcharihi's premises, for example, agents discovered a notarized statement of provenance signed by a neighbor and dated March 5, 2016, regarding a "mosaic carpet" (USA 2018: 7–8). It stated that in 2009 the neighbor had sold Alcharihi a rolled "mosaic carpet" that had been in her family's possession since the 1970s. The neighbor told the FBI that she had sold Alcharihi a carpet, but not a mosaic, and that Alcharihi had prepared the misleading statement she had subsequently signed.

The Trade Out of Syria

Looted antiquities pass from source countries to transit and ultimately destination countries through an often complex chain of dealers (middlemen or intermediaries) and smugglers (couriers or runners). The division of labour between dealers and smugglers makes sense logistically as the roles require different skill-sets and commercial networks, and it can also act to protect

Looting and Trafficking of Syrian Antiquities 27

dealers from being caught in possession of stolen material. Sometimes, however, a single person can embody both roles (see Loughnane, Chapter 5, this volume). Once on the transit market, some of the trade is long distance, point-to-point, passing from one dealer in a transit country straight to another one active on the destination market. Other trade is down-the-line, transiting through the hands of several dealers or criminal groups before reaching the destination market. All means of transport are utilized, including automobiles, buses, cargo trucks, mail and courier services, personal luggage, and air and sea freight. Some smugglers are generalists, willing to carry a range of illegal commodities, including consumer products, cigarettes, pharmaceuticals and narcotics alongside antiquities (Baker and Anjar 2012; Mabillard 2013)[4], others specialize in antiquities (Limoges et al. 2018), while those who transport high-value goods such as weapons, will not want to compromise an expensive safe route for lower-value material like antiquities (Bajjaly 2013). It has been reported several times that refugees have been used to smuggle antiquities out of Syria (Stoughton 2015; Cox 2015; Parkinson *et al.* 2015; Faucon *et al.* 2017)[5].

Some of the transit trade is facilitated by ethnic and linguistic continuities across borders and more wide-ranging diasporas. Traditionally, smuggling across borders into Lebanon, Jordan and Iraq has been in the hands of Bedouin and Druze (Moos 2020: 32), and Kurdish groups in Syria are reported to be working with Kurds in Turkey and Germany (Clark 2016)[6]. The large-scale movement of Syrian refugees into Turkey must be considered under this heading too. Sometimes destination market dealing is a family business for ethnic minorities, passing down through more than one generation, but allowing continuing familial and commercial contacts with a dealer's county of origin. Back in the 1990s, for example, many of the Turkish dealers in Germany and the United States belonged to Syriac or Kurdish families from Mardin (Acar and Kaylan 1990). Language and family relationships between Syrian nationals resident in Syria and Turkey are reported to have enabled trade both out of Syria and onwards to Europe, and the role of wider diaspora communities remains to be investigated[7].

The immediate transit routes out of Syria are through neighboring countries, particularly Lebanon, Turkey and, although less-well documented, Jordan. Lebanon has been a long-time conduit for Syrian antiquities, particularly during the period 1976 to 2005 when it was under Syrian occupation. Antiquities trading was legal in Lebanon until 1988 (Seif 2015: 66–67), and with the ancient cultural continuities between Syria and Lebanon it is easy to create fictitious sales histories for Syrian antiquities dating back to an invented Lebanese purchase sometime prior to 1988. From Lebanon, material passes to Europe or North America by sea or by air. The importance of Lebanon as a transit route diminished after the Syrian withdrawal in 2005, but it has not fallen into disuse. In one year, for example, 2013, there were several major seizures of material from Syria, including objects thought to be from Apamea and Palmyra, and a large quantity of fakes (Seif 2015: 71–75).

28   *Neil Brodie*

In January 2013, Lebanese officials seized 18 Syrian mosaics crossing into Lebanon in a bus registered in Idlib Governorate (Seif 2015: 72; Bajjaly 2013). Looking at the conflict geography of the area, since 2011 the Syrian side of the Lebanese border has mainly been under the control of the Syrian government, particularly after Hezbollah occupied the border zone inside Syria in 2012 (Stoughton 2015; Moos 2020: 31). Thus it should be expected that since 2011 Lebanon has been the favoured route for material looted in areas of Syria subject to government control. Looters and dealers resident in opposition-controlled Idlib Governorate confirm that since 2011 access to Lebanon has become more difficult (Brodie and Sabrine 2018: 79).

Turkey, too, has been a major transit country since 2011, helped by the fact that overland routes from Turkey to Germany through the Balkans became available in the 1990s after the lapse there of Soviet control (Mladenov 2015; and see Cengiz, this volume, Chapter 4, for an in-depth discussion of the antiquities trade through Turkey, and Cengiz and Roth 2019 for an analysis of organized crime in Turkey). After 2011, routes out of Syria through Turkey were strengthened by Syrian dealers relocating over the border. As Lebanon was closing down to opposition groups, Turkey became correspondingly more important and most trade from areas controlled by ISIS and JAN looks to have passed through Turkey. Until 2015, the Turkish border was open to people and material moving in and out of Syria, possibly as deliberate Turkish policy to support opposition groups (including ISIS and other Salafists) fighting inside Syria[8]. Corrupt Turkish border guards and police are well reported (Giglio 2014)[9]. Several seizures of looted antiquities inside Turkey and at its borders have been noted by Turkish media (Topal 2015; Sabah 2016, 2018) and more are reported by Cengiz (Chapter 4). Outside Turkey, in March 2015, Bulgarian police seized 9,000 ancient coins, dozens of Roman statues and what looked to be Sumerian relief from Iraq in the district of Shumen in north-east Bulgaria. The Roman statues were thought to be from Turkey or another Middle Eastern country (Dikov 2015a, 2015b). Three people were arrested, including a Turk with Bulgarian citizenship. Not everything has been moving overland out of Turkey through the Balkans, with material transported by sea to Spain and Italy in the west and Russia and the Ukraine to the north. The Byzantine mosaic purchased by Alcharihi arrived at Long Beach, California after having been shipped by sea from Iskenderun in Turkey (USA 2018). In 2015, Turkey started strengthening border controls and constructing a barrier in some places (AP 2016; Arango and Schmitt 2015). On the Syrian side, Kurdish People's Protection Units (YPG) closed their section of border after June 2015 (Soguel 2015). The stronger border controls were reported to have dampened smuggling out of opposition-controlled areas (Brodie and Sabrine 2018: 82). The border situation since the 2018 Turkish invasion of Afrin is unclear, though it has probably increased opportunities for smuggling from areas under Turkish military occupation[10]. Cengiz discusses these developments in more detail (this volume, Chapter 4).

Through the 1990s into the early 2000s, Jordan was an important transit route for Iraqi (and Jordanian) antiquities passing into Israel or being flown out of Amman to London (Brodie 2006: 214–216). Its continuing role as a transit state was confirmed by reports in 2013 that Syrian antiquities were being smuggled out of opposition-controlled areas into Jordan, often with refugees, either for transhipment elsewhere or for purchase by collectors in Amman (Luck 2013a, 2013b; Fisk 2013).

Beyond Syria's immediately neighboring countries, the tracks of the trade become harder to follow. Dubai and the United Arab Emirates maintain large free trade zones that facilitate the duty-free transhipment of material and it is assumed that Syrian antiquities might pass through there, though nothing has been confirmed. Thailand does not have an established record of being a transit country for Syrian or Middle Eastern antiquities, but there is evidence to suggest that it is assuming the role[11]. In March 2016, two pieces of relief from a church in the Syrian Euphrates Valley were seized at Charles de Gaulle Airport in Paris, where they were in transit from Lebanon to Thailand. French customs thought the intended final destination was probably in the United States (Revenu 2016; Faucon et al. 2017). This seizure highlights the possible transit role of European countries. In Spain, too, in November 2019, Moroccan national and Alicante resident Nourdine Chikar was convicted of financial crimes relating to the supply of military uniforms to ISIS in Syria and also cultural property, though the exact nature of his involvement in trafficking antiquities has yet to be made public (Moreno 2019). He was using the hawala system to move money.

The Changing Nature of the Antiquities Trade

The nature of the antiquities trade has changed considerably since 1990 as developing technologies, economic deregulation and political reconfigurations – post-Cold-War processes conventionally grouped together under the heading of "globalization" – have provided profitable new opportunities for conducting business. It is not clear that policies and actions aimed at diminishing the trade have adapted accordingly (Brodie 2017a).

Before the 2000s, antiquities were sold mainly by auction houses and specialized dealers operating out of brick-and-mortar establishments. It was common during this time to see unprovenanced mosaics and other antiquities offered for sale at auction described as Syrian, possibly recently looted, but they rarely attracted any action, attention or adverse comment, with one exception. Between 1991 and 1996, 86 pieces of Syrian Late Roman floor mosaic arrived in Montreal from Lebanon. Canadian customs agents recovered most of them and returned them to Syria, including five pieces that were intercepted at the border by US customs. But one piece was allegedly sold at auction by Sotheby's in New York and together with nine other pieces remains missing (Fossey 2015: 209). Auctions comprise the public face of the destination market, but at the same time there was a thriving private or

30 *Neil Brodie*

invisible antiquities trade, with dealers selling directly to collectors. What if any Syrian antiquities were being traded invisibly cannot be assessed at the present time. It is assumed the nine mosaics that eluded the Montreal seizures entered private collections (Fossey 2015: 209). These mosaics are typical of the type of material being trafficked at the time – large, monetarily-valuable and culturally-significant pieces.

At the turn of the millennium, the nature of the antiquities trade was changing, partly because of political detente and trade deregulation at the end of the Cold War, but mainly because of the increasing availability of new technologies, particularly metal detectors and the Internet. By 2003, there was a maturing Internet antiquities market, with on-line dealers and auctioneers selling direct to the public. The Internet offers easier market access for a much larger number of customers than brick-and-mortar establishments, and antiquities sold on the Internet are generally of poorer quality and thus less valuable than those that have been traditionally traded. While there has been a move towards providing more provenance-related information in the catalogues of the major auction houses (Mackenzie et al. 2020: 64–69), the Internet remains a largely provenance-free sales platform (Brodie 2015b: 250–251).

The continuance of Internet sales into the 2010s confirms their profitability and shows that buyers generally have a relaxed attitude towards the extremely poor standards of provenance that prevail. The fact that customers are generally accepting of unprovenanced antiquities means that the Internet is ideally suited for selling looted and trafficked material and it also provides an uncritical environment for passing fakes. By 2016 there were large numbers of purportedly Syrian antiquities and coins of uncertain provenance for sale on the Internet (Brodie 2017b: 196–201; Wartenberg 2015; Topçuoğlu and Vorderstrasse 2019; this volume, Chapters 7 and 8). Whether they were fake or authentic, looted or legitimate, was usually hard if not impossible to decide.

On into the 2010s, as the Internet market continued to grow in size, more developing technologies, particularly cellular smart phones and their associated digital communication and social media apps, further refashioned the trade (see Waddell and Hashemi, this volume, Chapter 8). Facebook, for example, has been widely adopted as a trading platform across source and transit market countries. The use of Facebook in Syria and neighboring countries for communicating about antiquities trading and for actual commerce increased markedly from 2016 onwards, and by 2019 Facebook was bedded in, with at least 95 Arabic-language predominantly closed groups (Al-Azm and Paul 2019: 6). Five of the groups comprised more than 100,000 members (Al-Azm and Paul 2019: 6). Close analysis of four Syria-based Facebook groups showed their active members to be concentrated regionally in and around Syria, though with some located in other countries around the world (Al-Azm and Paul 2019: 27–37). HTS might also be using Facebook to advertise finds (Al-Azm and Paul 2019: 43–44). Instagram is another popular social media platform for transacting antiquities, and YouTube too occasionally advertises material. Vetted membership Internet discussion forums are also used for establishing contact between buyers and sellers. Social media has accelerated "glocalization" of the source market (Robertson 2012), with users participating simultaneously in local and global networks of communication and commerce.

Social media apps such as Facebook and Instagram need to be publicly accessible if they are to attract customers. When secrecy is required, WhatsApp, Facebook Messenger, Telegram or other encrypted means of electronic messaging are used to arrange deals (Giglio and Al-Awad 2015; Al-Azm and Paul 2019: 8, 14; Moos 2020; Sargent et al. 2020: 54–63). On Facebook and Instagram, sometimes it is possible to see purchasing negotiations commence, but then not proceed, presumably continuing to a successful conclusion away from the site on private, more secure platforms. On May 16, 2015, US Special Forces raided the Syrian compound of Abu Sayyaf, head of the ISIS Diwan al Rikaz (Ministry of Natural Resources and Minerals, including its Antiquities Division), where they discovered images of stolen antiquities in the WhatsApp folder of his cell phone (Keller 2015).

With more people buying more material, particularly material that in the past would not have been considered worth trading, the expanding global coverage of the Internet and cellular communication technologies has extended the commercial reach of the antiquities market, augmenting the pre-existing brick-and-mortar trade to increase the volume of antiquities being looted and trafficked and to offer more opportunities for faking. This developing process of commercial persistence and diversification is symptomatic of illicit trades more generally, allowing them to "operate as if on steroids" (Shelley 2018: 2).

Despite suggestions to the contrary, there is no evidence of antiquities having been traded in large quantities on the Darknet (Brodie et al. 2019: 108; Sargent et al. 2020: 44–49; Waddell and Hashemi, this volume, Chapter 8). There are several possible explanations for this general absence of material on the Darknet, besides the obvious one that it is very effectively hidden. Since the antiquities trade is a grey trade, as described earlier, rather than an overtly illegal one, on the destination market customers can easily buy material without any stigma of criminality, privately or on open sales platforms, whether they be brick-and-mortar or electronic. Potential customers might be scared off by the illegal and harder-to-find Darknet. Further down the trading chain, on the source and transit markets, social media and easily accessible secure messaging apps can reach a much wider audience than the Darknet as described in Chapter 8.

The Changing Nature of Traded Material

Despite the well-documented damage caused to archaeological sites by looting since the 2011 onset of fighting in Syria, there have been hardly any reports of large, valuable Syrian antiquities such as the "Montreal mosaics"

32   Neil Brodie

entering the United States or Europe (McAndrew 2014; Bakare 2020). Several suspicious-looking pieces of Palmyran sculpture have been offered for sale, but with provenances claiming they moved out of Syria long before 2011, and it is hard to prove otherwise (Albertson 2016; Brodie 2017b: 196). To explain the apparent market absence of large (and valuable) objects, there have been unsubstantiated claims that material is being stockpiled regionally for sale in the future when limitation periods have expired and international attention has drifted elsewhere (CBS 2015; Myers and Kulish 2016; Moos 2020: 27; Brodie et al. 2019: 103; Brodie and Sabrine 2018: 82; Yoon 2015), or is entering regional collections in the Gulf or elsewhere (McAndrew 2014; AFP 2015; Yoon 2015). There have, for example, been allegations that private museums in neighbouring countries such as the newly established Nabu Museum in Lebanon and the Bible Lands Museum in Israel have been acquiring looted material (Sewell 2019; Press 2019). Investigation of regional collecting practices is urgently required. This conjectured pattern of regional demand and acquisition has been used by commercial lobbyists to argue for measures aimed at market interdiction and suppression at source rather than destination (CCP 2015, 2017; Macquisten 2017; McAndrew 2014).

But another reason for the seeming non-appearance in the United States and Europe of large Syrian antiquities is that the type of material being traded has changed, with coins and other small objects suitable for sale on the Internet achieving more commercial dominance as described in Chapters 7 and 8. Larger and more expensive objects are more difficult to transport, more readily recognizable, and thus less in demand. Although on the ground in Syria there are many reports of bulldozers or other heavy digging machines being used to open sites (Giglio and Al-Awad 2015; Baker and Anjar 2012; Chivers 2013; ASOR 2016b: 55), the widespread use of metal detectors to search for coins and other metal objects has been equally well documented (Harkin 2014; Giglio and Al-Awad 2015; Brodie and Sabrine 2018; Cuneo and Danti 2019: 276). Metal detectors were developed in the 1970s, but the changing market conditions of the 2000s with an increasing demand for smaller antiquities have increasingly favoured their use while looting archaeological sites. More than 300 people were reported using metal detectors while digging at Dura Europos in early 2014 and selling their finds to dealers at the site (some of them at least arriving from neighboring countries – the international "mafia" noted previously) (DGAM 2014)[12]. Dealers were also said to be selling metal detectors to aspiring looters[13]. It is thought that the looting there was driven by the search for coins and jewelry (Daniels and Hansen 2015: 90–91). The ASOR CHI database suggests more generally that most material traded from Syria could be classed as "low and middle tier" (Cuneo and Danti 2019: 276). Many of the antiquities recovered from the possession of Abu Sayyaf were coins from Syria and Iraq, and there were electronic images of gold coins and jewelry on his computer (USA 2016). The trade on Facebook since 2015 has been dominated by coins and other small antiquities (Al-Azm and Paul 2019: 37–38).

Looting and Trafficking of Syrian Antiquities 33

Perhaps on the ground there is an expectation of more valuable finds. The Abu Sayyaf documents, for example, contain reference to a find of gold objects that was valued within Syria at between $120,000 to $200,000. If such large sums of money are changing hands inside Syria for found material, even if only occasionally, they would provide a powerful incentive for looters intent upon finding a valuable "treasure" to continue digging, even when the monetary value of objects actually found is comparatively disappointing. But even without buried treasure, the looting of large numbers of small, relatively low-value coins and antiquities would still in aggregate generate appreciable profits for anybody involved in their trade (Greenland et al. 2019).

Outside Syria, media reports from the border area of southern Turkey emphasize the trafficking of coins, jewelry and other small objects (Ruiz 2016). Between 2011 and the end of 2015, Turkish authorities seized 6,800 antiquities of possibly Syrian origin, the majority of them coins (Myers and Kulish 2016). By 2020, there had been more seizures and the number of coins would be larger still. In May 2017, for example, Turkish police at GAP Airport in Sanliurfa province seized 90 Hellenistic and Roman coins that had been smuggled out of Syria[14]. The Syrian suspect stated he had bought the coins from a local smuggler who had contacts with ISIS. In June 2017, two people were arrested in Aksaray province of Turkey, with 3,745 Byzantine coins and 408 other antiquities from Syria in their possession, bought from a Syrian smuggler in Hatay province[15]. In May 2018, Bulgarian customs intercepted a car carrying 11,037 coins and 141 other antiquities entering the country from Turkey. The coins may have originated in Turkey, Iraq or Syria (Dikov 2018). There is evidence of increased quantities of Syrian coins appearing for sale post-2011 in Europe and North America (Brodie 2017b: 196–201; Topçuoğlu and Vorderstrasse 2019; Wartenberg 2015; Wartenberg and Brederova, this volume, Chapter 8).

The conflict in Syria has also been associated with an increase in antiquities faking as criminals moved to maximize supply (Giglio and Al-Awad 2015; Cockburn 2016). Provenance-free and distanced trading on the Internet and social media has made it easier to infiltrate fakes into commerce than was previously the case through face-to-face trading in the physical market. In 2015, the Syrian Director-General for Antiquities and Museums estimated that approximately 80 per cent of objects being seized internally were fake, compared to about 30 per cent at the start of the conflict (Cockburn 2016). The trade in fake Judaeo-Christian manuscripts through Turkey has been particularly remarked upon (Hardy 2018). Counterfeit antiquities are filtered into the genuine trade, increasing profitability for those involved. By 2019, it was claimed that genuine antiquities appearing on Facebook were rapidly being copied for sale (Moos 2020: 28).

Thus, it is likely that looting and trafficking from Syria post-2011 has preferentially targeted coins and smaller, lower-value antiquities and increasingly enabled the passing of fakes, a shift enabled by the widespread availability of the Internet, cellular communication technologies and metal

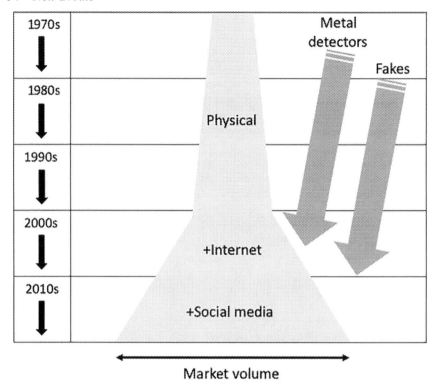

Figure 1.2 The changing shape of the antiquities trade since 1970, showing how Internet and social media trading have increased the importance of metal detectors and created more opportunities for marketing fakes.

detectors (Figure 1.2). Coins and other small antiquities can be easily concealed and transported out of Syria before being offered for sale on the Internet and delivered by mail or courier to customers on the destination market. Observations that law enforcement agencies in destination countries are not seeing any looted Syrian objects (McAndrew 2014; Giglio and Al-Awad 2015; Bakare 2020) might simply mean that the agencies concerned are not looking for the right type of material. In 2015, for example, the French government asked dealers to watch out for mosaics, statues and bas-reliefs (Chazan 2015). By way of contrast, there are reports of small unprovenanced Syrian antiquities and coins on open sale in some London sales galleries (Shabi 2015), and although it is not possible to say without doubt that they were looted in Syria after 2011, it is simply wrong to say that they weren't.

The Criminal Organization and Operation of the Antiquities trade

On the source and transit markets, it is possible to conceptualize three separate though interacting and interdependent spheres of economic networking

Looting and Trafficking of Syrian Antiquities 35

or organization, each with its own motivating rationale and means of mobilizing and allocating resources (Brodie and Sabrine 2018; Goodhand 2003, 2005: 202–209). First there is a "conflict economy", constructed and maintained with the aim of supporting armed violence in pursuit of a political objective. Second, there is a "criminal economy", the work of criminal entrepreneurs bent on profiting personally from opportunities created by conflict. Finally, there is a "coping economy", offering poor households and communities whose traditional livelihoods have been destroyed by conflict opportunities to engage in illegal activities as a means of ensuring their ongoing survival. This tripartite conceptualization is idealized, overly compartmentalized perhaps, and individual actors can certainly embody multiple roles, motivations and relationships, but it does offer a useful heuristic for thinking about how the antiquities trade out of Syria is organized, how it operates, and how it might best be tackled.

The reality of people looting archaeological sites during peacetime as a means of enhancing their wellbeing has been well-described in the archaeological literature as "subsistence digging" (Staley 1993; Brodie 2012: 244–247; Field et al. 2016) and the participation of Syrians in a wartime coping economy should not come as a surprise (Giglio and Al-Awad 2015; Limoges et al. 2018; Brodie and Sabrine 2018). By 2016, three million Syrians had lost their jobs to conflict, about 50 per cent of the labor force (Gobat and Kostial 2016: 7). Ultimately, however, the coping economy is dependent upon the criminal economy for expertise and disposal of looted material (Brodie and Sabrine 2018: 81). For antiquities trafficking, it is the organized criminal networks comprising the criminal economy that enable the trade out of Syria and through onto the destination market. Organized crime provides access to specialized services (e.g. money laundering and counterfeiting) and operational support (e.g. access to smuggling networks). Long-established criminal dealers in Syria and its immediately neighboring countries are essential for the ongoing functioning of the trade and by extension the coping and conflict economies (Giglio and Al-Awad 2015; Brodie and Sabrine 2018: 7; Cengiz, this volume, Chapter 4). They possess the expertise necessary to authenticate and value material, the out-of-country contacts necessary to arrange for ongoing trade and are generally trusted by other participants (Moos 2020: 11, 27–28). To a certain extent, they are the human glue holding the economies together. The criminal economy probably includes locally corrupt or criminal government agents or army personnel, with any proceeds benefiting them personally, and not necessarily implicating the Syrian government.

The traditional, pre-2000, low-volume trade of large, expensive objects presupposes the participation of a limited number of criminals, perhaps acting in long-term cooperation, exercising a good degree of control over the organization and operation of trade, and with significant transport and storage capabilities. It would be vulnerable to targeted law enforcement aiming to disrupt trade by apprehending offenders. The new higher-volume trade of

36 *Neil Brodie*

smaller objects such as coins instantiates the more general criminal move away from fixed hierarchies towards distributed and decentralized networks (Naím 2005: 7; Shelley 2015: 99) and is harder to tackle. It is most likely dispersed, involving a larger number of people, and more loosely organized with less onerous transport and storage requirements. It will be flexible and opportunistic and better able to survive the occasional removal of participating criminals.

Having said that, network analysis of Facebook group memberships shows a high degree of centrality and connectivity (Al-Azm and Paul 2019: 16–19). If this communication network reflects a deeper illegal trading operation, the post-2000 trade might not be so distributed as is supposed[16]. In late 2018, open-source analysis of Facebook data was used to examine the activities of three coin dealers, one based in Canada, one in the United Kingdom and one in Germany[17]. The dealers were working together selling ancient coins on the open market in Europe and North America, including coins from Middle Eastern countries. The German had 4,993 Facebook friends. The Facebook pages of many of these friends in turn revealed information about their participation in antiquities looting and trafficking. From a sample of 500 of these friends, 313 provided information about location. At least 131 were based in Arabic-speaking countries, including eight in Syria, 18 in Jordan and two in Lebanon. There were many more in Turkey. The Canadian dealer's Facebook friends were not accessible, but it was obvious from his timeline that he was often visiting Middle Eastern countries. The British dealer's friends were mainly located outside the Middle East and from his timeline at least he never visited there. What this analysis revealed was a small group of destination-market dealers with an extremely wide-ranging communication network penetrating deep into source and transit countries. Presumably it reached down into the regional Facebook groups revealed by Al-Azm and Paul (2019). Again, if this Facebook communication network reflected an underlying illegal trading operation, it would show how a small, tightly-organized group of destination-market dealers was obtaining material from a much less organized source market, though it would not necessarily imply a control hierarchy – perhaps more of an arrangement of interlocking trusted-partner trading relationships. A BBC investigation into the trade of ancient coins out of Gaza showed how the Canadian dealer was known there as a buyer or receiver (BBC 2020), perhaps highlighting once more the importance of reputation or trust for dealers in local source-market trading operations.

The Financial Structure of the Antiquities Trade

Traditionally on the antiquities market, mark-ups of several hundred per cent between source and destination prices have not been unusual (Brodie 2014: 34–35). These mark-ups represent profit to be divided between the various dealers, smugglers and facilitators that constitute the trade, including payments through bribery, extortion or taxation necessary to allow its operation, together with fees paid to professional experts for activities related to marketing. In the Californian mosaic case previously described, for example, Alcharihi paid a dealer in Turkey $12,000 for a large mosaic, two smaller mosaics and 81 pottery vessels. Once the mosaic had arrived in the United States, he paid a US-based conservation company $40,000 to restore it, and after restoration independent appraisals suggested the mosaic to be worth between $70,000 and $200,000. The Alcharihi mosaic demonstrates the large mark-up in price expected on the destination market, including the added-value of expert restoration. To explore further, it was reported in 2015 that a Turkish dealer was in possession of a Syrian mosaic (presumably not the Alcharihi one) that had been smuggled across the border rolled up in a carpet. He said he had bought it for $21,000 from a dealer in Syria and hoped to sell it for $30,000 (Giglio and Al-Awad 2015). If that reported fifty-per-cent mark-up between Syria and Turkey was real and representative of the financial structure of the cross-border trade more generally, it would imply that the Alcharihi mosaic had been sold inside Syria for $8,000. If Alcharihi had managed to sell the piece for its appraised value of between $70,000 and $200,000, the mark-up between Syria and California would have ranged from several hundred up to a couple of thousand per cent. Exactly what would be expected from what is known from other sources about the general price structure of the antiquities trade.

But for ancient coins and other small antiquities, the financial structure of the trade out of Syria since 2011 is not so clear cut. One digger in Daraa Governorate complained that for 20 gold Byzantine coins he had been paid only 10 per cent of the value in Amman (Moos 2020: 29), which seems normal, but generally the prices reported on-the-ground by journalists and other researchers seem very high when compared to those on the destination market (Brodie and Sabrine 2018: 82). It has been reported from Idlib Governorate in 2019, for example, that 42 pure (24 carat) gold coins were sold for $300,000 to the representative of a German dealer who subsequently resold them at auction in the Netherlands (Moos 2020 25). That would be an on-the-ground purchase price of just over $7,000 for each coin. In December 2019, on the Sixbid Internet coin auction aggregator site, Byzantine gold solidi dating to the second half of the first millennium AD of a type likely to be found in Syria, which are nearly pure gold (Morrison 2002), were selling for a few hundred US dollars each, about $400 on average. At the same time, Abbasid gold dinars were selling for about $100 less. So, if the reported on-the-ground prices are to be believed, the German dealer would have incurred a serious loss on his investment. Perhaps instead the prices on the ground have been misreported, and the German did in fact make a profit. But delving further back into the Sixbid sales archive, it is possible to find rare examples of both Byzantine solidi and Abbasid dinars selling for tens of thousands of US dollars each, up to as much as $100,000 in some cases. So, it is also possible that the German dealer was able to recognize and willing to

38 *Neil Brodie*

pay a premium price for 40 rare coins with a high resale value and did in fact make a considerable profit. But staying with this rare coin scenario for a moment, if it is correct, it would be unusual and not generally representative of prices being paid on the ground – the prices paid for more common coin types would be much lower. It seems likely also that a significant number of previously rare coins being sold at auction on the destination market would be noticed, and perhaps even act to depress prices.

More contradictory information about prices is forthcoming from the investigation of an image of a Hellenistic-Roman gold ring discovered on Abu Sayyaf's computer hard drive, which revealed it to be part of an assemblage of 18 pieces of gold jewelry believed to have been sold in Deir ez-Zor Governorate for approximately $260,000 (USA 2017c). The ring, weighing 37 g, was subsequently smuggled into Turkey by a Syrian national, who is said to have sold it for $250,000 in early 2015. He later sold the remaining pieces of the assemblage. In early 2016, Turkish police in Gaziantep confiscated the ring. This price of $250,000 inside Turkey is difficult to reconcile with the prices of similar gold rings sold at auction in New York. In Ancient Jewelry sales, for example, held by Christie's New York in 2011 and 2012, prices for five materially-similar rings were in the thousands to tens-of-thousands of dollars' range. The highest-priced ring sold for $62,500 (Christie's 2011: lot 390). Nothing like the $250,000 sale price claimed for the Abu Sayyaf ring in Turkey.

It is not certain how reliable these prices quoted inside Syria are; in fact, they seem distinctly unreliable. Dealers inside Syria and Turkey might be exaggerating prices for an expected sale, maybe as an opening gambit in a sales negotiation, or to bolster future prices. If dealers inside Syria or other countries are monitoring prices on the destination market in sales catalogues or on the Internet, they might be discounting or unaware of the hidden costs of restoration or other services such as shipping and storage and demanding unrealistic high prices for on-the-ground transactions. Perhaps it is simply that currency conversions are misleading. But when these high prices on-the-ground have been reported in the Arabic media they have incentivized further looting (Dandachi 2020: 136–137).

If the high prices reported for ancient coins and jewelry inside Syria are in fact generally correct, there are at least four possible explanations. First, the new modalities of trade, low-value objects transacted directly through social media, messaging apps or the Internet, might be diminishing price differentials between source and destination markets, primarily by eliminating the profitable role of intermediaries or brokers, and helped by better information obtained on-line about prices on the destination market. Second, the practice instituted by ISIS but also perhaps by other groups of requiring dealers from Turkey to travel into Syria to acquire material might have increased prices on the ground. Third, at the other end of the trade, perhaps higher prices in emerging though under-reported destination markets in the Gulf, Russia and East Asia are trickling down to the source market. Finally, the possibility of trade-based money laundering should not be excluded (TraCCC 2019).

Financial evidence in the form of invoices, receipts etc. necessary to investigate the use of antiquities trading for money laundering is not generally available, but the fact that the trade is clandestine and transnational with an open end-market makes it an eminently suitable vehicle for such a purpose. The apparent monetary loss suffered by the German dealer on the sale of gold coins in the Netherlands, for example, would be explicable if the dealer was using the trade to launder dirty money. Syria is primarily a cash economy (ICSR 2018), and the dealer would have needed to pay (potentially dirty) cash on the ground, while presumably receiving (clean) payment after sale in the Netherlands by wire transfer or cheque. The monetary shortfall would have been the acceptable cost of laundering. Unfortunately, these possibilities of commercial reconfigurations and money laundering are all speculative. The pricing structure of the trade out of Syria remains obscure.

ANSA and Terrorist Profiting from the Antiquities Trade

The mechanisms by which ANSA groups operating a conflict economy profit from the trade scale qualitatively according to their combat capability, territorial control and political project (Naylor 2002: 45–52). Where groups are militarily weak and facing strong and determined state opposition, they engage in "predatory" activities such as theft, or in this case archaeological looting. Early on in the Syria conflict, several reports suggested that FSA and later JAN members were engaging in predatory activities by digging and selling antiquities to trade for money to fund weapons' purchases (Baker and Anjar 2012; Bajjaly 2013; van Tets 2013; RT 2014; Luck 2013b). As groups become stronger and able to exert territorial control they develop more systematic means of profiting from "parasitical" methods of extortion through ultimately to regularized "symbiotic" regimes of taxation. During the conflict, in areas remaining under government control, dealers were forced to pay off parasitical Shabiha groups (Baker and Anjar 2012), but it is in areas occupied by ISIS and HTS that true symbiotic systems of taxation were developed.

Pseudo-state ANSA groups such as ISIS or HTS in occupation of territory and intending to achieve permanent control are concerned to achieve some semblance of civil legitimacy and order by maintaining provision of peacetime goods and services. To achieve this end, they will legalize or suppress criminal enterprises and raise money through taxation of legitimate economic activity. ISIS moved quickly to legitimize and control archaeological looting and trading through a permit system and to impose a 20 per cent "khums tax" on any proceeds (Al-Azm et al. 2014), establishing an office in the city of Manbij close to Turkish border to coordinate its antiquities activities (Al-Azm 2015). In effect, ISIS incorporated the pre-existing coping economy into its own system of governance and encouraged its newly acquired "citizenry" to participate in what it had decreed was to be a legal endeavour. To maximize tax revenue, it tried to ensure that sales of looted

40 *Neil Brodie*

material were conducted within its jurisdiction (Al-Tamimi 2015). Thus it allowed ingress for non-affiliated dealers or smugglers (Faucon et al. 2017). In February 2016, a YPG unit seized ISIS documents including an official paper allowing safe passage for a Turkish dealer through ISIS held territory (RT 2016). Another tactic to secure revenue was for ISIS to buy objects itself at a 20 per cent (tax) discount and then arrange for ongoing sale (Faucon et al. 2017). ISIS also taxed material passing through its territory from other areas (Limoges et al. 2018).

From taxing the trade, ISIS moved quickly to exert control over looting and trafficking by instituting a permit system (Faucon et al. 2017). The 2015 raid on the Syrian compound of Abu Sayyaf by US Special Forces discovered documentary evidence of ISIS's antiquities operation, showing how it controlled the trade to extract maximum profit (Keller 2015). As well as issuing permits to individuals to excavate sites, ISIS took action to prevent unauthorized excavation. One memorandum dated September 13, 2014, prohibited people from excavating archaeological sites without prior permission, and prohibited unauthorized ISIS members from giving permission. Anybody violating these prohibitions would be subject to a penalty according to Sharia law.

ISIS might also have been defrauding its subjects. The Abu Sayyaf raid recovered the transcript of a judgment resolving a dispute over the value and ownership of some gold antiquities (USA 2016). The antiquities had been dug up by a group of women, who claimed to have refused an offer of $120,000 to $180,000 made by Syrian dealers from Idlib Governorate. After occupying their area of residence, ISIS subsequently offered them $70,000 (which, allowing for tax deducted in advance, would have been $87,500), hoping to sell the material to a Turkish dealer for $200,000 (thereby raising an extra $100,000 at the finders' expense).

JAN was also using permits to control digging by at least 2015, a practice continued and developed by its successor organization HTS (Moos 2020: 15). By 2019, HTS was taxing all finds made on private land at 20 per cent, though confiscating material found on public land (Moos 2020: 14–15). Increasingly, however, HTS was coming to favour a permitting system, allowing people to dig but taking two-thirds of any sales proceeds (Moos 2020: 15, 18).

ANSAs are specialists in political violence. To obtain funding they must incorporate criminal expertise or co-opt or forge alliances with criminal groups. Increasingly, as ANSAs adopt criminal financing methods, and vice versa, hybrid organizations or cooperations of convenience emerge – the "crime–terror nexus" (Makarenko 2012; Ruggiero 2020) or "dirty entanglements" of crime, corruption and terrorism (Shelley 2015). ANSA and criminal groups might work together to market material, or individual actors might move between groups. For the antiquities trade, like any other, criminal dealers and smugglers are generally in business to make money, are not politically motivated, and are willing to trade material from any source (Giglio and Al-Awad 2015). Criminal groups have been reported in Turkey with Syrian and Turkish members of different political affiliations, including the Syrian government and former ISIS members[18]. One loose network of dealers inside Turkey has approximately 130 members, including 11 Syrians, with several members affiliated with ISIS and JAN[19]. Syrians in Hatay province active in antiquities trading are reported to have established front companies with Turkish bank accounts for transferring money abroad[20].

As ISIS has been pushed back, incoming groups have continued to profit from antiquities trading. Smugglers who in the past paid tax to ISIS now pay bribes to government forces, or taxes to other opposition groups, including the FSA and HTS (Limoges et al. 2018; Moos 2020: 29–30). It is becoming increasingly clear, if it was not clear already, that political boundaries are permeable and that criminal actors are changing allegiance when it is profitable, expedient, or necessary for them to do so[21]. Nevertheless, for a looter or smuggler, it is a fine line between a tax paid to ISIS or HTS or a bribe paid to a corrupt army officer or government official.

The facts that all armed factions have been profiting from looting and smuggling and that their areas of territorial control have fluctuated through time mean that it is not practical to pick apart discrete flows of antiquities that are differentially financing ANSA and non-ANSA (criminal) groups. By the time they are passing through the transit market, antiquities from different sources that have profited different groups will have become mixed together, fake and genuine, with trading histories suppressed and invented for passage onto the grey destination market.

The Overall Monetary Value of ANSA and Terrorist Profiting

In 2014, media outlets began publishing estimates of the financial worth of antiquities trading to ISIS, with figures ranging from the millions to billions of US dollars annually. Most of these claims can be traced back to an ambiguously-worded statement attributed to an unnamed Iraqi "intelligence official" reported in the *Guardian* newspaper, which declared that in Syria ISIS "had taken $36m from al-Nabuk alone [an area in the Qalamoun mountains west of Damascus]. The antiquities there are up to 8,000 years old" (Chulov 2014). This figure of $36 million was never verified or corroborated and is at variance with what is known of the pricing structure of the trade, where, as already explained, most profits are made on the destination market, not at source. Nevertheless, the article was frequently referenced and exaggerated by subsequent claims of a multi-billion-dollar trafficking operation (Howard et al. 2014; Hall 2015; Grantham 2016; Faucon et al. 2017; Loveluck 2015; Moody 2014). Politicians began accepting these figures as fact (Jenrick 2015; Charbonneau 2016). In 2016, the US House of Representatives Committee on Homeland Security (HSC) published a report on ISIS funding which drew from media and other open-source documentation, stating that "At one point, U.S. officials judged that ISIS was probably reaping over $100 million a year from such illicit trading" (HSC 2016: 9).

42   Neil Brodie

The evidence underpinning these political claims was never made available for critical scrutiny – if in fact it even existed. The HSC report, for example, simply referenced a newspaper article, which stated that "The total volume of illicit trade is impossible to accurately assess but is thought to have mushroomed to more than $100 million a year, according to U.S. officials" (Parkinson et al. 2015). The circularity is patent. Journalists and politicians quoting each other with no material reference open to independent verification as to its evidential reliability. Thus media reports that ISIS was making millions or even billions of dollars annually from the antiquities trade must be viewed with suspicion and perhaps even discounted (van Lit 2016; Brodie et al. 2019: 113–115). A calmer and more evidence-based assessment of ISIS profiting is much needed.

The documents seized during the Abu Sayyaf raid included a book of receipts, dated to between December 6, 2014, and March 26, 2015, recording $265,000 tax revenue made from antiquities sales. Extrapolating, it would suggest that ISIS was making approximately $880,000 annually. Only three of the receipts were published, and it has since been implied that some of the money recorded on the receipts might have been raised through sale of gold or other precious metals (Taub 2015), which has caused lobbyists for the antiquities trade to question the $265,000 figure (CCP 2017). More receipts have been published since then, however, with the English translations consistently reporting "relics" or "antiquities" (USA 2016). As previously described, the Abu Sayyaf documents also contain reference to a find of gold objects that was valued within Syria for between $120,000 and $180,000, with ISIS hoping to expropriate the material for below-value compensation and sell on, making $117,500 in the process.

As already noted, some individual coins can be sold on the destination market for prices in the tens-of-thousands of US dollars' range, with some achieving prices in excess of $100,000. But most low-denomination and common coins sell for considerably less. As relatively low-value objects, these coins are easily discounted as major income generators. But coins are traded in large quantities and aggregate revenue might be substantial, as some hypothetical accounting can easily show. In June 2018, for example, one coin dealer in North America was offering for sale 63 Greek coins said to be from "Syria and Phoenicia", with a low price of $115, a high price of $6,000, a mean price of $571 and a total value of $39,994. If it is assumed that these coins had been sold in Syria for 10 per cent of their destination market value, in other words $3,999, and further assumed that ISIS levied a 20 per cent tax, then the coins would have provided tax revenue of $800. This calculation is not to suggest that the coins actually were traded from ISIS-held territory, it simply aims to assess their potential financial worth to the group. Hypothesizing further, it is informative to look at the 14,872 coins recovered in the three Bulgarian and Turkish seizures of 2017 and 2018 referenced previously. Again, assuming each coin was found in ISIS-held territory, with a destination market price of $571 and a price inside Syria of $5, then inside Syria the coins would have generated \$74,360, which would have provided \$14,872 of tax revenue for ISIS. That is a significant sum of money and certainly a worthwhile one for ISIS to collect. Even with a lower average destination market price of \$100 and inside Syria a price of \$1 each, ISIS would have collected \$2,974. If prices inside Syria were actually higher, as previously discussed, the revenue for ISIS would likewise have been higher.

When interviewed, high-ranking ISIS operative Abdul Nasser Qardash (captured in 2020) made some confusing but not contradictory statements about the potential though not actual value of antiquities trafficking for the group (Al-Hashimi 2020):

> We did not need to grow hashish, cocaine, or Indian hemp. We had an obscene abundance of antiquities. We tried to transfer the relics to Europe to sell them, but we failed in four major attempts. This is especially true for Syrian relics, which are well known and documented as a world heritage. So we resorted to destroying them and punishing those who trade in them.
>
> But what I know is that there are four sources at least in eastern Syria that finance the organization: the proceeds of oil smuggling; arms and goods smuggling; ransom money from kidnapping of media personalities, journalists, members of humanitarian, human rights, and relief missions, and local officials; and proceeds from selling the bodies of dead and killed people – so-called selling the infidel's corpse which is viewed as war spoils. In addition, other sources include the spoils of raids and taxes on peasants, farmers, and merchants.

These statements together seem to imply that while ISIS recognized the potential financial importance of antiquities trading it failed to exert any effective control, so that antiquities trading did not become a major source of income (though it is worth remembering the interviewer's warning that "Qardash's claims should be taken with a grain of salt").

From what is known from the Abu Sayyaf documents and some hypothetical accounting, an annual income for ISIS in the high hundreds-of-thousands of dollars' range would not be an outlandish estimate, perhaps even as much as a million or just over. But certainly nothing like the millions or billions of dollars reported in the media.

Long-term Policy Failure?

A long international history of ignoring the trafficking of Syrian antiquities, both legislatively and for law enforcement operationally, laid the groundwork for post-2011 looting (Brodie 2015a, 2017a). There was a healthy international trade in Syrian antiquities before 2011, with no serious or systematic attempts at disguising their origin. It was common to see Syria offered as country of origin in sales descriptions of objects that could have been found in Syria. Syria was even

44   Neil Brodie

used in sales and customs descriptions to disguise the origins of material most likely from Iraq or another adjacent country. In 2001, for example, CBP agents at JFK International Airport reported the arrival from the United Kingdom of more than 100 Iraqi cylinder seals misdescribed as Syrian (Studevent-Hickman 2018: 208–211). On December 20, 2010, CBP agents at Detroit Metropolitan Airport stopped Michigan-based dealer Salem Alshdaifat while entering the United States from Jordan and seized Byzantine coins he was carrying. Alshdaifat claimed the coins were Syrian, but they were confiscated because he provided two different invoices at two different inspections – not because they were Syrian (St Hilaire 2011). In February 2000, New York dealer Hicham Aboutaam arrived at JFK International Airport with an Iranian silver vessel, which he misdescribed to customs as Syrian. He was allowed through but arrested afterwards in December 2003 when it became known that the vessel was in fact from Iran and its import had been illegal under the Iranian Transactions Regulations (Lufkin 2004).

Thus the evidence suggests that before 2011 the trade in Syrian objects was considered unproblematic by customs and dealers alike. The previously discussed mosaics seized in Montreal between 1991 and 1996 seem to have been the exception to the rule. There are examples of Syrian objects that were in transit or on the market before 2011, but not seized until after 2011. In April 2014, an inscribed Syrian stele offered for sale at London's Bonhams auction house was seized by the Metropolitan Police when evidence came to light that it had probably been looted in 1999 (Lamb 2014b). It had been offered at Christie's New York in 2000 but had failed to sell. Sometime between 2013 and 2016, three funerary reliefs from Palmyra were seized in the Geneva Freeport. They had arrived there in 2009 and 2010 from Qatar (AFP 2016). Thus, on the destination market, there was an open trade in Syrian antiquities in the decades leading up to 2011, but very little was done to stop it. Inside Turkey on the transit market, Antakya and Gaziantep have since 2011 emerged as a major hubs of the cross-border antiquities trade (Hunter 2015; and see Cengiz this volume, Chapter 4), in Gaziantep at least due in part to a well-established network of dealers and smugglers working with corrupt government officials and law enforcement officers (Sputnik 2016)[22]. The corrupting influence of these long-established collaborations of wealthy and politically influential dealers and smugglers (and collectors) has been reported in other countries in the region[23]. Protected as they were, no successful attempts were made before 2011 to extirpate their networks, and they have continued in operation. Thus many of the people criminally involved before 2011 were still active in 2011, inside Syria, but also outside Syria on the transit and destination markets. They constituted a skeletal yet experienced organizational structure that was available to encourage and support the rapid increase in looting and smuggling seen after 2011.

If the trade in Syrian antiquities was left generally unmolested before 2011, the changing nature of the trade during the early 2000s made it even harder to tackle after 2011. Coins and smaller antiquities were easier to move and harder to detect. The small amounts of money involved in individual transactions on the destination market diminishes the apparent seriousness of crimes and reduces the public interest requirement for committing adequate resources to their investigation and prosecution. Furthermore, because the seriousness of a crime determines the severity of sentencing, weak particularly non-custodial sentences pose little deterrent effect on destination-market dealers. Thus the trade in low-value coins and antiquities weakens both the case for and the effectiveness of targeted law enforcement. It is worth revisiting in this context observations that looted Syrian antiquities have not been appearing on the market in Europe or the United States (McAndrew 2014; Bakare 2020), while at the same time, as already described, Turkish law enforcement agencies have been seizing what by now must be tens of thousands of smuggled ancient coins and other antiquities. The contrast is stark. Perhaps Turkey is being so successful at interdicting the trade on its own territory that nothing is reaching the United States or Europe, though that seems unlikely, to say the least. The contrast most likely speaks instead to different priorities, competences and operational procedures, with Turkish agencies either better resourced and incentivized or better trained and experienced than their US and European counterparts for engaging with low-value antiquities trading.

It is difficult to prove criminal intent on the part of dealers or collectors on the destination market. The grey trade facilitates honest or dishonest defences of innocent purchase. As a result, while most seized antiquities are returned to their lawful owners, there is hardly ever an associated criminal investigation or conviction. This policy has been termed "seize and send" (St Hilaire 2016) or "recovery and return" (Brodie 2015a: 324–326). It can be justified by arguments that the return of an antiquity of great cultural worth to its dispossessed owner should not be jeopardized by the uncertain outcome of a criminal trial or that the confiscation of a valuable antiquity will deter future wrongdoing. But it is debateable to what extent the antiquities seized through customs and other law enforcement actions match such high cultural standards. Dealers and smugglers can accept the occasional loss of material through "seize and send" as a cost of doing business, and continue trading, thereby generating proceeds at source for terrorist groups to appropriate. ANSA and terrorist profiting from the looting and smuggling of antiquities out of Syria would have been much reduced if action had been taken against the trade before 2011, with the pre-existing criminal economy weakened through the energetic prosecution and deterrent sentencing of criminal dealers. By the time ISIS was extracting its hundreds-of-thousands of dollars, it was too late – the world was playing catch-up. Antiquities looting and trafficking will never be stopped while the dealers and smugglers responsible are left at large. It is a matter of some urgency that appropriate and effective countermeasures should be planned and implemented, focusing on eliminating trade (and terrorist financing) rather than recovering looted material.

46   *Neil Brodie*

Conclusion

This chapter has attempted to provide an evidence-based account of the looting and trafficking of Syrian antiquities since the onset of civil conflict in Syria in 2011. It should be apparent to any reader that reliable "evidence" is in short supply. Most information is derived from media reporting, which is sometimes good but often simply repetitive or at worst sensationalist. Sam Hardy (2015b) has warned about the dangers of relying too much upon "churnalism" in this context, though in the general absence of good quality research there is often no other option. Nevertheless, triangulation and redundancy of sources offer some reassurance about the general accuracy of information being reported, and overall the picture is clear. On-the-ground reporting and particularly satellite imagery have between them documented without doubt the severity of archaeological looting since 2011. The involvement of a broad constituency of civilian, criminal and political actors is also well established. It is unfortunate, however, that most media and scholarly attention has been focused upon the situation in Syria and its immediately neighboring countries, with very little paid to the destination market. There have, for example, been a large number of admittedly abbreviated interviews with source-market dealers and smugglers published, but almost none with dealers based in London, Paris or New York[24]. Arguably, this reporting imbalance has serious consequences as it creates the mistaken impression that the problem is purely a regional one affecting only Syria and its neighbors, and thus is one that needs to be tackled regionally by any introduced policies or implemented actions. Causative demand on the destination market is left untouched and the problem persists. This under-reporting and under-investigation of the destination market is in urgent need of rectification.

What evidence is available points to the commercial importance of ancient coins and other small antiquities. Money paid in the United States or Europe for such antiquities excavated in or traded through territory controlled by terrorists or ANSAs must "trickle down" to the ANSAs involved. But important questions remain unanswered, particularly those relating to the economics of the trade. How much is it worth, both globally and locally? Who profits, and by how much? The level of financial support looting and trafficking provides ANSAs remains unaccounted and many quoted figures seem hopelessly inflated or exaggerated. There is at present no reliable evidence to support claims that ISIS or any other ANSA might have been making millions or even billions of dollars annually from the trade, or that the trade might have been a major source of revenue. Nevertheless, the evidence that both ISIS and HTS have been profiting from the trade is incontrovertible, and the degree of profitability has certainly been high enough for both groups to exert command and control.

It is worth bearing in mind Peter Neumann's admonition about "small-dollar terrorism" when he talks about the low cost of violent terrorist attacks in Europe (ICSR 2018). The bottom line remains that it takes only $1,000 to buy a Kalashnikov (McCarthy 2017). It can be argued by some scholars and others that the monetary value of the trade is of no consequence as the damage caused can only be measured in terms of cultural or intellectual loss. For many politicians and members of the general public, however, concerned about terrorist financing and the threats posed by terrorism to the ongoing security of civil society, money is of fundamental importance and the financial questions are not going to go away any time soon. Trade-based money laundering has only been touched upon in this chapter, largely because evidence is lacking, but that is not to say that it doesn't exist. While ISIS seems to have depended largely upon exploiting human and natural resources in territory under its control, money laundering through transnational trade might be a significant source of income for other ANSAs or for criminals more generally. The challenge now is to devise robust methodologies for answering these financial questions. It is time to stop following the antiquities and to start following the money. That will not be easy, but highlighting the issue is at least a first step.

Notes

1 This chapter is based upon a report submitted as part of the US State Department funded project Countering Looting of Antiquities from Syria and Iraq (CLASI), conceived and delivered by the Terrorism, Transnational Crime and Corruption Center (TraCCC) of George Mason University. It is based in part on original research conducted by the CLASI project via media, Internet, and social media monitoring, as well as interviews with knowledgeable "project informants" (PIs) living inside Turkey, Syria and Iraq.
2 There is not enough space in this chapter to deal adequately with the political and ideological configurations and reconfigurations of the many armed opposition groups and their constituent actors that have fought in Syria since 2011. Only the larger groups are considered.
3 By 2020, a lot of information about the looting of Syrian archaeological sites and museums had been assembled and made available on resources like the American Society of Overseas Research's Cultural Heritage Initiatives (ASOR CHI) database and the Association for the Protection of Syrian Archaeology (APSA) report into Syrian museums (Ali 2020), though it remained largely undigested. This chapter is primarily concerned with trade, not looting, so no attempt has been made to produce a comprehensive, synthetic account of the chronology, extent or intensity of looting. Nevertheless, the general outlines are clear.
4 PIs 2, 9, 13, 17, 18, 19, 20, 21.
5 PIs 11, 12, 13.
6 PIs 1, 2, 4, 6, 8.
7 PIs 11, 12, 13.
8 PIs 3, 6, 8.
9 PIs 1, 2, 6, 8, 9, 13, 18.
10 PIs 2, 4, 6, 9, 10.
11 PI 23.
12 PIs 14, 25.
13 PI 14.
14 PIs 4, 5, 7.

48   *Neil Brodie*

15 Pls 3, 5.
16 In April 2020 Facebook announced a new policy as regards its use as a platform for trading antiquities, stating that it would remove content on Facebook and Instagram attempting to buy or sell antiquities (Mashberg 2020). How this policy plays out in practice remains to be seen. One worry is that by removing rather than deactivating content Facebook will be removing evidence of criminal activity and make it harder to investigate (Al-Azm and Paul 2019: 46).
17 This previously unpublished research was conducted by the author for a talk entitled "The Structure and Organisation of the Antiquities Trade: Results of Some Recent Research" presented at the November 2018 UNESCO meeting Fighting the Illicit Trafficking of Cultural Property.
18 Pls 2, 3, 4, 5, 7, 8.
19 Pls 1, 6, 8.
20 Pls 3, 5, 8.
21 Pls 2, 3, 5, 7, 8.
22 Pls 1, 6, 8.
23 Pls 23, 24.
24 Though see the BBC interactive investigation into Hellenistic coins looted in Gaza (BBC 2020).

References

AAAS. 2014. *Ancient History, Modern Destruction: Assessing the Status of Syria's Tentative World Heritage Sites Using High-Resolution Satellite Imagery: Part One.* Washington DC: American Association for the Advancement of Science. https://www.aaas.org/resources/ancient-history-modern-destruction-assessing-status-syrias-tentative-world-heritage-sites.

Abdulkareem, Inas. 2020. Mercenaries of the Turkish Occupation Excavate Efrin Antiquities to loot them, *Syria Times,* June 28. http://syriatimes.sy/index.php/news/local/49515-mercenaries-of-the-turkish-occupation-excavate-efrin-antiquities-to-loot-them.

Abdulrahman, Ammar. 2001. The New Syrian Law on Antiquities. In *Trade in Illicit Antiquities: The Destruction of the World's Archaeological Heritage,* edited by Neil Brodie, Jennifer Doole and Colin Renfrew. Cambridge: McDonald Institute for Archaeological Research, 111–114.

Acar, Özgen and Melik Kaylan. 1990. The Turkish Connection: An Investigative Report on the Smuggling of Classical Antiquities. *Connoisseur* October, 128–137.

Afeiche, Anne-Marie. 2018. La restitution au Liban de cinq sculptures d'Echmoun. *Baal* 18, 5–18.

AFP. 2012. Syria's Archaeological Heritage Falls Prey to War, Agence France-Presse, September 24. http://www.hurriyetdailynews.com/syrias-archaeological-heritage-falls-prey-to-war-30846.

AFP. 2015. In Syria, Race to Save Antiquities from Looting, Damage, Agence France-Presse, March 26. https://www.timesofisrael.com/in-syria-race-to-save-antiquities-from-looting-damage/.

AFP. 2016. Looted Palmyra Relics Seized by Swiss Authorities at Geneva Ports. *Guardian,* December 3. https://www.theguardian.com/world/2016/dec/03/looted-palmyra-relics-seized-by-swiss-authorities-at-geneva-ports.

AGI. 2012. L'allarme di Paolo Matthiae: "Stanno rubando I mosaici di Palmira e Apamea", *Il Giornale dell' Arte,* August 7. https://www.ilgiornaledellarte.com/articoli/articoli/2012/8/114052.html.

Looting and Trafficking of Syrian Antiquities 49

Al-Azm, Amr. 2015. *The Pillaging of Syria's Cultural Heritage*, May 22. Middle East Institute. https://www.mei.edu/publications/pillaging-syrias-cultural-heritage.

Al-Azm, Amr, Salam al-Kuntar and Brian Daniels. 2014. ISIS' Antiquities Sideline, *New York Times*, September 2.

Al-Azm, Amr and Katie Paul. 2019. Facebook's Black Market in Antiquities. Trafficking, Terrorism and War Crimes. Antiquities Trafficking and Heritage Anthropology Research (ATHAR) Project. http://atharproject.org/report2019/.

Albertson, Lynda. 2016. Auction alert I: Ancient Palmyran Limestone Head ca. 3rd-5th Century A.D.?ARCA blog, November 30. http://art-crime.blogspot.com/2016/11/auction-alert-i-ancient-palmyran.html.

Al-Haj Salih, Yassin. 2015. The Syrian Shabiha and their State: Statehood and Participation. Heinrich Böll Stiftung, March 3. http://lb.boell.org/en/2014/03/03/syrian-shabiha-and-their-statestatehood-participation.

Al-Hashimi, Husham. 2020. Interview: ISIS's Abdul Nasser Qardash. Centre for Global Policy, June 4. https://cgpolicy.org/articles/interview-isiss-abdul-nasser-qardash/.

Al-Tamimi, Aymenn Jawad. 2015. The Archivist: Unseen Documents from the Islamic State's Diwan at-Rikaz. Jihadology blog, October 12. https://jihadology.net/2015/10/12/the-archivist-unseen-documents-from-the-islamic-states-diwan-al-rikaz.

Ali, Cheikhmous. 2015. *Palmyra: Heritage Adrift*, ASOR Cultural Heritage Initiatives, June 29. http://www.asor-syrianheritage.org/palmyra-heritage-adrift.

Ali, Cheikmous. 2020. *Rapport détaillé sur tous les dégâts que les musées syriens ont subis depuis 2011 jusqu'à 2020*. Association for the Protection of Syrian Archaeology, June 2. https://www.facebook.com/apsa2011/?__tn__=kC-R&eid=ARBAmlktpYzZqGu-D9 1cy_Kmc_Plq5K-oiT5c8h3IzybYuW3eat29gi4SKZl-Opz1iiaSxZH0EjWkI-J&hc_ref= ARQxx8ttJXePQmOxKMqm6MHLtzacqtXL4IfpmDpybRYF6rNSCuH_VTHm50R sgk6Ttn0&fref=nf&__xts__[0]=68.ARAYD1L8zbLWOUqy0Mvdn5nqDFucG8JxOgY twqrRliv77bGw8rjlnXCM4oCnBg-uj9sGN4jjj_Bxc42_DE5RYFo_4MmuhjWD-sZjm BZv6SKFgpsBaN_SPKctwZxl3ZN0-vTZXqt8mdepFGAIXuv3kwGUkiDXv4VkNa TYai0z2AQru1zgD25no1SCzGrG8QxebYFVTihpiLq9uUFk5PC8gsyMLb94b4uqHu z1aN9bKj_65-e5Cje1Z5n1mDZdMsYCXuIwf0l_ZKgoQ6SZu2PJMpBRIMzv2cH1X g9fYSHOkZT49wP9yGdTfpS1535p63jiSx96j0sobYwD9hgEzlhH10UaSA.

Ali, Zulfiqar. 2020. Syria: Who's in Control of Idlib?, BBC News, February 18. https://www.bbc.co.uk/news/world-45401474.

AP. 2016. Islamic State Pressured after Turkey Tightens Jihadi Highway, Associated Press, July 6. http://www.dailymail.co.uk/wires/ap/article-3676506/Islamic-State-pressured-Turkey-tightens-jihadi-highway.html.

Arango, Tim and Eric Schmitt. 2015. A Path to ISIS, Through a Porous Turkish Border, *New York Times*, March 9. https://www.nytimes.com/2015/03/10/world/europe/despite-crackdown-path-to-join-isis-often-winds-through-porous-turkish-border.html.

ASOR. 2014. ASOR Cultural Heritage Initiatives Weekly Report7, September 22. http://www.asor-syrianheritage.org/shi-weekly-report-7-september-22-2014/.

ASOR. 2016a. The Day After Heritage Protection Initiative Observer's Project in Idlib City: A Field Survey of the Historic City of Apamea, *ASOR Cultural Heritage Initiatives Weekly Report*, 79–80, February 3–16. http://www.asor-syrianheritage.org/wp-content/uploads/2016/03/ASOR_CHI_Weekly_Report_79%E2%80%938 0r.pdf.

ASOR. 2016b. ASOR Cultural Heritage Initiatives Weekly Report83–84, March 2–15. http://www.asor-syrianheritage.org/wp-content/uploads/2016/03/ASOR_CHI_Week ly_Report_83%E2%80%9384r.pdf.

50 *Neil Brodie*

Bajjaly, Joanne. 2013. Arms for Antiquities: Syrian Artifacts Smuggling Bleeds Sites Dry, *Al-Akhbar English*, September 3. https://english.al-akhbar.com/node/16918.

Bakare, Lanre. 2020. UK Curator Criticises "Misleading" Reports About Looted Items, *Guardian*, April 10. https://www.theguardian.com/world/2020/apr/10/uk-curator-criticises-misleading-reports-about-looted-items.

Baker, Aryn and Majdal Anjar. 2012. Syria's Looted Past: How Ancient Artifacts are Being Traded for Guns, *Time*, September 12. http://world.time.com/2012/09/12/syrias-looted-past-how-ancient-artifacts-are-being-traded-for-guns.

Barnard, Anne. 2014. Syrian War Takes Heavy Toll at a Crossroad of Cultures, *New York Times*, April 16. http://www.ilgiornaledellarte.com/articoli/2012/8/114052.html.

BBC. 2012. Syria Unrest: Who are the Shabiha? BBC News, May 29. https://www.bbc.co.uk/news/world-middle-east-14482968.

BBC. 2020. *Treasure Hunters: An Interactive Investigation into the Disappearance of a Rare Hoard of Ancient Coins*, BBC website, no date. https://www.bbc.co.uk/news/resources/idt-d4a6df1b-995d-4d0d-a562-43bd47b86afb.

Bogdanos, Matthew. 2005. The Terrorist in the Art Gallery, *New York Times*, December 10. https://www.nytimes.com/2005/12/10/opinion/the-terrorist-in-the-art-gallery.html.

Brodie, Neil. 2006. Iraq 1990–2004 and the London Antiquities Market. In *Archaeology, Cultural Heritage, and the Antiquities Trade*, edited by Neil Brodie, Morag Kersel, Christina Luke and Kathryn W. Tubb. Gainesville: University Press of Florida, 206–226.

Brodie, Neil. 2012. Uncovering the Antiquities Market. In *Oxford Handbook of Public Archaeology*, edited by Robin Skeates, Carol McDavid and John Carman. Oxford: Oxford University Press, 230–252.

Brodie, Neil. 2014. The Antiquities Market: It's All in a Price, *Heritage and Society*, 7 (1), 32–46.

Brodie, Neil. 2015a. Syria and Its Regional Neighbors: A Case of Cultural Property Protection Policy Failure?, *International Journal of Cultural Property*, 22, 317–335.

Brodie, Neil. 2015b. The Internet Market in Precolumbian Antiquities. In *Cultural Property Crime: An Overview and Analysis on Contemporary Perspectives and Trends*, edited by Joris Kila and Marc Balcells. Leiden: Brill, 237–262.

Brodie, Neil. 2017a. Protection not Prevention: The Failure of Public Policy to Prevent the Plunder and Traffic of Cultural Property from the MENA Region (1990–2015). In *The Routledge Companion to Cultural Property*, edited by Jane Anderson and Haidy Geismar. London: Routledge, 89–107.

Brodie, Neil. 2017b. Virtually Gone! The Internet Market in Antiquities. In *Proceedings of the 6th International Conference of Experts on the Return of Cultural Property*. Seoul: Overseas Korean Cultural Heritage Foundation, 190–204.

Brodie, Neil and Isber Sabrine. 2018. The Illegal Excavation and Trade of Syrian Cultural Objects: A View from the Ground, *Journal of Field Archaeology*, 43, 74–84.

Brodie, Neil, Donna Yates, Brigitte Slot, Olga Batura, Niels van Wanrooij and Gabriëlle op 't Hoog. 2019. *Illicit Trade in Cultural Goods in Europe*. Luxembourg: European Union. https://op.europa.eu/en/publication-detail/-/publication/d79a105a-a6aa-11e9-9d01-01aa75ed71a1/language-en/format-PDF/source-114932158.

Burke, Jason. 2017. Rise and Fall of ISIS: Its Dream of a Caliphate is Over, So What Now? *Guardian*, October 21. https://www.theguardian.com/world/2017/oct/21/isis-caliphate-islamic-state-raqqa-iraq-islamist.

Butterlin, Pascal and Mathilde Mura. 2019. Mari et al crise syrienne. In *Archéologie des Conflits/Archéologie en Conflit*, edited by Julie Bessenay-Prolonge, Jean-Jacques Herr and Mathilde Mura. Paris: Routes de l'Orient, 199–224.

Casana, Jesse and Mitra Panahipour. 2014. Notes on a Disappearing Past: Satellite-based Monitoring of Looting and Damage to Archaeological Sites in Syria, *Journal of Eastern Mediterranean Archaeology and Heritage Studies*, 2, 128–151.

Casana, Jesse and Elise Jakoby Laugier. 2017. Satellite Imagery-based Monitoring of Archaeological Site Damage in the Syrian Civil War, *PLoS ONE*, 12 (11), e0188589. https://doi.org/10.1371/journal.pone.0188589.

CBS. 2015. Dangerous "Uphill Battle" to Save Syria's History, CBS News, March 20. https://www.cbsnews.com/news/syria-antiquities-looted-destroyed-war-isis-modern-monuments-men/.

CCP. 2015. Media Alert: Poor Data on Syria Triggers Widespread Disinformation Campaign, Committee for Cultural Policy, press release, February 11.

CCP. 2017. *Bearing False Witness: The Media, ISIS and Antiquities*, Committee for Cultural Policy special report, December 1. https://culturalpropertynews.org/bea ring-false-witness-the-media-isis-and-antiquities.

Cengiz, Mahmut and Mitchel P. Roth. 2019. *The Illicit Economy in Turkey: How Criminals, Terrorists, and the Syrian Conflict Fuel Underground Markets*. Maryland: Lexington Books.

Charbonneau, Louis. 2016. *Islamic State Nets Millions from Antiquities: Russia*. Reuters, April 6. https://www.reuters.com/article/us-mideast-crisis-antiquities-russia /islamic-state-nets-millions-from-antiquities-russia-idUSKCN0X32HK.

Chazan, David. 2015. ISIL Antiques "Sold to Western Collectors" Warns French Finance Minister, *Daily Telegraph*, December 4. https://www.telegraph.co.uk/news/ worldnews/europe/france/12034421/Isil-antiques-sold-to-western-collectors-warns-F rench-finance-minister.html.

Chivers, C.J. 2013. Grave Robbers and War Steal Syria's History, *New York Times*, April 6. https://www.nytimes.com/2013/04/07/world/middleeast/syrian-war-devasta tes-ancient-sites.html.

Christie's. 2011. *Ancient Jewelry*, December 7. New York: Christie's.

Chulov, Martin. 2014. How an Arrest in Iraq Revealed ISIS's $2bn Jihadist Network, *Guardian*, June 15.

Clark, Justin. 2016. How the Antiquities Black Market Thrives on Syria: "We have the Collapse of State Institutions and the Society Holding them all Together", Syria Direct, December 8. http://syriadirect.org/news/how-the-antiquities-black-ma rket-thrives-on-syria-%E2%80%98we-have-the-collapse-of-state-institutions-and-th e-society-holding-them-all-together%E2%80%99.

CNN. 2019. *ISIS Fast Facts*, CNN, May 1. https://edition.cnn.com/2014/08/08/world/ isis-fast-facts/index.html.

Cockburn, Patrick. 2014. The Destruction of the Idols: Syria's Patrimony at Risk from Extremists, *Independent*, February 11. https://www.independent.co.uk/news/ science/archaeology/news/the-destruction-of-the-idols-syria-s-patrimony-at-risk-fro m-extremists-9122275.html.

Cockburn, Patrick. 2016. Fake Antiquities Flood Out of Syria, as Smugglers Fail to Steal Masterpieces Amid the Chaos of War, *Independent*, September 6. https:// www.independent.co.uk/news/world/middle-east/syria-isis-civil-war-antiquities-fake s-palmyra-a7228336.html.

52 Neil Brodie

Cox, Simon. 2015. *The Men who Smuggle the Loot that Funds IS*, BBC News, February 17. https://www.bbc.co.uk/news/magazine-31485439.

Cuneo, Allison and Michael Danti. 2019Tracking Heritage Loss in the Middle of Armed Conflict. In *Archéologie des Conflits/Archéologie en Conflit*, edited by Julie Bessenay-Prolonge, Jean-Jacques Herr and Mathilde Mura. Paris: Routes de l'Orient, 265–284.

Cuneo, Allison, Susan Penacho, Michael Danti, Marina Gabriel and Jamie O'Connell. 2016. *The Recapture of Palmyra*. ASOR Cultural Heritage Initiatives Special report, March. http://www.asor.org/chi/reports/special-reports/The-Recapture-of-Pa lmyra.

Cunliffe, Emma. 2012. *Damage to the Soul: Syria's Cultural Heritage in Conflict*. Palo Alto: Global Heritage Fund. http://ghn.globalheritagefund.com/uploads/docum ents/document_2107.pdf.

Dandachi, Nidaa. 2020. Syrian Antiquities and the Media. In *Working with Cultural Objects and Manuscripts*, edited by Visa Immonen, Rick Bonnie, Helen Dixon, Ulla Tervahauta and Suzie Thomas. Helsinki: Finnish Museums Association, 131–138.

Daniels, Brian and Katharyn Hanson. 2015. Archaeological Site Looting in Syria and Iraq: A Review of the Evidence. In *Countering Illicit Traffic in Cultural Goods*, edited by France Desmarais. Paris: ICOM, 83–94.

Darke, Diana. 2020. Syria War: Forgotten Amid the Bombs: Idlib's Ancient, Ruined Riches. BBC News, February 8. https://www.bbc.co.uk/news/world-middle-ea st-51177433.

Davis, Tess and Simon Mackenzie. 2015. Crime and Conflict Temple Looting in Cambodia. In *Cultural Property Crime: An Overview and Analysis of Contemporary Perspectives and Trends*, edited by Joris D. Kila and Marc Balcells. Leiden: Brill, 292–306.

DGAM. 2014. Violations Cause Grave Damage to Mari and Dura Europos Sites, Deir ez-Zor, Directorate-General of Antiquities and Museums, Syria, press release, January 28.

DGAM. 2015. Illegal Excavations are Still Going on at Mari and Dura Europos Archaeological Sites. Directorate-General of Antiquities and Museums, Syria, press release, February 17.

Dikov, Ivan. 2015a. Bulgarian Police Seize Ancient Roman Archaeology Artifacts, Slab with Sumerian Motifs from Treasure Hunters, *Archaeology in Bulgaria*, March 24. http://archaeologyinbulgaria.com/2015/03/24/bulgarian-police-seize-ancient-roman-arc haeology-artifacts-slab-with-sumerian-motifs-from-treasure-hunters/.

Dikov, Ivan. 2015b. Bulgarian Archaeologist Concludes Roman Artifacts Seized from Smugglers Authentic, Originated in Asia Minor and the Middle East, *Archaeology in Bulgaria*, August 12. http://archaeologyinbulgaria.com/2015/08/12/bulgarian-a rchaeologist-concludes-roman-artifacts-seized-from-smugglers-authentic-originated -in-asia-minor-and-the-middle-east/.

Dikov, Ivan. 2018. 11,000 Coins, Archaeological Artifacts Seized on Bulgaria's Border in Attempted Smuggling from Turkey into EU, *Archaeology in Bulgaria*, May 26. http://archaeologyinbulgaria.com/2018/05/26/11000-coins-archaeological-a rtifacts-seized-on-bulgarias-border-in-attempted-smuggling-from-turkey-into-eu.

Dupree, Nancy. 1996. Museum Under Siege, *Archaeology*, 49 (2), 47. https://archive. archaeology.org/online/features/afghan/.

Dupree, Nancy. 1998. The Plunder Continues, *Archaeology* on-line, May 26. https://a rchive.archaeology.org/online/features/afghan/update.html.

Faucon, Benoit, Georgi Kantchev and Alistair MacDonald. 2017. Antiquities: The Men who Trade ISIS Loot – The Middlemen who Buy and Sell Antiquities Looted by ISIS from Syria and Iraq Explain how the Smuggling Supply Chain Works, *Wall Street Journal*, August 7.

Field, Les, Cristóbal Gnecco and Joe Watkins. 2016. *Challenging the Dichotomy. The Licit and the Illicit in Archaeological and Heritage Discourses*. Tucson: University of Arizona.

Fisk, Robert. 2013. The Cost of War must be Measured by Human Tragedy, not Artifacts, *Independent*, March 18. https://www.independent.co.uk/voices/comment/robert-fisk-the-cost-of-war-must-be-measured-by-human-tragedy-not-artefacts-853 7986.html.

Fossey, John M. 2015. Illicit Traffic in Antiquities: Some Canadian Experiences. In *Cultural Property Crime: An Overview and Analysis of Contemporary Perspectives and Trends*, edited by Joris D. Kila and Marc Balcells. Leiden: Brill, 206–220.

Giglio, Mike. 2014. This is How ISIS Smuggles Oil, *BuzzFeedNews*, November 3. http s://www.buzzfeed.com/mikegiglio/this-is-how-isis-smuggles-oil?utm_term=.kixy1G XRM#.ctw7xpzko.

Giglio, Mike and Munzer Al-Awad. 2015. Inside the Underground Trade to Sell off Syria's History, *BuzzFeedNews*, July 30. https://www.buzzfeed.com/mikegiglio/the-trade-in-stolen-syrian-artifacts?utm_term=.jnpDr3wjx#.jpAj8Qp9R.

Gobat, Jeanne and Kristina Kostial. 2016. *Syria's Conflict Economy*. IMF Working Paper. International Monetary Fund. https://www.imf.org/external/pubs/ft/wp/2016/wp16123.pdf.

Goodhand Jonathan. 2003. *From War Economy to Peace Economy?*, paper presented at London School of Economics and Political Science and University of Bonn conference: State reconstruction and international engagement in Afghanistan, May 30–June. http://eprints.lse.ac.uk/28364.

Goodhand, Jonathan. 2005. Frontiers and Wars: The Opium Economy in Afghanistan, *Journal of Agrarian Change*, 5 (2), 191–216.

Grantham, David. 2016. *Shutting Down ISIS' Antiquities Trade*. National Center for Policy Analysis, Issue Brief no. 185. January. http://www.ncpathinktank.org/pdfs/ib185.pdf.

Greenland, Fiona, James Marrone, Oya Topçuoğlu and Tasha Vorderstrasse. 2019. A Site-level Market Model of the Antiquities Trade, *International Journal of Cultural Property* 26, 21–47.

Hall, John. 2015. The ISIS Smugglers Making up to $1million per Item Selling Ancient Antiquities Looted from the Rubble of Syria. *Daily Mail*, February 17. https://www.dailymail.co.uk/news/article-2957240/The-ISIS-smugglers-making-1mil lion-item-selling-ancient-antiquities-looted-rubble-Syria.html.

Hardy, Sam. 2015a. The Conflict Antiquities Trade: An Historical Overview. In *Countering Illicit Traffic in Cultural Goods*, edited by France Desmarais. Paris: ICOM, 21–32.

Hardy, Sam. 2015b. Palmyra: Looting Under the Rebels, the Assad Regime and the Islamic State?, Conflict Antiquities blog, July 3. https://conflictantiquities.wordp ress.com/2015/07/03/palmyra-looting-rebels-regime-islamic-state-propaganda.

Hardy, Sam. 2018. *Conflict Antiquities and Fake Conflict Antiquities are Marketed From and Through Turkey*, Conflict Antiquities blog, February 28. https://conflicta ntiquities.wordpress.com/2018/02/28/fake-conflict-antiquities-market.

Harkin, James. 2014. *Stealing Syria's Past*. Pulitzer Center on Crisis Reporting, August 27. http://pulitzercenter.org/reporting/middle-east-syria-war-theft-archeolo gy-assyria.

54 *Neil Brodie*

Herbert, M. 2014. Partisans, Profiteers, and Criminals: Syria's Illicit Economy, *Fletcher Forum of World Affairs*, 38 (1), 69–86.

Howard, Russell D., Jonathan Prohov and Marc Elliott. 2014. Opinion: How ISIS Funds Terror through Black Market Antiquities Trade, USNI News, October 27. https://news.usni.org/2014/10/27/isis-funds-terror-black-market-antiquities-trade.

HSC. 2016. *Cash to Chaos: Dismantling ISIS' Financial Infrastructure.* House Homeland Security Committee Majority Staff Report. October. https://info.pub licintelligence.net/US-ISIS-FinancialDismantling.pdf.

Hunter, Isabel. 2015. Syria Conflict: The Illicit Art Trade that is a Major Source of Income for Today's Terror Groups is Nothing New, *Independent*, April 26.

ICSR. 2018. *Beyond Banking: Professor Neumann's Opening Keynote Address at "No Money for Terror"* Summit in Paris, International Centre for the Study of Radicalisation website, April 26. https://icsr.info/2018/04/26/beyond-banking-professor-neumanns-opening-keynote-address-no-money-terror-summit-paris.

Jaba, Hala and George Arbuthnott. 2013. Syrians Loot Roman Treasures to Buy Guns, *Sunday Times*, May 5.

Jenrick, Robert. 2015. No One Group has Done More to Put Our Heritage at Risk than Islamic State, *Art Newspaper*, January 28.

Kadi, Samar. 2015. Narrowing Markets for Illicit Trade of Syrian Antiquities, *Daily Star*, March 14. https://www.dailystar.com.lb/News/Lebanon-News/2015/Mar-14/290754-narrowing-markets-for-illicit-trade-of-syrian-antiquities.ashx.

Kaercher, Kyra, Susan Penacho, Katherine Burge, Jamie O'Connell and Marina Gabriel. 2018. Update: Ebla. An Evaluation of Damage, ASOR Cultural Heritage Initiatives. http://www.asor.org/chi/updates/2018/05/ebla.

Keller, Andrew. 2015. *Documenting ISIL's Antiquities Trafficking: The Looting and Destruction of Iraqi and Syrian Cultural Heritage: What we know and What can be Done*, U.S. Department of State, September 29. https://2009-2017.state.gov/e/eb/rls/rm/2015/247610.htm.

Lamb, Franklin. 2014a. Raqqa is Being Slaughtered Silently, *Scoop*, May 10. http://www.scoop.co.nz/stories/HL1405/S00084/raqqa-is-being-slaughtered-silently.htm.

Lamb, Franklin. 2014b. A Syrian Victory at a Posh London Auction House?, *Counterpunch*, April 9. http://www.counterpunch.org/2014/04/09/a-syrian-victory-at-a-posh-london-auction-house/.

Limoges, Barrett, Amjad Alhawamdeh and Waleed Khaled a-Noufal. 2018. While the Islamic State Fades in Syria, its Legacy of Antiquities Smuggling Flourishes, Syria Direct, May 30. https://syriadirect.org/news/while-the-islamic-state-fades-in-syria-its-legacy-of-antiquities-smuggling-flourishes.

Loveluck, Louisa. 2015. Islamic State Sets Up "Ministry of Antiquities" to Reap the Profits of Pillaging, *Telegraph*, May 30.

Luck, Taylor. 2013a. Police Seize Large Cache of Syrian Artefacts, *Jordan Times*, February 9.

Luck, Taylor. 2013b. Syrian Rebels Loot Artifacts to Raise Money for Fight Against Assad, *Washington Post*, February 12. https://www.washingtonpost.com/world/m iddle_east/syrian-rebels-loot-artifacts-to-raise-money-for-fight-against-assad/2013/02/12/ae0cf01e-6ede-11e2-8b8d-e0b59a1b8e2a_story.html?noredirect=on&utm_ter m=.9671ec3a102a.

Lufkin, Martha. 2004. Antiquities Dealer Arrested for Smuggling Iranian Object, *Art Newspaper*, no. 145, March 8.

Mabillard, Boris. 2013. Snapshot of a Syrian Smuggler: Arms, Antiquities and Jihad along Turkey's Border, *Le Temps*, August 31.

McAndrew, James. 2014. Syria and Iraq's Neighbours Can Help Contain the Looting, *Art Newspaper*, no. 263, December.

McCarthy, Niall. 2017. The Cost of an AK-47 on The Black Market around the World, *Forbes*, March 30. https://www.forbes.com/sites/niallmccarthy/2017/03/30/the-cost-of-an-ak-47-on-the-black-market-across-the-world-infographic.

Mackenzie, Simon and Donna Yates. 2016. What is Grey about the "Grey Market" in Antiquities. In *The Architecture of Illegal Markets: Towards an Economic Sociology of Illegality in the Economy*, edited by Jens Beckert and Matias Dewey. Oxford: Oxford University Press, 70–86.

Mackenzie, Simon, Neil Brodie and Donna Yates, with Christos Tsirogiannis. 2020. *Trafficking Culture*. London: Routledge.

Macquisten, Ivan. 2017. No EU Problem with Terrorist Antiquities, So Let's Legislate for It. Cultural Property News website, September 21. https://culturalpropertynews.org/no-eu-problem-with-terrorist-antiquities-so-lets-legislate-for-it-says-commission.

Makarenko, Tamara. 2012. *Europe's Crime–Terror Nexus: Links Between Terrorist and Organised Crime Groups in the European Union*. Brussels: European Parliament. http://www.europarl.europa.eu/document/activities/cont/201211/20121127ATT56707/20121127ATT56707EN.pdf.

Mashberg, Tom. 2020. Facebook, Citing Looting Concerns, Bans Historical Artifact Sales, *New York Times*, June 23.

Mladenov, Andrei. 2015. Trafficking of Cultural Artifacts through Bulgaria and Other Balkan States – Challenges. In *Fighting the Looting of Syria's Cultural Heritage*, edited by Dima Chahin and Inge Lindblom. Norwegian Institute for Cultural Heritage Research, 18–19. https://pure.au.dk/ws/files/98457295/Sofiareport_2016.pdf.

Moody, Oliver. 2014. Isis Fills War Chest by Selling Looted Antiquities to the West, *Times*, December 17.

Moos, Olivier. 2020. *Antiquities Trafficking in Syria*. Fribourg: Reigioscope. https://www.religioscope.org/cahiers/2020_02_Moos_Antiquities_Syria.pdf.

Moreno, Sonia. 2019. Detenido Nourdine Chikar, el "Sastre" Marroquí que Vestía al ISIS Enviando Ropa Desde España, *El Español*, November 24. https://www.elespanol.com/espana/20191124/detenido-nourdine-chikar-marroqui-isis-enviando-espana/446705801_0.html.

Morrison, Cecile. 2002. Byzantine Money: Its Production and Circulation. In *The Economic History of Byzantium: From the Seventh through the Fifteenth Century*, edited by Angeliki Laiou. Washington DC: Dumbarton Oaks, 909–966.

Myers, Steven Lee and Nicholas Kulish. 2016. "Broken System" Allows ISIS to Profit from Looted Antiquities, *New York Times*, January 9. https://www.nytimes.com/2016/01/10/world/europe/iraq-syria-antiquities-islamic-state.html.

Naím, Moisés. 2005. *Illicit*. London: Heinemann.

Nassar, Alaa and Nada Atieh. 2020. *Idlib's Antiquities: A Forgotten Tragedy in Northwest Syria*, Syria Direct, March 17. https://syriadirect.org/news/idlib-antiquities-a-forgotten-tragedy-in-northwest-syria%C2%A0/.

Naylor, R.T. 2002. *Wages of Crime*. Ithaca, NY: Cornell.

Parkinson, Joe, Ayla Albayrak and Duncan Mavin. 2015. Culture Brigade: Syrian "Monuments Men" Race to Protect Antiquities as Looting Bankrolls Terror, *Wall Street Journal*, February 10.

56 Neil Brodie

Press, Michael. 2019. In Jerusalem, a Museum's Ethics Go Astray, *Hyperallergic*, January 14. https://hyperallergic.com/479466/jerusalem-bible-lands-museum-finds-gone-astray.

Revenu, Nathalie. 2016. Un trésor archéologique saisi à Roissy, *Le Parisien*, September 29. http://www.leparisien.fr/faits-divers/un-tresor-archeologique-saisi-a-roissy-21-09-201 6-6136959.php.

Robertson, Roland 2012. Globalisation or Glocalisation?, *Journal of International Communication*, 18, 191–208.

RT. 2014. *Relics for Rifles: Syrian Rebels Trade Antique Treasures for Weapons*, October 23. https://www.rt.com/news/198496-syria-rebels-antiquities-trade/.

RT. 2016. ISIS "Department of Artifacts" Document Exposes Antique Loot Trade via Turkey, March 31. https://www.rt.com/news/337829-isis-artifacts-trade-turkey.

Ruggiero, Vincenzo. 2020. Hybrids: On the Crime–Terror Nexus. In *Organized Crime and Terrorist Networks*, edited by Vincenzo Ruggiero. London: Routledge, 26–41.

Ruiz, Christina. 2016. What Do We Really Know About Islamic State's Role In Illicit Antiquities Trade?, *Art Newspaper*, March 1.

Sabah. 2016. Turkish Culture Minister: No Tolerance for Antiquity Smuggling from Syria, *Daily Sabah*, April 18. https://www.dailysabah.com/turkey/2016/04/18/tur kish-culture-minister-no-tolerance-for-antiquity-smuggling-from-syria.

Sabah. 2018. Istanbul Police Destroy Smuggling Ring Planning to Sell Ancient Sumerian, Akkadian Artifacts. *Daily Sabah*, January 26. https://www.dailysabah. com/history/2018/01/26/istanbul-police-destroy-smuggling-ring-planning-to-sell-anc ient-sumerian-akkadian-artifacts.

Sargent, Matthew, James V. Marrone, Alexandra Evans, Bilyana Lilly, Erik Nemeth and Stephen Dalzell. 2020. *Tracking and Disrupting the Illicit Antiquities Trade with Open-Source Data*. Santa Monica, CA: Rand. https://www.rand.org/pubs/ research_reports/RR2706.html.

Seif, Assad. 2015. Illicit Traffic in Cultural Property in Lebanon: A Diachronic Study. In *Countering Illicit Traffic in Cultural Goods*, edited by France Desmarais. Paris: ICOM, 71–75.

Sewell, Abby. 2019. Museum Tangled in Debate Over Heritage, *Daily Star*, April 11. https://www.dailystar.com.lb/News/Lebanon-News/2019/Apr-11/480893-museum-ta ngled-in-debate-over-heritage.ashx.

Shabi, Rachel. 2015. Looted in Syria – and Sold in London: The British Antiques Shops Dealing in Artefacts Smuggled by ISIS, *Guardian*, July 3.

Soguel, Dominique. 2014. Syrian Smugglers Enjoy a Free-for-all Among Ancient Ruins, *Christian Science Monitor*, April 27. https://www.csmonitor.com/World/Mid dle-East/2014/0427/Syrian-smugglers-enjoy-a-free-for-all-among-ancient-ruins.

Soguel, Dominique. 2015. Jihadis Face Detour at Turkey Border, But "Highway" Still in Business, *Christian Science Monitor*, June 23. https://www.csmonitor.com/World/ Middle-East/2015/0623/Jihadists-face-detour-at-Turkey-border-but-highway-still-in -business.

Sputnik. 2016. Why Gaziantep Became Hub for Smugglers Selling Historical Syrian Artifacts, April 11. https://sputniknews.com/middleeast/201604111037838400-syria n-artifacts-illegal-smuggling.

St Hilaire, Rick. 2011. *Khouli +3 Update: Search Warrant Affidavit Describes HSI Investigation*, Cultural Heritage Lawyer blog, September 23. http://culturalherita gelawyer.blogspot.com/2011/09/khouli-3-case-update-search-warrant.html.

Looting and Trafficking of Syrian Antiquities 57

St Hilaire, Rick. 2014. Conflict and the Heritage Trade: Rise in US imports of Middle East "Antiques" and "Collectors' Pieces" Raises Questions, Cultural Heritage Lawyer blog, October 6. http://culturalheritagelawyer.blogspot.com/2014/10/conflict-and-heritage-trade-rise-in-us.html.

St Hilaire, Rick. 2016. *How to End Impunity for Antiquities Traffickers: Assemble a Cultural Heritage Crimes Prosecution Team*, Antiquities Coalition Policy Brief no. 1, November. http://thinktank.theantiquitiescoalition.org/wp-content/uploads/2015/10/Policy-Brief-1Nov.17-2016.pdf.

Shelley, Louise. 2015. *Dirty Entanglements*. Cambridge: Cambridge University Press.

Shelley, Louise. 2018. *Dark Commerce*. Princeton, NJ: Princeton University Press.

Staley, David. 1993. St Lawrence Island's Subsistence Diggers: A New Perspective on Human Effects on Archaeological Sites, *Journal of Field Archaeology*, 20, 347–355.

Stoughton, India. 2015. Lebanon Wages War on Antiquities Smuggling, *Daily Star*, May 8. https://www.dailystar.com.lb/Arts-and-Ent/Culture/2015/May-08/297209-lebanon-wages-war-on-antiquities-smuggling.ashx.

Studevent-Hickman, Benjamin. 2018. *Sumerian Texts from Ancient Iraq: From Ur III to 9/11*, (*Journal of Cuneiform Studies*Supplemental Series Number 5). Atlanta, GA: Lockwood Press.

Taub, Ben. 2015. The Real Value of the ISIS Antiquities Trade, *New Yorker*, December 4. https://www.newyorker.com/news/news-desk/the-real-value-of-the-isis-antiquities-trade.

Topal, Ahmet. 2015. Artifact Smuggling, Recovery Both on the Rise, *Daily Sabah*, July 20.

Topçuoğlu, Oya and Tasha Vorderstrasse. 2019. Small Finds, Big Values: Cylinder Seals and Coins from Iraq and Syria on the Online Market, *International Journal of Cultural Property*, 26 (3), 239–263.

TraCCC. 2019. *Trade Based Money Laundering*. Fairfax, VA: George Mason University.

USA. 2011. *United States of America against Mousa Khouli, also known as 'Morris Khouli', Salem Alshdaifat, Joseph A. Lewis II and Ayman Ramadan*, United States District Court, Eastern District of New York (1:11-cr-00340-ERK).

USA. 2016. *United States of America v. One Gold Ring with Carved Gemstone, an Asset of ISIL, Discovered on Electronic Media of Abu Sayyaf, President of ISIL Antiquities Department; One Gold Coin Featuring Antoninus Pius, an Asset of ISIL, Discovered on Electronic Media of Abu Sayyaf, President of ISIL Antiquities Department; One Gold Coin Featuring Emperor Hadrian Augustus Caesar, an Asset of ISIL, Discovered on Electronic Media of Abu Sayyaf, President Of ISIL Antiquities Department; One Carved Neo-Assyrian Stone Stela, an Asset of ISIL, Discovered on Electronic Media of Abu Sayyaf, President of ISIL Antiquities Department, United States District Court for the District of Columbia* (1:16-cv-02442), December 15. https://www.justice.gov/usao-dc/press-release/file/918536/download.

USA. 2017a. *In the Matter of an Application for a Warrant to Search the Premises Located at the Metropolitan Museum of Art*, 1000 5th Avenue New York, New York 10028 ("The Target Premises"), Supreme Court of the State of New York, County of New York, Part 65, September 22.

USA. 2017b. *United States of America against Approximately Four Hundred Fifty (450) Ancient Cuneiform Tablets; and Approximately Three Thousand (3,000)*

58 *Neil Brodie*

Ancient Clay Bullae, United States District Court, Eastern District of New York (17-CV-3980).

USA. 2017c. *United States of America v. One Gold Ring with Carved Gemstone, an Asset of ISIL, Discovered on Electronic Media of Abu Sayyaf, President of ISIL Antiquities Department, United States District Court for the District of Columbia* (1:16-cv-02442-TFH), December 6.

USA. 2018. *United States of America v One Ancient Mosaic*, United States District Court, Central District of California, Western Division (18-CV-04420).

USA. n.d. Foreign Terrorist Organizations. U.S. Department of State. https://www.state.gov/foreign-terrorist-organizations/.

van Lit, Tim. 2016. *Destruction, Plunder and Trafficking of Cultural Property and Heritage by Islamic State in Syria and Iraq – A War Crimes Perspective.* Driebergen: Dutch National Police.

van Tets, Fernande. 2013. The Art of Civil War, *Foreign Policy*, May 8. http://foreignpolicy.com/2013/05/08/the-art-of-civil-war.

Wartenberg, Ute. 2015. *Collecting Coins and the Conflict in Syria.* https://eca.state.gov/files/bureau/wartenbergsyria-coincollecting.pdf.

Yoon, Sangwon. 2015. Islamic State is Selling Looted Art Online for Needed Cash, Bloomberg, June 29. https://www.bloomberg.com/news/articles/2015-06-28/isis-has-new-cash-cow-art-loot-it-s-peddling-on-ebay-facebook.

Zablit, Jocelyne. 2012. Experts Sound Alarm over Syria Archaeological Treasures, *Daily Star*, April 6. https://www.dailystar.com.lb/Culture/Art/2012/Apr-06/169378-experts-sound-alarm-over-syria-archaeological-treasures.ashx.

2 Hobby Lobby, the Museum of the Bible and the Law

A Case Study of the Looting of Archaeological Artifacts from Iraq

Patty Gerstenblith

In the summer of 2017, the U.S. Government filed a civil forfeiture complaint against approximately 3,000 ancient clay bullae and 450 cuneiform tablets that Hobby Lobby Stores Inc. had imported or attempted to import into the United States between late 2010 and early 2011. In a stipulation Hobby Lobby agreed not to contest the forfeiture (U.S. Government 2017a, 2017b Complaint and Stipulation).[1] In March 2020, Steve Green, one of the owners of Hobby Lobby and Chairman of the Board of the Museum of the Bible, announced that the Museum would voluntarily return 5,000 papyrus fragments to Egypt and 6,500 clay objects to Iraq (Museum of the Bible 2020).[2] Two months later, the U.S. Government filed a forfeiture complaint against a cuneiform tablet, known as the "Gilgamesh Dream Tablet" ("Tablet"), owned by Hobby Lobby but on loan to the Museum of the Bible (U.S. Government 2020 Complaint). Hobby Lobby was and continues to be a corporation well-known for its ubiquitous craft stores (Moss and Baden 2017: 2–14) and its earlier challenge, in Burwell v. Hobby Lobby Stores, Inc., 573 U.S. 682 (2014), to the Affordable Care Act. Based on the strongly held Evangelical Protestant beliefs of the Green family, Hobby Lobby's founders and owners, Hobby Lobby challenged the ACA's requirement that employers provide health insurance to cover the cost of birth control. The 2017 and 2020 forfeiture cases concerning the import and attempted import of archaeological artifacts involved multiple violations of U.S. law, although none of the individuals involved in the schemes was criminally charged.

The story of these artifacts, the several individuals involved and the applicable law provide the basis for a case study of the looting and trafficking of archaeological artifacts particularly from Iraq, which has been subject to armed conflict, international economic sanctions and political instability since 1990. This pattern of looting and trafficking emerged on a large scale in Iraq in the 1990s, the period of sanctions imposed on Iraq after its 1990 invasion of Kuwait. Large-scale looting re-emerged during the U.S.-led invasion of Iraq in 2003 and has continued during the armed conflict in Iraq and Syria, involving such diverse actors as the Islamic State of Iraq and the Levant (ISIL), Syrian regime forces, some or all of the rebel forces in Syria, and other State and non-State actors. While estimates of the numbers of

DOI: 10.4324/9781003023043-4

60   *Patty Gerstenblith*

antiquities looted from Iraq and Syria during this time period begin at 400,000 in the aftermath of the 2003 invasion (Gerstenblith 2006: 292–294), there is much we do not know about the fates of these objects (Greenland et al. 2019; Topçuoglu and Vorderstrasse 2019). We do not know where, when and whether these artifacts will surface on the visible art market, and whether they will be recovered through law enforcement efforts and returned to their proper owners—the countries where these objects were discovered. Because of the legal proceedings in the Hobby Lobby cases, more information than is typically known has come to light concerning these artifacts, providing a background from which we can hypothesize the fates of more recently looted antiquities.

I. Background to the Case Study

In 2009–2010, Hobby Lobby embarked on the building of a collection of art, manuscripts and other artifacts related to the Bible (Moss and Baden 2017: 15). This effort was spearheaded by Steve Green, the son of Hobby Lobby founder, David Green. The Green family planned to found a museum devoted to the Bible. Originally the museum was to be located in Dallas (Fabrikant 2010), but later the Greens decided to locate it in Washington DC, not far from the National Mall. As early as 2010, the Green family discussed openly their collection that included illuminated manuscripts, Torah scrolls, New Testament papyri and other works, estimated to be worth $20 million to $40 million. At that time, the Greens estimated their collection included more than 30,000 objects (Fabrikant 2010).[3] Some have suggested that the Greens' aggressive buying pushed up market prices for such objects (Fabrikant 2010; Moss and Baden 2017: 29).

The Green collection has been involved in numerous legal controversies over the years including the acquisition of forged and stolen artifacts. Included in these controversies were "Dead Sea Scroll" fragments, all of which were determined to be forgeries (Greshko 2020; Rollston 2020),[4] several papyrus fragments stolen from the Oxyrynchus collection belonging to the Egypt Exploration Society housed at Oxford University (Higgins 2020), and a manuscript stolen in 1991 from the University of Athens (Kellner 2018). With such large-scale and hasty acquisitions by the Greens, one might easily suggest that mistakes concerning authenticity and legality were virtually inevitable.[5]

A. The 2017 Forfeiture

On July 15, 2010, Steve Green and Scott Carroll inspected a collection of antiquities in the United Arab Emirates (U.S. Government 2017a Complaint ¶ 20). A pair of dealers from Israel (Dealers #1 and #2)[6] and one from the UAE were present and displayed some 5,548 artifacts, consisting of 1,500 cuneiform tablets, 500 cuneiform bricks, 3,000 clay bullae, 35 clay envelope seals, 13 extra-large cuneiform tablets and 500 stone cylinder seals. On July 18, on his way back to the United States, Green attempted to import a Bible worth more than $1,000,000 into the U.S. (U.S. Government 2017a Complaint ¶ 21). He did not file any paperwork for formal entry and did not declare the Bible with Customs. Customs authorities allowed him to bring the Bible into the United States but explained to him the proper import procedures and requirements for declaration. On August 23, Carroll reported meeting with the two Israeli dealers in Israel. These dealers told Carroll that the objects he and Green viewed in the UAE were from an old collection belonging to a different dealer in Israel (Dealer #3). The dealers further told Carroll that the collection had been in Washington DC and was shipped to the UAE from Washington for the July 2010 inspection. Carroll also reported that the asking price was $2,091,000, the collection could be appraised for $11,820,000, but Hobby Lobby could acquire the collection for $1,600,000 (U.S. Government 2017a Complaint ¶ 24).

On August 30, Israeli Dealer #1 sent a provenance[7] statement from Israeli Dealer #3 outlining the artifacts' ownership history for approximately 5,513 of the artifacts, omitting the 35 clay envelope seals. The provenance statement indicated that the collection had been legally acquired from local markets by the father of Israeli Dealer #3 in the late 1960s and had been stored

Figure 2.1 Cuneiform tablet, acquired by Hobby Lobby in 2010–11, returned to Iraq in May 2018
Source: Photo courtesy of the U.S. Department of Justice.

Figure 2.2 Cuneiform bulla, acquired by Hobby Lobby in 2010–11, returned to Iraq in May 2018
Source: Photo courtesy of the U.S. Department of Justice.

in Mississippi in the 1970s (U.S. Government 2017a Complaint ¶ 25). No Hobby Lobby representative ever met or communicated with Israeli Dealer #3. Hobby Lobby also never contacted the Alleged Custodian in Mississippi to determine whether the provenance statement was correct (U.S. Government 2017a Complaint ¶ 25). In fact, the Alleged Custodian first met Israeli Dealer #3 in 2007 and had never stored any artifacts for the dealer. On December 8, Israeli Dealer #2 and Green signed a purchase agreement (U.S. Government 2017a Complaint ¶ 27). The attached invoice said the seller was Israeli Dealer #3 and that the artifacts originated in Israel. Green authorized payment of $1,600,000, which was wired to seven different accounts associated with five different individuals (U.S. Government 2017a Complaint ¶ 28). Payments were made to Israeli Dealers #1 and #2, the UAE Dealer and two other individuals, but not to Dealer #3, although the invoice stated that Dealer #3 was the seller. The inconsistencies in the different provenance statements, the utter lack of credibility of some of the statements (in particular, that the collection had been in the United States but was then shipped to the UAE for inspection by a prospective U.S. purchaser), and the wiring of funds to numerous accounts seem not to have been a matter of concern to Green nor a reason to inquire further as to the true origin of the artifacts. In reality, all of these were red flags that would have alerted any reasonable purchaser or businessperson to questionable and possibly illegal practices (Orenstein 2020).

At the time, U.S. Customs allowed goods worth less than $2,000 to be imported by means of an informal entry process. The shipments of artifacts purchased by Green were worth considerably more, but their values were incorrectly stated to be lower so as to take advantage of informal entry. Multiple shipments utilizing the informal entry process were sent to different addresses in late 2010 and early 2011. The objects were incorrectly declared to be ceramic tiles or tile samples. Hobby Lobby's own International Department was not used because its Customs Broker had warned that the artifacts could be detained by U.S. Customs and Border Protection (U.S. Government 2017a Complaint ¶ 32). The shipment paperwork was therefore handled by the Israeli and UAE dealers. The forfeiture complaint discusses two groups of artifacts: the "Seized Defendants *in Rem*" and the "Additional Defendants *in Rem*".

The "Additional Defendants *in Rem*" were sent in eight shipments between November 23, 2010, and September 1, 2011. The forfeiture complaint does not state the exact number of artifacts contained in each shipment. On November 23, 2010, the UAE Dealer sent the first package of artifacts consisting of 13 or 23 pieces, described as "ceramic tiles" (U.S. Government 2017a Complaint ¶ 33). On December 19, the UAE Dealer shipped three packages with the contents described as "Tiles (Sample)". These were shipped to three different business entities associated with Hobby Lobby (U.S. Government 2017a Complaint ¶ 34). Three more shipments were sent in late December, similarly misdescribed and without formal entry (U.S. Government 2017a Complaint ¶ 35). The final package of "Additional Defendants *in Rem*" consisted of 1,000 clay bullae and was sent in September 2011 with an export license from Israel, which was falsely declared to be the country of origin (U.S. Government 2017a Complaint ¶ 36).[8] All of the "Additional Defendants *in Rem*" were processed at the international mail facility at JFK in Queens, New York, and received by Hobby Lobby (U.S. Government 2017a Complaint ¶ 37).

The UAE dealer shipped eight packages between December 26, 2010, and January 5, 2011, by means of Federal Express from the UAE to a purchaser in Oklahoma City. The first three packages were delivered to Hobby Lobby, while five packages were detained in Memphis at the FedEx shipping facility. The five packages detained at FedEx had a combined total of approximately 223 cuneiform tablets and 300 clay bullae, known as the "Seized Defendants *in Rem*" (U.S. Government 2017a Complaint ¶¶ 40–42). The contents of the packages were described inaccurately as "clay tiles" or samples, they were stated to have been manufactured in Turkey, and their value was significantly understated. In July 2017 the U.S. Government announced the filing of the forfeiture complaint against these artifacts and Hobby Lobby's agreement not to contest the forfeiture.[9]

64 *Patty Gerstenblith*

B. The Gilgamesh Dream Tablet

In May 2020, the U.S. Government filed a forfeiture complaint against a cuneiform tablet ("the Tablet") that contains a portion of the Gilgamesh epic written in Akkadian (U.S. Government 2020 Complaint ¶¶ 2–5). The Tablet was on loan to the Museum of the Bible from Hobby Lobby. While the Museum did not contest the seizure and forfeiture, Hobby Lobby initially contested the forfeiture. Hobby Lobby is also suing Christie's and the consignor[10] of the Tablet for breach of express and implied warranties and for fraud (U.S. Government 2021c). The Tablet seems to have first been known outside of Iraq when a U.S. antiquities dealer viewed it along with other tablets and items at the apartment of a Jordanian dealer, Ghassan Rihani, in London in or prior to 2001. The U.S. dealer subsequently viewed the objects again in London in 2003, after Rihani's death, in the company of a cuneiform expert, later identified as Renee Kovacs. Although the tablets were unreadable, the dealer and the cuneiform expert suspected that the tablets were literary texts rather than the more typical economic and administrative texts.[11] They therefore decided the tablets were "potentially rare and valuable" and purchased all of the tablets and some other items for $50,350 (U.S. Government 2020 Complaint ¶¶ 15–16).

After purchasing and shipping the tablets back to the United States, the cuneiform expert baked and cleaned the Tablet, recognizing that the Tablet contained part of the Gilgamesh epic. In 2005, the cuneiform expert sent the Tablet to Princeton, New Jersey, where it was studied by Andrew George, who later published it (George 2007). In 2007, the U.S. antiquities dealer sold the Tablet alone to two buyers for $50,000 without any provenance information. However, one of the buyers later requested a provenance statement from the dealer (U.S. Government 2020 Complaint ¶ 19). The dealer therefore created a false provenance letter stating that the Tablet was purchased in 1981 at a Butterfield & Butterfield auction in San Francisco as part of lot 1503; however, the Butterfield auction catalog indicated that this lot consisted of miscellaneous ancient bronze fragments.

Later in 2007, the Tablet was published in a catalog for Michael Sharpe Rare & Antiquated Books (Sharpe 2007). The catalog identified Renee Kovacs as the cuneiform expert who authenticated the Tablet and mentioned the upcoming publication by George (Sharpe 2007: 51). The catalog also stated that the Tablet had a "clear provenance" and listed a price of $450,000 (Sharpe 2007: 51). It may be surmised that announcement of the upcoming publication of the Tablet by George contributed significantly or entirely to the nine-fold increase in the value of the Tablet within the space of a few months, although the price at which the Tablet sold is not stated in the Complaint.

In 2013, a new owner of the Tablet contacted an international auction house, which Hobby Lobby later identified as Christie's auction house in London. This owner was later identified as a Tel Aviv art collector, Joseph David Hackmey. The head of Christie's Antiquities Department at that time contacted the original dealer to verify the provenance of the Tablet. According to the Government complaint, the dealer responded that "the provenance was not verifiable and would not hold up to scrutiny in a public auction." According to the Government's Complaint, the Christie's Department Head advised the dealer that the Tablet "would not be offered in a public auction, but a private sale." (U. S. Government 2020 Complaint ¶ 26). If the facts as alleged in the forfeiture complaint are accurate,[12] this exchange sheds an interesting light on possible auction house practices. Because auction sales are public and therefore information concerning the works the auction houses sell is also public to the extent the consignor is willing to make such information public, it is often assumed that information indicating a questionable background for an artifact would deter an auction house from accepting the artifact for sale. Yet private sales are a substantial and increasing part of auction house business.[13] This sale illustrates what Nørskov and Brodie describe as the invisible market: "the 'high-end' trade of exceptional and expensive artifacts sold away from public scrutiny by private treaty sales to wealthy museums and private collectors." (Brodie 2011c: 5; Nørskov 2002: 291–292). This detail from the Tablet forfeiture complaint may indicate that, while an auction house may have several reasons for selling an artifact privately rather than publicly, an auction house that has questions about the legitimacy of an artifact does not necessarily refuse to sell the object. Rather, it may choose to sell the artifact privately in order to avoid public scrutiny. Market sellers may dispute this characterization on the grounds that the background of a questionable antiquity will become public sooner or later and that therefore objects sold privately should meet the same standards as those sold publicly. Nonetheless, questionable background may influence the business model chosen by an auction house rather than the decision whether to sell.

A representative of the Green Collection/Museum of the Bible viewed the Tablet in London in 2014. Hobby Lobby agreed no later than July 2014 to purchase the Tablet for $1,674,000 (U.S. Government 2020 Complaint ¶¶ 27–28). To fill in the timeline, this purchase occurred after the 2010/2011 shipments had been seized and while the U.S. government's investigation that led to the 2017 forfeiture was ongoing. This also coincides with the purchases of the artifacts, most of them tablets, whose return was announced in March 2020. Jeff Kloha, the later chief curator of the Museum, stated that these purchases occurred between 2009 to 2014 (Arraf 2020). After its purchase, Christie's shipped the Tablet to its New York office and a representative hand carried it to Hobby Lobby in Oklahoma so that Hobby Lobby could avoid paying New York sales tax.

In response to a query from a Museum of the Bible registrar in 2014 for more information concerning the Tablet's background, a Christie's business manager changed the sale invoice to indicate that the Tablet's country of origin was Iraq and its date was c. 1600 BCE. A Christie's employee at about the same time emailed Hobby Lobby and the Museum the provenance information indicating that the Tablet was sold at a Butterfields auction in 1981 and that the Tablet was therefore outside of Iraq before that date. Soon

Figure 2.3 "Gilgamesh Dream Tablet" Museum of the Bible
Source: (c) 2017 P. Gerstenblith

Figure 2.4 Empty stand of the "Gilgamesh Dream Tablet" Museum of the Bible
Source: (c) 2020 M.M. Kersel

after, Hobby Lobby completed the purchase (U.S. Government 2020 Complaint ¶¶ 29–37).

In October 2017, shortly before the Museum opened to the public and as part of a new effort to conduct provenance research spurred by the publicity surrounding announcement of the 2017 forfeitures, a curator and collections

68 *Patty Gerstenblith*

management staff at the Museum made additional inquiries of Christie's in order to complete and verify the provenance information. In the process, the Museum staff noticed the discrepancy in the Butterfield's catalogue that indicated that lot 1503 was composed of bronze fragments. The U.S. Government seized the Tablet in September 2019 and filed the forfeiture complaint in May 2020 (U.S. Government 2020 Complaint). Hobby Lobby initially contested the forfeiture (United States v. One Cuneiform Tablet Known as the Gilgamesh Dream Tablet, Answer of Claimant Hobby Lobby Stores, Inc., Civ. No. 20–2222 (E.D.N.Y. 2020). In July 2021, the U.S. Government filed an amended complaint (U.S. Government 2021a Amended Complaint). Hobby Lobby subsequently relinquished its claim to the Tablet and a decree of forfeiture was issued (U.S. Government 2021b).

II. The Legal Framework

The legal bases discussed in both forfeitures represent the three most typical legal violations involved in the illegal import of cultural artifacts: (1) importation contrary to law because the artifacts are stolen property; (2) importation contrary to law because the artifacts were improperly declared upon entry into the US and (3) import in violation of an import restriction imposed under the Convention on Cultural Property Implementation Act (19 U.S.C. §§ 2601–13), the U.S. domestic legislation implementing the 1970 UNESCO Convention on the Means of Prohibiting and Preventing the Illicit Import, Export and Transfer of Ownership of Cultural Property. The specific legal basis in both forfeitures was that the artifacts were imported contrary to law. In the 2017 forfeiture, the importation contrary to law was based on false and incomplete declarations to Customs. In the 2020 forfeiture, the importation contrary to law is based on the government's characterization of the Gilgamesh Tablet as stolen property.

The looting of archaeological sites raises particular public policy and legal concerns. When a site is looted, the objects are ripped from their stratigraphic association with other artifacts, faunal and floral remains, architectural features, and at times human remains. This loss of stratigraphic context means that our ability to reconstruct and understand the past is severely impaired. It is only through scientific recovery of all data that a site contains that the history of the site can be best understood and reconstructed. Looted archaeological artifacts are unknown and undocumented before they appear in smuggling networks, at the border of a transit or destination market country, in a private or public collection, or for sale on the international market. This lack of documentation makes it difficult for law enforcement to trace such objects, establish their legal status and apprehend the individuals involved in the looting and smuggling operation. Because much site looting is carried out for economic rewards and in recognition of the challenges posed by illegal activity involving undocumented artifacts (Gerstenblith 2007: 170–77), the law has developed unique doctrines to respond to these particular public policy concerns.

A. The 1970 UNESCO Convention and Its Implementation

The 1970 UNESCO Convention[14] is the preeminent legal instrument that addresses the international movement of cultural objects. Following the Second World War, the growth of the international art market proved to have a devastating effect on cultural heritage. In 1969, Clemency C. Coggins brought attention to the destruction of Maya architectural remains in Central America, writing,

> In the last ten years there has been an incalculable increase in the number of monuments systematically stolen, mutilated, and illicitly exported from Guatemala and Mexico in order to feed the international art market. Not since the sixteenth century has Latin America been so ruthlessly plundered. ... The theft and mutilation of monuments is not confined to little known, or unknown sites where their loss, and the concomitant tomb-robbing, destroys all archeological evidence.
>
> (Coggins 1969: 94)

The world community under the leadership of UNESCO sought to find a way to deal with the illegal trade in art works, archaeological artifacts and ethnographic objects.

The 1970 UNESCO Convention, in Article 1, defines cultural property as "property which, on religious or secular grounds, is specifically designated by each State as being of importance for archaeology, prehistory, history, literature, art or science" and which falls into a category of cultural objects, such as paintings, drawings, original works of sculpture, rare manuscripts, coins more than one hundred years old, ethnological objects, products of archaeological excavations and elements of artistic or historical monuments that have been dismembered. To all States Parties, with the exception of the United States, the core provision of the Convention is Article 3, which states: "The import, export or transfer of ownership of cultural property effected contrary to the provisions adopted under this convention by the States Parties thereto, shall be illicit." According to the legal scholar Patrick O'Keefe, this provision means that States Parties shall not permit the import of cultural property that was illegally exported from another State Party (O'Keefe 2017: 135–138). Most States Parties have implemented the Convention by adopting reciprocal import restrictions, thus automatically prohibiting the import of any cultural property illegally exported from another State Party. Such import restrictions are both broad, in that they apply to a broad range of cultural materials, and proactive, meaning that in case of a situation of crisis that engenders looting and destruction, import restrictions are already in place and do not need to be implemented to respond to the crisis (Gerstenblith 2017).

The United States' response to the problem of looting of undocumented artifacts, enacted through the Convention on Cultural Property

70 *Patty Gerstenblith*

Implementation Act (CCPIA), requires the United States to enter into a bilateral agreement following a request from another State Party to impose import restrictions on designated categories of archaeological and/or ethnological materials (19 U.S.C. §§ 2602–03).[15] These import restrictions do not apply to specific identified objects but rather to categories of object types and so prevent the import of previously unknown and undocumented objects that have been looted directly from archaeological sites (Gerstenblith 2017). A State Party initiates the process for a bilateral agreement by submitting a request to the United States through diplomatic channels, which means that the United States and the requesting country must have diplomatic relations. The CCPIA also allows the United States to impose import restrictions, without the negotiation of a bilateral agreement, in emergency circumstances but only after the other State Party has submitted a request for a bilateral agreement. Because of this requirement, in the case of two of the greatest cultural heritage crises in recent decades, the widespread looting and destruction of sites, religious institutions, historic structures and museums in Syria and Iraq, the U.S. was not able to respond in a timely manner to prevent the import of looted cultural materials.

Following the looting of the Iraq Museum in April 2003 and reports of large-scale site looting during the U.S.-led invasion, the U.N. Security Council adopted Resolution 1483, UN Doc S/RES/1483 (22 May 2003), ¶ 7, http://unscr.com/en/resolutions/doc/1483. This Resolution, among other provisions, called for all U.N. Member States to enact import restrictions on cultural materials illegally removed from Iraq after 1990, the date of the original sanctions against Iraq following its invasion of Kuwait. In response, the United States enacted the Emergency Protection for Iraqi Cultural Antiquities Act in late 2004, Pub. L. No 108–429, 118 Stat 2434, §§ 3001–03, that directed the President to impose permanent restrictions under the CCPIA on the importation of cultural materials illegally removed from Iraq after August 1990, although Iraq had not submitted a request for a bilateral agreement.[16] These import restrictions went into effect in April 2008 and are permanent. 19 C.F.R. Part 12, Fed. Reg. 73, No. 84, 23334 (April 30, 2008) https://www.govinfo.gov/content/pkg/FR-2008-04-30/pdf/E8-9343.pdf.

A similar situation arose with respect to the looting of Syrian sites and cultural repositories during the civil war. In compliance with U.N. Security Council Resolution 2199, UN Doc S/RES/2199 (12 February 2015), 15–17 http://unscr.com/en/resolutions/doc/2199, the U.S. enacted the Protect and Preserve International Cultural Property Act, modelled on the Iraq legislation, Pub. L. 114–151, 130 Stat 369 (2016). This legislation directed the Department of State to impose comparable import restrictions on cultural materials illegally removed from Syria after March 2011, although Syria had not submitted a request for a bilateral agreement. 19 C.F.R. Part 12, Vol. 81, No. 157, 53916 (August 15, 2016) https://www.govinfo.gov/content/pkg/FR-2016-08-15/pdf/2016-19491.pdf. Unlike the import restrictions for Iraq, the Syria import restrictions have the potential to sunset if the President determines that Syria is in a position to bring a request for a bilateral agreement using the normal CCPIA process and that it is not against the interest of the United States to enter into such an agreement. Pub. L. 114–151, 130 Stat 369, § 3(b). The need for special legislation to respond to these crisis situations demonstrates the significant inadequacy of the U.S. system of implementing the 1970 UNESCO Convention.

B. Importation Contrary to Law: Stolen Property

In order to remove the economic incentive and thereby discourage the looting of sites, many nations with a rich archaeological heritage have vested ownership of artifacts that were as yet "undiscovered" in the State. In two decisions involving criminal prosecutions of dealers in the 1970s,[17] the U.S. federal courts accepted the principle that an archaeological object removed in violation of a national ownership law would be characterized as stolen property under federal law, such as the National Stolen Property Act (NSPA), 18 U.S.C. §§ 2314–15, as well as state laws. This principle was later applied by the Second Circuit Court of Appeals, whose jurisdiction includes New York, in the successful prosecution of the prominent dealer, Frederick Schultz, for conspiring to deal in antiquities illegally removed from Egypt after enactment of its vesting law, Law 117, in 1983.[18] Therefore, an archaeological object that is subject to national ownership but removed from its country of origin without permission is considered to be stolen property. One who knowingly transports across a state or international boundary or sells, buys, possesses or otherwise handles a stolen object that has been transported across a state or international boundary and that is worth more than $5,000 may be prosecuted.

The decisions in *United States v. McClain* and *United States v. Schultz* establish four criteria required for recognition of foreign national ownership of archaeological artifacts: (1) the vesting law must be clearly an ownership law on its face; (2) the nation's ownership rights must be enforced domestically and not only upon illegal export; (3) the object must have been found within the country claiming ownership and (4) the object must have been located within the country at the time the law was enacted. The purpose of the first requirement is that the vesting law must be clear and unambiguous so as to give notice to U.S. citizens who might be adversely affected by these laws, particularly in a criminal prosecution.[19] The purpose of the second requirement is to distinguish national ownership from export controls because export controls are generally not enforced by another nation absent a specific agreement to do so.[20] The purpose of the third requirement is to ensure that the national ownership law is not given extraterritorial effect and of the fourth requirement to ensure that the national ownership law is not given retroactive effect. The characterization of an archaeological artifact as stolen when it was removed from its country of discovery in violation of a national ownership law allows the object to be civilly forfeited under the

72   Patty Gerstenblith

Customs statute, 19 U.S.C. § 1595a(c), which prohibits the import of merchandise contrary to law.[21]

C. Importation Contrary to Law: Improper Declaration

Countries typically require the declaration upon import of commercial goods or goods with a value above a certain amount. While the details vary considerably by country, the requirements for a declaration include what the goods are, the country of origin and the value of the goods. These declarations determine whether the goods are importable and the amount of customs duty or tariff that the importer must pay (Pike and Friedman 2012: 25, 71). In the case of typical commercial goods, "country of origin" usually refers to the place of manufacture or a place where substantial changes were made to the goods (Pike and Friedman 2012: 281). However, in the case of antiquities, the country of origin is the provenience or country of modern discovery, rather than the place of manufacture or production in antiquity. While an importer may make a false declaration in order to mislead a Customs agent and thereby evade scrutiny, the false declaration is itself another violation of the law and may constitute a distinct basis for forfeiture.[22]

In one of the earlier modern cultural property cases, New York collector Michael Steinhardt purchased a gold phiale that was discovered in Sicily.[23] The phiale was imported into the United States through the use of false declarations as to the country of origin, which was stated to be Switzerland, through which the phiale was transported, rather than Italy, where the bowl was discovered, and as to value, which was declared as $250,000, although the dealer had purchased it for $1.2 million. The courts reviewing the case held that the misstatements of value and country of origin were material; the bowl was forfeited and returned to Italy.

Three similar attempts to smuggle ancient artifacts by means of false Customs declarations were interdicted in the United Kingdom. One involved a group of cuneiform tablets, which were falsely declared upon entry at Heathrow Airport. Their country of origin was declared to be the United Arab Emirates, they were described as handmade miniature clay tiles and they were given an implausible valuation. Scholars at the British Museum subsequently identified them as originating at the sites of Umma, Larsa and the unknown site of Iri-Saĝrig, all of which are located within modern Iraq, and are likely to be associated with the Hobby Lobby tablets forfeited in 2017 and possibly others (Taylor 2019). In another example, a *kudurru* stone, an official document recording a grant of land or other gift from the king, was declared upon attempted import as a "carved stone for home decoration" originating in Turkey and with a misstated value (Alberge 2019). The stone is likely from the region of Nippur in southern Iraq and dates between 1126–1103 BCE. In a final example, U.K. customs authorities seized and returned an ancient Greek sculpture that was discovered at the site of Cyrene in Libya. Upon import into the United Kingdom, its country of origin was

Looting of Archaeological Artifacts from Iraq 73

Figure 2.5 The Phiale of Achyris. Hellenistic, Gold, 23 cm × 4 cm
Source: Photo copyright (c) 1997 Ira Block. Reproduced by permission of Ira Block.

Figure 2.6 Cuneiform tablets seized by British authorities for declaration as ceramic tiles in 2011, originated from Umma, Larsa and Irisagrig, and probably looted in 2003 or soon after; returned to Iraq August 2019
Source: Photo courtesy of Trustees of the British Museum.

74   *Patty Gerstenblith*

declared to be Turkey and its value to be £72,000, rather than its actual worth that was later estimated to be £1.5 million.[24]

III. Hobby Lobby and the Law

A. Hobby Lobby and the Looting of Artifacts from Iraq

Near the close of the 1991 Gulf War, eleven of thirteen regional museums in Iraq were looted. More than 3,000 objects were stolen, of which some 400 were documented in the *Lost Heritage* series. At least one documented object later appeared on the market in New York.[25] Because of the sanctions imposed on Iraq in response to Saddam Hussein's invasion of Kuwait, between 1990 and 2003 the economic situation in Iraq deteriorated and the ability of Iraqi authorities to acquire equipment to pursue archaeological research and excavations and to protect archaeological sites was severely hampered. Largely as a result of these economic pressures, the archaeological sites in southern Iraq were looted on a large scale and the market was flooded with what seemed to be illegally obtained artifacts from Iraq, despite the fact that the UN trade sanctions should have prevented the import of antiquities from Iraq (Gibson 2008: 35; Brodie 2008: 41–43). The Gilgamesh Dream Tablet and the other artifacts sold with it seemed to be in London in 2001 or earlier and may therefore be associated with the period of looting during the 1990s. The Jordanian dealer, Ghassan Rihani, who first showed the Tablet and other artifacts to the U.S. dealer, is associated with other sales of artifacts looted from Iraq during this time period. Perhaps most notorious is the Schøyen collection of Aramaic incantation bowls, which were looted from Iraq in the 1990s (Brodie and Kersel 2014: 206–207).[26] Looting of sites in southern Iraq mushroomed again following the 2003 U.S. invasion and then diminished but without entirely stopping (Stone 2015: 180). Most of the 1990 sanctions were lifted in May 2003 shortly after the U.S.-led invasion, but the restrictions on import of cultural objects remained in place.

In her initial study of site looting in Iraq in 2003 and later, Elizabeth Stone concluded that looters focused on sites of the Ur III (2112–2004 BCE)/Isin-Larsa (2004–1763 BCE) and Old Babylonian (1894–1595 BCE) periods, "the high-point of Mesopotamian civilization" (Stone 2015: 180). The looters also focused on later sites of the historic periods (the Parthian to Early Islamic periods). The earlier period sites are rich sources of cuneiform tablets, cylinder seals and similar objects, while the later sites are sources of coins, jewellery and glass, all of which, Stone commented, "are very marketable" (Stone 2015: 181) and, one might add, easily transported. Looting of archaeological sites in northern Iraq increased following the incursion of ISIL and the breakdown of civil order in 2014.

While it has been difficult to associate any particular artifacts that surfaced on the market with specific looting episodes, the Hobby Lobby artifacts may present an opportunity to do so. In this case we may hypothesize as to the time lag between looting and public appearance on the market as well as some of the mechanisms by which such artifacts reach the market. The timeline for the looting and sale of the Gilgamesh Tablet and that for the looting and sale of the artifacts forfeited in 2017 are different. The Gilgamesh Tablet was first known outside of Iraq in 2001, thereby likely associating it with the looting of sites in Iraq during the 1990s. That it was recognized fairly easily by the U.S. dealer and cuneiform expert as "rare and valuable" makes it unlikely that the Tablet was languishing in a private collection for decades. The artifacts forfeited in 2017 were first known in 2010. These are therefore likely associated with the looting that occurred soon after the 2003 Gulf War.

Despite the extensive looting of archaeological sites engendered by the 2003 invasion of Iraq, the appearance of Iraqi antiquities at the major auction houses of Christie's in London and Sotheby's in New York plummeted in 2003. This market reaction followed the publicity given to the looting of the Iraq Museum in Baghdad and the adoption of UN Security Council Resolution 1483 and associated legal measures taken by individual States (Brodie 2011a: 117–120). Nonetheless, it seems that private sales through dealers, who often do not make their sales public, continued. As early as 2011, Neil Brodie commented on the appearance in 2008 of cuneiform tablets and foundation cones on the market, primarily at the Barakat Gallery with locations in London, Los Angeles and elsewhere (Brodie 2011a: 126–127). Most of the tablets offered by Barakat were dated to the first half of the twenty-first century BCE and, although they were linked through the appearance of the same personal names, different proveniences were given for this corpus, the most common being "East Mediterranean" (Brodie, 2011a: 126–127). From this evidence, Brodie surmised that the corpus originated in an archive from a single archaeological site (Brodie 2011a: 126). Most of the Barakat cuneiform objects sold between 2008 and 2009 (Brodie 2011a: 129–129).

While Brodie did not realize it at the time,[27] Manuel Molina subsequently established a link between the appearance on the market of large quantities of cuneiform tablets of the Ur III period with looting that occurred possibly in the 1990s or, more likely, soon after the 2003 invasion. Of particular interest is a large quantity of tablets that are associated with an as-yet unlocated site in southern Iraq whose ancient name was Iri-Saĝrig. Scholars have debated the location but today believe Iri-Saĝrig is in southern Iraq along the ancient course of the Tigris River; some suggest that it was a provincial capital with an important economic and cultic role (Viano 2019; Molina 2013; Brodie 2020). Eckart Frahm, an Assyriologist who studied the seized Hobby Lobby tablets for the government, identified many of them as coming from Iri-Saĝrig and suggested that they had been part of the same archive (Connally 2018). According to Molina, the first publication of a tablet from the ancient city of Iri-Saĝrig occurred in 2002,[28] and a tablet was auctioned on eBay in 2004 (Molina 2019: 239). In 2005, 166 tablets from Iri-Saĝrig that had been confiscated by Jordanian authorities on July 7, 2003, were

76 *Patty Gerstenblith*

published (Molina 2019: 241; Parapetti 2008: 229–230).[29] Given the timing of this interception at the Iraq–Jordan border, these tablets were likely looted in the months immediately following the 2003 invasion.

Additional Iri-Saĝrig tablets appeared for sale on the internet in 2005 and tablets were being offered in Australia, Canada and New York. The Barakat Gallery offered 181 Iri-Saĝrig tablets in 2008, thirty-four in 2017, and sixty-seven in 2018. Other galleries offering these tablets included the Malter Galleries, Arte Primitivo—H.S. Rose Gallery, and Aphrodite Gallery in the United States and additional galleries and auction houses in Barcelona, Melbourne, the United Kingdom, Tel Aviv, Madrid and Hamburg (Molina 2019: 239–240). Molina listed among the major collections of Iri-Saĝrig tablets Cornell University (77 tablets), the Iraq Museum (182, composed to a large extent of the tablets intercepted and returned by Jordanian authorities), Sulaimaniah Museum in the Kurdish region of Iraq (9), Nabu Museum in Lebanon (135), and the Randy Best Collection, Tandy Archaeological Museum at the Southwestern Baptist Theological Seminary, Fort Worth Texas (18) (Molina 2019: 241; Abboud 2020: 204).

The publication of Iri-Saĝrig tablets spiked with 186 in 2005, 23 in 2006, 15 in 2007, followed by 204 in 2008, 583 in 2013 (Owen 2013; Molina 2019: 241), and the largest quantity, probably 1,420 out of 2,000 tablets, published in 2020 (Sigrist and Ozaki 2019). The date of publication supplies only a *terminus ante quem* for the appearance of the tablets on the market, not a definitive date, with the date of looting occurring at some earlier time. At this point, a scholarly consensus seems to posit that the Iri-Saĝrig tablets were looted shortly after the 2003 invasion (Brodie 2020). Given the known appearance of only two tablets associated with Iri-Saĝrig (one in 1932) before the 2003 Gulf War and their questionable attributions, it is possible that the site of Iri-Saĝrig was discovered before 2003, but the interception of a significant quantity of tablets by Jordanian authorities in July 2003 indicates that the bulk or all of the looting occurred in the immediate aftermath of the 2003 invasion.[30]

In 2019, Marcel Sigrist and Tohru Ozaki[31] published a corpus of approximately 2,000 tablets. The publication announcement described the corpus "from Iri-Saĝrig [as] present[ing] an extraordinary range of new sources, depicting a cosmopolitan Sumerian/Akkadian city unlike any other from this period." (Sigrist and Ozaki 2019). The announcement indicates that the 2,000 tablets are "mostly" from Iri-Saĝrig (Sigrist and Ozaki 2019). Owen Jarus wrote that 1,400 of these tablets are from Iri-Saĝrig and the remaining 600 are from various other sites (Jarus 2020). Based on the texts recorded in the Cuneiform Digital Library Initiative, Brodie concluded that this number is 1420 (Brodie 2020).[32] All of these were part of the Hobby Lobby or Museum of the Bible collection. We do not know whether the tablets Sigrist and Ozaki studied in Oklahoma City between 2012 and 2016 included the "Additional Defendants *in Rem*" because we do not know when these artifacts were transferred to New York or to Washington DC and therefore

Looting of Archaeological Artifacts from Iraq   77

whether they were still in Oklahoma at that time.[33] It is likely that, as Brodie has suggested, the Sigrist and Ozaki tablets and possibly others that Hobby Lobby had donated to the Museum are among the 6,500 artifacts (later identified as 8,000) that the Museum of the Bible announced in March 2020 that it was returning to Iraq (Museum of the Bible 2020; Brodie 2020).

Many mysteries remain concerning the precise number of tablets and other artifacts seized and forfeited by the U.S. government, the exact number returned to Iraq, and the different groups of tablets published in various places including the Cornell series. These questions are not idle in that at least two sites that are known to have major corpora of ancient texts, Mari and Ebla, located respectively in eastern and western Syria, were looted by ISIL (Mari) and likely the Syrian regime forces or possibly Free Syrian Army forces (Ebla) during the years of the Syrian civil war.[34] If the pattern of looting, acquisition on the market and publication of Iri-Saĝrig tablets repeats itself, we can anticipate the appearance of similar hoards of cuneiform tablets to appear on the market within the next several years—tablets that contain a limited amount of intrinsic information in their texts but that, without their context and associated artifacts, cannot tell their full story. The looting of both textual and non-textual archaeological artifacts from sites destroys their context and poses a significant loss to our ability to reconstruct and understand the past. These tablets, as with the Iri-Saĝrig tablets, may be attributed to incorrect points of origin, split up and mixed in with tablets from other sites, thereby further obfuscating the information that could have been learned if they had been scientifically excavated.

B. Hobby Lobby and the Law

Based on the previous discussion of the international and domestic legal framework for controlling the trade in looted and smuggled archaeological artifacts, one can see that the Hobby Lobby acquisitions violated one or more of the three primary aspects of this framework. The US sanctions prohibiting the import of any goods, including cultural materials illegally exported from Iraq after 1990, were continued in effect by the import restrictions imposed in April 2008 (U.S. Government 2017a Complaint ¶ 17). While it is not certain that the objects forfeited in 2017 were looted and exported after the 2003 invasion, there is a high probability they were exported from Iraq after 1990 and their import was thus clearly in violation of the import restrictions imposed under the CCPIA, as well as the original sanctions. The Gilgamesh Tablet would have violated the same import restrictions as it was imported into the United Kingdom in approximately 2001 and into the United States in 2003 (and re-imported in 2014) and seems likely to have been exported out of Iraq after 1990.

The objects from the 2017 forfeiture, the tablets published by Sigrist and Ozaki and the Gilgamesh Tablet can also be defined as stolen property under Iraq's national ownership law. The 2017 forfeiture complaint cited Article 3

78   *Patty Gerstenblith*

of Iraq's Antiquities Law No. 59 of 1936, which vested title of all antiquities in the Iraqi State, and Article 26, which prohibits export of antiquities (U.S. Government 2017a Complaint ¶ 18). The same complaint also cites to Iraq's Antiquities and Heritage Law No. 55 of 2002 as containing similar provisions, but this would not apply to the Gilgamesh Tablet. The complaint gives only a brief description of Iraq's ownership law, in comparison to the court's detailed analysis of Egypt's ownership law in the *Schultz* decision, 333 F.3d at 399–402. Nonetheless, the Iraqi law is clearly a vesting law and its application to the Hobby Lobby artifacts is neither retroactive nor extraterritorial as the artifacts were located in Iraq at the time of the earlier law's enactment. The complaint did not address the remaining *Schultz* criterion—whether the law was internally enforced.

The third legal element raises the question of improper declaration upon import into the United States. Here, again, the import of the 2017 forfeited artifacts did not comply with the requirements for proper declaration. As the Government explained in its Complaint:

> Persons who import cultural property into the United States believing that the property is or may be stolen, or who may wish to avoid detention and scrutiny of the property for other reasons, ... often seek to avoid detection and targeting by Customs by means of false statements regarding the description, value and country of origin of the goods in their shipments. ... [S]uch importers may split shipments so that the packages' individual values remain below the threshold for formal entry or falsely state that each shipment's value is below that threshold. To avoid scrutiny of packages based on the identity of the importer, such importers may ship packages to or through other addresses.
>
> (U.S. Government 2017a Complaint ¶ 16)

In the case of these artifacts, those responsible for the shipment and import of the objects engaged in every method of improper importation. They divided the artifacts into numerous packages and falsely declared each package with a value below that required for formal entry. The contents were described as ceramic tiles or as tile samples; the country of origin was stated as either Israel or Turkey rather than Iraq; the artifacts were consistently undervalued so as to remain below the $2000 threshold for use of the informal importation process (U.S. Government 2017a Complaint ¶¶ 33–42). The question of forfeiture was never litigated because the government and Hobby Lobby entered into a stipulation of settlement, whereby Hobby Lobby agreed not to contest the forfeiture and agreed to other measures, such as undertaking compliance training. The 2021 Amended Complaint for the Gilgamesh Tablet indicates that it was imported in 2003 without a formal entry in violation of the law and that the provenance information given was incomplete because it omitted the name of the American dealer. (U.S. Government 2021 Amended a Complaint ¶¶ 21–23, 35).

C. The 2017 Stipulation Agreement and the "Missing" Artifacts

While most of the provisions of the 2017 stipulation agreement are routine, one provision caught the eye of those closely following this story. In addition to forfeiting the approximately 3,450 artifacts, Hobby Lobby also agreed to forfeit an additional 144 cylinder seals and, perhaps of greater interest, $3,000,000 "as a substitute *res* for dissipated property or merchandise that was introduced or attempted to be introduced into the United States contrary to law in 2009 through 2011." (U.S. Government 2017b Stipulation ¶ 11). The Stipulation does not specify the artifacts for which $3,000,000 was substituted, but the Stipulation's language indicates that these artifacts were no longer owned by Hobby Lobby as they are described as "dissipated" and that the forfeiture amount of $3,000,000 represents the benefit Hobby Lobby received from these objects, either by selling or by donating them.

Dissipation by sale does not fit within the modus operandi previously described for Hobby Lobby, so one may further posit that, in line with the creation of the Museum of the Bible,[35] these artifacts were donated to a charitable organization, such as the Museum.[36] To obtain a sense of the values involved, one may recall Scott Carroll's statement to Steve Green in August 2010 that the artifacts they inspected in July in the UAE were being offered at $2,091,000, he believed they could be appraised at $11,820,000, but he also believed Hobby Lobby could negotiate a purchase price of $1,600,000, which is the price that Hobby Lobby paid for this group of artifacts (U.S. Government 2017a Complaint ¶ 24). This gives an idea of the appraised value of the donated artifacts but not how many or which types of artifacts would have been donated. Yet another complicating factor is the allegation of the Israel Antiquities Authority that the dealers involved in the sale wrote invoices worth $20,000,000 (Estrin 2017). If this allegation is true, then either the invoices were used to support the valuation for the deduction claimed by Hobby Lobby when it donated the artifacts to the Museum or the same group of Israeli dealers was involved in the sale of additional artifacts, perhaps some or all of the artifacts whose return was announced in March 2020.

The "dissipated" assets may relate to some or all of the 8,000 objects owned by the Museum and that the Museum announced in March 2020 would be returned. This group may include some or all of the 2,000 cuneiform tablets published by Sigrist and Ozaki. That the artifacts, including the tablets published by Sigrist and Ozaki, could have been located in Oklahoma City is not inconsistent with their having been donated to the Museum (Ozaki 2016: 127 nn. 2–3). Given the relatively small number of objects from the Green collection on display in the Museum of the Bible and the relatively large number of artifacts reported to be in the Green collection, it seems likely that many donated objects were and may still be physically located at Hobby Lobby headquarters in Oklahoma City. However, the Gilgamesh Tablet would not be among the "dissipated" assets because it was still owned

80   *Patty Gerstenblith*

by Hobby Lobby in 2019, although loaned to the Museum. The Gilgamesh Tablet was on display at the Museum at the time the Museum opened in late 2017 until its seizure in 2019. Answers to these many questions are crucial in order to complete the full story of the looting, smuggling and trafficking of the forfeited artifacts and other objects that once were or may still be in the collection of Hobby Lobby, the Green family or the Museum.

IV. Lessons Learned and Lessons Not Learned

A. Market Routes and Timelines

The first set of lessons learned focuses on the international market in antiquities. The Hobby Lobby cases inform us about the timeline and routes that such artifacts take in reaching their ultimate markets. The Gilgamesh Tablet was likely looted from an archaeological site in southern Iraq in the 1990s or stolen from a regional museum in 1991, smuggled through Jordan to London, and then sent to the U.S. The Tablet was then taken out of the U.S., made its way to Israel and perhaps other countries and then brought back to the U.S. via London in 2014.

The Hobby Lobby 2017 forfeited objects were likely looted in southern Iraq at the time of or within 2–3 months after the U.S. invasion in 2003. Molina has identified the date Jordanian authorities intercepted Iri-Saĝrig tablets as July 7, 2003 (Molina 2013: 72). He has suggested possible locations for Iri-Saĝrig based on internal textual references to other known sites, archaeological surveys and satellite imagery showing looting, and the appearance of Iri-Saĝrig tablets on the market. (Molina 2013: 71–76). From southern Iraq, these tablets may have travelled through Jordan to Israel and then to the UAE and possibly back to Israel (or possibly to another Gulf State, then to Israel and then back to the UAE) and possibly to London en route to Hobby Lobby in the United States. These tablets were most likely intended for donation to the Museum of the Bible. These artifacts took what might be termed a "southern" or "eastern" route from Iraq in that at some point they went south toward the Gulf. While we do not know where they were kept between 2003 and 2010, they could well have been stored in the UAE or elsewhere in the region, awaiting a buyer. The fact that other artifacts, particularly tablets, from this corpus ended up in London, where they were intercepted, and other locations, including Lebanon, further complicates the attempt to determine the routes by which artifacts travel from the source to the buyer.

Some artifacts looted in Syria may have followed a similar route, possibly passing through Iraq first. Artifacts from Iraq and Syria have been transported through Jordan, which shares a border with both Iraq and Syria. From Jordan, artifacts then move either directly to Europe or pass first through Israel. As with the Iri-Saĝrig tablets from Iraq intercepted by Jordan in 2003, Jordan has intercepted at its border with Syria artifacts looted in

Syria. An alternate, northern route out of Syria likely went through Turkey, then to the Balkans and/or Bulgaria and then to western Europe. A third route from Syria would have passed through Lebanon and from there possibly to countries such as Cyprus and Italy or to the Balkans. We will only fully learn what smuggling routes were used for artifacts from Syria in later years as looted antiquities surface on the market and are intercepted by law enforcement and their itineraries reconstructed. These routes are likely to change as the legal landscape changes, law enforcement methods evolve and new "havens" are identified through which looted antiquities can pass relatively freely, their title laundered and their history obscured.

The false documentation provided to U.S. Customs for the Hobby Lobby objects forfeited in 2017 claimed an origin in Turkey and Israel. At that time, a declaration of Turkey or Israel as the country of origin (that is, country of discovery) of archaeological artifacts upon entry into the United States would raise less suspicion than a declaration of Iraq or Syria. In the 1990s, a declaration of Turkey as the country of origin for antiquities would have been a red flag to Customs agents but, in light of the publicity given to site looting in other parts of the Middle East and North Africa, Turkey is less of a red flag now. The status of Turkey will change again as Turkey and the United States entered into a bilateral agreement to prevent the import into the United States of illegally exported archaeological and ethnological materials in early 2021 (U.S. Dept of State 2021).

The naming of Israel as a country of origin (or discovery) is not a surprise. Israel is known to have a legal trade in archaeological artifacts and to grant export licenses, although in 2012 it adopted new regulations to prevent the trade in illegal archaeological materials that enter Israel from other countries (Kersel 2007: 83–84; Klein 2014). Unlike Turkey and the other countries of the Middle East and North Africa, Israel is not a State Party to the 1970 UNESCO Convention, which means it cannot have a bilateral agreement under the Convention with the United States, nor are its artifacts subject to import restriction in other States Parties. Therefore, fewer legal constraints apply to the import of archaeological artifacts from Israel and Customs agents are less likely to scrutinize artifacts with Israel as the declared country of origin. For this reason, declaration of Israel as the country of origin will continue to be a frequently used subterfuge for trafficking in looted and illegal artifacts that originate in other countries in the region.

The timeline for the Iri-Saĝrig tablets from looting to ultimate destination market is more difficult to establish than their routes. Two tablets known before the large-scale looting of 2003 have been attributed to Iri-Saĝrig, although their actual provenience is not known. Evidence indicates that most of the Iri-Saĝrig tablets were looted in the few months after the March 2003 invasion, which led to a significant increase in such artifacts on the market. The lesson concerning timeline would therefore seem to be that while the shortest time lag from site to the market, particularly a transit market country such as Jordan, may be only a few months, it may also be several years,

82 *Patty Gerstenblith*

easily the seven years in the case of the Hobby Lobby tablets, before looted antiquities reach a destination market country, such as the United States and the United Kingdom.

The case of the Gilgamesh Tablet poses even thornier questions of time-line. While it seems to have been looted in the 1990s and was in London no later than 2001, its visible presence on the market may be dated to 2007 (when it was published by George and appeared in the Michael Sharpe catalog), 2014 (when Hobby Lobby purchased it), 2017 (when it went on public display at the Museum of the Bible) or 2020 (when the US government filed a forfeiture complaint). This puts the time between looting and public knowledge possibly as short as ten years or as long as twenty-nine years. The lesson here is therefore that neither the market nor law enforcement can rely on length of time to provide legitimacy or legality to undocumented artifacts on the market.

B. Deterrent Effect

The main lesson learned from this case study is that the lessons from past illegal conduct in the market for antiquities have not been learned. In all likelihood, both Hobby Lobby forfeitures have reinforced the negative lesson that it is very easy to succeed in trafficking in illegal antiquities with little or no adverse consequences, even if caught. As particularly Simon Mackenzie has pointed out, the white-collar criminals involved in illegal antiquities trafficking are not concerned with economic consequences, such as loss of the value of the trafficked objects and a financial penalty, unless they face a relatively certain threat of criminal punishment through conviction and incarceration (Mackenzie 2005: 212–213; 243–246). This was the lesson that the conviction and incarceration of Fred Schultz, the scion of a wealthy and prominent New York family led by a member of the Federal Reserve Board of New York (Bohlen 2002), was supposed to teach, but its lessons have been forgotten or perhaps not adequately taught in the first place.

Before the acquisition and import of the artifacts in 2010–2011, U.S. Customs stopped Steve Green for attempting to import improperly a Bible and instructed him as to import procedures. I informed Green and others in the Hobby Lobby organization of the illegalities involved in the import of antiquities and of anti-quities from Iraq in particular (U.S. Government 2017a Complaint ¶¶ 22–23, 26). Hobby Lobby's International Department and Customs Broker warned that such shipments would be intercepted by U.S. Customs. The response of those involved in shipping the artifacts was to bypass Hobby Lobby's usual shipping mechanisms and have the Israeli dealers (who were outside of the jur-isdiction of the U.S. government) handle the shipping (U.S. Government 2017a Complaint ¶¶ 31–32). According to a news report, "After the Dubai trip in 2010, Mr. Carroll said he twice told [Steve] Green to end the purchase negotia-tions because of 'issues of provenance' with the cuneiform tablets. He said Mr. Green told him, 'My family is not averse to risk.' Mr. Green did not dispute Mr.

Carroll's account."[37] At no point did Hobby Lobby decide not to acquire the artifacts. Having been told four times, Steve Green's excuse for these purchases that he was poorly advised is not credible. While in many cases involving antiquities trafficking it is difficult to establish the knowledge or *scienter* requirement needed for a criminal conviction, this should not have been one of those cases. In the *Schultz* decision, the jury instruction given by the trial court judge relied on the doctrine of conscious avoidance and instructed the jury that it could find that the defendant had the requisite knowledge if the defendant intentionally avoided learning the truth as to whether the antiquities involved were stolen property. United States v. Schultz, 333 F.3d at 413–14.[38] It would seem the same logic applied here.

It will remain a mystery why no one in the Hobby Lobby operation was indicted and prosecuted—whether the company was too large, its resources too deep, or its prior entanglement with the federal government in its challenge to the Affordable Care Act made the government prosecutors wary of an attempted prosecution. While we do not know the answers, the resolution of this case will almost certainly encourage others to engage in trafficking of illegal antiquities, feeling confident that, even if caught, they will only have to give up the artifacts involved and not face any personal consequences. Relinquishing the artifacts and their value is only the cost of doing business; Hobby Lobby's loss of the artifacts and the forfeited $3 million is of minor consequence to a corporation that is so large and financially successful, although Hobby Lobby sued Christie's and the consignor of the Tablet to Christie's to recover the value of the Tablet (Hobby Lobby Stores 2021). This case was subsequently settled but the terms were not disclosed.

C. The Role of Scholars

This case study also points out the complicity of academics and other scholars who enable the market in illegal artifacts and show disdain for legalities (Brodie 2011b: 414–415). The story of the Gilgamesh Tablet illustrates this all too well. Whether the value of the Tablet was recognized when it was first looted and trafficked is unclear. However, its authentication by Renee Kovacs and later publication by Andrew George pushed its market price within a few months from about $50,000 to $450,000, the price at which Michael Sharpe Rare & Antiquarian Books advertised it. Nothing can explain this escalation in such a short period of time other than its authentication and publication by a known prominent scholar, as noted in the catalog.

Some text scholars believe that they can derive much historical information from a text without knowing its findspot. They also believe that such texts are considerably more difficult to forge and that the information that can be gleaned should not be ignored in the interest of preserving archaeological context or, apparently, of observing the law (Owen 2009; Owen 2013: 335–356; Boardman 2009; Westenholz 2010). As the cuneiform scholar Aage

84 *Patty Gerstenblith*

Westenholz wrote, "Though undeniably a part of illicit trade merchandise, objects with inscriptions are indeed different from other 'works of art' – they are not easily faked, and they hold information more or less independent of their archaeological context." (Westenholz 2010: 260). Furthermore, the publication of these texts takes the intellectual value of the texts from the country of origin, the true owner, and the country is denied this value even if the physical objects are later returned (Brodie 2020).

David Owen of Cornell University and other scholars have felt no reluctance to publish in the Cornell University Studies in Assyriology and Sumerology extensive collections of cuneiform texts, whose findspots and ownership histories are not publicly known, from unlocated sites in southern Iraq, including Garšana and Iri-Saĝrig (Owen and Mayr 2007; Brodie 2011b: 417–420). The comment of Marcel Sigrist referring to the Green family, as quoted by Owen Jarus, summed it up: "'They bought these tablets — I never knew how it happened. It was not really my business.'" (Jarus 2020). However, if a scholar is aware of the illegal nature of the artifacts he or she handles or engages in conscious avoidance of learning the relevant facts, the scholar is as guilty of breaking the law as the looters, sellers, smugglers and purchasers who traffic in such objects—in fact, it is very much the scholar's business to avoid handling stolen or otherwise illegal artifacts. No significance of the Gilgamesh Tablet or the Iri-Saĝrig tablets justifies the role of scholars in incentivizing the future destruction of sites and artifacts, possibly including tablet fragments that are of equal or greater significance for knowledge and understanding of the ancient world. So long as there are scholars willing to authenticate and publish such artifacts and so long as scholars continue to evade the reach of the law despite their handling of stolen property, scholars will continue to confer value, and the illegal trade will continue while the world and the countries of origin suffer the consequences of loss of knowledge about the past.

Notes

1 The author is the "Expert" mentioned in the forfeiture complaint (U.S. Government 2017 Complaint ¶¶ 22–23, 26). All information presented in this essay derives from publicly available sources. Other individuals mentioned in the complaint include the "President" who is Steve Green, the President of the Hobby Lobby Corporation, and the "Consultant" who was Scott Carroll. I want to thank Morag Kersel, Jane Levine, Layla Hashemi and Louise Shelly for commenting on earlier drafts of this article, Neil Brodie for assisting me with bibliographic references and Dr. Katharyn Hanson and Professor McGuire Gibson for correcting the placement of the image of the cuneiform tablet (Figure 2.1). I also want to thank Dr. Kersel for giving me permission to publish the photograph of the empty stand for the Gilgamesh Tablet at the Museum of the Bible.

2 This number was later stated by the chief curator, Jeff Kloha, to be 8,106 artifacts. Kloha was quoted as saying, "Hobby Lobby acquired them so haphazardly for the museum … that it may never be known how they came onto the market."

(Arraf 2020) The papyrus fragments and other artifacts were returned to Egypt in early 2021 (Goldstein 2021). The objects forfeited in 2017, the approximately 8,000 objects at the Museum of the Bible, and an additional approximately 5,000 tablets held at Cornell University were returned to Iraq in July 2021 (Arraf 2021).

3 Moss and Baden described the collection as "the largest privately held collection of biblical antiquities in the world." (Moss and Baden 2017: 15). Moss and Baden stated that the Greens began acquiring biblical manuscripts in 2009 and that the collection eventually included 40,000 artifacts related to the Bible (Moss and Baden 2017: 25).

4 The research group Lying Pen of Scribes: Manuscript Forgeries, Digital Imaging, and Critical Research, under the leadership of Årstein Justnes and Ludvik A. Kheldsberg, initiated consideration of whether the "Dead Sea Scroll" fragments purchased primarily by US Evangelical Protestant institutions post-2002 were forgeries https://lyingpen.com/2020/07/02/post-2002-dead-sea-scrolls-like-fragments-online-a-really-exhausting-guide-for-the-perplexed accessed July 10, 2020. In March 2020, the Museum of the Bible announced that after extensive scientific testing, all of its "Dead Sea Scroll" fragments were forgeries. A Journey for the Truth: Investigating the Recent Dead Sea Scrolls Fragments https://museumofthebible.org/dead-sea-scroll-fragments accessed July 10, 2020.

5 For years before the Greens began acquiring antiquities, they had purchased properties that could be bought for less than their appraised value; they would then rehabilitate the buildings and donate them to charities, thus earning a charitable deduction from their taxable income and a saving in their income tax liability. According to Baden and Moss, "The magic ratio for the Greens was 1:3: for a given investment to be financially viable, they had to be able to write it off at three times the amount that they purchased it for." (Moss and Baden 2017: 24). According to Moss and Baden, it was Donald Jonathan Shipman who proposed to the Greens, sometime between 2005 and 2008, that the same business model could be applied to their acquisition of manuscripts and antiquities, which could then be donated to a charitable institution created by the Greens (Moss and Baden 2017: 22–27). A different version of the origin of the idea for the museum is given by Pond 2019.

According to Moss and Baden, both acquisitions and donations were determined by the financial advantages they brought—what could be bought relatively cheaply and donated with a relatively high appraised value, such as Torah scrolls that could be purchased for $1500–$5000 but, after restoration, valued from $80,000–$500,000 (Moss and Baden 2017: 26–27). The Green family had the goal of creating a museum that would be devoted to the history and role of the Protestant Bible. The Museum of the Bible opened in Washington, D.C. in December 2017. According to the decision in *Burwell*, Hobby Lobby is a closely held corporation, in this case, an S corporation. S corporations do not pay income tax but, rather, their profits and losses are passed through to the shareholders who, in this case, are the Green family members. These profits and losses are reported on the shareholders' personal income tax returns (DeSilver 2014). From a tax perspective, it does not matter whether the artifacts involved were owned by the Greens or the Hobby Lobby corporation; according to the 2017 forfeiture complaint and stipulation of agreement, it seems that those forfeited artifacts were owned by Hobby Lobby. The approximately 8,000 objects whose return was announced in March 2020 were owned by the Museum of the Bible. The tablets published by Sigrist and Ozaki seem to have been owned by the Museum of the Bible, although they were located in Oklahoma City at the time they were studied (Ozaki 2016: 127 nn 2–3). The Gilgamesh Tablet was also owned by Hobby Lobby but was on loan to the Museum of the Bible at the time of its seizure.

86 *Patty Gerstenblith*

6 In July 2017, the Israel Antiquities Authority arrested five Palestinian antiquities dealers in Jerusalem in connection with these sales to Hobby Lobby. It was reported that their sales to Steve Green took place between 2010 and 2014 and amounted to some $20 million. They were arrested for tax evasion for failing to report earnings to the tax authorities. It was reported that they were engaged in money laundering "for an alleged scheme in which fictitious receipts and invoices were issued for antiquities sold to Green." It was further alleged that these invoices were used by "an American ... to receive large-scale tax breaks—and paid dealers kickbacks in return." Three prominent Palestinian families long involved in the antiquities trade were named: the Baidun, Hroub and Barakat families (Estrin 2017). The Complaint refers to some of the dealers as Israeli Dealers; this news report indicates that they are Palestinians in the Old City of Jerusalem. I will use the term "Israeli Dealer" where the Complaint does so (U.S. Government 2017 Complaint ¶¶ 20, 24–25, 27–30).

7 The term "provenance" should indicate the ownership history of a work of art or an artifact, while provenience indicates the archaeological findspot or at least the modern country within which an artifact was discovered (Gerstenblith 2020). The terminology used here follows that of the Complaint, which seems to refer to the ownership history of the artifacts involved, although this is not definitive.

8 According to the US government complaint, the names of people, places and months used on the cuneiform tablets "confirm that these tablets originated in the area that is now Iraq." U.S. Government 2017a Complaint ¶ 2a. Therefore, the statement of Turkey as the country of discovery (or country of origin) was incorrect. See also Brodie 2020; Viano 2019; Connally 2018.

9 Forfeiture is an *in rem* action brought by the government in which the defendant is the property to be forfeited. Someone with an interest in the property can enter the litigation as a claimant. Civil forfeiture, which was used in the Hobby Lobby case, is a quasi-criminal action in which the property was involved in criminal activity, but the government has not pursued a criminal case against any individuals (Cassella 2004: 132; Cassella 2016: 32–33, 37–42; Cassella 2020). The result of a forfeiture action is to transfer title to the U.S. Government, after which the government decides the disposition of the property. When the forfeited property is cultural property, the government typically returns the object to its rightful owner.

10 The consignor was subsequently identified in the litigation between Hobby Lobby and Christie's as Joseph David Hackmey, an art collector in Tel Aviv, Israel. Hobby Lobby Stores 2021 ¶¶ 6, 21.

11 Neil Brodie has suggested that these other texts, or some of them, may be omen tablets referred to by Andrew George in his publication of the Gilgamesh Tablet (George 2007), then published by George in 2013, and in the collection of the Department of Near Eastern Studies of Cornell University (Brodie 2021).

12 Some of the facts given in the forfeiture complaint are disputed. The original antiquities dealer denied having confirmed any of the details in the false provenance letter to the former Head of Christie's Antiquities Department. (U.S. Government 2020 Complaint ¶ 32). Christie's denied several of the statements in its response to Hobby Lobby's filing of its claim against Christie's. Christie's stated, in part, that "[a]ssertions within the filing that suggest Christie's had knowledge of the original fraud or illegal importation do not comport with our investigation." (Grant 2020)

13 According to the 2020 Art Basel report, Christie's and Sotheby's realized $1.8 billion in private sales and private sales were a source of increased revenue in 2019 in comparison to public auction sales. (McAndrew 2020).

14 Nov. 17, 1970, 823 U.N.T.S. 231, 10 I.L.M. 289 (1971). A second convention, the UNIDROIT Convention on Stolen or Illegally Exported Cultural Objects,

Looting of Archaeological Artifacts from Iraq 87

parallels the 1970 UNESCO Convention but has not yet achieved the same level of ratifications, especially among market nations.

15 Switzerland is the only other State Party that requires an additional bilateral agreement to impose import restrictions, but it implements Article 3, rather than Article 9. Therefore, its import restrictions apply to a broader range of cultural objects. For more discussion of the different methods of implementing the 1970 UNESCO Convention, see Gerstenblith 2017.

16 Rather than citing to the import restrictions imposed under the EPIC Antiquities Act and the Convention on Cultural Property implementation Act, the 2017 forfeiture cites to the Iraqi Sanctions Regulations, Title 31, Code of Federal Regulations, Section 575.533(b)(5), and the Iraq Stabilization and Insurgency Sanctions Regulations, Title 31, Code of Federal Regulations, Part 576.208. U.S. Government 2017a Complaint ¶ 17. The Government's amended complaint in the forfeiture of the Gilgamesh Tablet cited to the import restrictions imposed under the EPIC Antiquities Act and the Convention on Cultural Property implementation Act (U.S. Government 2021Amended Complaint ¶¶ 16-17).

17 United States. v. McClain, 545 F.2d 988 (5th Cir. 1977); 593 F.2d 658, 665–66 (5th Cir. 1979), and United States. v. Hollinshead, 495 F.2d 1154 (9th Cir. 1974).

18 United States. v. Schultz, 178 F. Supp. 2d 445 (S.D.N.Y. 2002), *aff'd*, 333 F.3d 393 (2d Cir. 2003). The principle of national ownership was also recognized by the British courts in a civil replevin action brought by the Republic of Iran against the Barakat Gallery to recover artifacts looted from the Jiroft region of Iran. Gov't of the Republic of Iran v. The Barakat Galleries Ltd., [2007] E.W.C.A. Civ. 1374; [2007] 1 All E.R. 1177. For more discussion of these two decisions, see Gerstenblith 2009.

19 Schultz, 178 F. Supp. 2d at 447; McClain, 545 F.2d at 997–1002. As these elements derive from two criminal prosecutions, *Schultz* and *McClain*, it is not certain whether the required standard of clarity is the same in non-criminal litigation, such as a civil replevin action or a civil forfeiture action.

20 While some commentators have suggested that an illegally exported cultural object should also be considered illegal in the United States, for most purposes (and for this discussion), it is accepted that if the *only* violation of law involved is illegal export, the object is not illegal in the United States unless the import violates a specific agreement to restrict the import of the object into the United States such as an agreement under the CCPIA. For further discussion of whether an illegally exported cultural object is illegal in the United States, see Gordley 2013.

21 19 U.S.C. § 1595a(c) (stating that "Merchandise which is introduced or attempted to be introduced into the United States contrary to law shall be treated as follows: (1) The merchandise shall be seized and forfeited if it—(A) is stolen, smuggled or clandestinely imported or introduced."). Stolen property may also be forfeitable directly under the National Stolen Property Act but, under the Civil Asset Forfeiture Reform Act, the government would have a higher burden of proof and the forfeiture would be subject to an innocent owner defense (Cassella 2020).

22 18 U.S.C. § 542 (stating that "Whoever enters or introduces ... into the commerce of the United States any imported merchandise by means of any fraudulent or false invoice, declaration ... or by means of any false statement ... or makes any false statement in any declaration without reasonable cause to believe the truth of such statement ... [shall be guilty of a crime]."). A false declaration constitutes an importation contrary to law and may be a violation of either 18 U.S.C. § 545 (stating that "Whoever fraudulently or knowingly imports or brings into the United States, any merchandise contrary to law ... [shall be subject to criminal penalties]. ... Merchandise introduced into the United States in violation of this section ... shall be forfeited to the United States"), or 19 U.S.C. § 1595a(c), *see supra* note 21. The former is a criminal provision while the latter authorizes civil forfeiture.

88 *Patty Gerstenblith*

23 United States v. An Antique Platter of Gold, known as a Gold Phiale Mesomphalos c. 400 B.C., 991 F. Supp. 222 (S.D.N.Y. 1997), *aff'd*, 184 F.3d 131, 133 (2d Cir. 1999), *cert. denied sub nom.*, Steinhardt v. United States, 528 U.S. 1136 (2000). The United States exempts works of art from the payment of tariffs so there would not have been a financial motive to understate the value of the phiale. Payne-Aldrich Tariff Act of 1909, ch. 6, 36 Stat. 11 §§ 714–717.

24 HM Revenue & Customs v. Al Qassas, unpublished, Westminster Magistrates Court (1 Sept. 2015); Brodie 2017: 118; Telegraph 2015. As in the case of forfeitures in the United States, the forfeited property becomes owned by the Crown and then returned to the rightful owners, in these cases Libya and Iraq.

25 Brodie noted the recovery of 54 items looted from Iraq's regional museums as of 2006 (Brodie 2006: 206). Some of the items stolen from the museums had been published by US, UK and Japanese scholars in the three fascicles published by the University of Chicago's Oriental Institute: *Lost Heritage: Antiquities Stolen from Iraq's Regional Museums* http://oi-archive.uchicago.edu/OI/IRAQ/lh.html accessed July 11, 2020. At least fourteen relief slabs were stolen from Sennacherib's palace at Nineveh, several of which were discovered on the market (Russell 1998), reliefs were stolen from storerooms at Nimrud, and archaeological sites in the south were looted, for example at the site of Umma where reportedly an archive of cuneiform tablets was discovered. A Sumerian foundation cone, which had been excavated at al-Hiba, stolen from the Kirkuk Museum in 1991 and was being sold at Christie's, was recovered in New York after it was identified in one of the *Lost Heritage* publications. A collection of Iraqi antiquities, including 302 cuneiform tablets, was intercepted upon its attempted import into the U.S. in March 2001. U.S. Immigration and Customs Enforcement, "ICE returns more than 1,000 artifacts to Iraq," Sept. 15, 2008 https://www.ice.gov/news/releases/ice-returns-more-1000-artifacts-iraq. This collection was stored in one of the World Trade Center buildings and was damaged during the September 11th attacks. After conservation work, the collection was returned to Iraq in 2010 (Cherry 2014: 227–228).

26 Although not many of these bowls are known from excavated contexts, all that have been excavated were discovered in Iraq. The Norwegian collector, Martin Schøyen, built a large collection during the 1990s, including 654 bowls, as well as other artifacts. (Brodie and Kersel 2014: 200–207). These bowls were the subject of a Parliamentary study, which concluded that "on the balance of probabilities" the bowls were removed from Iraq illegally and were illegally imported into the U.K. (Freeman 2005: 2). These bowls were acquired from Rihani (Freeman 2005: 8–9). In 2021, Norwegian authorities seized nearly one hundred archaeological artifacts from the Schøyen collection on suspicion that they were looted from Iraq (Ulvin 2021). Brodie (2011a: 118–120) documented the vibrancy of the trade in New York and London in artifacts from Iraq between 1990 and 2003, despite the sanctions imposed on all trade with Iraq in 1990.

27 I want to acknowledge my appreciation to Dr. Brodie for sharing this insight.

28 At the time of its publication in 2002, this tablet was thought to have been found at the site of Nippur. However, Molina considers it to have been found at Iri-Saĝrig (Molina 2019: 239, n. 14; De Sossi 2002). The Cuneiform Digital Library Initiative (CDLI) lists one other pre-2003 tablet, which is in the Ashmolean Museum collection. See https://cdli.ucla.edu/search/search_results.php?SearchMode=Text&ObjectID=P142867. It was published in 1996 (Grégoire 1996), but the publication is not available on-line. According to the Ashmolean's register books, this tablet was one of a group acquired by the Oxford-Field Museum expedition to Kish in 1932; the register book records for these tablets "no provenance known." (Personal Communication, Paul Collins. March 25, 2020). CDLI concurs that its provenience is uncertain but seems to have attributed this tablet to Iri-Saĝrig based on the content of the text.

Looting of Archaeological Artifacts from Iraq   89

29 Menegazzi published these tablets in 2005 among a group of 1451 objects recovered by Jordanian authorities between April and November 2003 and between March and October 2004. Parapetti states that only a few of these were identifiable as having been in the Iraq Museum collection and most therefore were looted from archaeological sites (Parapetti 2008: 230).

30 Because the news of the government's forfeiture of the Hobby Lobby artifacts became public in 2017, media reports sometimes mistakenly link these artifacts to the looting and destruction carried out by ISIL in Syria and Iraq in 2011 and following years. As Casana and Laugier point out, this is not correct (Casana and Laugier 2017: 12).

31 Sigrist spent the summer of 2015 in Oklahoma City with the Green Scholars Initiative. International Dominican Foundation, September 2015 https://www.internationaldominicanfoundation.org/wp-content/uploads/2015/09/2015-09-IDF-September-NEWSLETTER-FINAL.pdf. Ozaki acknowledged studying tablets with Sigrist over several years in both Jerusalem and Oklahoma City. He expressed his gratitude to the "Museum of the Bible of Oklahoma City" where the tablets were stored and to Hobby Lobby (Ozaki 2016: 127 nn. 1 and 2). At that time, Sigrist, Ozaki and Lance Allred, curator of the Museum, planned to publish one thousand tablets from the Museum of the Bible collection.

32 A search of the CDLI site in March 2020 revealed that the CDLI listed 2981 texts with the name Iri-Saĝrig, although some of these are seals, rather than tablets: https://cdli.ucla.edu/search/search_results.php?SearchMode=Line&PrimaryPublication=&MuseumNumber=&Provenience=Irisagrig&Period=&TextSearch=&ObjectID=&requestFrom=Submit+Query&Page=0&offset=0. Brodie examined the lists on the CDLI site and the Database of Neo-Sumerian Texts (BDTNS) site a few months later and concluded that 3021 cuneiform-inscribed objects were attributed to Iri-Saĝrig (Brodie 2020).

33 The publication announcement stated that the authors did not have time to clean, bake or photograph the tablets, but they made handwritten transliterations of the texts. The authors examined the tablets between 2012 and 2016 in storerooms of Hobby Lobby in Oklahoma City (Jarus 2020). According to Jarus, Hobby Lobby owned or owns the additional tablets, including those which were not from Iri-Saĝrig. However, Ozaki refers to them as belonging to the Museum of the Bible, although they were located in Oklahoma City. There seems to be a degree of uncertainty surrounding the exact numbers of tablets and other artifacts involved at the different stages. It is unfortunate that the precise number of artifacts forfeited in 2017 was not determined by those responsible for examining and packing the tablets before they were returned. Similarly, it is not clear which tablets were included among the 8,000 returned from the Museum to Iraq.

34 For Ebla (Tell Mardikh), see UNITAR 2014. For Mari, see Daniels and Hanson 2015: 86–88.

35 *See supra* note 5 for the pattern of charitable giving by the Green family.

36 The $3,000,000 may represent the tax savings that the owners of Hobby Lobby realized from the charitable deduction from their taxable income that they would have received for donating the artifacts. As a hypothetical exercise, if the "dissipated" objects had an appraised value of approximately $9,000,000 and, at the time of the donation the marginal tax rate for the owners of Hobby Lobby was the 35% tax bracket, that would have resulted in a saving of approximately $3,000,000.

37 Kelly Crow, "Hobby Lobby Scion Spent Millions on Biblical Relics – Then Came a Reckoning," Wall St. J. (Nov. 13, 2017) https://www.wsj.com/articles/hobby-lobby-scion-spent-millions-on-biblical-relicsthen-came-a-reckoning-15105899450, quoted in Orenstein 2020: 527.

38 The formulation of the jury instruction in *Schultz* on conscious avoidance, which in other circuits is typically referred to as wilful blindness, stated: "[A] defendant may

90 *Patty Gerstenblith*

not purposefully remain ignorant of either the facts or the law in order to escape the consequences of the law. Therefore, if you find that the defendant, not by mere negligence or imprudence but as a matter of choice, consciously avoided learning what Egyptian law provided as to the ownership of Egyptian antiquities, you may [infer], if you wish, that he did so because he implicitly knew that there was a high probability that the law of Egypt invested ownership of these antiquities in the Egyptian government. You may treat such deliberate avoidance of positive knowledge as the equivalent of such knowledge, unless you find that the defendant actually believed that the antiquities were not the property of the Egyptian government." United States v. Schultz, 333 F.3d 393, 413. The Second Circuit further reiterated that the essential element for a jury instruction on conscious avoidance is that "knowledge of the existence of a particular fact is established (1) if a person is aware of a high probability of its existence, (2) unless he actually believes that it does not exist." Id.

Bibliography

Abboud, Nelly. 2020. The Nabu Museum: the Alleged Guardian (Saviour) of the Mashriq. *Revista d'Arqueologia de Ponent* 30: 203–214.

Alberge, Dalya. 2019. Babylonian treasure seized at Heathrow to be returned to Iraq. *The Guardian.* March 10. https://www.theguardian.com/culture/2019/mar/10/babylonia n-treasure-seized-at-heathrow-to-be-returned-to-iraq, accessed March 24, 2020.

Arraf, Jane. 2020. After 'Missteps' and Controversies, Museum of the Bible Works to Clean up its Act. National Public Radio. June 23. https://www.npr.org/2020/06/23/ 877581382/after-missteps-and-controversies-museum-of-the-bible-works-to-clean-u p-its-act, accessed July 11, 2020.

Arraf, Jane. 2021. Iraq Reclaims 17,000 Looted Artifacts, Its Biggest-Ever Repatriation, *The New York Times,* August 3. https://www.nytimes.com/2021/08/03/world/m iddleeast/iraq-looted-artifacts-return.html, accessed Sept. 3, 2021.

Boardman, John. 2009. Archaeologists, Collectors, and Museums. In *Whose Culture? The Promise of Museums and the Debate over Antiquities*, Edited by James Cuno, 107–124. Princeton, NJ: Princeton University Press.

Bohlen, Celestine. 2002. Antiquities Dealer Sentenced to Prison. *New York Times,* June 12. https://www.nytimes.com/2002/06/12/arts/antiquities-dealer-is-sentenced-to-prison.html, accessed March 22, 2020.

Brodie, Neil. 2006. The Plunder of Iraq's Archaeological Heritage, 1991–2005, and the London Antiquities Trade. In *Archaeology, Cultural Heritage, and the Antiquities Trade,* edited by Neil Brodie, Morag M. Kersel, Christina Luke, and Kathryn Walker Tubb, 206–226. Gainesville, FL: University Press of Florida.

Brodie, Neil. 2008. The Market Background to the April 2003 Plunder of the Iraq National Museum. In *The Destruction of Cultural Heritage in Iraq*, edited by P.G. Stone and J. Farchakh Bajjaly, 41–54. Woodbridge: Broydell.

Brodie, Neil. 2011a. The Market in Iraqi Antiquities 1980–2009 and Academic Involvement in the Marketing Process. In *Crime in the Art and Antiquities World*, edited by Stefano Manacorda and Duncan Chappell, 117–133. New York: Springer.

Brodie, Neil. 2011b. Congenial Bedfellows? The Academy and the Antiquities Trade. *Journal of Contemporary Criminal Justice* 27: 408–437.

Brodie, Neil. 2011c. *Scholarship and Insurgency/ The study and trade of Iraqi antiquities.* https://traffickingculture.org/app/uploads/2015/02/Brodie-2011-Scholarship -and-insurgency.pdf.

Brodie, Neil. 2017. The role of conservators in facilitating the theft and trafficking of cultural objects: the case of a seized Libyan statue. *Libyan Studies* 48: 117.

Brodie, Neil. 2020. Restorative justice? Questions arising out of the Hobby Lobby return of cuneiform tablets to Iraq. *Revista memória em rede* 12 (23): 87–109.

Brodie, Neil. 2021. Bad omens for Cornell? *Market of Mass Destruction* March 12. https://marketmassdestruction.com/author/njb1012redux, accessed March 29, 2021.

Brodie, Neil J. and Morag M. Kersel. 2014. WikiLeaks, Text, and Archaeology: The Case of the Schøyen Incantation Bowls. In *Archaeologies of Text: Archaeology, Technology, and Ethics*. Edited by Matthew T. Rutz and Morag M. Kersel, 198–213. Haverton, PA: Oxbow Books.

Casana, Jesse and Elise Jakoby Laugier. 2017. Satellite Imagery-based Monitoring of Archaeological Site Damage in the Syrian Civil War. Plos One. November 30. https://journals.plos.org/plosone/article?id=10.1371/journal.pone.0188589, accessed February 26, 2020.

Cassella, Stefan D. 2004. Using the Forfeiture Laws to Protect Archaeological Resources. *Idaho Law Review* 41: 129–145.

Cassella, Stefan D. 2016. Using the Forfeiture Laws to Protect Cultural Heritage. *United States Attorneys' Bulletin* 64 (2): 31–43.

Cassella, Stefan D. 2020. Recovering Stolen Art & Antiquities Under the Forfeiture Laws: Who Is Entitled to the Property When There Are Conflicting Claims. *North Carolina Journal of International Law* 45: 395–442.

Cherry, John F. 2014. Publishing Undocumented Texts: Editorial Perspectives. In *Archaeologies of Text: Archaeology, Technology, and Ethics*. Edited by Matthew T. Rutz and Morag M. Kersel, 227–244. Haverton, PA: Oxbow Books.

Coggins, Clemency C. 1969. Illicit Traffic of Pre-Columbian Antiquities, *Art Journal* 29 (1): 94–98.

Connally, Bess. 2018. Yale Assyriologist Discovers Evidence of Lost City in Iraq. *YaleNews*. June 26, 2018. https://news.yale.edu/2018/06/26/yale-assyriologist-discovers-evidence-lost-city-iraq, accessed July 10, 2020.

Daniels, Brian I. and Katharyn Hanson. 2015. Archaeological Site Looting in Syria and Iraq: A Review of the Evidence. In *Countering Illicit Traffic in Cultural Goods: The Global Challenge of Protecting the World's Heritage*. Edited by France Desmarais, 83–94. Paris: ICOM.

DeSilver, Drew. 2014. What is a "closely held corporation," anyway, and how many are there? *FactTank*. https://www.pewresearch.org/fact-tank/2014/07/07/what-is-a-closely-held-corporation-anyway-and-how-many-are-there, accessed March 24, 2020.

De Sossi, Giovanni. 2002. One More Su-ba-ti Ur III Tablet. *Nouvelles Assyriologiques Brèves et Utilitaires (NABU)* 4: 74–75.

Estrin, Daniel. 2017. Israeli Authorities Arrest Antiquities Dealers in Connection with Hobby Lobby Scandal. NPR. July 31. https://www.npr.org/sections/parallels/2017/07/31/540579261/israeli-authorities-arrest-antiquities-dealers-in-connection-with-hobby-lobby-sc.

Fabrikant, Geraldine. 2010. Craft Shop Family Buys Up Ancient Bibles for Museum, *N.Y. Times*. June 11. https://www.nytimes.com/2010/06/12/business/12bibles.html.

Freeman, David John. 2005. An inquiry into the provenance of 654 Aramaic incantation bowls delivered into the possession of UCL by, or on the instruction of, Mr Martin Schøyen. House of Lords Library.

George, Andrew. 2007. The Civilizing of Ea-Enkidu: An Unusual Tablet of the Babylonian *Gilgameš* Epic. *Revue d'assyriologie et d'archéologie orientale* 101 (1): 59–80.

92 *Patty Gerstenblith*

Gerstenblith, Patty. 2006. From Bamiyan to Baghdad: Warfare and the Preservation of Cultural Heritage at the Beginning of the 21st Century. *Georgetown J. Int'l L.* 37 (2): 245–351.

Gerstenblith, Patty. 2007. Controlling the International Market in Antiquities: Reducing the Harm, Preserving the Past. *Chicago Journal of International Law* 8 (1): 169–195.

Gerstenblith, Patty. 2009. Schultz and Barakat: Universal Recognition of National Ownership of Antiquities. *Art Antiquity and Law* 14(1): 29–57.

Gerstenblith, Patty. 2017. Implementation of the 1970 UNESCO Convention by the United States and Other Market Nations. In *The Routledge Companion to Cultural Property.* Edited by Jane Anderson and Haidy Geismar. Abingdon, UK: Routledge.

Gerstenblith, Patty. 2020. Provenience and Provenance Intersecting with International Law in the Market for Antiquities. *North Carolina Journal of International Law* 45: 457–495.

Gibson, McGuire. 2008. The Acquisition of Antiquities in Iraq, 19th Century to 2003, Legal and Illegal. In *The Destruction of Cultural Heritage in Iraq*, edited by P.G. Stone and J. Farchakh Bajjaly, 31–40. Woodbridge: Broydell.

Goldstein, Caroline. 2021. The Museum of the Bible Must Once Again Return Artifacts, This Time an Entire Warehouse of 5,000 Egyptian Objects. *Artnet News*, January 29. https://news.artnet.com/art-world/museum-bible-returns-objects-egypt-1940432, accessed March 29, 2021.

Gordley, James. 2013. The Enforcement of Foreign Law: Reclaiming One Nation's Cultural Heritage in Another Nation's Courts. In *Enforcing International Cultural Heritage Law.* Edited by Francesco Francioni and James Gordley, 110–124. Oxford: Oxford University Press.

Grant, Daniel. 2020. Hobby Lobby Sues Christie's for Selling It an Antiquity Authorities Say Was Looted. *The Art Newspaper.* May 19. https://www.theartnewspaper.com/news/hobby-lobby-sues-christie-s-for-selling-it-a-looted-antiquity, accessed July 10, 2020.

Greenland, Fiona *et al.*, 2019. A Site-Level Market Model of the Antiquities Trade. *Int'l J. Cultural Property* 26 (1): 21–47.

Grégoire, J.-P. 1996. *Archives Administratives et Inscriptions Cunéiformes: Ashmolean Museum, Bodleian Collection, Oxford.* Paris: Librairie Orientaliste Paul Geuthner.

Greshko, Michael. 2020. "Dead Sea Scrolls" at the Museum of the Bible Are All Forgeries. *National Geographic.* March 13. https://www.nationalgeographic.com/history/2020/03/museum-of-the-bible-dead-sea-scrolls-forgeries/#close, accessed March 16, 2020.

Higgins, Charlotte. 2020. A Scandal in Oxford: The Curious Case of the Stolen Gospel, *The Guardian*, Jan. 9. https://www.theguardian.com/news/2020/jan/09/a-scandal-in-oxford-the-curious-case-of-the-stolen-gospel.

Hobby Lobby Stores. 2021. Hobby Lobby Stores, Inc. v. Christie's Inc. and Hackmey. First Amended Complaint. CV-20-2239 (E.D.N.Y.).

Jarus, Owen. 2020. 1,400 Ancient Cuneiform Tablets Identified from Lost City of Irisagrig in Iraq. Were They Stolen? *Live Science.* Jan. 7. https://www.livescience.com/lost-city-in-iraq-cuneiform-tablets.html?fbclid=IwAR1F4hwm4PyAIUyy0M_lkw34qsVacVynhxKDgzUBnho77Ww4UirpXi4Uli0, accessed February 26, 2020.

Kellner, Mark A. 2018. Museum of the Bible Returns Stolen Gospel Manuscript. *The Christian Century.* Aug. 14. https://www.christiancentury.org/article/news/museum-bible-returns-stolen-gospels-manuscript, accessed February 28, 2020.

Kersel, Morag. 2007. Transcending Borders: Objects on the Move. *Archaeologies* 3 (2): 81–98.

Klein, Eitan. 2014. Illicit Trafficking of Antiquities and the Antiquities Dealers: The Israel Experience. In *Proceedings of the 3ʳᵈ International Conference of Experts on the Return of Cultural Property,* edited by Souzána Choúlia-Kapelőnī, 226–230. Athens: Archaeological Receipts and Expropriations Fund.

Mackenzie, S.R.M. 2005. *Going, Going, Gone: Regulating the Market in Illicit Antiquities.* Leicester, UK: Institute of Art and Law.

McAndrew, Clare. 2020. *The Art Market 2020.* https://www.artbasel.com/about/initiatives/the-art-market, accessed July 10, 2020.

Molina, Manuel. 2013. On the Location of Irisağrig. In *From the 21st Century BC to the 21st Century AD. Proceedings of the International Conference on Neo-Sumerian Studies Held in Madrid, 22–24 July 2010.* Edited by Steven J. Garfinkle and Manuel Molina, 59–87. Winona Lake, IN: Eisenbrauns.

Molina, Manuel. 2019. The Looting of Ur III Tablets After the Gulf Wars. In *Dealing with Antiquity: Past, Present & Future. Proceedings of the 63ʳᵈ Rencontre Assyriologique Internationale, Alter Orient und Altes Testament* 460, edited by W. Sommerfeld, 233–262. Münster: Ugarit-Verlag.

Moss, Candida R. and Joel S. Baden. 2017. *Bible Nation: The United States of Hobby Lobby.* Princeton, NJ: Princeton University Press.

Museum of the Bible. 2020. *Statement on Past Acquisitions.* https://www.museumofthebible.org/press/press-releases/statement-on-past-acquisitions, accessed July 10, 2020.

Nørskov, Vinnie. 2002. *Greek Vases in New Contexts.* Aarhus, Netherlands: Aarhus University Press.

O'Keefe, Patrick J. 2017. *Protecting Cultural Objects: Before and After 1970.* Builth Wells, UK: Institute of Art and Law.

Orenstein, Karin. 2020. Risking Criminal Liability in Cultural Property Transactions. *North Carolina Journal of International Law* 45: 529–550.

Owen, David. 2009. Censoring Knowledge: The Case for the Publication of Unprovenanced Cuneiform Tablets. In *Whose Culture? The Promise of Museums and the Debate over Antiquities,* edited by James Cuno, 125–142. Princeton, NJ: Princeton University Press.

Owen, David. 2013. *Cuneiform Texts Primarily from Iri-Sağrig/Āl-Šarrākī and the History of the Ur III Period.* University Park, PA: Pennsylvania State University Press.

Owen, David and Rudolf H. Mayr. 2007. *The Garšana Archives.* Cornell University Studies in Assyriology and Sumerology 3. University Park, PA: Pennsylvania State University Press.

Ozaki, Tohru. 2016. On the Calendar of Urusağrig. *Zeitschrift für Assyriologie* 106 (2): 127–137.

Parapetti, Roberto. 2008. The Contribution of the Centro Scavi di Torino to the Reconstruction of Iraqi Antiquities. In *The Destruction of Cultural Heritage in Iraq,* edited by Peter G. Stone and Joanne Farchakh Bajjaly, 229–234. Woodbridge, UK: Boydell Press.

94 *Patty Gerstenblith*

Pike, Damon V. and Lawrence M. Friedman. 2012. *Customs Law*. Durham, NC: Carolina Academic Press.

Pond, Shelly. 2019. Museum of the Bible's Roots Extend into South Florida. *Good News*. April 2. https://www.goodnewsfl.org/museum-of-the-bibles-roots-extend-into-south-flor ida, accessed March 25, 2020.

Rollston, Christopher. 2020. *The Forger Among Us: The Museum of the Bible Dead Sea Scrolls and the Recent History of Epigraphic Forgeries*. March 15. http://www.rollstonepigraphy.com/?p=884, accessed March 16, 2020.

Russell, John M. 1998. *The Final Sack of Nineveh*. New Haven, CT: Yale University Press.

Sharpe, Michael. 2007. *Michael Sharpe Rare & Antiquarian Books Catalog* No. 1. https://twitter.com/incunabula/status/1243928139207671810/photo/3, accessed July 10, 2020.

Sigrist, Marcel and Tohru Ozaki. 2019. Publication Announcement: *Tablets from the Irisagrig Archive*, Cornell University Studies in Assyriology and Sumerology. Eisenbrauns. https://www.eisenbrauns.org/books/titles/978-1-57506-726-1.html, accessed 26 February 2020.

Stone, Elizabeth C. 2015. An Update on the Looting of Archaeological Sites in Iraq. *Near Eastern Archaeology* 78 (3): 178–186.

Taylor, Jonathan. 2019. Twitter, Aug. 30. https://twitter.com/JonTaylor_BM/status/1167405875168010240, accessed Sept. 28, 2019.

Telegraph. 2015. Ancient Greek Relic Looted from Libya to Be Returned, *Telegraph*, Sept. 1. https://www.telegraph.co.uk/news/earth/environment/archaeology/1183 7886/Ancient-Greek-relic-looted-from-Libya-to-be-returned.html, accessed Sept. 28, 2019.

Topçuoglu, Oya and Tasha Vorderstrasse. 2019. Small Finds, Big Values: Cylinder Seals and Coins from Iraq and Syria on the Online Market. *Int'l J. Cultural Property* 26: 239–263.

Ulvin, Philippe Bédos. 2021. Kjempebeslag av uvurderlige kulturgjenstander hos norsk storsamler. NRKSept. 3. https://www.nrk.no/norge/kjempebeslag-av-uvurder lige-kulturgjenstander-hos-norsk-storsamler-1.15635305, accessed Sept. 3, 2021.

UNITAR. 2014. http://unosat.web.cern.ch/unosat/unitar/downloads/chs/ebla.pdf, accessed March 24, 2020.

U.S. Dept of State. Bureau of Educational and Cultural Affairs. 2021. United States and Turkey Work Together to Protect Cultural Heritage. Jan. 19. https://eca.state.gov/high light/united-states-and-turkey-work-together-protect-cultural-heritage, accessed March 29, 2021.

U.S. Government. 2017a. United States v. Approximately Four Hundred Fifty (450) Cuneiform Tablets and Approximately Three Thousand (3,000) Ancient Clay Bullae. Verified Complaint in Rem. CV 17–3980 (E.D.N.Y.).

U.S. Government. 2017b. United States v. Approximately Four Hundred Fifty (450) Cuneiform Tablets and Approximately Three Thousand (3,000) Ancient Clay Bullae. Stipulation of Settlement CV 17–03980 (E.D.N.Y.).

U.S. Government. 2020. United States v. One Cuneiform Tablet known as the "Gilgamesh Dream Tablet". Verified Complaint in Rem. CV 20–2222 (E.D.N.Y.).

U.S. Government. 2021a. United States v. One Cuneiform Tablet Known as the "Gilgamesh Dream Tablet". Amended Verified Complaint in Rem. CV 20–2222 (E.D.N.Y.).

U.S. Government. 2021b. United States v. One Cuneiform Tablet Known as the "Gilgamesh Dream Tablet". Decree of Forfeiture. Civ. No. 20–2222 (E.D.N.Y.).

Viano, Maurizio. 2019. On the Location of Irisaĝrig Once Again. *Journal of Cuneiform Studies* 71: 35–52.

Westenholz, Aage. 2010. Illicit Cuneiform Tablets: Heirlooms or Stolen Goods? In *Why Should Someone Who Knows Something Conceal It?*. Edited by Alexandra Kleinerman and Jack M. Sasson, 257. Eisenbrauns.

3 The Hearing Hand

Scribes and Seal Cutters in the Ancient Near East

Ira Spar and Antonietta Catanzariti

Introduction

Conflict in the Near East over the last several decades has led to increased illicit excavation of ancient sites. With smuggling across borders made easier by war, the demand for antiquities remains unabated. Smuggling and forging of art objects such as large and small sculptures, monuments, cylinder and stamp seals, cuneiform tablets and even manuscripts has thrived. Hundreds of thousands of tablets in many sizes and shapes were produced in the ancient Near East. The small size of tablets and seals allows for their ease of transport making them desired objects for smuggling. The craving of collectors thirsty for new acquisitions and the need for extra income by those in war torn Middle Eastern countries led to an ongoing cycle of looting, smuggling and the forging of ancient Near Eastern artifacts.

According to a Sumerian proverb, "possessions are flying birds: they never find a place to settle."[1] By the late 19th century the demand for antiquities by dealers, collectors and museums to satisfy demand for confirmation of the historicity of the Bible was soaring. As soon as dealers in the Near East and Europe realized that there was a profitable collector's market in Europe and America for ancient Near Eastern antiquities, illicit excavations and forging of antiquities surged. In an article in the *American Journal of Semitic Languages* published in 1904, the adventurer, diplomat and art dealer Edgar J. Banks wrote, "Four-fifths of all the antiquities offered for sale in Baghdad are spurious." In the Near East, faking of tablets and seals continues today. This chapter looks at tablets, seals and fakes, the most common items being smuggled and targeted in the antiquities market in order to provide an overview of their historical importance and characteristics, and to emphasize the role of the subject matter specialist in the support of law enforcement in the fight against ancient Near Eastern antiquities trafficking.

Smuggling Goods in the Ancient Near East: A Case from the Old Assyrian period (ca. 1970–1700 B.C.E.)

Almost four thousand years ago, enterprising merchants in ancient Assyria found that there existed a potential lucrative market for their goods in the

DOI: 10.4324/9781003023043-5

cities of southeastern Anatolia, ca. 1,000 miles away. To facilitate enterprise, merchants formed companies with a main branch in their home town of Ashur and subsidiary branches in Kanesh and other towns in Anatolia. Their main exports were textiles and tin, which they exchanged for silver, gold and copper. Business partners communicated over the long distance by exchanging letters written on tablets encased in envelopes. The envelope contained the name of the sender and the addressee.[2]

Letters dealt with business and family matters. One individual named Buzazu, who appears to have been a "man about town," was admonished by his father to pay attention to his job, settle his strained relationship with his sister and stop stealing slaves. One letter reveals more about his character. He schemed to increase his company's profits by avoiding taxes on goods sent from Ashur to Kanesh by having his caravan take a circuitous, dangerous road through the mountains, skirting the dangers posed by robbers and wild beasts. This hazardous route allowed his caravaneers to avoid check points with tolls, and payment of import taxes on merchandise.

"Let them [the transporters] bring the tin via the narrow [mountain route smuggling] tract if it is clear. If not, let them make small packets of my tin and introduce them gradually into Kanesh, concealed in their underwear."[3]

In another letter a merchant is reprimanded by his business partners for his prohibited activities. "The orders of the harbor (authorities) are firm, your smuggling that you wrote about is not feasible, so we shall not write you about your smuggling. Make up your own mind! Do not rely on colleagues! Beware!"[4]

Other merchant letters reveal that smugglers were willing to bribe guards, fool customs officials by making false import declarations, and mix cleared goods with non-taxed merchandise to avoid additional import payments. The penalties if caught ranged from a fine to house arrest to possible incarceration. One merchant had his house raided by the authorities who found an abundance of smuggled goods. He was sentenced to serve time in jail.

Cuneiform Tablets: The Birth of Writing

Excavated from the mounds and sands of ancient Mesopotamia, the private correspondence, archives and records of one of humankind's first civilizations allow us to reveal the past.[5] Cuneiform records now in museum and private collections, allow entrance to the business and daily lives of families, insight into the private and public affairs of royalty, and the observation of the activities of traders, farmers, artisans, accountants, astronomers, mathematicians, scientists, physicians, scholars, priests and prophets. With the development of writing over five thousand years ago in the lands of southern Mesopotamia, the culture of one of the world's most ancient societies has come to light. Even after all physical traces of once great civilizations had perished; their legacy was preserved in writing and art.

Clay was the medium that made possible the preservation of writing. Plentiful, cheap, easily available and hardened when dried, ancient writing on

98 *Ira Spar and Antonietta Catanzariti*

clay has withstood the ravages of time. While ancient Mesopotamian records written on wood, leather, metal and even wax have mostly disintegrated, texts written on clay survive. Hundreds of thousands of documents written on clay have been both legally and illicitly excavated over the past two hundred years. Thousands still lie beneath the mounds and ruins of ancient cities.

The earliest tablets from southern Mesopotamia were administrative documents, practical minded book-keeping devices rather than literary masterpieces of abstract thought. They included both pictographic-type images and linear representations. The pictograms and wedge-signs usually inscribed on both the obverse and reverse sides of a tablet were randomly placed in box-shaped areas marked off with thin vertical and horizontal ruling lines. These square-shaped or rectangular boxes placed in rows were read from right to left.[6]

The development of writing from left to right on parallel lines (as in European languages) with cuneiform signs placed one after another with no punctuation markers did not appear for another thousand years. By this time there was a large reduction in the number of signs to about 600. Each Sumerian and Akkadian sign represented either a syllable or a word, not a letter in an alphabet.

During the 3rd millennium B.C.E., both the Sumerian and Akkadian languages were most commonly in use; most people were probably bilingual. As Sumerian became extinct as a spoken language, probably by the early part of the second millennium B.C.E., its practice was mainly restricted to temple sacred and ceremonial use and by scholars and their students who preserved past classical traditions. By the middle of the third millennium B.C.E., Akkadian scribes had adopted and adapted the corpus of Sumerian signs. Over the next millennium, variant forms of the signs were employed to write the differing Assyrian and Babylonian dialects of the Akkadian language. By the 7th century, Aramaic had replaced Akkadian as the primary spoken language. By the time of Alexander the Great's conquest of the Near East, Aramaic, primarily written on leather scrolls, had increasingly become the standard script, superseding cuneiform writing on clay (scholars are divided as to whether cuneiform was written on leather). Cuneiform writing continued to be used on monumental inscriptions, commercial, legal, scientific, astronomical and medical documents and the endless scribal copying of older literary and scholastic texts until the end of the first century C.E. By the second century C.E., texts written in cuneiform had become extinct, the ability to decipher and understand Akkadian and Sumerian texts was lost, not be recovered until the 19th –20th century C.E.

The earliest writing to survive, dating to the end of the 4th millennium B.C.E., was inscribed onto damp clay tablets with a pointed stick or reed cut to a point at its end. Recognizable objects included the head and foot of the human body, female genitalia, plants, animals, vessels and profiles of mountains.

Within a few hundred years, these sketches on clay were partially replaced by pressing a thicker stylus end into the clay rather than by drawling a crude naturalistic image. The new method left a wedge-shaped impression followed by an embedded tail. Curves become straight lines leading to a stylization which soon removed any pictorial representation. Early writing soon became a maze of stylized horizontal, vertical and slanting wedge-shaped marks which we call cuneiform. On clay tablets vertical wedges have their triangle-shaped head at the top, horizontal wedges have the wedge at the left and inclined wedges at their upper left end. Some characters retained the outer shapes of images but most evolved over time.

Over the millennia different sign forms emerged which were used to write numerous Near Eastern languages including Sumerian (whose origins remain unknown), Akkadian and Assyrian (written in the lands of modern Iraq and Syria) as well as Hittite and Luwian (written in ancient Anatolia, modern day Turkey and its environs), Urartian in Armenia, Eblite in Syria and Elamite and Old Persian (in Iran), and Hurrian and Ugaritic in Syria. Scribes in the royal court of Egypt during the 18th dynasty even corresponded in Akkadian with kings, princes and leaders in the Near East and Cyprus. In the city of Ugarit in Syria and probably in its environs as well, scribes in the 14th–12th centuries B.C.E. simplified Akkadian signs developing an alphabet using cuneiform type wedges.

To prepare a tablet for inscribing, student scribes began the process by taking lumps of river clay, sifting to remove most intrusive inclusions such as pebbles, pieces of wood and vegetation. They then kneaded, rolled and hand molded the refined clay into small pillow-shaped tablets, most of which fit easily into the palm of one's hand. Larger size texts such as bricks and prisms contain some chaff to provide strength. For scholarly tablets inscribed by master scribes, a paste of fine water-diluted clay was applied as a slip to provide a visually appealing smooth surface.[7] The scribe shaped a tablet's obverse so that the obverse was flat, the reverse convex. Tablets were kept moist prior to their inscription with a piece of moist cloth paced over the clay. A cloth imprint is still visible on some tablets. Tablet sizes and shapes vary by period. Neo and Late Babylonian commercial tablets from the 7th–2nd century B.C.E are usually inscribed in landscape mode, Old Babylonian (ca. 1900–1600 B.C.E.) tablets in portrait mode, Ur III (ca. 2100–2000 B.C.E.) messenger tablets are small, Ur III field survey texts are round, barley loans were sometimes inscribed on triangular dockets, scholarly tablets are large often written in columns with vertical rulings, some magical texts were inscribed on small clay balls about the size of a marble. School boy exercise tablets are lenticular in shape. For copies of long compositions, a small single oblique wedge could be added along the tablet edge every ten lines. A total number of lines were added at the end, an indication that a complete text had been reproduced. Signs are read from left to right and from top to bottom. The end of the obverse writing may continue onto the lower edge; the tablet is then turned over and writing continues on the reverse. There are, however, occasional exceptions to this rule.

Wedge-shaped signs were impressed into the moist clay with a stylus called a "tablet-reed." Unfortunately, reed styluses have not survived. It is still

Figure 3.1 Photo of tablets of various shapes. First row (left) from the top: Ur III Sumerian account of expenditures; below an Old Assyrian letter. Second row from the top: Neo-Babylonian record of expenditures of silver; Ur III receipt for a goat; Early Dynstic III (meaning unknown); Old Babylonian loan of silver. Row three from the top: Old Babylonian Private Letter; Achaemenid period field ease. Fourth row from the top: 3 Neo-Babylonian economic tablets: Agreement regarding disposition of slaves; Proxy contract for purchase of a slave; Promisory note for silver

The Metropolitan Museum of Art, photo, Ira Spar.
1st row: MMA 11.217.29; MMA66.245.11. 2nd row: MMA 86.11.107; MMA 11.217.9a; MMA 11.217.15. 3rd row: MMA 62.70.99; MMA 86.11.98. 4th row: MMA 79.7.10; MMA 79.7.11; MMA 79.7.8.

possible to see the remnants of the scribe's reed stylus. When through use the reed fibers separated, they left double-line striation-marks on the clay, still visible to the trained eye. Other styluses include those made from wood, bone, ivory or even metal. The stylus was pressed into the clay at different angles to create horizontal, vertical and slanting signs. At the end of the third millennium B.C.E. into the Early Dynastic Period a round-ended stylus was used to create number marks.[8] In the tablet below the scribe has made two round holes above an image of barley to indicate 300 liters of barley. Other signs include a foot, bowl, vessels and a pubic triangle. One can also see part of an image created by the rolling of a cylinder seal over the tablet surface prior to it being inscribed (see below).

Figure 3.2 Sumerian, eleven column register of field yields under the reign of Ibbi-Sin: Ca. 2028–2004 B.C.E. The tablet is almost a perfect square measuring ca. 12 × 12 inches in size.
Ur III, reign of Ibbi-Suen
British Museum
BM 110116

By the middle of the third millennium B.C.E., signs were written from left to right in a continuous flowing line without a break. There are no western-type punctuation marks such as commas or periods. During the Old Assyrian period, a vertical line signified word division. Erasures in which the scribe ran his finger over a group of signs on the still moist clay often appear on commercial texts. Scribal writing styles varied, during the Late Babylonian period the script leaned to the right, on Old Assyrian tablets they lean slightly to the left. Sumerian and Akkadian cuneiform signs could have more than one sound value and multiple meanings. Only in Ugaritic cuneiform do the signs indicate alphabetic letters. A rare group of twenty tablets have been found with a cuneiform text on one side and a transliteration into Greek on the reverse.[9]

Figure 3.3 Proto-cuneiform tablet with seal impressions: administrative account of barley distribution
The Metropolitan Museum of Art
Ca. 3100–2900 B.C.
Mesopotamia, probably from Uruk (modern Warka)
MMA1988.433.1

Some large portrait-shaped first millennium scholarly tablets are marked with what have been called "firing holes." Most are small round holes, others square. Originally, they were thought to have been placed to allow for air to escape during firing although few tablets were oven baked. This suggestion lacks confirmation. Another theory asserts that they were placed in open spaces to prevent unauthorized changes or additions. At present their meaning is unknown.

After a scribe wrote his account, the moist clay was left to air-dry. As long as the clay was of fine quality and not contaminated by inclusion of salts, records could last a long time. However, if a tablet contained old information no longer needed, it could be placed in a "dead letter file" or most commonly recycled after being left to soak in water. Tablets burnt in ancient fires, either due to an accidental fire or the result of a conflagration caused by an enemy, become hardened turning dark grey or black. Private business records could be archived by being stored in baskets, brick boxes or in pottery vessels.[10] Large library-type collections of tablets were also stored in specially designated rooms containing pigeon-hole type shelves cut into walls. Royal archives such as the one assembled by king Ashurbanipal in the 7th century B.C.E., contained political, commercial, legal and medical documents together with literary compositions including myths, epics, hymns, prayers, magical and medical compositions, astrological and astronomical texts, lengthy sign and word lists and especially divinatory omens. There were also some administrative records and historical inscriptions. In total it is estimated that the king had assembled between 5,000–10,000 tablets. Cuneiform tablet references indicate that there were also many writing boards in the collection. The destruction and burning of the city of Nineveh in 612 B.C.E. caused the disintegration of the writing boards and many of the clay tablets to be broken into thousands of fragments.

Figure 3.4 Ten joins from tablet fragments. Letter of King Sin-sharra-ishkun to King Nabopolassar
2nd century B.C.E.
The Metropolitan Museum of Art, photo Ira Spar
MMA 86.11.370A+MMA 86.11.370C+MMA 86.11.383C+MMA86.11.383D+MMA 86.11.383E

Writing Boards

Writing boards were once ubiquitous, being used for erudite compositions and record keeping. The boards were made of ivory or wood with a slight depression carved out, leaving a raised rim enclosing the rectangular board. Scratches incised onto the board allowed a soft layer of beeswax to more easily be adhered to the surface. A scribe could use his stylus to impress cuneiform wedges into the soft wax in the same manner as if he were writing on a clay tablet. A scribe could also use the tablet for non-cuneiform scripts such as Aramaic or Hieroglyphic Luwian. Individual boards were hinged to one another for lengthy compositions. Panels were folded together to form a book. An outer cover contained an inscription identifying the building location in which the book was stored and its contents. One surviving fragment indicates that the book contained the contents of a composition known as Enuma Anu Enlil, "When the Gods Anu and Enlil," a compilation of astrological omens found in seventy tablets. Scribes are shown on palace reliefs carrying the boards in battle scenes, presumably to be used like a modern notebook to record booty or numbers of captives. Texts refer to scholars using writing boards as portable reference books and teachers used them to instruct students. Tablets in remote collections were copied onto writing boards and sent to the royal libraries of King Ashurbanipal where other scribes recopied their inscriptions onto new tablets for storage and consultation. Wooden boards have mostly disappeared, only a few survive today from a shipwreck off the coast of Turkey dating to ca. 1300 B.C.E. At ancient Nimrud sixteen ivory boards and several walnut boards were found having been thrown down a well probably during the sack and destruction of the city in 612 B.C.E. Writing boards were also used in the Levant t and Greece (Iliad 6:178–80).[11]

Images of scribes writing on tablets or on writing boards are rare. In the image below two Assyrian scribes are shown recording information from a war campaign. The scribe on the left holds a portable writing board in his left hand. He carries a long stylus with a large blunt end in his right hand. Presumably, it was easier when in the field during war to record information, possibly from dictation, into the wax rather than to find and refine clay suitable for inscription. Unlike clay which dried out, the wax surface was malleable, did not dry out and was easily erasable. The scribe on the right holds a long ink pen or brush in between his thumb and forefinger to write in ink on a parchment roll. He is probably recording a tally in Aramaic in alphabetic script.

Some cuneiform tablets contain images impressed on their surface. The images were formed by rolling or impressing a small cylinder or stamp over its surface. An image, design or inscription carved by a seal cutter into a stone could act as a signature, or certify the authenticity of an obligation (see further below). On some tablets, presumably when a seal was not easily obtainable, one or more finger-nail impressions could serve in lieu of a seal.

Figure 3.5 Assyrian ivory and wax writing board found in a well at Nimrud
The Metropolitan Museum of Art
Ca. 721–705 B.C.E.
Nimrud (ancient Kalhu)
MMA 54.117.12a,b
Source: Photo: Ira Spar.

The hem of a garment or rarely a shell could also be used in place of a seal. The practice of using a seal substitute was discontinued by the Hellenistic period.

Some tablets, especially from the Ur III and Old Assyrian period were covered with a thin slip of clay molded to form a protective envelope. In personal correspondence the envelope served to conceal the contents of the

Figure 3.5a A funerary stela of Tarhunpiyas
Louvre Museum
Late 8th century B.C.E., Anatolia
Louvre AO 19222 www.louvre.fr/llv/oeuvres

In this funerary stela a mother embraces her son around his legs. The boy holds a leash in his left hand which is attached to the foot of the goshawk used in falconry. In his right hand he holds a stylus used to possibly record the flight of the bird to be used in augury. His writing tablet is pictured directly below the bird. The tablet is hinged indicating that it contained individual boards and it is closed with a latch.

The name of the deceased is written in hieroglyphic Luwian, an Indo-European language attested in Anatolia from the mid second millennium and in Neo-Hittite cities in Syria from the 9th to 7th century B.C.E.

Ancient Near East Scribes and Seal Cutters 107

Figure 3.6 Detail from a gypsum neo-Assyrian sculptured relief depicting two scribes recording booty(?) from one of Tiglath-Pileser III campaigns into southern Babylonia.
British Museum
Nimrud (ancient Kalhu)
8th century B.C.E.
BM 118882

108   *Ira Spar and Antonietta Catanzariti*

letter. The sender's identifying seal was impressed onto the envelope. A scribe also included the address of the recipient and or a short greeting on the envelope. In legal matters such as in contracts, a copy of the tablet's message or a summary was duplicated on the envelope which was then sealed by witnesses' cylinder seals.

Cuneiform signs were predominately impressed on clay using a stylus, but cuneiform written with brush(?) and ink on tablets and leather is also known. Aramaic notes written in ink or incised into the clay are also attested. It appears likely that stone carvers who could not understand how to read Akkadian, had scribes outline signs in ink on stone prior to the stonecutter carving them out. Akkadian texts also note that inked cuneiform signs were written on parchment to record an array of probably literary and scholastic texts.

Schools

> "The scribal art is enjoyable; one can never have enough of its charms"
> Babylonian saying[12]

Students learned the art of reading and writing cuneiform in schools located in private homes. It took many years for a student to progress from learning how to properly hold a stylus and impress simple signs to becoming a master scribe. School curriculums differed depending on local traditions and teachers, but the common element was memorization and the art of learning to copy the cuneiform script. A young novice discovered that a sign could contain only a few wedges or in some periods over a dozen individual wedges. In beginning lessons, the teacher taught the student simple signs and soon afterwards how to recognize their phonetic values. As learning proceeded the student had to learn that there was more than one value for a sign. Next came the copying of god names and personal names (Figure 3.8). Advancing to the next level the pupil copied a series of lexical lists with items in both Sumerian and Akkadian featuring legal terms and grouping of nouns that referred to items of material culture such as the names of animals, trees, foods and beverages. As copying progressed, learning included the elements of metrology and mathematics, lists of place names, professions and excerpts of literary works, proverbs, administrative formulae and model legal contracts. Finally, the student advanced to the copying of literary texts, incantations and hymns. In a literary document about school life written in Sumerian, one student was reprimanded and punished by his teacher for his poor handwriting, which "is not nice at all. And he struck me."

Sumerian began to disappear by the beginning of the 2nd millennium B.C. E. so the student had to learn both a dying language, and study a wide range of administrative, legal, lexical and literary texts in Akkadian and Sumerian. Many lexical and religious texts were bi-lingual written both in Sumerian and Akkadian.

Ancient Near East Scribes and Seal Cutters 109

Figure 3.7 Private letter regarding slaves and the management of a trading company.
Tablet with envelope and small "second page" found inside of the case
The Metropolitan Museum of Art
ca. 20th–19th century B.C.E.
Kültepe (Karum Kanesh), ancient Anatolia
MMA 1983.135.4a,b,c.
Photo: Ira Spar.

110   *Ira Spar and Antonietta Catanzariti*

Specialized instruction also took place in the homes of professionals such as physicians, exorcists, diviners, astrologers, lamentation experts and priests. Tutors could be a member of the family or a contracted specialist.

Literacy was not limited to the scribal realm. Findings of tablets in homes, temples and state archives indicate that some rulers, city officials and wealthy businessmen among others could read and write at different levels of proficiency.[13]

Omens

In the library archives of King Ashurbanipal, the majority of literary texts and fragments are omens. In ancient Mesopotamia it was believed that the gods communicated with humans by encoding messages about the future into the entrails of animals ready for sacrifice. Every event, every birth, every astronomical or strange observation out of the ordinary was thought to be ominous. Even daily occurrences such as such as opening a well, building a wall or the movement of birds, insects or reptiles held meaning. To decode some of the gods' message, diviners (*baru*) made clay models of the animal entrails, principally sheep or lambs. Each box on the liver indicated a blemish or protrusion on the liver's surface. The associated cuneiform text described the relationship of such anatomical features to future events, such as "If so-and-so occurred, then the following will happen." It was believed that the human source of belief and emotion resided in the liver. Scholars composed long multi-tablet editions of various omens.[14]

Temples, Palaces and Monuments

Mesopotamian monumental buildings were primarily constructed out of sundried clay bricks. Palaces were huge complexes serving as propaganda monuments to the king's glory. The palaces were official residence of the monarch and his family. They had rooms for official duties, administrative activities, ceremonial functions, courtyards and halls for reception of foreign dignitaries. Huge *lamassu* sculptures of winged human-headed bulls or lions guarded the palace entrances. Important rooms were decorated with large carved gypsum reliefs. The reliefs depicted battles, hunting activities, court ceremonies and rituals with images of mythological beings. Reliefs were painted with vivid colors. Cuneiform inscriptions were carved into the stone and over or around the figures in the reliefs.

Monuments

Cuneiform inscriptions are featured on large and small stone statues and on large monuments such as the Laws of Hammurabi (now in the Louvre) or the Black Obelisk of the Assyrian king Shalmaneser III (now in the British Museum). Many huge monuments were placed in city open areas for

Ancient Near East Scribes and Seal Cutters   111

Figure 3.8 Lenticular school exercise tablet with a god name Urash
The Metropolitan Museum of Art
Ca. 20th–16th century B.C.E.
MMA 86.11.251
On this tablet a schoolboy or schoolgirl (some apprentice scribes were female) had to turn the tablet over and attempt to copy the master's hand. In the image above the instructor has written two simple signs. On the left the star-shaped sign indicates a deity. The second sign represents the goddess Urash. A student needed to master this preliminary exercise before writing more elaborate documents on his or her own, led according to one myth by the goddess Nisaba, who guides their fingers on the clay to make the scribe "put beautiful wedges on the tablets."

propaganda purposes as well as in temples to make the gods aware of royal success in war and in service to the populace. The stela of Hammurabi contains 4,000 lines of cuneiform to commemorate his achievements as a "king of justice," It was deemed so important as a war prize, that conquering Elamite invaders from Iran carried it off to Susa in 1160 B.C.E.

Figure 3.9 Clay model of a sheep's liver
British Museum
ca. 1900–1600 B.C.E.
Sippar
BM 92668

Royalty, most of whom were illiterate, wanted their names and accomplishments to be honored and praised for generations. By inscribing their exploits on stone monuments, sculpture, vases and gems and dedicating them in temples to be viewed by their deities, kings ensured the favor of the temple's patron deity. In order to show their erudition and respect for an idealized past, some inscriptions were written in an archaizing script. This type of old fashioned writing enhanced the king's prestige by association with a revered past.

When members of the landowning elite received a grant of land from the king, a special exemption from taxes or labor obligations, a grant of temple income in return for temple service, a decision in a legal suit or a record of an expensive purchase of property, they commissioned a stone monument termed today a kudurru or boundary marker. In fact, the monument (*naru*) was not placed on the recipient's land but in a temple in the presence of a deity. The kudurru recorded a copy of the original royal decree and the

Figure 3.10 Gypsum alabaster neo-Assyrian relief, the king with his chief official
The Metropolitan Museum of Art
Reign of Ashurnasirpal, ca. 883–859 B.C.E.
Nimrud (ancient Kalhu)
MMA 32.143.4

location of the land if specified. The landowner received a clay copy for his personal records. Kudurrus made of black limestone were erected in temples from the mid second to the mid first millennium B.C.E. Some were carved on clay prisms. Carved at the top of the stone monument were symbols of the gods who served as witnesses and as protectors from desecration. A curse was included against those who disputed the gift or broke its contractual terms. One kudurru was found in the Iranian city of Susa, taken by invaders as a symbol of the Elamite king's defeat of his Kassite enemies.[15]

114 *Ira Spar and Antonietta Catanzariti*

Figure 3.11 Black limestone kudurru reign of Marduk-nadin-ahhe
British Museum
Ca. 1099–1082 B.C.E.
BM 90841
The top of this monument features images of the hierarchy of gods who preserve order in the world. Symbols representing deities begin with the highest astral gods and continue with representations of warrior gods and the gods of fertility. The king, bow and arrows in hand, is dressed in royal garb. To his right is an inscription indicating the name of the kudurru, "Establisher of the Boundary." The text records a deed for purchase of land by a certain royal official named Marduk-nasir.

Clay Cones, Nails, Bricks and Metal Weights

Beginning in the third millennium B.C.E., inscribed clay-shaped cones and clay-shaped nails were placed in the walls and in foundation boxes of many important religious buildings. Clay nails have a broad flat nail-head and a long, tapered body. They usually contain a short inscription written in columns naming a ruler, his buildings and occasionally his achievements. Clay cones may contain one or two column inscriptions on the widest part of the object usually attesting to the piety of the ruler, praise for his achievements and a claim of ownership for the building. In the case of one famous example now in the Louvre Museum, a broad multi- columned cone contains the record of an historical alliance and later land dispute between two Sumerian rulers dating to ca. 2400 B.C.E. Property owners too, during home construction would place an inscribed nail into its wall to attest to their ownership.

In the Neo-Babylonian period cones typically invoked the king as a donor and religious patron of temples. By erecting and restoring temples and ziqqurats as well as through public works projects such as extending the course of the Euphrates to provide fresh water the king declared that he was worthy of receiving the support of the gods. Thousands of cones have been unearthed, being among the first cuneiform inscribed objects collected by European travelers in Iraq in the early 19th century.

In ancient Mesopotamia, stone was scarce and too expensive for building construction. Its use was reserved for monuments and statues presented as votives to the gods. There were no modern type cornerstones. Instead, royal names, titles and a message to the gods asserting that king so-and-so had built a named temple were cut in reverse on a clay, stone or wood stamp which was then impressed onto countless bricks and placed in walls, covered from view with a layer of plaster. This printing press method ensured that eventually when a building was in need of repair, a future generation would become aware of the piety of a previous ruler who had commissioned the construction of the god's temple. Countless inscribed stamped bricks used in royal construction are preserved. Mud brick inscriptions were yet another way of propounding a royal ideology designed to glorify the sovereign by expounding upon his accomplishments to please the gods and assure praise from the public.

Cylinders and Prisms

From the Early Dynastic period onwards Mesopotamian ceramists produced a wide variety of cylinders and prisms with inscriptions of historical records intended to praise royal achievements. Sizes and shapes were varied. Most prisms were six to eight sided. The inscriptions detail, sometimes at great length, royal triumphs in war and battle, hunting prowess, praise for the king who revers his gods, success in restoring decaying cities, construction of

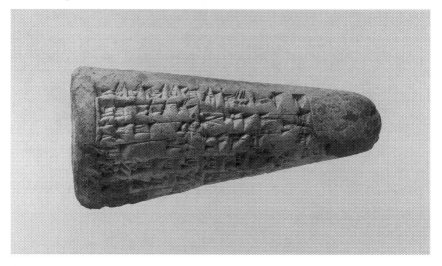

Figure 3.12 Clay votive cone of Lipit-Eshtar
The Metropolitan Museum of Art
Ca. 1870 B.C.–1860 B.C.E.
MMA 1971.71
This votive cone was dedicated by King Lipit-Eshtar who asserts that he is one who cares for his people and temples, establishes justice and built the E-nisisa temple ("House of Justice").

palaces and rebuilding temples together with public works projects and reforms designed to bring prosperity.

In this eight-sided prism, the Assyrian monarch, Esarhaddon described his rebuilding of the Esharra temple in Babylon, destroyed by his father. He claims that Babylon was destroyed not by his father, but by the god Marduk who raged against its citizens for their neglect of the god's rites and rituals. This prism contains part of a hieroglyphic design impressed on its base. The images, to be read counterclockwise from the top left feature a stylized tree, a striding lion, a mountain, a plow, a date-palm and partially preserved symbol. Various interpretations have been proposed. The signs probably form a cryptographic writing of Esarhaddon's name and titles.[16]

Weights

Stone weights were carved in the shape of animals such as a duck, a goose or a frog. They had inscriptions attesting to their "true" weight. Most weights were cylindrical. A rare metal weight is attested with an inscription in both Akkadian and in Aramaic.

Figure 3.13 Stamped Sumerian brick
The Metropolitan Museum of Art
Reign of Shulgi ca. 2094–2047 B.C.E.
Nippur
MMA 59.41.87

Forgeries

According to an ancient Babylonain proverb, "commit no crime and fear of your god will not consume you."[17] In spite of this admonition ancient and modern forgers continue to create fakes. The craving for increased wealth, ego, or the desire to prove the authenticity of a religious doctrine has led dealers, collectors and even ancient priests to produce forgeries. During the Neo-Babylonian period (6th century B.C.E.), priests of the temple of the Sun god in the ancient city of Sippar, forged a stone monument purported to be from the time of Manishtushu, king of Akkad (23rd century B.C.E.) granting the priests the rights to certain lands and privileges. The text ended with the statement, "this is not a lie."[18] Recently, pious philanthropists eager to prove

Figure 3.14 Neo-Assyrian eight-sided clay prism (bottom)
The Metropolitan Museum of Art
Ca. 674 B.C.E. or later
Reign of Esarhaddon
Babylon(?)
MMA 86.11.283

the truthfulness of the Bible purchased thousands of illicitly excavated cuneiform tablets, and fragments of the Dead Sea scrolls for display in the Museum of the Bible in Washington, D.C. On March 13, 2020 it was revealed that all of the Dead Sea Scroll manuscripts in the Museum's collections are forgeries! Similarly, a purported tiny papyrus fragment called by a renowned Harvard scholar in 2013, part of a "Gospel of Jesus' Wife," is also a forgery.[19] Use of modern ink, medieval papyrus, and use of a later language dialect by the forger, helped researchers to uncover the Jesus fraud.

Ever since the 19th century cuneiform forgeries have flooded the antiquities market with fakes that have entered into private and museum collections, libraries and monasteries. It became, and still is, a common dealer ruse is to offer for sale a small group of illicitly excavated cuneiform tablets, together with a much larger collection of freshly crafted forgeries. Few museums, dealers or collectors have the necessary expertise to detect these forgeries. The difficulty of recognizing the numerous individual wedges found in cuneiform signs and the proper orientation of the signs (wedge shapes should appear only on the top or left side of a sign) means that without expert assistance, a forger rarely has the ability to correctly reproduce a sign, nor produce any meaningful grammatically correct sequence of signs. The improper weight, thickness and color of a forged tablet, the misunderstanding of the way writing on a tablet turns from obverse to reverse as well as the incorrect direction of the wedges are additional signs of a forgery. Unfortunately, it is extremely difficult to determine the origin of forgeries or even if a supposed middleman or dealer knew that he or she was dealing in fakes. The grey antiquities market holds it secrets close to its chest! The best way to tell if a tablet is real or a modern forgery is to have a good photograph made and then send it to a Assyriologist for authentication. In order to provide a proper photograph, the tablet should be placed on a neutral colored paper, preferably light grey. The tablet should be positioned so that horizontal wedge-heads are oriented from left to right and vertical wedges should appear with the wedge-triangle hanging towards the top of a line. If the text has a series of lines, they should appear in parallel horizontal lines. Next, a light, diffused if possible, should be placed above and to the left side corner of the tablet at about a 45 degree angle. The light will cast a shadow into the wedges for the specialist to facilitate reading. If the tablet is large an overall photo and several section photos should be made. If a cylinder seal has an inscription, follow the above rules, but lower the light source to shed a raking light over the slightly indented surface.

Cuneiform tablets, cylinders and inscribed objects can sell on the market for slightly over one hundred to hundreds of thousands of dollars. The appearance of illicitly excavated cuneiform texts on the market attests to desperate need for income for those caught in the vice of Near Eastern war, corruption and civil strife. The destruction of ancient sites to obtain artifacts of the past also attests to the contempt of certain political groups for their pre-Islamic past and the desires of middlemen and dealers to profit from corruption. But it is content of texts and seals that help us to reveal and gain insight into the lives and achievements of those who lived, wrote and created the arts of the past.

Introduction: Ancient Near Eastern Seals on the Antiquities Market

This chapter section offers a close look at ancient Near Eastern seals in order to provide an overview of some of the characteristics of this frequently trafficked item.[20] The information that follows is based on data collected during the monitoring of ancient Near Eastern objects on online selling platforms in 2018. The monitoring made clear that the array of ancient Near Eastern objects being smuggled is quite varied. The objects include, but are not limited to, figurines, ceramic vessels, coins, seals and tablets, and they are

120 *Ira Spar and Antonietta Catanzariti*

available together with a high number of fake items. Most commonly, ancient Near Eastern seals have been sold in venues such as Christie's (see auction catalogues from 1989, 1997–1999, 2011, 2013, 2016, etc.), Sotheby's (see auction catalogues from 1997–1999, 2000) and Bonhams (2010, 2015), just to mention a few of the auction houses that offer these objects. More recently, and particularly during times of conflict and civil unrest, social media and online auction and marketplace websites such as Etsy, Catawiki and eBay (see Chapter 8, which discusses online platforms) have become the preferred method for selling ancient artefacts. These platforms, where object provenance is overshadowed by false information, have proven to be a simple method to market illegal artefacts. As pointed out by Topçuoğlu and Vorderstrasse (2019), the number of cylinder seals and coins sold on the internet has increased steadily since 2011, reaching a peak in 2016–2017. Neil Brodie (2015, see also Chapter 1 in this book) notes that small objects looted from Iraq and Syria have been sold openly and in great quantities on the internet since 2005. During the monitoring of these platforms in 2018 and at intervals in 2019 and 2020, the seals that have been offered online are generally described as being Akkadian, Sassanian or Prehistoric, or more generally they are called ancient Near Eastern/Mesopotamian seals dated to the *x* millennia. Based on the types of seals sold online, the tendency seems to be towards the trade of objects from the Akkadian and Old Babylonian periods. Therefore, the following section of this chapter will concentrate on a specific set of seals and, in particular, seals from the Akkadian (ca. 2340–2200 B.C.E.) period and early II millennium B.C.E. seals, which include the Isin-Larsa (ca. 2004–1763 B.C.E.), Old Babylonian (ca. 2000–1900 B.C.E.) and Old Classical Syrian (ca. 1894–1595 B.C.E.) seals.

Ancient Near Eastern Seals and Sealings

Seals have an important role in the study of the ancient Near East. Their small appearance belies the overwhelming amount of information that they hold, for example, about economic, religious, cultural and artistic trends, as well as individual identity. As early as the seventh millennium B.C.E., we can trace the presence of engraved stones being used to stamp impressions on clay. Indeed, the stamp seal type is the earliest form of sealing adopted in the ancient Near East. Later on, stamp seals were used along with cylinder seals, which were introduced around 3500 B.C.E. at the site of Uruk in southern Mesopotamia and at Susa in southwestern Iran when the practice of writing was introduced. Seals existed throughout the ancient Near East (Mesopotamia, Levant, Anatolia and ancient Iran), and the practice spread to the neighboring regions. Seals deriving from archaeological excavations have been found in locations such as administrative buildings, palaces, temples and burial sites. These findings underline the wide use of seals by members of different social classes. Stamp and cylinder seals were impressed or rolled onto lumps of clay that were used to close jars, doors and baskets, to seal legal transactions and to impress over tablets. Seals of various shapes were carved from different organic and inorganic materials. Stone (e.g., marble, limestone, lapis lazuli, agate, chalcedony, hematite and serpentine) was the most common medium used to carve seals. Metals (e.g., copper, bronze, iron, silver and gold) organic substances (e.g., bone and wood), and other substances (e.g., faience and glass) were also used. Generally between 1.5 cm to 4 cm in dimension, seals were produced in different shapes. Stamp seals were in conoid, pyramid, anthropomorphic, zoomorphic, lentoid, hemispheroid, rectangular, circular and kidney form (Figure 3.15), while cylinder seals are also available in a barrel shape and often had deep, vertical grooves creating three panels (Figure 3.16); each panel section was used as a distinctive stamp. These are just few of the most common shapes of stamp and cylinder seals attested.

The complexity of the seals and their iconography (which will be discussed further on) are only two of the aspects that render these objects so fascinating and unique. Two other aspects that contribute to making these artifacts distinctive are the manufacturing and the carving techniques used to create ancient Near Eastern seals. A glimpse at the techniques use for carving seals is available in two tomb paintings from Saqqara, Egypt, dating to the mid-third millennium B.C.E., that depict seal cutters (Merrillees 2006, Seevers and Korhonen 2016). Here, the craftsmen are shown sitting on the ground using one or both knees to brace their hands as they work. Each uses a hand-held tool to work on a cylindrical object, or a drill to bore the hole on a cylinder seal held in a fixture. Another representation comes from a decoration of an Egyptian tomb (1420 B.C.E.) illustrating the production of beads (Wilkinson 1971). In this image, the use of a bow-drill is depicted, suggesting that this same tool could have been used to perforate seals. In fact, seals were perforated on the back or through the seal and may have had an attachment. Cylinder seals were perforated through or had a V-shaped perforation on both ends of the seal, where a cap attachment was placed. Materials science studies further suggest that seals could have been engraved through drilling or wheel-cutting, microchipping or sawing and filing (Sax et al. 2000, 157). The surfaces of the seals were carefully carved with a large array of motifs that were intricately detailed and sophisticated. Cylinders provided a larger space where more complex seal designs could be carved, but producing such detail would not have been possible using simple drills or engraving tools alone. Based on studies conducted on the carvings, abrasives such as emery or sand were used to achieve the detail by continuously rubbing them on the surface of the seal (Gorelick 1978; Collon et al. 1986).

Seals had several functions and were modified, changed or adapted according to the region that adopted such objects. Primarily, they were known as administrative instruments used to record goods and to identify the seal owner. Scholars have reconstructed how seals were used thanks also to the study of the lumps of clay (also known as sealings) on which the seals were impressed. The recovery of such remains in archaeological contexts has helped scholars to determine some of the uses of the seals. Both cylinder and stamp seals were employed to certify the administrative transaction of goods, as well as to signal ownership, obligation or authority. As administrative tools, seals have their origin in the sixth millennium B.C.E. in the Syro-Mesopotamian heartland. Stamp seals in geometric shapes are the earliest documented seals. Cylindrically shaped seals were introduced at the same time as proto-cuneiform writing in the middle of the fourth millennium B.C.E. Seals were impressed on a lump of wet clay and pressed against the surface of the item to be sealed. To secure its content, a cloth/textile (remnants of which can sometimes still be seen impressed on the underside of the sealing) was fastened with a rope around the item and then sealed, or the impression on clay was pressed against a basket, the grain of wood or string. The purpose of this practice was to insure, through the integrity of the seal, that the contents had not been altered. In the instance of tablets, seals were

Figure 3.15 Kidney-shaped stamp seal and modern impression with animal motifs
Ca. 3100–2900 B.C.E.
Limestone or marble
Freer Gallery of Art, Smithsonian Institution, Washington, D.C.: Gift of Dr. and Mrs. Leonard Gorelick, F1999.6.7

Figure 3.16 Cylinder seal with three panels showing figures engaging in work activities
3100–2900 B.C.E.
Marble
Freer Gallery of Art, Smithsonian Institution, Washington, D.C.: Gift of Dr. and Mrs. Leonard Gorelick, F1999.6.59

sometimes rolled before the tablets were inscribed; in other cases, the seal was rolled across the text of the tablet (Collon 2005, 113–119).

Identifying Ancient Near Eastern Seals

Over the millennia during which seals were used throughout the ancient Near East, these objects evolved, being reinvented and adapted, making the plethora of types of seals too vast to be introduced here. Therefore, for the purpose of this chapter, this section will discuss the Akkadian and the early second millennium B.C.E. seals, as these are the most commonly found in the antiquities market. The complexity of these small tools can only be understood through the close observation of the many details that compose the surface of the period seals discussed below.

Akkadian Period Seals

Produced mainly during the Akkadian period (ca. 2340–2200 B.C.E.) in Mesopotamia, seals documented from this period were made from chert, jasper, rock crystal, speckled black and white diorite, lapis lazuli, serpentine, metadiorite and gypsum alabaster. Shell was another medium used. Besides the physical differences (size and shape) that characterize the different period seals, another key element that distinguishes seals from one period to another is found in the iconographic motifs engraved. Akkadian seals are generally distinguished by the presence of contest, mythological, banquet and presentation scenes before deities.[21] Although there are instances where the scenes in the Akkadian period are divided into two registers, the most common organization is that of a single scene with simple border outlines. The contest scene (Figure 3.17) generally displays a hero grappling with real and mythical animals. Within the contest scene, there are different compositions. For example, the scene can include three figures: two heroes and an opponent. The key image is the hero, who is one of the most commonly represented figures in Akkadian seals. There are two main heroes: one is the full-faced, bearded hero with curls, usually naked except for a belt, and the other is beardless and shown in profile wearing a short kilt/skirt and a cap. The bull-man, a composite figure, is the hero's great ally, while the lion is the main opponent. The figures represented in these scenes display modeled bodies that show indications of the musculature. Seals with mythological scenes include several deities, either in a victorious stance or battling each other. Representations of the gods Shamash (sun god) and Ea (water god), as well as vegetation gods and goddesses, became popular during this period and are presented either standing, enthroned or scaling a peak. Some will display their attributes, allowing the identification of a specific god, as in the case of the sun god, Shamash, who is illustrated with rays behind his back. The water god, Ea, is usually depicted with streamers and water pouring from his back. At times, the symbolism used to represent some of the gods is too general and it is not possible to discern their specific identity. A banquet scene during this period often portrays several deities, while the presentation scenes include a worshipper who is being introduced to a seated deity. Although there are instances where the scenes in the Akkadian period are divided into two registers, the most common organization is that of a single scene with simple border outlines.

When inscribed, seals from the Akkadian period bear the name of the king that the person served, personal name and the name of the owner of the seal, thus allowing the identification of the owner of the seal. Other seals may just mention names of officials or personal names and titles that could indicate the role of the individual in the Akkadian administrative organization (Rakic 2018, 87–92).

Early Second Millennium B.C.E. Seals

Seals commonly assigned to the first half of the second millennium B.C.E. include the Isin-Larsa (2004–1763 B.C.E.), Old Babylonian (ca. 1900–1600 B.C.E.) and Classical Syrian (1894–1595 B.C.E.) seals (Otto 2000), produced in the Mesopotamian and Levantine regions of the ancient Near East.[22] Hematite is the preferred stone, but other stones adopted are calcite and serpentine. Isin-Larsa seals use jasper, agate and crystal (Collon et al. 1986, 4–11). Also, seals during this time have more standardized shapes and proportions (Collon et al. 1986, 12), ranging from 2.5 to 3.0 cm in size with perforations bored on each end.

The most typical scene of this period is the presentation scene, which includes a seated deity and a goddess leading a worshipper. This composition is generally associated with the Isin-Larsa period, while the Old Babylonian seals include two standing figures (Figure 3.18),[23] that of a king and a suppliant goddess (see Collon 2005, Teissier 1985). The representation of the sun god Shamash becomes popular during this period, and he is portrayed as carrying a small saw. Other gods found in presentation scenes include the water god Ea, the suppliant god, and the god with a crook. When a

Figure 3.17 Cylinder seal and modern impression with contest scene
Akkadian Period ca. 2340–2200 B.C.E.
Chlorite or serpentinite
Freer Gallery of Art, Smithsonian Institution, Washington, D.C.: Gift of Dr. and Mrs. Leonard Gorelick, F1999.6.18

cuneiform inscription is available, it will include the following types of information: names of deities; personal name plus family relationship; personal name plus title or profession; personal name plus family relationship plus title or profession plus servant of the deity (Collon et al. 1986, 15–17).

In addition to the Isin-Larsa and Old Babylonian seals, during this time we also find the classical Syrian seals, which are mainly documented in the Syrian region. These seals display a greater variety in the iconographic motifs represented. Some of these motifs depict kneeling heroic figures with fantastic creatures, kneeling griffins and female figures, royal figures and worship scenes with deities. Animals are commonly presented and include monkeys, caprids, scorpions and fantastic creatures. Smaller objects inserted into the field include heads and hands, ball staffs and Egyptian details, such as the ankh symbol and astral elements. Motifs are shown in rows or columns divided by various rope-like dividers or guilloche.

Suspect and Counterfeit Seals

Both Beatrice Teissier in *Ancient Near Eastern Cylinder Seals* (1985) and Dominique Collon in *First Impressions* (2005) have discussed this subject and have delineated some of the main features that characterize both suspect and counterfeit seals. These two types of problematic seals will be discussed here, as they can be often encountered in the online (or physical) antiquities market.

Suspect seals include all those seals that in the first instance are believed to have all the elements that resemble a composition that is traditionally found on authentic seals of a specific period but concurrently present possible discrepancies in the motifs illustrated and the composition represented; in some

Figure 3.18 Inscribed cylinder seal and modern seal impression with a royal figure and suppliant
Old Babylonian Period ca. 1900–1600 B.C.E.
Hematite
Freer Gallery of Art, Smithsonian Institution, Washington, D.C.: Gift of the Duncan M. Whittome Revocable Trust in memory of Ambassador and Mrs. James S. Moose, Jr., F1993.18.2

126 *Ira Spar and Antonietta Catanzariti*

cases, however, it could be either a composition that is previously unknown to us or unusual.[24] Counterfeits or forgeries are those seals that technically are not well executed but attempt to reproduce an original based on an illustration found in a book or on the actual object. Many counterfeiters attempt to emulate the iconography and the cutting style of the seals being reproduced, but if we pay close attention to the details, we can detect small imprecisions in the composition of the seals or note inaccuracies in the writing, which sometimes may be illegible or senseless. For example, seals were meant to produce a mirror image of the motif and of the inscription, therefore, by performing an impression of a suspect seal or counterfeit seal, these flaws can be easily revealed. A motif or scene on a cylinder seal needs to be carved into the curving plane of the cylinder, providing evidence that the carving visible on ancient seals is a complex work of art that makes use of high technical skills developed over the years. In the ancient Near East, when conceiving the scene to be reproduced on the surface of a seal, the carver most probably imagined and engraved it as if reversed, so that the negative carving would produce a convincing positive image on the impression.

The display of inconsistencies in the iconography and composition of the scenes are two elements that can be fundamental in the identification of nongenuine seals. Another telling factor is the rough technical execution of the seal, revealing the unskilled hand of the falsifier or the inadequacy of the tool used to perform the carving. Seals, cut in a crude manner, are evidenced by the sharp edges of the motifs carved. The central perforation performed from both ends in ancient times may, in modern pieces, be executed from only one end or, if attempted from both ends, be incomplete. The size of the perforation can be very narrow rather than being splayed. The ends of the seals are uneven or roughly cut or sometimes too straight (Gorelick 1978). Finally, ancient seals were carved on stones that were precious or that had an apotropaic value. The stones used for the suspect and counterfeit seals are usually not precious and are of low quality.

Along with the circulation of suspect goods and forgeries, other types of seals that can be found on the market and may be easily overlooked are unfinished ancient seals, including recut and unfinished recut seals. This is the case, for example, of cylinder seals which were recut and modified. These were produced either after a change of ownership or as a result of abrasion, and in the latter instance, if the abrasion was not complete, one could see the signs or traces of the former design that was not properly removed. Another instance is that of the incomplete ancient seals that were in the process of being produced but were never finalized. These stones are generally of high quality but lack any carved motif, offering the possible forger the surface of an empty canvas that can be used to depict motifs uncommon to the ancient Near East's artistic tradition (see Table 3.1 for a layout of some of the most common characteristics of counterfeit seals). Only a close examination by experienced eyes can identify signs of a recut seal, such as past traces and indications of an inscription or iconographic motifs along with combinations of incompatible engraving styles that appear together on the same seal, and exceptional anomalies on scenes that do not fit the rule of the seal design (Feingold 2019, 42).

Experts in the materials science field can provide additional help by using scientific tools to probe signs related to the manufacturing techniques used to carve the seal and/or any modifications made on the surface of the seals.[25] This type of examination is seldom performed on objects under investigation by authorities who might not have the resources to carry out any scientific examinations. For this reason, law enforcement, subject matter specialists and conservators should work together on the identification of objects.

With the increase in use of online auction houses, the presence of the above-mentioned types of seals on these platforms has also grown. Along with the issue of the problematic authenticity of objects, another matter that needs scrutiny is their provenance. An object found on an online sales platform will commonly have information that indicates the auction house where it was acquired and the date. The object may be said to be from a private collection with the city name and country of the collector posted. It may also state that the collection was put together over a long period of time (e.g., 50 years). More suspicious is the terminology used to define the seals, for example, "Ancient Near Eastern", "Mesopotamian", "Sasanian" or "intaglio". These terms do not reflect either the region, the type, the typology or the time period needed to truly identify the seals on sale.

The prices seen on online selling platforms for seals are varied. They may go up to $2,600 on the platform Artemission.com ("Old Babylonian Cylinder Seal with Goddess and Worshippers, c. 18th–16th Century B.C." – item number 29.35801), while on eBay they can be as low as $200–900 (eBay 2018 item number 232418803535) and rise up to $9,999 (eBay 2018 item number

Table 3.1 Layout of main differences between genuine seals and forgeries

Seals' Features	Forgeries	Genuine
Motif	Unconventional and unfamiliar to the ancient Near East's artistic tradition	Reflect motifs and artistic trends of the period in which they are produced
Stone type	Both high- and low-quality stones	When made of stone, these are generally of high quality
Cut	Roughly carved; often a modern tool is used to engrave the motifs	Drilling marks and abrasion
Inscription	Script attempts to imitate cuneiform wedges but are not correct and the script has no meaning	A formula is discernible
Impression	No mirror image	A mirror image

128 *Ira Spar and Antonietta Catanzariti*

322660216764 "Genuine, rare, Near East Black stone cylinder God seal"). Seals that present completely invented iconographies are being produced in Thailand and are advertised as beads. One such advertisement reads: "Ancient Old Jasper Stone Babylonian God Intaglio Cylinder Seal Bead" (eBay item number:193384784437). This particular item sells for $150 as of 2020, while in 2018, seals shipped from Thailand were sold for as little as $1. Since 2018, the price of such fake items has grown, contributing to the circulation and demand for "ancient" seals. An in-depth discussion on eBay and online selling platforms is presented in Chapters 7 and 8 of this volume, the latter providing a discussion on how such online platforms provide low barriers to entry for getting involved in the antiquities trade.

Conclusions

This chapter describes some of the most common examples of ancient Near Eastern trafficked items: cuneiform tablets, inscribed objects and seals. These are just a small portion of the larger variety of ancient Near Eastern object types circulating in the antiquities market, but, because these are the most iconic artifacts of ancient Near Eastern material culture, they are the main target of the illegal market. A first section of this chapter provides a brief description of the types of inscribed objects found in the ancient Near East: tablets, clay cones, nails, bricks and metal weights, inscribed large and small stone statues, and large monuments. When on the market, these are offered in small groups from illicitly excavated sites along with freshly crafted forgeries. Few museum workers, dealers or collectors have the necessary expertise to detect forgeries. The inability to recognize the numerous individual wedges found in cuneiform signs can easily trick the untrained eyes of the buyer to accept them as authentic and to purchase fake items. The forger rarely has the capacity to correctly reproduce a sign, or to produce any meaningful, grammatically correct sequence of signs. The improper weight of a real tablet, the way it turns from obverse to reverse and the direction of the wedges are additional signs of a forgery.

A second section of this chapter deals with seals. These small items, since the time of their creation, have held multiple functions. For example, they were used to denote individual identity, as administrative tools essential in transactions, and as decorative and protective amulets. Although small in size, these objects were highly valued in ancient times and today they are relevant to the understanding of the ancient Near Eastern societies that adopted them. The variety of seal types available and produced in the ancient Near East is vast; here only a few have been discussed (Akkadian and early second millennium B.C.E. examples), as they represent those seals that are commonly found in the antiquities market. Such diversity and variety can easily lead forgers to attempt to reproduce seals and/or carve new ones with motifs unfamiliar to the ancient Near East's artistic tradition. Commonly sold by auction houses, seals are increasingly being found on online auction

Ancient Near East Scribes and Seal Cutters 129

platforms and commercial selling websites. This phenomenon has contributed to the increase production of fake seals, but most worrisome is the ease with which authentic, ancient cultural heritage material is being sold online. Increased control and monitoring of illicit antiquities trafficking on online sales platforms by ancient Near Eastern field researchers and experts on the illegal trade of goods has brought more awareness to this issue. The unlawful exportation of cultural heritage objects from Iraq and Syria, as well as the creation of fakes, continues. Indeed, an area that deserves more attention is the increased presence and production of fake objects.[26] Fakes are being easily exported and offered for sale, as was made evident during the 2018 CLASI project monitoring of online sale sites. Some objects sold for just a few dollars in 2018 but by 2020, sale prices for fakes increased notably. Unaware buyers continue purchasing fakes, thus increasing the demand and production of such items. The need to properly identify and track the production of fake antiquities is urgent and requires the collaboration of experts in the field of the ancient Near East, conservators and law enforcement personnel.

Notes

1 Black, J.A., Cunningham, G., Robson, E., Zólymoni, G.G. et. al. *The Electronic Corpus of Sumerian Literature, 1988–2006.* http:/etcsl.orinst.ox.uk, Proverbs: Collection 1 Segment A, 22.
2 Black, J.A., Cunningham, G., Robson, E., Zólymoni, G.G. et. al.
3 British Museum Blog https://blog.britishmuseum.org/trade-and-contraband-in-a ncient-assyria. Reprinted, 2018. Chapter Four "Life of a Salesman: Trade and Contraband in Ancient Assyria," in Editor's Selection Vol. 1: *Five Articles from The Ancient Near East Today A Publication of Friends of ASOR* ebook pdf.
4 Larsen, M.T. 1988. "Old Assyrian Texts," in I. Spar (ed.). *Cuneiform Texts in The Metropolitan Museum of Art* 1. New York: The Metropolitan Museum of Art, p. 94.
5 For the scribal arts in Mesopotamian culture, see in general: Radner, K. and E. Robson. 2011. *The Oxford Handbook of Cuneiform Culture.* Oxford: Oxford University Press; Charpin, D. 2008. *Lire et écrire à Babylone.* Paris: Press Universitaires de France; English edition. 2011. *Reading and Writing in Babylon,* tr. J. M. Todd. Cambridge, MA: Harvard University Press; Finkel, I. and J. Taylor. 2015. *Cuneiform.* Los Angeles: J. Paul Getty Museum; Walker, C.B.F. 1987. *Cuneiform (Reading the Past).* Berkeley: University of California Press/British Museum.
6 Englund, R. 1993. *Archaic Bookkeeping: Early Writing and Techniques of Economic Administration in the Ancient Near East.* Chicago: University of Chicago Press.
7 Taylor, Jonathan. 2011."Tablets as Artefacts, Scribes as Artisans," in Radner and Robson (2011); de Lapérouse, Jean-Francois. 2014."Cuneiform Documents as Artifacts," in I. Spar and M. Jursa. 2014. *Cuneiform Texts in The Metropolitan Museum of Art* 4. New York and Winona Lake, Indiana: The Metropolitan Museum of Art and Eisenbrauns, pp. 243–247.
8 Englund, R.K. 2011, "Accounting in Proto-Cuneifrom," in Radner and Robson (2011), 32–50.
9 Geller, M. J., 1997. "The Last Wedge," *Zeitschrift für Assyriologie* 87, 43–95.
10 For storage of tablets in brick boxes, see Tanret, M. 2011. "Learned, Rich, Famous, and Unhappy: Ur-Utu of Sippar," in Radner and Robson (2011), 270–

130 *Ira Spar and Antonietta Catanzariti*

287; Tanret, M. 2008, "Fin the Tablet Box ... New Aspects of Archive-Keeping in Old Babylonian Sippar Amnanum," in R. van der Spek (ed.). *Studies in Ancient Near Eastern World View and Society Presented to Marten Stol on the Occasion of his 65th Birthday.* Bethesda, MD: CDL Press, 131–147.

11 Wiseman, D.J. 1955. "Assyrian Writing-boards," *Iraq* 17, 3–13. Pulak, C. 2008. "Writing Board," in J. Aruz, K. Benzel, and J.M Evans. *Beyond Babylon: Art, Trade, and Diplomacy in the Second Millennium B.C.* New York, The Metropolitan Museum of Art, 367–368.

12 Foster, B. 2005. *Before the Muses: An Anthology of Akkadian Literature.* 3rd edn. Bethesda, MD: CDL Press, p. 1023.

13 For literacy in ancient Mesopotamia see, Veldhuis, N. 2011. "Levels of Literacy," in Radner and Robson (2011), 68–89. For the Mesopotamian school, see Veldhuis, N. 2016. "Old Babylonian School Curricula," in S. Yamada and D. Shibata (eds.). 2016. *Cultures and Societies in the Middle Euphrates and Habur Areas in the Second Millennium BC* 1, 1–12; Veldhuis, N. 2015, "Scribal Education and Scribal Traditions," *Studia Chaburensia* 5. Wiesbaden: Harrossowitz, pp. 1–13; Gesche, P. D. 2000. *Schulunterricht in Babylonien im ersten Jahrtausend v. Chr.*, Alter Orient und Altes Testamen 275. Münster: Ugarit-verlag.

14 For omens see, Koch, Ulla. S. 2011. "Sheep and Sky: Systems of Divinatory Interpretation," in Radner and Robson 2011, pp. 447–469.

15 See Slanski, K. 2003. *Babylonian Entitlement Narus (Kudurrus): A Study in their Form and Function.* Boston: American Schools of Oriental Research.

16 For cuneiform writing on cones, bricks, cylinders, prisms and weights, see Finkel and Taylor (2015).

17 Lambert, W.G. 1960. *Babylonian Wisdom Literature.* Oxford: Oxford University Press, p. 247.

18 See https://www.britishmuseum.org/collection/object/W_1881-0428-118-b. Compare the similar Donations of Constantine, a 8th century C.E. forgery of a Roman imperial decree of the Emperor Constantine the Great granting Pope Sylvester I (314–335) and his successors vast territory, spiritual authority and temporal power over Rome. For the text of the forgery and a short commentary see, https://sourcebooks.fordham.edu/source/donatconst.asp.

19 See further discussion by Patty Gerstenblith in Chapter 2 of this volume.

20 Due to the large variety of objects trafficked, the authors suggest a close collaboration of subject matter specialists with official authorities in the identification process of such items.

21 See the following resources for images and examples of such scenes: Collon, Dominique. 1982. *Cylinder Seals II: Akkadian-Post Akkadian, Ur III periods.* London: British Museum Publications; Collon, Dominique. 2005. *First Impressions: Cylinder Seals in the Ancient Near East.* London: British Museum Press; Porada, Edith. 1948. *Corpus of Ancient Near Eastern Seals in North American Collections.* Washington D.C.: Pantheon Books; Pittman, Holly. 1987. *Ancient Art in Miniature: Ancient Near Eastern Seals from the Collection of Martin and Sarah.* New York: Metropolitan Museum of Art. Several resources are also available online through the museum websites with images available under their collection page. See for examples the Metropolitan Museum of Art, British Museum, The Morgan Library & Museum (https://www.themorgan.org/collection/ancient-near-eastern-seals-and-tablets). Online projects include the Sceaux et Empreintes de sceau du Proche-Orient ancient (http://sespoa.huma-num.fr), Achemenet (http://www.achemenet.com/en/tree/?/achaemenid-museum/object-categories/seals), Digitizing Ancient Near Eastern Seals and Sealings – DigANES (http://www.diganes.gwi.uni-muenchen.de) and for additional online resources on ancient Near Eastern seals see: Seals and Sealings in the Ancient Near East (http://cdli.ox.ac.uk/wiki/doku.php?id=seals_and_sealings_in_the_ancient_near_east).

Ancient Near East Scribes and Seal Cutters   131

22 See the following resources for images and examples of such scenes: Collon, Dominique. 2005. *First Impressions: Cylinder Seals in the Ancient Near East.* London: British Museum Press; Collon, Dominique, Margaret Sax, and C.B.F. Walker. 1986. *Catalogue of Western Asiatic Seals in the British Museum. Cylinder Seals III, Isin/Larsa and Old Babylonian Periods.* London: British Museum Publications; Teissier, Beatrice. 1996. *Egyptian Iconography on Syro-Palestinian Cylinder Seals of the Middle Bronze Age.* Fribourg, Switzerland: University Press; Porada, Edith. 1948. *Corpus of Ancient Near Eastern seals in North American Collections.* Washington D.C. Pantheon Books; Pittman, Holly. 1987. *Ancient Art in Miniature: Ancient Near Eastern Seals from the Collection of Martin and Sarah Cherkasky.* United States: Metropolitan Museum of Art. On collections of seals from Syrian Museums see: Hammade, H. 1994. *Cylinder Seals from the Collections of the Aleppo Museum, Syrian Arab Republic, Vol. 2: Seals of Known Provenance.* Oxford: Tempus Reparatum; Hammade, H. 1987. *Cylinder Seals from the Collections of the Aleppo Museum, Syrian Arab Republic, Vol. 2: Seals of Unknown Provenience.* Oxford: B.A.R. As for the Akkadian period seals, examples of early second millennium B.C.E. seals are available with images at several museum websites under their collection page. See for examples the Metropolitan Museum of Art, British Museum, The Morgan Library & Museum.
23 The cuneiform text of the cylinder seal reads: Iddin-Shamash – Son of IZ-ZA-AK-KA-AN – Servant of Shamshi-Adad. For more information about this seal see: https://archive.asia.si.edu/publications/seals/object.php?q=F1993.18.2.
24 Teissier (1985), pp. 109–110 for some of the characteristics that makes a suspect and a forgery.
25 On this subject see: Gorelick, L. and Gwinnett, A.J. 1986. "Further Investigation of the Method of Manufacture of an Ancient Near Eastern Artefact Cast Glass Vessel," *Iraq* 48: 15–18; Gorelick, L. 1983. "Ancient Egyptian Stone-drilling," *Expedition* 25.3: 40–47; Gorelick, L. and Gwinnett, A.J. 1979. "Functional Analysis of Drilling Using Scanning Electron Microscopy," *Scanning Electron Microscopy* I: 405–409; Gorelick, L. and Gwinnett, A.J. 1981. "Close Work Without Magnifying Lenses?" *Expedition* 23.3: 27–34; Gorelick, L. 1975. "Near Eastern Cylinder Seals Studied with Dental Radiography," *Dental Radiography and Photography* 48.1: 17–21; Gorelick, L. and Gwinnett, A.J. 1978. "Ancient Seals and Modern Science: Using the Scanning Electron Microscope as an Aid in the Study of Ancient Seals," *Expedition* 20.2: 38–47; Kenoyer, J.M. and Vidale, M. 1992. "A New Look at Stone Drills of the Indus Valley Tradition," *Materials Research Society Symposium* 267: 495–518; Lahanier, C. 1976. "Note sur l'emploi de l'heulandite et de la mordénite dans la fabrication de sceaux cylindres proto-élamite," *Annales du Laboratoire de Recherche des Musées de France.* 65–66; Lambert, W.G. 1979. "The training of a seal-cutter," *Revue d'Assyriologie* 73: 89; Mahrzahn, J. 1997. "Der "Siegelschneider» nach keilschriftlichen Quellen," in *Mit Sieben Siegeln versehen: Das Siegel in Wirtschaft und Kunst des Alten Orients.* Ed. E. Klengel-Brandt. Berlin: Staatliche Museen zu Berlin, Vorderasiatisches Museum; Sax, M. 1991. "Innovative Technqiues Used to Decorate the Perforations of Some Akkadian Rock Crystal Cylinder Seals," *Iraq* 53: 91–95; Sax, M., Collon, D. and Leese, M.N. 1993. "The Availability of Raw Materials for Near Eastern Cylinder Seals During the Akkadian, Post Akkadian and Ur III Periods," *Iraq* 55: 77–90; Sax, M., Meeks, N.D., and Collon, D. 2000. "The Early Development of the Lapidary Engraving Wheel in Mesopotamia," *Iraq* 62: 157–176; Sax, M. and Meeks, N.D. 1994. "The Introduction of Wheel Cutting as a Technique for Engraving Cylinder Seals: Its Distinction from Filing," *Iraq* 56: 153–166; Sax, M., McNabb J. and Meeks, N.D. 1998. "Methods of Engraving Mesopotamian Cylinder Seals: Experimental Confirmation," *Archaeometry* 40: 1–21.

132 *Ira Spar and Antonietta Catanzariti*

26 On May 5th, 2020, St John Simpson reported via the British Museum blog that on July 1st, 2019, two metal trunks were opened at Heathrow Airport. The trunks, which were consigned from Bahrain to a private address in the UK, were filled with fake objects that imitated ancient Mesopotamia artifacts. See the British Museum blog: Fake antiquities made for unsuspecting collectors (https://blog.britishmuseum.org/fake-antiquities-made-for-unsuspecting-collectors).

Bibliography

Black, J.A., Cunningham G., Robson E., and Zólymomi G.G. *et al. The Electronic Text Corpus of Sumerian Literature*, 1988–2006. http://etcsl.orinst.ox.uk. Proverbs: Collection 1 Segment A, 22.

British Museum Blog. Trade and contraband in ancient Assyria. https://blog.britishmuseum.org/trade-and-contraband-in-ancient-assyria.

Brodie, Neil. 2015. "The Internet Market in Antiquities." In *Countering Illicit Traffic in Cultural Goods: The Global Challenge of Protecting the World's Heritage*, edited by F. Desmarais, 11–20. Paris: International Council of Museums.

Charpin, Dominique. 2008. *Lire et écrire à Babylone*. Paris: Press Universitaires de France; English edition. 2011. *Reading and Writing in Babylon*, tr. J.M. Todd. Cambridge, MA: Harvard University Press.

Collon, Dominique. 1982. *Catalogue of Western Asiatic Seals in the British Museum. Cylinder Seals II: Akkadian–Post Akkadian, Ur III periods*. London: British Museum Publications.

Collon, Dominique. 2005. *First Impressions: Cylinder Seals in the Ancient Near East*. London: British Museum Press.

Collon, Dominique, et al. 1986. *Catalogue of Western Asiatic Seals in the British Museum. Cylinder Seals III, Isin/Larsa and Old Babylonian Periods*. London: British Museum Publications.

de Lapérouse, Jean-Francois. 2014. "Cuneiform Documents as Artifacts." In *Cuneiform Texts in The Metropolitan Museum of Art* 4, edited by Ira Spar and Michel Jursa. New York: Metropolitan Museum of Art and Eisenbrauns.

Englund, Robert. 1993. *Archaic Bookkeeping: Early Writing and Techniques of Economic Administration in the Ancient Near East*. Chicago: University of Chicago Press.

Englund, Robert K. 2011, "Accounting in Proto-Cuneifrom." In *The Oxford Handbook of Cuneiform Culture*, edited by Karen Radner and Eleanor Robson. Oxford: Oxford University Press.

Feingold, Rony. 2019. *Engraved on Stone: Mesopotamian Cylinder Seals and Seal Inscriptions in the Old Babylonian Period*. Piscataway, NJ: Gorgias Press. https://public.ebookcentral.proquest.com/choice/publicfullrecord.aspx?p=5906929.

Finkel, Irving and Jonathan Taylor. 2015. *Cuneiform*. Los Angeles, CA: J. Paul Getty Museum.

Foster, Benjamin. 2005. *Before the Muses: An Anthology of Akkadian Literature*. 3rd ed. Bethesda, MD: CDL Press, 1023.

Geller, Mark J. 1997. "The Last Wedge." *Zeitschrift für Assyriologie* 87:43–95.

Gesche, Petra D. 2000. *Schulunterricht in Babylonien im ersten Jahrtausend v. Chr.* Alter Orient und Altes Testament275. Münster: Ugarit-verlag.

Gorelick, Leonard. 1978. "Ancient Seals and Modern Science," *Expedition Magazine* 20 (2): 38–47.

Koch, Ulla S. 2011. "Sheep and Sky: Systems of Divinatory Interpretation." In *The Oxford Handbook of Cuneiform Culture*, edited by Karen Radner and Eleanor Robson. Oxford: Oxford University Press, 447–469.

Lambert, Wilfred G. 1960. *Babylonian Wisdom Literature*. Oxford: Oxford University Press.

Larsen, M.T. 1988. "Old Assyrian Texts." In Ira Spar (ed.). *Cuneiform Texts in The Metropolitan Museum of Art* 1. New York: Metropolitan Museum of Art.

Merrillees, R.S. 2006. "Representations of a Seal Cutter in Old Kingdom Tomb Reliefs from Saqqara." In *Timelines: Studies in Honour of Manfred Bietak*, edited by E. Černy, I. Hein, H. Hunger, D. Melman, and A. Schwab, 217–224. Leuven: Peeters.

Otto, Adelheid. 2000. *Die Entstehung und Entwicklung der Klassisch-syrischen Glyptik*. Berlin: De Gruyter.

Porada, Edith. 1993. "Why Cylinder Seals? Engraved Cylindrical Seal Stones of the Ancient Near East, Fourth to First Millennium B.C." *The Art Bulletin* 75 (4): 563–582.

Pulak, Cemal. 2008. "Writing Board." In *Beyond Babylon: Art, Trade, and Diplomacy in the Second Millennium B.C.*, edited by Joan Aruz, Kim Benzel, Jean M. Evans, 367–368. New York: Metropolitan Museum of Art.

Radner, Karen and Eleanor Robson (eds.) 2011. *The Oxford Handbook of Cuneiform Culture*. Oxford: Oxford University Press.

Rakic, Yelena Z. 2018. "Sealing Practices in the Akkadian Period." In *Seals and Sealing in the Ancient World: Case Studies from the Near East, Egypt, the Aegean, and South Asia*, edited by Marta Ameri, Sarah Kielt Costello, Gregg Jamison, and Sarah Jarmer Scott, 81–94. Cambridge: Cambridge University Press.

Sax, Margaret and N.D. Meeks. 1994. "The Introduction of Wheel Cutting as a Technique for Engraving Cylinder Seals: Its Distinction from Filing." *Iraq* 56: 153–166.

Sax, Margaret, Dominique Collon, and M.N. Leese. 1993. "The Availability of Raw Materials for near Eastern Cylinder Seals during the Akkadian, Post Akkadian and Ur III Periods," *Iraq* 55: 77–90.

Sax, Margaret, N.D. Meeks, and Dominique Collon. 2000. "The Early Development of the Lapidary Engraving Wheel in Mesopotamia." *Iraq* 62: 157–176.

Seevers, Boyd and Rachel Korhonen. 2016. "Seals in Ancient Israel and the Near East: Their Manufacture, Use, and Apparent Paradox of Pagan Symbolism." *NEASB* 61: 1–17.

Slanski, Kathryn. 2003. *Babylonian Entitlement Narus (Kudurrus): A Study in their Form and Function*. Boston: American Schools of Oriental Research.

Tanret, M. 2008, "Fin the Tablet Box ... New Aspects of Archive-Keeping in Old Babylonian Sippar Amnanum." In *Studies in Ancient Near Eastern World View and Society Presented to Marten Stol on the Occasion of his 65th Birthday*, edited by R. van der Spek, 131–147. Bethesda, MD: CDL Press.

Tanret, M. 2011, "Learned, Rich, Famous, and Unhappy: Ur-Utu of Sippar." In *The Oxford Handbook of Cuneiform Culture*, edited by Karen Radner and Eleanor Robson, 270–287. Oxford: Oxford University Press.

Taylor, Jonathan. 2011. "Tablets as Artefacts, Scribes as Artisans." In *The Oxford Handbook of Cuneiform Culture*, edited by Karen Radner and Eleanor Robson, 5–31. Oxford: Oxford University Press.

Teissier, Beatrice. 1985. *Ancient Near Eastern Cylinder Seals from the Marcopoli Collection*. Berkeley: University of California.

Topçuoğlu, Oya and Tasha Vorderstrasse. 2019. "Small Finds, Big Values: Cylinder Seals and Coins from Iraq and Syria on the Online Market." *International Journal of Cultural Property* 26 (3): 239–263.

Veenhof, Klaas R. 2017. "The Old Assyrian Period (20th–18th Century BCE)." In *A Companion to Assyria*, edited by Ekart Frahm, 57–79. New Haven, CT: Yale University Press.

Veenhof, Klaas R. and Jasper Eidem. (2008). *Mesopotamia: The Old Assyrian Period.* Fribourg, Switzerland: Academic Press.

Veldhuis, Niek. 2011."Levels of Literacy." In *The Oxford Handbook of Cuneiform Culture*, edited by Karen Radner and Eleanor Robson, 68–89. Oxford: Oxford University Press.

Veldhuis, Neik. 2016. "Old Babylonian School Curricula." In *Cultures and Societies in the Middle Euphrates and Habur Areas in the Second Millennium BC*. I, Scribal Education and Scribal Traditions, edited by Shigeo Yamada and Daisuke Shibata, 1–12. Wiesbaden: Harrossowitz.

Walker, Christopher B.F. 1987. *Cuneiform (Reading the Past)*. Berkeley: University of California Press/British Museum.

Wilkinson, Alix. 1971. *Ancient Egyptian Jewelry*. London: Methuen.

Wiseman, Donald J. 1955. "Assyrian Writing-boards." *Iraq* 17: 3–13.

Part II
The Illicit Antiquities Trade

4 Antiquities Trafficking from Syria Along the Northern Route

Mahmut Cengiz

This chapter analyses the illicit economy and antiquities trafficking in Syria and Turkey and examines the routes that have been used and the actors involved in antiquities trafficking along the northern route. Antiquities trafficking has been a profitable activity for local smugglers and government officials and a lucrative financial resource for insurgents and terrorists in Middle Eastern conflict zones, including Syria. When the now ongoing civil war erupted in Syria in March 2011, the Islamic State in Iraq and Syria (ISIS) and its well-established networks of like-minded groups began to engage in antiquities trafficking, seeing it as a funding source for the organization. That same year, the southern trafficking route through Lebanon was abandoned, and a northern route through Turkey was used instead to transport Syrian artefacts to Western European countries. This chapter finds that various groups of antiquities traffickers are networked to each other and actively use the northern route. Additionally, the study highlights that Syrians have been the dominant group involved in the antiquities trafficking along this route.

Introduction

The regime changes sought by the Arab Uprisings in the early 2010s raised hopes around the world for an end to conflict and rule by long-term dictators in several Middle Eastern countries. The demonstrators' efforts failed in several countries, including Syria, which remains the epicenter of conflict between regime forces and insurgency and terrorist groups.

Syria has been a stage for clashes between many insurgent groups and terrorist organizations and for proxy wars between the states that sponsor terrorism. It is difficult to know precisely the number of jihadist groups operating in Syria. The Global Terrorism Database (GTD) has recorded more than 50 different terrorist groups fighting in the country between 2013 and 2017 (GTD 2018). Another legacy akin to what has occurred in Iraq is the looting of historical artefacts. In addition to revenue from oil production, extortion operations, and taxation, funds raised from the sale of stolen and smuggled antiquities made ISIS the richest terrorist organization during the years that the organization controlled huge expanses of territory in Iraq and Syria.

DOI: 10.4324/9781003023043-7

138   *Mahmut Cengiz*

Trafficking in antiquities is an ongoing activity for criminals and terrorists. Conflicts in the Middle East have resulted in the looting of antiquities, art objects, and other cultural property in the region. In Iraq alone during the early 2000s, for example, thousands of such items are reported to have been stolen and smuggled out of the country (Cuno 2008: 53).

It appears that while the looting of historical artefacts has continued, the actors involved and the land routes used to traffic the artefacts have changed. The networks that had previously existed among wealthy buyers, local smugglers, and corrupt Syrian officials have been replaced by ISIS militants. Syria's regime forces that seized provinces from ISIS in 2018 and the al Qaeda-affiliated group Hay'at Tahrir al-Sham (HTS) are the new actors engaged in the plundering of Syrian antiquities. When civil war broke out in Syria in 2011, the preferred trafficking route for the new actors shifted from the south through Lebanon to the north through Turkey, given Turkey's permissive policies which allow jihadist groups to cross its borders for the transferring of its militants, money, and explosives. This chapter analyzes the actors involved in the trafficking of Syrian antiquities and how those antiquities are transferred over a northern route that starts in Syria, passes through Turkey and then on to various destination countries in Western Europe and the United States.

Methodology

Mixed methods were used examining both quantitative data and qualitative data. Quantitative data were obtained from the annual reports prepared by the Anti-Smuggling and Organized Crime Department (ASOD) of the Turkish National Police. Cases from the early 1990s through 2018 were examined. Qualitative data were obtained from seven open-ended ethnographic interviews: four former Turkish antiquities traffickers who live in Gaziantep, Turkey, and three former Syrian smugglers who had been involved with the trafficking of antiquities who now live in Hatay, Turkey.

Both provinces are located on the border with Syria and are frequently used as entry points for goods (e.g., commodities, merchandise, supplies) smuggled from Syria into Turkey. The interview subjects were selected through snowball sampling because the technique was believed to be the best way to find potential participants. The author worked long years at ASOD and conducted research on ISIS financing and antiquities trafficking in the provinces bordering Syria. His former contacts helped him locate these subjects. The interviewees participated in the research voluntarily but agreed to do so only if their identities would remain confidential. The interviews were conducted with WhatsApp in Turkish and each interview lasted approximately 1.5 hours. To ensure the participants' confidentiality, the respondents were codified using letters and numbers. For example, TF1 refers to the first Turkish Trafficker, and ST1 refers to the first Syrian Trafficker.

Antiquities Trafficking from Syria 139

The Illicit Economy and Antiquities Trafficking in Syria

Smuggling networks have operated in Syria since the state was founded in 1961 (Herbert 2014: 71). Even in the 1980s, when Hafez Assad ruled the country, the market value of the illicit trade was around $1 billion (Martin 1986). Smuggling groups represent a longstanding illicit economy that permeates Syria's borderlands. These groups have engaged in drug- and weapons-trafficking, tobacco and consumer-goods smuggling, and human smuggling and trafficking (Reuter and Petrie 1999: 11). The Syrian government has ignored and exploited these smuggling groups within its borders (Herbert 2014: 69). In the early 2000s, the shadow economy was estimated as 24% of the overall economic activity in Syria (Schneider and Savasan 2007). The country's ongoing civil war has created new opportunities for smuggling groups and conflict entrepreneurs who were transformed into business moguls with the capacity to shape the post-conflict trajectory of the Syrian state (Herbert 2014: 70).

The most prominent components of the shadow economy in Syria are human smuggling, oil smuggling, drug trafficking, and antiquities trafficking. First, Syria is home to well-developed criminal networks of human smugglers. Syrians within the country and those in refugee camps in neighbouring countries often turn to smugglers for passage to European countries. Transnational human smuggling networks meet the demand in the region. In the early years of the Syrian civil war, a Syrian needed to pay $5,500 to escape a refugee camp in Jordan and then be smuggled to Denmark via Egypt (Sherlock and Malouf 2013).

Oil smuggling occurs frequently in Syria, and large quantities of the commodity have been transferred surreptitiously to other countries. The civil war in Syria led to an increase in the amount of oil smuggled out of the country. A comparison of oil seizures in cities across the border in Turkey between the two years leading up to the Syrian civil war (2009–2011) and the two years after the war began in 2011 shows a 900% increase after the conflict started (ASOD 2009, 2010, 2012, 2013).

The level of drug trafficking in Syria has been high since the early 2000s. Cocaine, heroin, and Captagon (an amphetamine-based drug) are the drugs most often trafficked in or through Syria. The booming market for amphetamines in the Gulf states made Syria one of the most active routes for traffickers. In 2006, Syrian police discovered a Captagon lab in the country (United Nations Office on Drugs and Crime [UNODC] Report; UNODC 2009) and, in 2009, investigators seized 22 million Captagon tablets (UNODC 2011). After the start the Syrian civil war began in 2011, the smuggling of synthetic drugs in or through Syria increased (ASOD 2013), as did the number of drug seizures in Turkish cities on the border with Syria. The increase in such seizures was substantial. In the period from 2009 to 2010, for example, four Syrians were arrested in Turkey with 26 kg of cannabis in their possession (ASOD 2009, 2010); in the period from 2011 to 2013, 36 Syrians were arrested in Turkey with 1.7 tons of the drug in their

140 Mahmut Cengiz

possession (ASOD 2011, 2013). Syrian involvement in drug trafficking continued to rise across the country. In 2014, 86% of the foreign cannabis traffickers and 80% of the foreign Captagon traffickers arrested in Turkey were of Syrian descent (ASOD 2014).

In terms of antiquities, Syria's 4,500 documented archaeological sites make the country one of the largest source countries in the world (Shelley and Metz 2017: 79). Like in other Middle Eastern countries, Syria's archaeological heritage has been destroyed with looted objects for sale on the international market. The ongoing civil war has worsened the situation (Brodie and Sabrine 2018: 74). Various groups generate revenue and among them are Salafi-jihadist groups and factions who are the major traffickers of antiquities in Syria today (Moos 2020).

According to Syria's Director of Antiquities, antiquities trafficking has continued in the post-ISIS period. Whether knowingly or unknowingly, some traffickers have transported fake antiquities out of the country (Swann 2019). For example, Turkish police in 2018 seized 14,894 fake coins in a Turkish town on the border with Syria (ASOD 2018: 48). A number of authentic and valuable Syrian antiquities remain in Syria, though they remain vulnerable for removal by traffickers. Purloined antiquities—authentic and fake—are sold not only in person but also on Facebook. In 2019, for example, Facebook removed 49 groups that had been selling Syrian antiquities illegally (Swann 2019). Currently, the destination countries for Syrian antiquities range from Thailand and China to the United Kingdom, France, and Germany. Turkey, Lebanon, and United Arab Emirates (Dubai) are the most popular transit points (Brodie 2018).

The Illicit Economy and Antiquities Trafficking in Turkey

The illicit economy in Turkey was valued at around \$5.2 billion in 2010, according to the Istanbul Accountants Association (Cengiz and Roth 2019: 33). Each year, Turkish police investigate thousands of cases involving the smuggling of human beings, cigarettes, oil, arms, pharmaceuticals, and antiquities. In 2017, for example, Turkish police conducted more than 14,000 investigations of various types of smugglers and traffickers (ASOD 2017: 25).

Economic, geographical, and social factors have led to the growth of smuggling and trafficking in Turkey. Economic factors include supply and demand, high taxes on goods, and rising unemployment and underemployed refugees in recent years. Drug trafficking and human trafficking can be explained by supply and demand. The large number of drug addicts in Turkey[1] created a demand for various types of drugs, which in turn affected the supply of such drugs. Similarly, high taxes on oil and cigarettes created a demand for cheaper goods, and smugglers willingly provided the supply. High unemployment in the eastern and south-eastern regions of the country prompted some of the country's citizens to operate or participate in smuggling and trafficking groups (Cengiz and Roth 2019: 34–35).

Geographical factors created a favorable environment for smugglers and traffickers to operate. Turkey is situated on the traditional Balkan trafficking route that connects Afghanistan to Western European countries. Significant quantities of drugs[2] have been transferred through Iran, Turkey, and the Balkan countries along this route.

Turkey also is surrounded by some of the most corrupt countries in the world, a situation that does inspire cooperation among law enforcement agencies (Cengiz and Roth 2019: 36). According to Transparency International's 2019 Corruption Perceptions Index (CPI), three of Turkey's neighbours—Iraq, Iran, and Syria—are perceived as being highly corrupt.[3] Iraq, with a score of 20, is ranked at 162; Iran, with a score of 26, is ranked 146; and Syria, with a score of 13, is ranked 178 (CPI 2019). By comparison, Turkey is ranked at 91, with a score of 39. A lack of collaboration among police agencies in the four countries to address cross-border smuggling and trafficking makes it easier for such criminal activity to continue. Moreover, Turkey has been on the edge of conflict zones since 2003. The U.S. invasion in Iraq 2003 and the ongoing civil war in Syria have contributed to the ability of opportunistic criminal groups to flourish in the borderland areas between Turkey and Iraq and Syria (Cengiz and Roth 2019: 36). Social factors also have helped to create an environment conducive to illicit trade activity in Turkey. The smuggling of oil and cigarettes is perceived as a routine daily activity among Turkish citizens who reside in cities and towns along the country's borders with Iran, Iraq, and Syria (Cengiz and Roth 2019: 36).

These three factors, therefore, not only facilitate the development of sectors within Turkey's illicit economy but also lead ultimately to the development of transnational criminal networks. Each year Turkey arrests a large number of foreign criminals operating within its borders and many Turkish criminals are arrested abroad reflecting the transnational nature of the phenomenon.

One of the illicit trade sectors that has had a significant negative impact on Turkey for several decades is antiquities trafficking—both locally and regionally. Local trafficking groups operate within the country and target historical artefacts, coins, and antiquities obtained through metal detectors or illegal excavations. Local interest in antiquities continues to grow, driven in large part by an increase in the number of Turkish websites devoted to the topic (ASOD 2014: 62).

The development of antiquities trafficking in Turkey spans two distinct periods. The first period, in the 1990s, was marked by a significant increase in the number of stolen antiquities. During this period, the most common destination countries for Turkish antiquities traffickers were the United States, Germany, Russia, Austria, Denmark, and the United Kingdom (ASOD 1997: 37–38). Six antiquities were repatriated from the United States to Turkey between 1994 and 1997 (ASOD 1997: 37). By the late 1990s, the trafficking of antiquities had morphed into a nationwide phenomenon, as

142   *Mahmut Cengiz*

exemplified by Turkish police reports of 55 seizures in the country's 81 provinces (ASOD 1997: 40). Analyses of these cases showed that antiquities traffickers were mostly tomb robbers and illegal excavators who operated individually and locally. Most antiquities dealers were located in urban centres, which facilitated the development of close contacts with international traffickers who eased the sale of the dealers' antiquities abroad.

There are signs in Turkish museums reflecting the theft in antiquities from this earlier period. In the Antalya Museum with many wonderful antiquities, there are signs that point out that related objects from this site are now housed at named museums in the United States. In Ankara, at the Museum of Anatolian Civilizations, there are a significant number of labelled objects indicating that they had been returned from overseas after having been smuggled abroad. The role of the Turkish police in recovering some of these objects and preventing their smuggling is indicated.

The second period of antiquities trafficking in Turkey runs from the year 2000 to the present and is marked by the involvement of organized crime groups, including cases related to the impact of the 2003 U.S. invasion of Iraq, during which a considerable number of antiquities were looted by criminal groups and marketed in Western countries. Antiquities trafficking during this period also was used as a source of revenue for insurgency groups in Iraq (Bogdanos 2005: 249). After the Iraqi government collapsed, looting of the country's museums increased at an unprecedented rate (Polk and Shuster 2005: 17). Antiquities smuggling groups active in Iraq used Syria and Turkey as transit routes to bring their stolen goods to the open market (Williams 2009: 175). Turkish statistics from the early 2000s affirm that Turkey was used as an alternative transit country for the transfer of many Iraqi antiquities and that use of the Turkish route grew over time. For example, the number of cases of trafficked antiquities in which used Turkey was used as a transit route doubled from 252 cases in 2003 to 525 cases in 2004. The number of historical artefacts and coins seized and the number of suspects detained by the police during this period also rose sharply (ASOD 2004: 13). These increases continued in the years after 2004. For example, the number of antiquities seized in Turkey reached 17,936 in 2007 (ASOD 2007: 78).

The second period of antiquities trafficking in Turkey was also marked by collaboration among local smugglers and criminal organizations in metropolitan cities and the development of Turkey's reputation as a reliable transit country for stolen antiquities. Based on that reputation, antiquities trafficking in Turkey expanded with the assistance of transnational criminal groups. This assistance then led to the transformation of Turkish organized crime groups into transnational criminal groups. Antiquities trafficking groups, for example, now collaborate with criminal groups for distribution of the stolen items and selection of target countries. Efforts to stop antiquities trafficking by organized crime and transnational criminal groups have, in some cases, been successful. In a three-county cooperative police investigation, for example, 16 antiquities traffickers were arrested in Turkey, Bulgaria, and

France. The group was transferring historical artefacts from Turkey to Bulgaria. The police operation seized around 5,000 historical pieces from the homes of the traffickers. The group leader was arrested in Bulgaria (Anadolu Ajansi 2017). These transnational criminal groups, however, are by nature opportunistic and readily take advantage of the effect of the ongoing Syrian civil war on Turkey as it attempts to deal with the influx of millions of Syrian refugees.[4]

Turkey continues to be exposed to the uncontrolled consequences of the ongoing conflict in Syria. Since 2016, for example, Turkey has been the site of various kinds of smuggling and trafficking and was the preferred route for antiquities smuggling (Brodie and Sabrine, 2018). That status was confirmed by the number antiquities trafficking cases recorded in 2018 in provinces (e. g., Gaziantep and Hatay) that lie along the country's border with Syria. For example, the police seized 17,080 historical artefacts, including antiquities and coins in these two provinces. Antiquities traffickers operating in or passing through Turkey continue to target the same Western European and U.S. destinations as they did in the 1990s and the early 2000s. These destinations include Germany, France, the United Kingdom, Switzerland, and the United States (ASOD 2017: 43).

Traffickers and purchasers in Turkey sometimes disguise their purchases. For example, Syrian pieces are registered as Turkish antiquities from the border region with Syria, legitimizing their subsequent resale within Turkey. Recently antiquities trafficking in Turkey has been widespread, resulting in hundreds of police investigations. In 2018, for example, Turkish police conducted 604 investigations and arrested 1,251 traffickers. The top 20 provinces in terms of the number of antiquities investigations are those with ports (e.g., Izmir, Aydin, Mugla, and Antalya), metropolitan cities (e.g., Istanbul, Ankara, and Bursa), on the border with Syria and therefore serve as entry points into Turkey (e.g., Sanliurfa, Hatay, and Gaziantep), and on the border with Bulgaria and therefore serve as exit points from Turkey (e.g., Kirklareli), as seen in Figure 4.1 (ASOD 2018: 49). Important economic centers such as Istanbul, Ankara and Izmir have communities with the disposable income to buy antiquities and law enforcement sophisticated enough to have personnel looking for illicit antiquities.

Facilitators are collectors and dealers of art and antiquities who either operate individually or are linked to traffickers. Their role is to provide national and international connections for the marketing of antiquities. They use land- or sea-based transportation to transfer antiquities to international dealers. Also they ship items through DHL. Given that most of the seizures of antiquities in Turkey have been made in the cities of Istanbul, Izmir, Antalya, and Mugla, it is reasonable to conclude that the facilitators operate in metropolitan, harbour cities and tourist destinations that have significant art markets (ASOD 2014: 61).

The smuggling of coins[5] has continued at a steady pace into the new decade. Each year, Turkish police seize tens of thousands of coins from the hands of local and international smugglers. The police seized 70,372 coins in Turkey in 2018 (ASOD 2018: 52). Among individual cases, for example, a British tourist was arrested in 2017 while attempting to smuggle 13 coins out of Turkey (BBC 2017). This is illustrative how the tourism industry is linked with this illegal trade.

Data for 2018 also show that 20% of all antiquities trafficking incidents in Turkey involved illegal excavations, while 80% involved the illegal sales of antiquities; police investigators seized 50 metal detectors and four screening equipment (ASOD 2018: 47); six traffickers who used social media to sell antiquities were arrested with 298 historical pieces (ASOD 2018: 48); and police investigators arrested 11 collectors and 12 antiquities sellers (ASOD 2018: 48). Almost all of the historical materials involved in these and other antiquities trafficking incidents are easily transferable items such as coins and small objects (ASOD 2018: 47). Antiquities trafficking on the regional level typically involves items that originated in Turkey's neighboring countries. The large number of police seizures along Turkey's eastern and southern borders confirms that antiquities trafficking from Iran, Iraq, and Syria into Turkey is ongoing.

Antiquities Traffickers along the Northern Route

Items reflective of Syria's cultural heritage have been smuggled out of Syria along the northern route through Turkey and along the southern route through Lebanon. The absence of army troops in the borderlands enabled the traffickers to use a variety of smuggling strategies (Kennedy 2012).[6] Syrian cultural artefacts were trafficked across the Lebanese border until high-ranking Syrian military officers took control of the area in 2011. Lower-ranking Syrian military officers who also participated in the sale of their country's artefacts opted instead for a less risky northern trafficking route

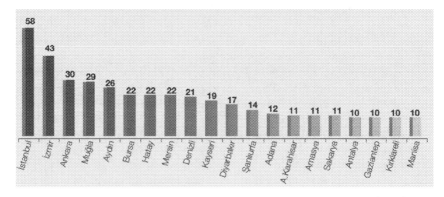

Figure 4.1 Top 20 Turkish provinces with the most antiquities trafficking investigations (ASOD 2018: 49)

Antiquities Trafficking from Syria 145

through Turkey (Brodie and Sabrine 2018: 79). These lower-ranking officers, however, did not abandon the southern route entirely and instead aided other antiquities traffickers who continued to use the route through Lebanon. Smuggled items that have been seized in Lebanon since 2011 provide evidence that the southern route remains in use (Seif 2015: 71–75); however, the northern route through Turkey has become the preferred option among Syrian antiquities traffickers.

Figure 4.2 shows the Turkish provinces in which Syrian antiquities were seized from traffickers. A significant amount of antiquities seizures were made in Gaziantep and Hatay, both of which are located on the border with Syria. A comparison of the number of antiquities seizures in these two Turkish provinces points to an increase in trafficking. In 2010 (the year before the Syria's civil war), the combined number of antiquities seized was 878; two years later in 2012, the combined number of antiquities seized was 4,524 (ASOD 2010, 2012). Arrest data from subsequent years indicates the continued involvement of Syrians in the trafficking of their country's antiquities. In Gaziantep in 2015, for example, a Syrian smuggler in possession of antiquities and a statue was arrested by Turkish police (Sabah 2016). In 2019, three Syrians in possession of 21 coins and antiquities were arrested and the items seized by Turkish police. The group had attempted to sell the items for 5 million Turkish liras, or around $1 million (CNN Turk 2019). In 2020, Turkish police arrested four traffickers in possession of 26 coins and small objects (Hurriyet 2020).

Individuals and groups involved in transporting Syrian antiquities to destinations in Western Europe and the United States typically take one of three routes: (1) the Balkans land route through Bulgaria, Romania, and Austria to Germany, France, and Switzerland; (2) the Mediterranean Sea route from

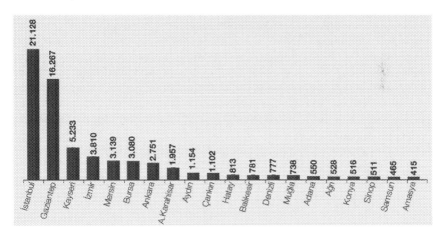

Figure 4.2 Top 20 Turkish provinces with the most antiquities seized from traffickers (ASOD 2018: 50)

146 *Mahmut Cengiz*

Turkish harbor cities to Italy and then to Germany, Scotland, the United Kingdom, and the United States; and (3) the Black Sea route from Turkish harbor cities to ports in Romania, Russia, or Ukraine and then to Germany, Scotland, the United Kingdom and the United States (ASOD 2013: 50). The existence of alternative routes demonstrates that traffickers have well-networked linkages for transporting stolen antiquities through Syria and Turkey and on to a variety of final destinations. The actors responsible for carrying out antiquities trafficking operations include local Syrian citizens, corrupt Syrian officials, transnational criminals, terrorists, insurgents, excavators, traders, and smuggling groups. Art dealers can also be important facilitators.

Locals, Criminals, and Corrupt Officials

Members of cross-border communities who operate on a local basis are the primary participants in efforts to smuggle antiquities through Syria's borderlands and out of the country (Anonymous 2009: 87–88). These local communities have been linked to fixers, financiers, and organizers who established business relations with regional and international networks. Some of the fixers were members of the Syrian government who became involved in direct facilitation of smuggling operations and direct taxation of the smugglers (Herbert 2014: 75). These fixers have facilitated the smuggling of Syrian cultural artefacts since the 1980s (Brodie 2015) and have turned a blind eye to smugglers who cross the Lebanese border. By the 1990s, the fixers also looked the other way when smugglers tried to bring Syrian antiquities across the country's border into Iraq. The illicit revenue generated by the fixers represents a sizable percentage of Syria's gross domestic product (Herbert 2014: 75).

The extent to which Syrian locals and corrupt officials are involved in trafficking of the country's antiquities can be seen from the results of interviews that Brodie and Sabrine (2018) conducted with seven participants who were either directly involved in illegally excavating archaeological sites and/or trading excavated objects. From those interviews, the researchers learned the following:

- Two groups of buyers with control over excavations in Syria were interested in antiquities. Established wealthy buyers were active before the civil war broke out in Syria and have remained the wealthiest purchasers of antiquities and dominate the market for these items. Individuals who have been grappling with poverty also are involved in this sector as excavators. Wealthy buyers are considered to be the most important buyers because of their international linkages. They have mutually beneficial relationships with buyers outside of Syria. In addition, these buyers have employed excavators whose daily wage was $17. Excavating historical artefacts is very common. In some Syrian villages, around 100 excavators and 20 buyers work to find objects. Excavators buy equipment to detect antiquities in Turkey. The price is around $1,000. Another group is comprised of small buyers who travel to small villages to find cheaper artefacts, which they then sell to the larger and wealthy buyers who are connected to dealers in Turkey and Europe (Brodie and Sabrine, 2018).

- Excavators want to find coins, glass vessels, and bronze and copper figures. The majority of found objects are coins, such as a silver Roman coin with the image of Nero worth $1,500; a silver Greek coin with the image of Alexander worth $350; late Roman and early Byzantine gold coins weighing 4 grams each and worth $1,500 each; coins from the late Umayyad and early Abbasid periods that had been minted in Damascus, Aleppo, and Homs and wroth about $150 each. One of the Umayyad coins was sold to a buyer in the Arabian Gulf for $50,000 (Brodie and Sabrine, 2018).
- In addition to Syrian army officers, Syrian-based diplomats from Arab countries exported antiquities from Syria. Syrian army officers and members from the Free Syrian Army (FSA) have collaborated in the trafficking of Syrian artefacts (Brodie and Sabrine 2018).

Local Syrian smugglers are networked with Turkish antiquities traffickers along the northern route. In Turkey, antiquities traffickers consist of amateurs, facilitators, criminal groups, local and international dealers. Amateurs, who conduct their business through personal networks or websites that facilitate the marketing of antiquities, are predominantly illegal excavators who are interested in antiquities. Amateurs are the most pervasive group of traffickers in Turkey (Cengiz and Roth 2019).

Criminal groups work as illegal excavators, collectors, and marketers. Their activities include selecting archaeological preservation areas, employing local individuals for excavations, maintaining their activities by means of agents in other regions, and transferring antiquities abroad. Police investigations have confirmed that Turkish antiquities traffickers have operated in networks since at least 2010, when investigators found criminal networks engaged in antiquities trafficking between Turkey and Europe (ASOD 2010: 100). In 2012, Turkish police discovered two transnational antiquities trafficking groups and arrested the member of both groups. In 2015, one transnational group was discovered and all of its members were arrested (ASOD 2012: 44 and ASOD 2015: 39).[7]

International dealers engaged in antiquities trafficking have close linkages to Turkey and to the Turkish diaspora in European countries and the United States. These dealers contact each other confidentially and prefer meeting in small cells or gathering in clandestine locations around the Grand Bazaar in Istanbul in order to locate customers or connect with dealers in Turkey and abroad. They frequently change their meeting locations and are careful to avoid police scrutiny. They communicate via encrypted social media.

Interviews by the author with three Syrian antiquities traffickers and four Turkish antiquities traffickers, all of whom operated in borderland areas, revealed two complicated networks: one small-scale and the other big-scale. Small-scale networks rely on small buyers who in turn rely on excavators to provide antiquities for trafficking. Small buyers are interested mostly in authentic coins and small pieces that are easy to transfer, but they also will sell fake pieces (see Figure 4.3). These small traffickers use oil trucks to transfer these materials. All of the respondents said that border controls are lax and customs officials are corrupt. Therefore, they said, customs officials are not making detailed checks. The drivers of the oil trucks, the traffickers said, already have ongoing corrupt relationships with customs officials who turn a blind eye to the contents of the trucks, making it easy for the drivers to transfer smuggled coins through border gates. The respondents also underlined that police officers and customs officials are reluctant to check the contents of oil trucks[8] and they may then be used to smuggle antiquities. (Interview by the Author, T1, T3, S2, and S3, 2020). Figure 4.3 shows the steps and networks involved in small-scale trafficking of Syrian antiquities.

Small-scale buyers are linked to either Turkish local traffickers who have operated in the borderland areas for many years or Syrian refugees. The local Turkish traffickers are linked to their Turkish facilitators and the Syrian refugees to their Syrian facilitators. These facilitators also actively use social media such as Facebook and Instagram to reach out local antiquities sellers.[9] Turkish facilitators are interested in acquiring the antiquities Syrian refugees have to offer. Turkish and Syrian facilitators then use their connections with international dealers to complete the process of trafficking Syrian antiquities abroad. Two groups of international dealers are involved in these transactions: European buyers who are interested in acquiring Greek and Byzantine objects and buyers from the Gulf States who prefer Islamic objects (Interview by the Author, T2, T3, S1, and S3, 2020).

Large-scale networks rely on wealthy antiquities buyers in Syria to initiate trafficking transactions (see Figure 4.4). These high-end buyers are interested in expensive and authentic pieces and rely on excavators and small buyers to procure the pieces. They then use their established networks with Turkish

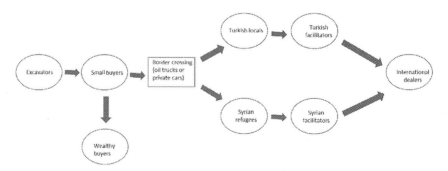

Figure 4.3 Flowchart of small-scale trafficking of Syrian antiquities

traffickers in the region to help transport the pieces to Syria's border with Turkey. Turkish customs officials then facilitate the trafficking of these pieces across the border where the pieces will be sold to wealthy buyers directly linked to either Syrian facilitators or criminal groups (Interview by the Author, T1, T4, S2, and S3, 2020). In the early years of the civil war, these criminal groups were Turkish-based trafficking groups. Today, the criminal groups may be Syrian trafficking groups whose members are Syrian refugees or mixed groups comprised of Syrian and Turkish traffickers.[10] After the Syrian facilitators or the criminal groups enter Turkey, they can transport the pieces to Istanbul unimpeded, as no checkpoints have been set up to stop them. From Istanbul, the trafficked items change hands again. The Syrian facilitators transfer the pieces they trafficked to international dealers, while the criminal groups transfer the pieces they trafficked to transnational criminal groups. International dealers and transnational criminal groups use various routes for the final leg of the trafficking transaction. The most popular land route is through Bulgaria; the most popular sea route starts at a Turkish port city (typically Izmir, Mugla, or Aydin). The sea vessel navigates from the port, travels through the Greek islands, and then sails on to final destinations in Western European countries (Interview by the Author, T1, T2, T3, and S1, 2020).

Insurgents and Terrorists

Syria's civil war is fuelled by grievances, but smuggling enables it. Decades of regional-level trafficking and smuggling in the areas of drugs, cigarettes, oil, arms, and antiquities have led to the emergence of criminal networks. These networks have created opportunities for insurgents and terrorists not only to obtain arms and ammunitions but also to acquire financial resources. The ongoing civil war and overfocus on jihadist groups in Syria have distracted attention from and minimized the importance of smuggling and trafficking in the borderlands. An expanding insurgency forced the withdrawal of the Syrian army from the Turkish and Iraqi borders (Herbert 2014).

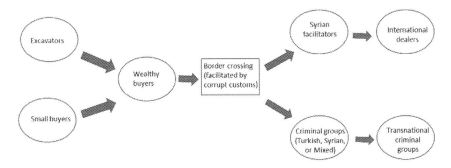

Figure 4.4 Flowchart of large-scale trafficking of Syrian antiquities

150 *Mahmut Cengiz*

A number of insurgent and terrorist groups have operated in Syria. These groups range from salafi-jihadist groups backed by Gulf states and Turkey (e.g., *ISIS an Al Qaeda-affiliated* [11] *groups*; Singh and Stroul 2019) to Shia groups backed by Iran (e.g., Hezbollah, Lashkar-i Fatimuyyun, Liwa al-Imam al-Hussein, and Kataib Hezbollah; Smyth 2015). Evidence shows that some of these groups are linked to antiquities trafficking in Syria. In addition to terrorist groups, the Syrian government and the Free Syrian Army (FSA) have been accused of looting the country's cultural heritage (Brodie and Sabrine 2018: 79).

ISIS was considered to be the richest terrorist organization in the world (Al-Bayati 2017: 81). The organization increasingly became involved in the sale of counterfeit cigarettes, cell phones, pharmaceuticals, foreign passports and Syrian antiquities (Shelley 2014a). The sale of antiquities in Turkey was aided by the favorable environment the Turkish government had created for such transactions (Cengiz and Roth 2019).

ISIS has been among the most active groups taking advantage of the utter lack of security at archaeological sites and museums. Documents found during the raid of an ISIS cell revealed that ISIS's antiquities trafficking apparatus is well organized and relies on established administrative and logistical resources. According to the documents, ISIS created subunits responsible for the marketing, identification, and excavation of new sites, research on and investigation of known sites, and administration (Keller 2015).

During the period when ISIS controlled a significant share of Syrian territory, the terrorist group emboldened thieves and smugglers in the plundering of archaeological sites, earning commissions from them. According to Brodie and Sabrine (2018), ISIS assigned one of its members to control the issuance of excavation permits; excavators were required to pay 20% of the value of any objects they found; at some cultural sites, at least 400 groups would be searching for coins under the control of ISIS; at one cultural site, ISIS used 35 digging gangs of 45 members each to work on-site in 10-person shifts. Most of the items found at the archaeological sites were transferred to Turkey by means of fuel tanks. ISIS then sold some of the items to a Syrian army officer who engaged in the ongoing trade and transport of the plundered items. Four years earlier, ISIS itself used bulldozers to excavate archaeological sites, selling the antiquities it found to local middlemen who then marketed the items in neighboring countries (United Nations Security Council 2014). Turkey served then, as it does now, as a gateway for transporting plundered antiquities to international markets (Amineddoleh 2016).

In 2013 and 2014, ISIS militants exploited previously established criminal networks between Turkey and Syria to move looted antiquities between the two countries. These criminal networks consisted primarily of smugglers who were well versed in different types of smuggling. Local smugglers transferred antiquities to brokers linked to antiquities trafficking groups. In 2016 and 2017, ISIS eliminated the use of local smugglers, turning instead to ISIS actors in Turkey in order to increase revenue by cutting out middlemen (Interview by the author, 2020). From Turkey, the smuggled antiquities were transported to Western countries, including the United Kingdom (The Guardian 2016). Media reports confirm ISIS's active involvement in Turkey. In one story, a correspondent contacted an ISIS smuggler in a southern Turkish town near the Syrian border who had attempted to sell a relief statue trafficked from Palmyra (NBC 2016).

After ISIS lost its power and popularity in Syria, al Qaeda-affiliated groups began to fill the void. Hay'at Tahrir al-Sham (HTS), a group formerly known as Jabhat al Nusra that broke away from al Qaeda in 2017, is one of the active groups operating in Syria. HTS has strong relations with Turkey and welcomed the Turkish army's presence in the fight against regime forces in Syria (Ulbricht 2019). Recent research suggests that HTS has been heavily involved in the looting of Syrian cultural assets in northwest Syria (Moos 2020).

Persons interviewed by the author described how they believe that HTS and Turkish-backed insurgent groups (e.g., the Syrian National Army [SNA], formerly known as the Free Syrian Army, or FSA) are involved in ongoing antiquities trafficking (see Figure 4.5). HTS and SNA members take advantage of their close relationship with the Turkish government but each operates separately. They are allowed to cross the two country's borders freely and have developed networks of financial resources (Interview by the Author, T1, T2, S2, and S3, 2020). Whereas HTS taxes local buyers and excavators and is itself involved in antiquities trafficking, SNA is directly involved in trafficking but does not use (and therefore does not tax) local buyers and excavators.

Both HTS and SNA use their relationships with Turkish intelligence officials to meet their respective group's objectives. Both groups, for example, freely transfer antiquities through customs checkpoints facilitated by corrupt officials. In some cases, HTS illegally transfers antiquities from the borderlands. Former Turkish jihadists who had operated in Syria provide networks in Turkey for the handling of antiquities that HTS has smuggled out of Syria and into Turkey. Former FSA members do the same for antiquities that SNA has smuggled out of Syria and into Turkey. Next, former Turkish jihadists transfer the HTS-acquired antiquities to Turkish criminal groups with whom they have ties; the criminal groups then hand off the antiquities to transnational criminal groups. For FSA-acquired antiquities, the process is slightly different in that former FSA members transfer the antiquities either to Syrian criminal groups or to Syrian facilitators. Syrian criminal groups then hand off the antiquities to transnational criminal groups, while Syrian facilitators hand off the antiquities to international dealers (Interview by the Author, T2, T4, S1, and S3, 2020).

Conclusion

Antiquities trafficking has been one of the most lucrative sources of income for criminals and terrorists in the Middle East and elsewhere. Ongoing conflicts in many parts of the world have resulted in the looting of art objects and antiquities and the destruction of the cultural heritage of affected

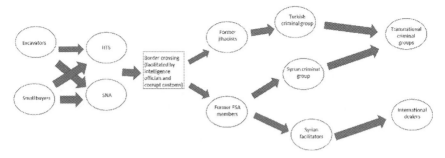

Figure 4.5 Flowchart of antiquities trafficking by Hay'at Tahrir al-Sham (HTS) and the Syrian National Army (SNA) and FSA (Free Syrian Army)

countries. The trafficking of these art objects and antiquities has in turn fueled the conflicts that triggered the looting. The Middle East is one of the hotbeds of antiquities trafficking. Starting with the U.S. invasion of Iraq in 2003, criminals, terrorists, and corrupt government officials have plundered and stolen Iraqi artefacts from the country's museums. Similarly, Syria remains at risk of losing its rich cultural heritage at the hands of antiquities traffickers. The repeated seizure of Syrian antiquities in Turkey and Lebanon indicate that the threat to the country's cultural heritage is ongoing.

What has changed over time is the preferred route for transporting Syrian antiquities out of the country. Until 2011, antiquities traffickers used a southern route from Syria through Lebanon. That route fell out of favor because the smuggled antiquities were subject to looting by government officials, local and wealthy buyers, excavators, and criminal groups. After civil war erupted in Syria in 2011, a northern route through Turkey became the favored, and less risky, option. For example, Turkey's supportive jihadist groups did not enforce strict border controls. At the same time, a significant number of al Qaeda and ISIS militants crossed the Turkish border into Syria after receiving weapons and logistics from Turkish intelligence officials. Smugglers and traffickers also took advantage of the porous borders and increased their capacity to smuggle drugs, cigarettes, arms, and antiquities. This strategic shift in trade routes shows the adaptability of trafficking networks and demonstrates the importance of national policy development and implementation (see comment below – criminal groups take advantage of lax policy implementation like in Turkey).

Various individuals and groups—excavators hired by local or wealthy buyers, facilitators, international dealers, and local, regional, and international criminal groups, Syrian refugees—are involved in the trafficking of antiquities over the northern route. Syrian refugees are the most active participants. Turkey's controversial immigration policies permitted the country to open its border to more than 4 million Syrians. Most of these refugees are not vetted and registered, and the police have paid little attention to the refugees' activities. Since 2013, for example, some Syrian refugees in Turkey

Antiquities Trafficking from Syria 153

have been operating smuggling networks for Syrian antiquities traffickers, while others have formed or joined existing Syrian criminal groups in Turkey. Still other Syrian refugees have taken on the role of facilitators who can link local smugglers to international dealers. Both Turkish and Syrian facilitators actively use social media to reach out local antiquities sellers.

When U.S. President Donald Trump declared in December 2018 that ISIS had been defeated in Syria, a reduction in the involvement of terrorist groups in antiquities trafficking was expected. That did not happen. HTS, an al Qaeda-affiliated group, strengthened its presence in Syria and mirrored ISIS's strategy by taxing local traffickers and becoming directly involved in the trafficking of Syrian antiquities. At the same time, the Turkey-backed insurgent group SNA (formerly known as FSA) used smuggling networks that it had established under the FSA group name. They are now run by former FSA members who remain involved in the trafficking of Syrian antiquities. The involvement of HTS and SNA in antiquities smuggling and their financial gain from this activity, however, are much lower than ISIS's revenues. The danger lies in the ongoing nature of HTS and SNA involvement in the trafficking of Syrian antiquities. As long as the Syrian civil war continues and Turkey maintains its immigration policies for the country's southern border, the Syrian cultural heritage will be trafficked through the northern route.

Notes

1 The number of addicts who applied to drug treatment centers between 2004 and 2016, for example, increased 92% (Elibol 2018).
2 It has been estimated that 37% of heroin coming from Afghanistan was transported over the Balkans route to final destinations in Western European countries (Michelotos 2012).
3 The rankings are based on a score ranging from zero (highly corrupt) to 100 (very clean).
4 Turkey opened its doors to 3.6 million of the 6.7 million Syrians who have fled their country since the Syrian civil war began in 2011 (Todd 2019), costing the country $25 billion on housing and other services (Cengiz 2018). Only 10% of the Syrian refugees in Turkey are housed in government-run camps, with the remainder mostly dispersed in Turkish cities on the border with Syria and some in other cities across the country (Kirisci and Ferris 2015). The Syrian refugees in Turkey often have little education and live in economically poor communities, conditions that could lead to criminal activity. As it has been seen in other diaspora communities in developed countries, Syrian refugees in Turkey are likely to engage in transnational trafficking. Data show, for example, that Syrian refugees are involved in drug trafficking more often than any other foreign minority group (ASOD 2014: 18).
5 It should be noted that one of the principal elements of Turkey's cultural heritage is its numismatic collection—most notably, coins. Many of these coins were discovered in the 1990s during legal excavations and controlled agricultural activities and by casual or professional treasure hunters. It is impossible to know the exact number of coins that were brought to foreign markets during the 1990s; however, the value of plundered Turkish coins must have been enormous (Lightfoot 1991: 1).
6 The procurement of arms for insurgents in Syria provides clues about how local and regional antiquities trafficking networks worked in Syria. The local trafficking

154 *Mahmut Cengiz*

groups operated on a small scale and generally were apolitical (Daou 2011). The local trafficking groups were connected to so-called fixers who operated regionally to source weapons from legal weapons sellers and from black-market entrepreneurs in Lebanon, Iraq, and Turkey (Diab 2011). The formation of tribes was an outgrowth of traditional cross-border groups that already existed in the area. At least 20% of the weapons procured for antiquities traffickers were transferred to insurgents through the involvement of tribes located in Syria's borderlands with Turkey, Lebanon, and Jordan (Willis 2012).

7 Some criminal groups in Turkey do not limit themselves to the trafficking and smuggling of drugs or humans. In the 1990s, for example, the police seized nuclear materials and antiquities from one such group, indicating a willingness among traffickers to branch into other areas of smuggling (Shelley 2014b: 261).

8 From the interviews, it was clear that Turkey's intelligence officials transferred arms and weapons to jihadist groups in Syria. When the police raided and frisked these oil trucks, all of the officers were put in jails on orders from the Turkish government. The government's message to all officers in the borderlands was to turn a blind eye on what was being transferred. The government's mandate has enabled traffickers and smugglers to operate without the risk of being arrested by the police.

9 An estimated 4 million Syrians are living in Turkey, many residing in the east of the country. Many have not been vetted by Turkish law enforcement, and most are not registered in the civil registry. Lacking legal status and facing economic difficulties, a significant number of Syrian refugees have no alternatives than to work in the illicit economy. They are active in human smuggling networks, as well as drug and antiquities trafficking. Some Syrian refugees also work as facilitators for drug and antiquities traffickers.

10 Several police officers in Gaziantep and Hatay are members the mixed group.

11 Al Qaeda operates as an umbrella organization for jihadist groups in conflict zones who pledge allegiance or declare loyalty to its leadership. In Syria, Jabhat al Nusra was one of the organizations that operated under the banner of al Qaeda but then changed its name as Hay'at Tahrir al Sham (HTS).

Bibliography

Al-Bayati, Hamid. 2017. *A New Counterterrorism Strategy*. California: ABC-CLIO.

Amineddoleh, Leila. 2016. How Western Art Collectors Are Helping to Fund ISIS. *The Guardian*. February 26. https://www.theguardian.com/artanddesign/2016/feb/26/western-art-funding-terrorism-isis-middle-east, accessed July 5, 2016.

Anadolu Ajansi. 2017. Türk ve Bulgar Polisinden Tarihi Eser Kaçakçilarina Operasyon. *Anadolu Ajansi*. https://www.aa.com.tr/tr/pg/foto-galeri/turk-ve-bulgar-polisinden-tarihi-eser-kacakcilarina-operasyon, accessed February 4, 2020.

Anonymous. 2009. Smuggling, Syria, and Spending. in *Bombers, Bank Accounts, and Bleedout: Al Qa'idas Road In and Out of Iraq*, edited by Brian Fishman. Darby, PA: Diane Publishing Company. https://ctc.usma.edu/wp-content/uploads/2011/12/Sinjar_2_FINAL.pdf, accessed August 2021.

ASOD (Anti-Smuggling and Organized Crime Department). 1997. *ASOD Report*. Ankara: ASOD Publications.

ASOD (Anti-Smuggling and Organized Crime Department). 2004. *ASOD Report*. Ankara: ASOD Publications.

ASOD (Anti-Smuggling and Organized Crime Department). 2007. *ASOD Report*. Ankara: ASOD Publications.

Antiquities Trafficking from Syria   155

ASOD (Anti-Smuggling and Organized Crime Department). 2009. *ASOD Report.* Ankara: ASOD Publications.

ASOD (Anti-Smuggling and Organized Crime Department). 2010. *ASOD Report.* Ankara: ASOD Publications.

ASOD (Anti-Smuggling and Organized Crime Department). 2011. *ASOD Report.* Ankara: ASOD Publications.

ASOD (Anti-Smuggling and Organized Crime Department). 2012. *ASOD Report.* Ankara: ASOD Publications.

ASOD (Anti-Smuggling and Organized Crime Department). 2013. *ASOD Report.* Ankara: ASOD Publications.

ASOD (Anti-Smuggling and Organized Crime Department). 2014. *ASOD Report.* Ankara: ASOD Publications.

ASOD (Anti-Smuggling and Organized Crime Department). 2015. *ASOD Report.* Ankara: ASOD Publications.

ASOD (Anti-Smuggling and Organized Crime Department). 2017. *ASOD Report.* Ankara: ASOD Publications.

ASOD (Anti-Smuggling and Organized Crime Department). 2018. *ASOD Report.* Ankara: ASOD Publications.

BBC. 2017. Sussex Man Held in Turkey for Smuggling Ancient Coins. *BBC News.* August 2017. www.bbc.com/news/uk-england-sussex-41026849, accessed May 2, 2020.

Bogdanos, Matthew. 2005. *Thieves of Baghdad.* New York: Bloomsbury.

Brodie, Neil. 2015. Syria and Its Regional Neighbors: A Case of Cultural Property Protection Policy Failure? *International Journal of Cultural Property* 22: 317–335.

Brodie, Neil. 2018. Interview by Mahmut Cengiz, Personal Interview, February 13, 2018.

Brodie, Neil and Isber Sabrine. 2018. The Illegal Excavation and Trade of Syrian Cultural Objects: A View from the Ground. *Journal of Field Archaeology* 43(1): 74–84.

Cengiz, M. and Mitchel P. Roth. 2019. *The Illicit Economy in Turkey: How Criminals, Terrorists, and the Syrian Conflict Fuel Underground Markets.* Maryland: Lexington Books.

Cengiz, Mahmut. 2018. The Smuggling of Syrians Evolve into Economic and Social Conundrum in Turkey and Europe". *Vocale Europe.* July 1. https://www.voca leurope.eu/the-smuggling-of-syrians-evolves-into-an-economic-and-social-con undrum-in-turkey-and-europe, accessed April 25, 2020.

CNN. 2015. Inside the $2 Billion ISIS War Machine. *CNN.* December 6. http://m oney.cnn.com/2015/12/06/news/isis-funding, accessed May 1, 2020.

CNN Turk. 2019. Hatay'da Tarihi Eser Operasyonu. *CNN Turk.* August 3. https://www. cnnturk.com/turkiye/hatayda-tarihi-eser-operasyonu?page=1, accessed January 5, 2020.

CPI (Corruption Perception Index). 2019. *Transparency International.* https://www.tra nsparency.org/cpi2019, accessed February 12, 2020.

Cuno, James. 2008. *Who Owns Antiquity?*New Jersey: Princeton University Press.

Daou, Rita. 2011. Arms Smuggling into Syria Flourishes: Experts. *The Daily Star.* October 16. http://www.dailystar.com.lb/News/Middle-East/2011/Oct-16/151423-a rms-smuggling-into-syria-flourishes-experts.ashx, accessed March 17, 2020.

Diab, Afif. 2011. Arms Smugglers Thrive on Syrian Uprising. *Reuters.* November 25. https://www.reuters.com/article/us-syria-weapons-idUSTRE7AO1GA20111125, accessed December 16, 2019.

Elibol, Kamil. 2018. Uyusuturucu Tedavisi Goren Bagimli Sayisi 10 Yilda 25 Kat Artti. *Sozcu Gazetesi.* May 21 https://www.sozcu.com.tr/2018/gundem/uyustur

156 *Mahmut Cengiz*

ucu-tedavisi-goren-bagimli-sayisi-10-yilda-25-kat-artti-2419460, accessed August 26, 2021.

GTD (Global Terrorism Database). 2018. GTD Access. *START, Maryland University*, https://www.start.umd.edu/gtd/access, accessed April 21, 2020.

Herbert, Matt. 2014. Partisans, Profiteers, and Criminals: Syria's Illicit Economy. *The Fletcher Forum of World Affairs* 38(1): 69–86.

Hurriyet. 2020. Hatay'da Tarihi Eser Kacakciligi Operasyonunda 4 Supheli Gozaltina Alindi. *Hurriyet Gazetesi*. March 9. https://www.hurriyet.com.tr/gundem/hatayda-ta rihi-eser-kacakciligi-operasyonunda-4-supheli-gozaltina-alindi-41464325, accessed April 25, 2020.

Keller, Andrew. 2015. Documenting ISIL's Antiquities Trafficking: The Looting and Destruction of Iraqi and Syrian Cultural Heritage. US State Department. http://www.state.gov/e/eb/rls/rm/2015/247610.htm, accessed April 3, 2020.

Kennedy, Elizabeth. 2012. With Smuggling Choked, Syrian Rebels Feels Arms Curb. *Associated Press*, May 24. https://www.yahoo.com/news/smuggling-choked-syria -rebels-feel-arms-curb-070846101.html, accessed April 11, 2020.

Kirisci, Kemal and E. Ferris. 2015. What Turkey's Open-door Policy Means for Syrian Refugees. *Brookings Institute.* https://www.brookings.edu/blog/order-from -chaos/2015/07/08/what-turkeys-open-door-policy-means-for-syrian-refugees, accessed April 28, 2020.

Lightfoot, Chris S. 1991. *Recent Turkish Coin Hoards and Numismatic Studies.* Ankara: British Institute of Archaeology.

Martin, Patrick. 1986. Bankrupt Syria Buys Supplies Using Black Market Currency. *The Globe and Mail.* May 12, A12.

Michelotos, Ioanni. 2012. Heroin Trade and Illegal Immigration in Southeastern Europe. *World Press.* January 17. https://www.worldpress.org/Europe/3869.cfm, accessed March 18, 2020.

Moos, Olivier. 2020. Antiquities Trafficking in Syria: Salafists, Tomb Raiders, and Buried Treasurers. *Religouscope.* https://www.religion.info/pdf/2020_02_Moos_ Antiquities_Syria.pdf, accessed April 2, 2020.

NBC. 2016. Smuggler of Stolen Artefacts from Palmyra Speaks out About ISIS' Illicit Operation. *NBC News.* April 6. http://www.nbcnews.com/storyline/isis-terror/sm uggler-stolen-artefacts-palmyra-speaks-out-about-isis-illicit-operation-n551806, accessed April 7, 2020.

Polk, Millbury and Angela M. H. Schuster. 2005. *The Looting of the Iraq Museum, Baghdad: The Lost Legacy of Ancient Mesopotamia.* New York: Biblio.

Reuter, Peter and Carole Petrie. 1999. *Transnational Organized Crime: Summary of a Workshop.* Washington, DC: National Academy Press.

Sabah. 2015. Gaziantep'te tarihi eser kaçakçılığı. *Sabah Gazetesi.* May 5. http://www.saba h.com.tr/yasam/2015/05/06/gaziantepte-tarihi-eser-kacakciligi, accessed February 21, 2020.

Schneider, Friedrich and Fatih Savasan. 2007. Dynamic Estimates of the Size of Shadow Economies of Turkey and of Her Neighbouring Countries. *International Research Journal of Finance and Economics* 9: 126–143.

Seif, Assad. 2015. Illicit Trafficking in Cultural Property in Lebanon: A Diachronic Study, in *Countering Illicit Trade in Cultural Goods: The Global Challenge of Protecting the World's Heritage*, edited by Frances Desmarais. Paris: International Observatory on Illicit Trade in Cultural Goods, 65–82.

Shelley, Fred M. and Reagan Metz. 2017. *Geography of Trafficking: From Drug Smuggling to Modern-Slavery.* California: ABC Clio.

Shelley, Louise. 2014a. Blood Money How ISIS Makes Bank, in *The ISIS Crisis,* edited by G. Rose. Foreign Affairs, 28–31.

Shelley, Louise. 2014b. *Dirty Entanglements: Corruption, Crime, and Terrorism.* New York: Cambridge University Press.

Sherlock, Ruth and Carol Malouf. 2013. Rich Refugees Pay Thousands to Flee War-torn Syria in Luxury. *The Telegraph.* November 14. https://www.telegraph.co.uk/m iddle-east, accessed April 15, 2020.

Singh, Michael and Dana Stroul. 2019. Syria Study Group 2019: Final Report and Recommendations. *Washington Institute for Near East Policy.* https://www.wa shingtoninstitute.org/uploads/Documents/testimony/Syria-Study-Group-final-repor t-2019.pdf, accessed April 3, 2020.

Smyth, Phillip. 2015. Understanding the Organizations Deployed to Syria. *Washington Institute for Near East Policy.* https://www.washingtoninstitute.org/uploads/Docum ents/pubs/PF138Appendices/PF138_Appendix_2.pdf, accessed March 3, 2020.

Swann, Steve. 2019. Antiquities Looted in Syria and Iraq Are Sold on Facebook. *BBC.* May 2. https://www.bbc.com/news/world-middle-east-47628369, accessed April 4, 2020.

Todd, Zoe. 2019. By the Numbers Syrian Refugees Around the World. *Frontline.* https:// www.pbs.org/wgbh/frontline/article/numbers-syrian-refugees-around-world, accessed April 3, 2020.

Ulbricht, Bailey. 2019. Justifying Relations With an Apostate During a Jihad: A Salafi-Jihadist Group's Relations With Turkey in Syria. *Middle East Institute.* http s://www.mei.edu/sites/default/files/2019-03/Justifying%20Relations%20with%20an% 20Apostate%20During%20a%20Jihad.pdf, accessed March 17, 2020.

United Nations Security Council. 2014. The Islamic State in Iraq and the Levant and the Al-Nusrah Front for the People of the Levant. United Nations Security Council Syrian Report. http://www.securitycouncilreport.org/atf/cf/%7B65BFCF9B-6D27-4E9 C-8CD3-, accessed May 2, 2020.

UNODC. (United Nations Office on Drugs and Crime). 2009. *World Drug Report. Global Illicit Drug Trends.* UN Office of Drugs and Crime. (United Nations pub-lication E/02/XI.9). https://www.unodc.org/documents/wdr/WDR_2009/WDR2009 _eng_web.pdf, accessed August 2021.

UNODC. (United Nations Office on Drugs and Crime). 2011. *World Drug Report.* UN Office of Drugs and Crime. (United Nations publication E/11/XI.10). https:// www.unodc.org/documents/data-and-analysis/WDR2011/World_Drug_Report_201 1_ebook.pdf, accessed August 2021.

The Guardian. 2015. Looted in Syria – and Sold in London: The British Antiques Shops Dealing in Artefacts Smuggled by Isis. *The Guardian.* July 3. https://www. theguardian.com/world/2015/jul/03/antiquities-looted-by-isis-end-up-in-london-sho ps, accessed April 25, 2016.

Williams, Phil. 2009. Criminals, Militias, and Insurgents: Organized Crime in Iraq. *Strate-gic Studies Institute.* https://www.globalsecurity.org/jhtml/jframe.html#https://www.globa lsecurity.org/military/library/report/2009/ssi_williams.pdf, accessed March 25, 2020.

Willis, Richard S. 2012. Syrian Opposition Receiving Arms Through Country's Neighbours. *The Media Line,* July 18, 2012.

5 The Value of Financial Investigations in the Battle Against Artifact Smuggling

Michael Loughnane

Antiquities smuggling requires illicit networks to avoid detection, launder money in order to succeed. Criminal networks and terror organizations, from local to transnational, rely upon some level of business structure. Without at least the most basic internal organization to generate money from smuggling, not only can antiquities crime fail, but there is a high likelihood of participants getting caught and assets seized. This chapter discusses the financial, communication and business structures necessary for illicit networks engaged in antiquities smuggling to operate. It also considers effective financial investigation techniques that can be used to disrupt and destroy the structures on which this type of crime stands.

Criminal networks vary in size and sophistication. Consider a small-time looter in Syria who digs up ancient coins at a nearby excavation. These coins have no value to him if he cannot find a buyer. He may not have the necessary contacts to find a buyer in another country or sell online to the legitimate market. He does, however, know a shop owner to whom he can sell the coins. Therefore, and perhaps without understanding the true value of the coins, he begins a supply chain as he sells the coins to this shop keeper. His role in the supply chain ends at the point when he walks away with payment and starts to look for more artifacts. The supply chain moves forward with the shop owner who is in a better position to sells the coins in his shop or online, or as they move further into the supply chain perhaps into a new, possibly larger, transnational network.

In this simple supply chain example, consider the role played by the shop owner who who comes into possession of the coins. He will likely seek to sell them to obtain his profits as part of the supply chain. He may sell them in his shop, move them up the chain by selling them to another shop owner, or offer them to a larger market, for example, through online sale. To realize this sale, he may need to fabricate documentation (provenance) to "authenticate" that the coins were legitimately obtained to prove them saleable and set a price. Finally, the shop keeper will have in place a financial system that can account for the coins, his costs, the listing price, final sale price, and the method and process of payment.

DOI: 10.4324/9781003023043-8

The Value of Financial Investigations 159

From a financial crime perspective, information from the shop keeper can offer a wealth of information to an investigation. First, in looking at the shop keeper and his records, investigators may identify the source of the coin and their receipt. These records can also possibly indicate how active a small-time looter is and the sources of his coins.

Did the looter have to pay a member of a terrorist or insurgent group, or a military or government official for the ability to access an archeological site to excavate the coins?
Are there regular means by which the shop keeper obtains coins and other artifacts?
How does he account for this inventory in his business records?
What records exist documenting receipt of the coins and the true source?
How are they accounted for in the shop inventory?
What was the item's listing and sale price?
What are the coins worth?
Were the coins appraised and by whom?
To whom were the coins sold?
Were they sold to repeat customers and/or another link in the supply chain?
How did the seller list, advertise, or otherwise make it known the coins were available for purchase?
Was there activity online in this process?
Was the sale accompanied by authentic representations and provenance?
Were these documents forged or counterfeit?
How did buyers make payments for the coins and how did the seller receive payment upon sale?
Investigation of the shop keeper's business practices can provide significant insight leading into larger networks. What are his methods to communicate with potential buyers, and who and where are they?
Are they additional middlemen and intermediaries or actual end user buyers?

Investigations at the front end of the supply chain can reveal the frequency and location of looting as well as the necessary requirements for gaining access to the site (e.g. bribe, "protection fee", etc.), which can lead to measures to identify exploited sites and take action to deter this activity and protect artifacts. Financial investigation can also be applied against the entire network and expose illicit activity far beyond the simple actions of small-time looters as we investigate the larger supply chain.

Similarities Between Antiquities Smuggling Other Illicit Networks

This example of the small-time looter and shop keeper can be expanded to describe larger supply chains used by transnational criminal organizations. Such networks will hire experts in the antiquities market to determine the value of the items and take measures to ensure the network remains safe

160   *Michael Loughnane*

from detection. This may involve multiple businesses positioned around the world, including front and shell companies. Key information for investigation includes the valuation of antiquities and protection of items during smuggling, whether free trade zones have been used in a trade-based money laundering scheme, and if fictitious provenance and business documents have been created to present to customs and law enforcement or perspective buyers. The criminal network must then facilitate the sale, receipt of money and laundering of proceeds through various methods to protect the network.

The process of trade-based money laundering in the illegal antiquities supply chain resembles that of other illicit commodities from narcotics to wildlife to humans. Commodities, such as antiquities, are placed into the supply chain and at the end of the process, the result of the sale generates revenue that needs to be safely transferred back to the illegal actors. Illicit activities can be impaired or ceased by focusing on and disrupting supply chain processes. An overriding finding of the research discussed in this volume is that local illicit networks are typically engaged in the initial acquisition of artifacts, but then intermediaries from more developed countries are needed to get the artifacts to market.[1]

Terror and insurgent networks are more engaged at the front end of the supply chain. As cited in the report:

> There are two distinct sectors of the market where terrorist groups and individual jihadis are most likely to be profiting at present in Syria:
>
> 1   At the initial stage, where antiquities are dug up from the ground in Syria, and to a lesser extent Iraq, by individuals or small teams with access to excavators and metal detectors, and are subject to "taxation" by whatever armed group controls the territory at the time.
> 2   As intermediaries, during the transport and early-stage marketing of the antiquities, where ISIL sympathizers, who remained in the Mideast after the defeat of ISIL (Islamic State in the Levant), are likely using the networks they developed during ISIL's heyday to profit from the trade.[2]

The network components are neither new nor innovative. Common to all trafficking of items of value is that commodities are acquired, marketed and sold in a manner that masks the network, including source, transport and payment methods. Cultural property crime uses similar business, financial and communication models found in these other networks to maintain operations. Therefore, an investigator with knowledge of the market may use known financial investigation techniques to acquire evidence to target and disrupt the underlying criminal networks connected to the antiquities trade.

Effective application of financial investigation techniques against cultural property networks can impact the profitability of this type of crime by interfering with their operation. Rather than focusing exclusively on the

The Value of Financial Investigations   161

acquisition of artifacts, it is important to identify key components within the supply chain such as the source of false provenance, the bank accounts used to hold and move payments, and the storage and transportation system utilized. Remove any one of these capabilities from the network and the network will need to either regroup, rebuild, or perhaps even abandon its activities. By targeting these key nodes, it is possible to make cultural property crime more risky and less profitable. With higher risk and perhaps little or no profit, criminal and terror networks may start to look elsewhere for means to generate revenue. The financial bottom line of these trafficking networks will be undermined by attacking and dismantling the underlying business supply chain and financial structures necessary to perpetrate this type of crime.

A Target-rich Market

The cultural property market provides a target rich opportunity for criminals to accomplish their objectives and currently operates in a sector with limited visibility or interest to law enforcement. A July 2020 staff report of the U.S. Senate Permanent Subcommittee on Investigations clearly described how vulnerable the art sector is to corruption:

> The art industry is considered the largest, legal unregulated industry in the United States. Unlike financial institutions, the art industry is not subject to Bank Secrecy Act's ("BSA") requirements, which mandate detailed procedures to prevent money laundering and to verify a customer's identity.
>
> (Portman and Carper 2020; 2)

Law Enforcement and Cultural Property Crime

It is easy to see how the lack of government oversight impacts the antiquities sector and allows their networks to operate effectively. The International Council of Museums describes some types of criminal activity in this sector, impacting museums, monuments, religious sites and other public or privately held places of conservation:

- Illicit excavations of archaeological objects, including underwater excavations;
- Removal of cultural property during armed conflicts or military occupation;
- Illicit export and import of cultural property;
- Illegal transfer of ownership of cultural property (sale, purchase, assumption of mortgage debt, exchange, donation or legacy);
- Production, trade and use of forged documentation;
- Traffic of fake or forged cultural property.[3]

162   *Michael Loughnane*

Law enforcement is overwhelmed with a multitude of crime considered to pose threats to global security, undermine personal safety or fund terrorism. Despite these negative consequences and cultural loss, law enforcement around the world directs most of its efforts elsewhere and direct limited resources to address cultural property crime. Global Financial Integrity (GFI) estimates that cultural property crime generates between $1.2 billion to $1.6 billion annually in revenues. GFI positions this type of crime toward the bottom of its extensive list of illicit activities in terms of revenue. More lucrative forms of illicit trade consist of trafficking of counterfeit goods and drugs, for which the revenues are hundreds of billions or even over a trillion dollars annually (Kar 2017).

The US Customs and Border Protection Strategy for 2020–2025 references its ongoing crime challenges as narcotics, counterfeit goods and human trafficking. There is no reference to cultural property in the Protection Strategy, although this crime falls within their jurisdiction (US Customs and Border Protection 2019). Antiquities trade is a less policed form of crime and hence a viable illicit profit center for crime (Shelley 2014: 261–264). It is much less visible to the public as actions take place in online markets or auctions that draw specific buyers and do not generate wide publicity.

Also explaining law enforcement's inattention is the fact that cultural property investigations usually require specialized knowledge about art and antiquities. The unique complexities of the market include item value, transport, methods of sale and care. Investigators need to understand the intricacies of markets, online sales and auctions, appraisal and authentication of artifacts and provenance as Nathan Elkins so clearly points out in Chapter 6.

In the United States, principal responsibility for investigations at the federal level rests with the Department of Homeland Security, and its attention to this type of crime is limited. During congressional testimony in 2017, ICE Homeland Security Investigations International Operations Assistant Director described the responsibilities of its Homeland Security Investigations, Immigration and Customs Enforcement (HSI) Cultural Property, Art and Antiquities (CPAA) program operational since 2007 as the protection, investigation and prosecution of those responsible for these crimes. One of their tasks in promotion of this goal is to increase awareness and support increased law enforcement capacity. As Assistant Director Raymond Villanueva noted, CPAA attempts to do this by:

> conducting training on the preservation, protection, and investigation of cultural heritage and property; to coordinate and support investigations involving the illicit trafficking of cultural property from countries around the world; and to facilitate the repatriation of illicit cultural items seized as a result of HSI investigations to the objects' and artifacts' lawful and rightful owners.
>
> (Villanueva 2017)

The Value of Financial Investigations 163

Through the CPAA, HSI supports 6,000 special agents as part of their collateral duties as well as training to personnel in other branches of law enforcement. HSI has the expertise and maintains a smaller, specialized unit for art and antiquities in its New York City field office (DHS 2017). Similarly, the Federal Bureau of Investigation, with its government-wide mission to investigate virtually all alleged violations of federal crime, also maintains a smaller specialized unit. The FBI Art Crime Team comprises 20 special agents, a small fraction of the FBI's 35,000 employees.[4] The Art Crime Team website reports that since its inception in 2004, it has recovered over 15,000 objects worth over $800 million.[5] This total is only a small share of the existing market as limited resources are allocated to its detection.

Specialized art and antiquities units operate in other countries and at the international level as well. Italy, for example, has one of the oldest law enforcement units. Founded in 1969, the Carabinieri Command for the Protection of Cultural Heritage was formed to "deal with the alarming phenomenon of the depletion of the largest museum in the world: Italy" (Amineddoleh 2020).[6] In its formation, Italy became the first nation to have a police force specialized in this specific sector.[7]

From an international perspective, INTERPOL supports international cultural property efforts by coordinating international investigations and providing a database of stolen works of art that combines descriptions and pictures of more than 50,000 items. It is the only database at the international level with certified police information on stolen and missing objects of art.[8]

Object ID is a program external to law enforcement that provides substantial support to international investigations. Established in 1993, Object ID is described as "an international standard for describing art, antiques and antiquities." The program is controlled by the International Council of Museums and is a collaboration of the museum community, police and customs agencies, the art trade, insurance industry, and appraisers of art and antiques.[9] With the Object ID checklist the identification of known art and artifacts is standardized for law enforcement and the antiquities community. Even more important from an investigative perspective, Object ID supports the creation of critical documentation applied to each item, providing important investigative lead material.

As previously discussed, law enforcement addressing cultural property crime is usually concentrated into smaller investigative units within larger law enforcement structures. With so few numbers in the law enforcement community, it is difficult for the members of these specialized units to have their operational needs met, such as acquiring funding for extensive investigations to pursue international networks. Financial analysts and investigators are often inexperienced or unavailable. Without specialized knowledge, one investigator explained to the author in an interview, in an asset seizure action they may recognize the $300,000 Lamborghini but leave the $12 million Monet on the wall.

164 *Michael Loughnane*

Law enforcement focus the expertise they have and apply it to investigate fraud and money laundering in the antiquities sector. Financial investigation methods can attack the entire illicit network structure rather than the specific item traded. As with crimes of every type, many investigations are initiated based on a "tip" from an informant. In this case, the tip may be a reporting that an artifact is being smuggled into the country or that the object is hidden in a shipment container masked as a lesser valued commodity. The focus, however, may be on the single reported activity and not extennded an investigation of the entire network. Traditional investigation methods may be applied such as setting up surveillance or providing information to customs and immigration authorities for interdiction and seizure. Other potential basic investigative methods include examination of any documents that accompany the smuggled item and possible arrest and interrogation of smugglers. The greater investigative impact more extensive investigations, dismantling transportation systems and interrupting the money flow as a deterrent against continued operation.

Current law enforcement efforts can often be viewed as a win-lose effort. An investigation may effectively disrupt a specific incident and arrest the perpetrators but may then leave the supporting network unscathed and able to continue its illicit activity.

To attack the complete network, investigators must develop detailed information on the financial and business operations of the cultural property trade and consult those with particular knowledge of art and antiquities. Financial investigations must gather evidence of the larger network operation and identify other predicate and related crimes and associated events. Investigators need to analyze information used in transactions with financial institutions and businesses, trade documents prepared for and by governments and internal business and communication records of networked businesses to identify the process through which stolen artifacts are bought, moved and sold. Investigators then need to follow the money to understand how the proceeds generated were moved.

The Criminal Supply Chain for Antiquities

The antiquities supply chain begins when the artifact is acquired from a source through a variety of means, including looting directly from the ground or stealing from private collections or museums. The next stage consists of the operational requirements of transport and storage. At this stage there is may be smuggling, movement of value through trade-based money laundering methods and possibly the warehousing of goods. The next phase is marketing and sales, where the artifacts usually become visible for sale and the sale converts the value of the artifact to money.

Artifacts may reach the market through a long and complex supply chain. It is not unusual in the Middle East for localized criminal and terror networks to control a specific territory where objects can be acquired. To access international connections to buyers beyond their immediate region, these

The Value of Financial Investigations 165

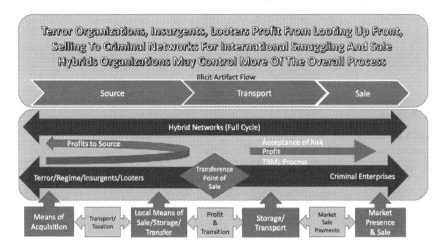

Figure 5.1 Illicit artifact flow
Source: M. Loughnane 2018.

criminal or terrorist groups may strategically intersect with larger, more capable networks with greater ability to move artifacts along a supply chain for sale globally. The local groups therefore sell locally, obtain their profit and leave the supply chain.

At this front end of the supply chain, criminal, insurgent and terrorist groups may generate revenue from charging for access to diggers at excavation sites under their control. This model was clearly used by ISIL by imposing "Taxes" on looters. "Licenses" to excavate were also issued (Sargent et al. 2020: 15). Once obtained, getting the artifacts to market could require the digger or the terrorist group itself to find middlemen to buy the item and then move it to sale. This could involve use of social media. These "middlemen," also commonly referred to as "gatekeepers" or "fixers," are a critical component to any illicit network. They are the experts that know how things need to look and how they actually work. As described in a report published in June 2019 by the ATHAR Project, networks interact between direct buyers as well as "middlemen" in order to sell artifacts using Facebook:

> Violent extremists currently include individuals associated with Syrian-based groups like Hay'at Tahrir Al Sham (HTS), Hurras Al-Din, the Zinki Brigade and other non-Syrian based Al-Qaeda or Islamic State in Iraq and Syria (ISIL) affiliates. All of these groups are using Facebook as a platform for antiquities trafficking, whether through direct interaction with buyers and sellers or through the use of middlemen who straddle transactions between the general public and terrorist groups.
> (Al-Azm and Paul 2019)

166 *Michael Loughnane*

From a financial investigation perspective, the red flags of the illegal antiquities trade share characteristics with other forms of illicit trade. For example, exhibiting wealth beyond one's known means is possibly indicative of a variety of illegal income sources, especially in areas where low incomes are common. This is often seen with poachers and members of wildlife trafficking networks in Africa. Understanding the means of generating revenues within geographic regions and effective net worth assessment techniques are important for suspicious activity identification.

More extensive crime networks will have some type of accounting system for their revenue and expenses. Seeking to minimize the risk of being caught for embezzlement or internal theft, they often keep detailed record of all revenues and expenses. In this manner they are able to control expenses and overhead costs and maximize profit. Financial investigators need to develop and understand the record keeping and financial controls maintained in these networks.

Once the artifact has moved past the initial point of acquisition at the source, it may be transferred through the rest of the supply chain. Before marketing and sale can begin, traffickers may need to create provenance, fictitious documents to establish legitimacy so the object may be listed for the maximum price. Manufactured documents create a wealth of information for financial investigators. As described previously, experts may be brought in for such work as restoration or appraisal and may be hired and paid as third parties. This creates a money trail, as they are likely paid for this work. Following a money trail may compromise the expert and create leverage, leading them to possibly cooperate in an investigation. It is also possible, as is often seen in illicit networks, that experts do not necessarily work exclusively for one network and their connections can lead to the discovery of other criminal networks.

If the network operates effectively the artifact, with all necessary documentation, is ready to be presented to the public at large for sale. To ensure profit, the object's price is adjusted based on the costs associated with acquisition, transportation, storage and preparation. The artifact can then be moved up the supply chain and sold to unsuspecting buyers.

Once the artifact has entered the supply chain, it simply becomes another commodity to be marketed, transported and sold. In this stage, third parties are often used to facilitate movement and storage. Several elements make it difficult for law enforcement to identify the movement of artifacts and track transactions, including the use of free trade zones, the long-term storage of goods before sale. To further obscure an artifact's source, objects are often not made immediately available and are instead stored in warehouses until the appropriate time for listing. This tendency to waitlist an item for sell presents an additional complication in investigating supply chains as investigations age and leads are lost. Additionally, new artifacts have not been previously identified or otherwise catalogued, have not otherwise been identified and noted as spirited away.

Once the artifact enters the market it will likely be moved and stored through the use of a number of techniques associated with TBML. This can

The types of records present in a TBML scheme are well known. These include false provenance documents, certificates of origin, bills of lading, airbills, manifests, invoices, and insurance documents. Some of these transactions are completed by complicit participants in the illicit supply chain. Some legitimate businesses are also unwitting parties to trade-based money laundering transactions, having been falsely assured of the contents and/or legitimacy of the antiquity shipped.

Antiquities are often stored on the short or long term in the many free trade zones in the Middle East or around the world. In these locales there are few challenges concerning the provenance or the documentation of commodities that move through them. Their storage there makes it difficult to trace the artifact back to its point of origin. Knowledge of the operations of free trade zones are critical in identifying suspicious business patterns and illicit supply chains.

The final point of sale can be the most risky element of the supply chain. At this point, the artifact becomes visible to buyers and the public. Some buyers may be uneducated, while others are experts and able to identify counterfeit, looted or stolen items. These experts can be affiliated with auction houses, insurance companies, banks, museums, or private buyers. Sales can be completed in a number or ways. The artifact may appear online on social media platforms, sold by a shopkeeper in a store or website or placed in a catalog for auction or sale. These and other methods can present their own risks of exposure. The cultural property community is closely connected and will frequently be aware who are the illicit actors and who should be avoided. Above all, a negative reputation can be one of the biggest impediments for a criminal network because no one will want to buy from them.

Payment processes also vary. The ability to track money through banking systems is a significant advantage in financial investigations. The money can be tracked through international banking systems and automated clearing houses aligned to the use of SWIFT messaging for transaction communications. Money can also be traced through the use of major alternate remittance systems such as Western Union that control money movement or use of other means of payment such as prepaid access cards or virtual assets such as Bitcoin and other virtual assets.

While the goal is profit for criminal enterprises or funds to support terror organization goals, money is needed to cover operational and overhead expenses in the illicit supply chain, such as paying for artifact acquisition, appraisal, creation of counterfeit provenance, shipping and storage, and any costs attributed to the sale. Money is also present at the end of the supply chain as payments are made through financial systems after purchase of the artifact.

168   *Michael Loughnane*

Illicit supply chain networks, are, at the basic level, business operations. As in any business, controls need to be maintained to manage structure, minimize costs and maximize profit. Top priority is given to the need to maintain a "legitimate" persona to avoid suspicion and detection. The supply chain needs to operate "under the radar" of the regulatory responsibilities of business, communication and finance while at the same time maintaining control of operations, costs, and profits. At the same time they need to also operate in the open as they market and sell activities, address due diligence concerns, work within the banking and financial structures to move and store their money. Given these needs, supply chain networks will employ business processes, measure profit and loss, oversee personnel, and function at an acceptable level of risk. Because these chains are profit driven, financial investigation techniques are highly effective methods to identify, track and disrupt their activity.

Earlier we described the shopkeeper who received an artifact from a digger and needed a network to sell it. As in his case, criminal networks need to control three elements for success: finances, communication and business processes. The financial component is one in which money is used to maintain the organization and its operations, including the generation and disbursement of profits. Communications are necessary to ensure that organization objectives are met, directions are followed and operational coordination is maintained. Business processes ensure the establishment, operation and maintenance of necessary structures such as the presence of specialized expertise and network gatekeepers, artifact specialists, experts in international trade documents and counterfeiters for fake artifacts or provenance. The business side also involves the establishment and operation of forward-facing front and shell companies necessary to evade due diligence programs and seemingly legitimate transactions with banks and insurance companies, auction houses and online platforms. Fronts and shell businesses are often necessary for criminal elements to operate internationally with minimal risk to the network.

These components also support terrorists and insurgents, such as charities that collect money that is diverted to support terror operations or businesses that purchase parts and equipment for sanctioned entities. Small, local networks may interact with larger transnational networks. As in our example, a local network acquired an artifact but lacked the international capability to sell the item. These sellers may negotiate a transaction with larger networks that have the capacity to move the artifact around the world.

Case Study One: Illicit Trade in an Egyptian Antiquity Transiting Through the UAE

The 2011–2012 New York case US v. Khouli, et. al.[10] resulted in a guilty plea by Mousa (Morris) Khouli, an antiquities dealer based in New York City. Khouli pled guilty in 2012 to charges related to smuggling Egyptian cultural property into the United States and making a false statement to law enforcement

The Value of Financial Investigations 169

authorities (St. Hilaire 2012). This section will examine one of the schemes for which Khouli was convicted. According to the federal indictment filed in 2012 at the Eastern District Court in Brooklyn, New York, Khouli, along with other defendants, smuggled antiquities "from abroad" (ICE Newsroom 2011). Another defendant, Ayman Ramadan, was an antiquities dealer who operated a business called Nafertiti Eastern Sculptures Trading ("NEST") located in Dubai, United Arab Emirates (St. Hilaire 2011).

Khouli was owner and operator of Windsor Antiquities, a gallery located in New York City. He sold antiquities from his gallery as well as over the Internet. As the prosecution's evidence showed, Windsor Antiquities was a front for Khouli. While the public facing business may have sold legitimate items, it was also knowingly selling stolen artifacts and reporting these sales as legitimate revenue in its business records.[11] Because of the complexities in this case, this chapter will focus on the acquisition, marketing and sale of one of the stolen artifacts, a Greco-Roman style Egyptian sarcophagus. The piece was sold to a collector in the United States (USDOJ 2011).[12] The business model supporting the scheme presented several challenges for Khouli's small criminal network, including securing shipment and creating false provenance. Obtaining credible provenance was critical to the sale as it was necessary to demonstrate the sarcophagus was not protected under a 1983 Egyptian law[13] which prohibited the sale of cultural artifacts including all elements of the process from transport through payment. Essentially, if an Egyptian artifact could be shown to have been in a private collection prior to 1983, it could legally be sold privately. Any artifacts acquired after 1983 are considered Egyptian property. Therefore, all provenance needed to indicate that the artifact was privately owned before 1983 in order to be sold legally.

The objective of the Khouli network was to sell a commodity (an antiquity protected under Egyptian law) at a profitable price. In order to do this, the network presented the sale as a legitimate business transaction and mitigated any suspicions of illicit trade. To achieve this aim, the network needed to control payment processes, communications, and business operations. Communications presented the most significant risk to the network, as emails and other communication were later used by investigators, providing incriminating evidence for prosecution. Once investigators determined email was a principal means used for communication, they were able to build a solid timeline and demonstrate elements of knowledge and intent by Khouli to participate in an illicit antiquities network.

The network also required a willing buyer. Khouli operated through Windsor Antiquities with an appearance of selling legitimate antiquities. With this outwardly legitimate appearance, Khouli could engage in negotiations and promise all necessary provenance to satisfy the intended buyer. The artifact was apparently only minimally exposed to the public through the use of direct marketing. The emails in February 2009 represented the sarcophagus, as a "coffin," to the potential buyer. After several emails, the collector agreed to purchase the artifact for $32,500 in March 2009.[14]

As a condition of sale, the collector requested provenance for the "coffin," a condition Khouli was willing to fulfill. Later, on the invoice to the buyer, Khouli described the coffin as coming from his own father's (Jack Khouli's) collection in Israel, dating back to the 1960s (this invoice also presented the sarcophagus as in a collection before the 1983 Egyptian law). There actually was no collection, and no Jack Khouli. When the buyer requested more detail with respect to the provenance, Khouli responded, "I have therefore established, to the best of my ability, that this item has not been illegally obtained from an excavation, architectural monument, public institution or private property."[15]

Figure 5.2 Windsor antiquities false provenance document
Source: Case 1:11-cr-00340-ERK-SMG US v Khouli et al., Declaration of Peter A. Chavkin Document Number 54, Exhibit 4 Filed 1/24/12 PageID # 326.

The Value of Financial Investigations 171

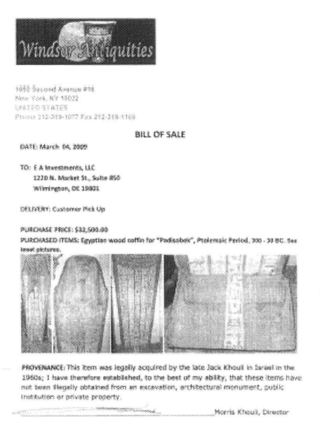

Figure 5.3 Windsor antiquities false provenance document
Source: Case 1:11-cr-00340-ERK-SMG US v Khouli et al., Declaration of Peter A. Chavkin Document Number 54, Exhibit 4 Filed 1/24/12 PageID # 332.

Emails also revealed the business process used by Khouli's network. The network needed to coordinate the movement of the Greco-Roman coffin from Dubai to the United States and create acceptable provenance to support the sale. At the start of the process Khouli even made an unsuccessful attempt to hire an expert to prepare the fake provenance. This probably resulted in Khouli eventually creating the lesser quality provenance he provided in the above bill of sale and invoice.

Business emails showed network efforts to mask the movement of the sarcophagus by falsifying the contents of relevant trade documents. This included the use of a third party, Agra Services, which moved the sarcophagus to

172 *Michael Loughnane*

a third location before movement to its US destination. The emails between Khouli and NEST (Nafertiti Eastern Sculptures Trading, the Dubai based business involved in acquiring the artifact) revealed the Greco-Roman sarcophagus was shipped from Dubai to the United States in November 2008, through Agra Services, with documentation falsely describing the sarcophagus as "antique wood panels." The email thread also provided an air bill number for tracking used as the artifact moved through the third-party shipper and then on to the US.[16] A tracking number was provided and a wire transfer of $3,400 was sent by Khouli to NEST to cover the cost of shipment. The shipment of "antique wood panels" originating from the United Arab Emirates eventually arrived in New Jersey. A "merchandise processing fee" of $3,400 was also noted in the shipping documents, the same amount that was wire transferred.[17] According to a search warrant affidavit, the special agent assigned to the investigation reported that in October 2008 Khouli purchased the Greco-Roman coffin from NEST, obviously revealing that the artifact was not from his father's collection. Khouli subsequently smuggled the coffin into the United States in November 2008, as described above.

The business process described in the email failed. It was apparently Khouli's intention to avoid Egyptian cultural property law and US customs detection. These actions served two purposes. First, it did not identify an item as coming from Egypt, therefore, preventing the application of Egyptian law. Second, the item could have been significantly undervalued in the paperwork during shipment, thereby lessening the risk of physical inspection by US Customs.

Under US law, an importer must disclose the contents of any package, country of origin, and value of the item shipped. Given the significant level of shipments, US Customs is dependent on the documentation provided to clear an item for entry into the country. The sarcophagus shipment apparently was not examined upon arrival, yet details from the documents that were entered into the Automated Targeting System used by Customs to track shipments describe the contents as "wood panels."[18] This description caught the eyes of US Customs and an investigation was initiated after customs officials suspected the assigned description of "wood panels" to the shipment. A special agent having expert knowledge knew that given the environmental conditions in the UAE, wood artifacts do not normally originate there.

Khouli was subsequently interviewed by HSI in February 2009. At that time, he physically presented to the special agent five old painted panels that he claimed were the contents of the shipment. However, in a follow up to this interview in a subsequent investigation, a special agent was able to demonstrate that Khouli actually had possession of the panels prior to the date of receipt of the shipment containing the coffin. Khouli later pled guilty to providing false statements to the special agent.[19] The day after the visit from the special agent, Khouli emailed the collector to determine his interest in purchasing the sarcophagus. The payment process in this transaction shows how important the business process is in supporting the network as a whole.

In this case, Khouli executed a wire transfer to NEST to cover shipping costs and a bill of sale seeking reimbursement. While this is a fairly normal transaction, it provided strong evidence for financial investigators that payment was directly tied to falsified trade documents. In its efforts to perform due diligence, the bank required the buyer to personally present the provenance for the sarcophagus before approval of the wire transfer for purchase.[20]

Case Study 2: Trafficking Italian Antiquities

Another example of a larger scale investigation was "Operation Achei" which revealed the activities of a much larger network involved in the illicit antiquities trade. In 2019, after a two-year multinational investigation led by the Italian Carabinieri Department for the Protection of Cultural Heritage with the support of Europol, 23 arrests were made in a trafficking ring that stole 10,000 artifacts from ancient Greek and Roman archeological sites in the Calabria region of southern Italy. "Operation Achei" found that traffickers had broken into sections of known archeological sites and used a "backhoe-like" excavator to dig. They then located objects by employing metal detectors. The stolen artifacts were then moved out of the country where they were sold in international auction houses at high value (Machemer 2019).

A Europol press release describes the complex nature of this network.

> The investigations revealed that the illegal excavations were managed by a well-structured organised crime group able to carry out all phases of the trafficking. The different rings included looters, fences, intermediaries and mules operating from different Italian regions. The key facilitators were also acting from Djion, Munich, London and Vršac, Serbia coordinating the supply chain.
>
> (EUROPOL 2019)

Comparing this with the operations of the smaller Khouli network, there are many similarities despite the difference in network size. Both networks shared the same concerns and challenges. They had to deal with the challenge of acquiring artifacts for sale. Both had to mask the sourcing and method of acquisition, protect the network from discovery during movement and storage of the artifacts, and engage in the public process of marketing and sales. Both networks have financial structures to pay network overhead costs and protect revenue generated from sales. To do this, they needed to process goods from product acquisition to sale and maintain methods to control operations to maximize efficiencies and costs.

Conclusion: The Benefits of Following the Value

The phrase, "Follow the Money" provides a limited view of financial investigations. If you ask someone its meaning, the usual response produces images of

174   *Michael Loughnane*

cash changing hands, briefcases full of currency and the moving of money through banks and remittance businesses. Since 1970, there has been such a focus on following the money that the world has taken extensive measures to hold financial institutions responsible for detecting suspicious activity. Such activity has created a wealth of valuable financial records for investigators.

With investigators focusing on movement of currency, the criminal world strategically operates in other areas to avoid detection. This broader criminal approach includes other items, from cars to diamonds, to art and antiquities. Therefore, as this chapter has shown, "following the value" is a much more useful concept. Financial investigation elements should be a high priority in the investigation of illicit supply chains.

Recent changes in international recommendations and laws are attempting to make the same rules that apply to the financial community apply to the arts and antiquities sector. These additions are critical since this sector is best suited to the detection of suspicious elements and reports to law enforcement. Unfortunately, law enforcement in most parts of the world is reactive rather than proactive. Therefore, the recommendations of the Financial Action Task Force established in 1989[21] that require countries to develop controls to regulate entities and monitor and report suspicious financial flows are key in addressing this illicit trade.

At the time of writing, countries are moving toward greater transparency for the art and antiquities sector and starting to require businesses to not only report significant transactions but also to maintain due diligence and report suspicious activity. In 2018 the European Union promulgated Directive (EU) 2018/843 required those in the business of arts and antiquities trade to incorporate risk-based approaches in their business models. Known as the 5th money laundering directorate, the detection and reporting requirements have been placed on,

> persons trading or acting as intermediaries in the trade of works of art, including when this is carried out by art galleries and auction houses as well as, persons storing, trading or acting as intermediaries in the trade of works of art when this is carried out by free ports, where the value of the transaction or a series of linked transactions amounts to 10,000 EUR or more.
>
> (Official Journal of the European Union 2018)[22]

These laws and regulations are in place around the world. Therefore, illicit supply networks need to be careful when engaging with businesses, banks, remitters, and others to disguise their suspicious and often criminal actions as there is much greater surveillance of their activities.

In the United States, the art sector has recently come under regulatory controls which may make transactions more transparent and disclose illicit activity. Under the Anti Money Laundering Act of 2020, the antiquities sector will be designated as Money Services Businesses and required to report cash transactions over a certain level, as well as any suspicious activities. While the specifics to any requirement is still under review at the time of this writing, it is anticipated the new responsibilities will be in line with industries of comparable risk and scale in the country such as sellers of precious metals, stones, and jewels, and pawn shops. It is also anticipated that these changes will provide significant opportunity for financial investigations to detect criminal network activity sooner and have immediate access to information to investigate false trade documents, false provenance, and related value movement.

Deployment of financial investigation methods in cultural property crime will reduce the profitability and increase the risk of antiquities trafficking. As a consequence, global supply chains for artifacts will become increasingly more complex. While this may not stop the presence of artifacts in illicit supply chains, it will make efforts by illicit actors more complex as they will need to fortify supply chains. Criminals will need stronger networks to withstand the increased scrutiny of an effective due diligence process. The financial community is preparing to address this issue more seriously as they attempt to close the gaps in the financial system that have facilitated the antiquities trade, thereby limiting future looting and illicit trade of antiquities.

Notes

1 Brodie, Neil. 2019. "CLASI Project Final Report." Terrorism, Transnational Crime and Corruption Center. https://traccc.gmu.edu/current-projects/counter ing-looting-antiquities-syria-and-iraq-clasi.
2 CLASI Gap Study, "Research and Training on Illicit Markets for Iraqi and Syrian Art and Antiquities," April 5, 2018.
3 CLASI Gap Study, "Research and Training on Illicit Markets for Iraqi and Syrian Art and Antiquities," April 5, 2018. https://traccc.gmu.edu/past-projects/ countering-looting-of-antiquities-from-syria-and-iraq-clasi.
4 "How Many People Work for the FBI?" Federal Bureau of Investigation. https:// www.fbi.gov/about/faqs/how-many-people-work-for-the-fbi.
5 "Art Theft.". Federal Bureau of Investigation. https://www.fbi.gov/investigate/vio lent-crime/art-theft.
6 "Introduzione." http://www.carabinieri.it/cittadino/tutela/patrimonio-culturale.
7 Ibid.
8 "Stolen Works of Art Database." https://www.interpol.int/en/Crimes/Cultura l-heritage-crime/Stolen-Works-of-Art-Database.
9 International Council of Museums, Object ID: http://icom.museum/object-id.
10 United States of America v. Mousa Khouli, Salem Alshdaifat, Joseph A. Lewis II and Ayman Ramadan, Case 1:11-cr-00340-ERK-SMG Document 10 Filed 05/04/2011.
11 Case 1:11-cr-00340-ERK-SMG Document 10 Filed 05/04/11 Page 1 of 17 PageID #: 18.
12 United States of America v. Mousa Khouli, Salem Alshdaifat, Joseph A. Lewis II and Ayman Ramadan, Case 1:11-cr-00340-ERK-SMG Document 10 Filed 05/04/ 2011, https://www.justice.gov/archive/usao/nye/pr/2011/2011jul14.html.
13 As of 1983, Article 1 of Egyptian Law 117, "The Law on the Protection of Ant-quities," all Egyptian antiquities are considered to be public property, i.e., prop-erty of the State of Egypt that cannot be publicly owned, possessed, or disposed of without state permission.

176 *Michael Loughnane*

14 It should be noted that the collector was indicted with the other defendants in this prosecution but after an extensive defense he was shown as to not being in the scheme itself.
15 Case 1:11-cr-00340-ERK-SMG US v Khouli et al., Memorandum in Support of Motion to Dismiss Based on Insufficient Evidence, Document Number 55 Filed 1/24/12 PageID # 790.
16 Case 1:11-cr-00340-ERK-SMG Document 79 Filed 04/27/12.
17 Case 1:11-cr-00340-ERK-SMG Document 83–6 Filed 04/30/12 Page 12 of 35 PageID #: 1285.
18 Case 1:11-cr-00340-ERK-SMG Document 83–6 Filed 04/30/12 Page 12 of 35 PageID #: 1285.
19 Case 1:11-cr-00340-ERK-SMG Document 83–6 Filed 04/30/12 Page 13 of 35 PageID #: 1285.
20 Case 1:11-cr-00340-ERK-SMG Document 54–10 Filed 01/24/12.
21 "With more than 200 countries and jurisdictions committed to implementing them. The FATF has developed Recommendations, or FATF Standards, which ensure a co-ordinated global response to prevent organised crime, corruption and terrorism. They help authorities go after the money of criminals dealing in illegal drugs, human trafficking and other crimes. https://www.fatf-gafi.org/publications/fatfrecommendations/documents/internationalstandardsoncombatingmoneyla underingandthefinancingofterrorismproliferation-thefatfrecommendations.html The FATF also works to stop funding for weapons of mass destruction." "About – Financial Action Task Force (FATF)." https://www.fatf-gafi.org/about/.
22 "Directive (EU) 2018/843 of the European Parliament and of the Council of 30 May 2018 Amending Directive (EU) 2015/849 on the Prevention of the Use of the Financial System for the Purposes of Money Laundering or Terrorist Financing, and Amending Directives 2009/138/EC and 2013/36/EU." 2018. *Official Journal of the European Union*: 32. https://eur-lex.europa.eu/legal-content/EN/TXT/PDF/?uri=CELEX:32018L0843.

References

Al-Azm, Amr and Katie Paul. 2019. Facebook's Black Market in Antiquities. Trafficking, Terrorism and War Crimes. Antiquities Trafficking and Heritage Anthropology Research (ATHAR) Project. http://atharproject.org/report2019/.

Amineddoleh, Leila. 2020. "How Italy's Art Crime Squad Has Protected Cultural Artifacts for Five Decades." *Artsy.* https://www.artsy.net/article/artsy-editorial-ita lys-art-crime-squad-protected-cultural-artifacts-five-decades.

DHS (Department of Homeland Security). 2017. "Written Testimony of ICE for a House Financial Services Subcommittee on Terrorism and Illicit Finance Hearing Titled 'The Exploitation of Cultural Property: Examining Illicit Activity in the Antiquities and Art Trade .'" Department of Homeland Security. June 23, 2017. https://www.dhs.gov/news/2017/06/23/written-testimony-ice-house-financial-services -subcommittee-terrorism-and-illicit.

EUROPOL. 2019. "23 Arrests and around 10 000 Cultural Items Seized in an Operation Targeting Italian Archaeological Trafficking." Europol. https://www.europol.europa.eu/newsroom/news/23-arrests-and-around-10-000-cultural-items-sei zed-in-operation-targeting-italian-archaeological-trafficking.

ICE Newsroom. 2011. "ICE Makes Arrests and Seizes Cultural Artifacts Stolen from Egypt." July 14, 2011. https://www.ice.gov/news/releases/ice-makes-arrests-and-sei zes-cultural-artifacts-stolen-egypt.

The Value of Financial Investigations 177

Kar, Dev. 2017. "Transnational Crime and the Developing World," *Global Financial Integrity*March 2017, p. 166. https://www.dmeforpeace.org/peacexchange/wp-con tent/uploads/2019/05/Transnational-Crime-and-the-Developing-World-Global-Fina ncial-Integrity.pdf.

Machemer, Theresa. 2019. "Authorities Recover 10,000 Artifacts Stolen by International Antiquities Trafficking Ring." *Smithsonian Magazine*. https://www.smithso nianmag.com/smart-news/authorities-recover-10000-artifacts-stolen-international-a ntiquities-trafficking-ring-180973636/.

Official Journal of the European Union. 2018. "Directive (EU) 2018/843 of the European Parliament and of the Council of 30 May 2018 Amending Directive (EU) 2015/849 on the Prevention of the Use of the Financial System for the Purposes of Money Laundering or Terrorist Financing, and Amending Directives 2009/138/EC and 2013/36/EU": *Official Journal of the European Union* 32.

Portman, Rob, and Tom Carper. 2020. "The Art Industry and U.S. Policies That Undermine Sanctions": 150. *United States Senate*, Permanent Subcommittee on Investigations, Committee on Homeland Security and Governmental Affairs. http://www.hsgac.senate.gov/download/majority-and-minority-staff-report_-the-a rt-industry-and-us-policies-that-undermine-sanctions/.

Sargent, Matthew, James V. Marrone, Alexandra T. Evans, Bilyana Lilly, Erik Nemeth, and Stephen Dalzell. 2020. Tracking and Disrupting the Illicit Antiquities Trade with Open Source Data. RAND Corporation. https://www.rand.org/pubs/ research_reports/RR2706.html.

Shelley, Louise I. 2014. *Dirty Entanglements: Corruption, Crime and Terrorism*. New York: Cambridge University Press.

St. Hilaire, Rick. 2011. "Ayman Ramadan and Nafertiti Eastern Sculptures Trading." *Cultural Heritage Lawyer*. https://culturalheritagelawyer.blogspot.com/2011/09/a yman-ramadan-and-nafertiti-eastern.html.

St. Hilaire, Rick. 2012. "U.S. v. Khouli et al. Update: Second Guilty Plea Expected Today in Egyptian Antiquities Case." https://culturalheritagelawyer.blogspot.com/ 2012/12/us-v-khouli-et-al-update-second-guilty.html.

U.S. Customs and Border Protection. 2019. "U. S. Customs and Border Protection Strategy 2020–2025." April 17, 2019. https://www.cbp.gov/document/publications/ u-s-customs-and-border-protection-strategy-2020-2025.

USDOJ (US Attorney's Office – Eastern District of New York). 2011. "Dealers and Collector Charged with Smuggling Egyptian Antiquities." https://www.justice.gov/a rchive/usao/nye/pr/2011/2011jul14.html.

U.S. Immigration and Customs Enforcement. 2012. Antiquities dealer pleaded guilty to smuggling Egyptian cultural property. April 4, 2012. https://www.ice.gov/news/ releases/antiquities-dealer-pleaded-guilty-smuggling-egyptian-cultural-property.

Villanueva, Raymond. 2017. "Written Testimony of ICE for a House Financial Services Subcommittee on Terrorism and Illicit Finance Hearing Titled 'The Exploitation of Cultural Property: Examining Illicit Activity in the Antiquities and Art Trade.'" Department of Homeland Security. June 23, 2017, https://financialservices. house.gov/uploadedfiles/06.23.2017_raymond_villanueva_testimony.pdf.

6 Working a Case on Looted and Smuggled Ancient Coins as an Expert Witness

Nathan T. Elkins[1]

Paid lobbyists for sellers have popularized the glib notion that ancient coins can be found anywhere in order to argue against international regulations on the import of recently looted material into the United States. While some coins did indeed circulate widely in antiquity, many coinages had much more regionalized or localized circulation patterns. Law enforcement and federal prosecutors have sometimes been reticent to pursue antiquities trafficking cases involving looted and smuggled ancient coins because of an unfamiliarity with the material and the false assumption that there is no way to identify a country of discovery. With more than a decade's experience of working with federal law enforcement, I present a methodology for working cases on ancient coins and identifying the country from which the material was looted and smuggled.

Introduction

In response to concerted lobbying efforts by American dealers of antiquities and ancient coins to exempt ancient coins from national and international protections, regardless of how they enter the supply chain, I entered the cultural property debate in 2007 as an archaeologist and historian specialized in Roman coinage. Since that time, study of the indiscriminate trade in ancient coins and its relationship to looting and the consequent erosion and loss of historical, archaeological, and numismatic information has been a small component of my broader research agenda (Elkins 2008; 2009; 2012; 2014; 2015a). As I first began to conduct research on the subject, I discovered that few studies had focused on the trade in ancient coins specifically; larger objects, such as sculpture and painted ceramics, had tended to be the focus of inquiry (for some earlier studies or remarks on the coin trade, see, for example, Finley 1975: 96; Butcher and Gill 1990; Beckmann 1998; von Kaenel 1994 or 1995; Dietrich 2002; Kersel 2006: 194–197; Center for the Study of Democracy 2007: 177–197). Even some numismatic scholars comfortable with partnerships in the trade had recognized the problems for the study of archaeology and history posed by a growing and unregulated trade in ancient coins from the 1970s onwards (e.g., Kraay 1976: xxiv; Walker 1977; Göbl 1987: 74ff.).

DOI: 10.4324/9781003023043-9

Working a Case as an Expert Witness   179

As my research and advocacy received some attention, a colleague in 2009 put me in contact with a special agent in Homeland Security Investigations who was working on antiquities smuggling cases. That investigator was interested only in quick seizures and repatriations, not in prosecuting criminal cases; he also had little interest in ancient coins, as they did not attract as much popular attention as more monumental objects. Furthermore, he believed, erroneously, the facile assertions that all ancient coins circulated very widely and that it was impossible to tell from where they might have been looted. Therefore, he felt that cases involving ancient coins were a waste of investigative efforts. Soon thereafter, I was contacted by another special agent from Homeland Security Investigations who was more ambitious in the pursuit of criminal prosecutions and who had learned that I had contacted his colleague; he had regularly encountered earth-encrusted shipments of ancient coins from the Middle East and Europe – more than any other type of artifact – and was eager to work with a specialist on ancient coins to start building cases for criminal prosecution, not just seizures and repatriations.

Through our many discussions, I learned that he had never been able to work with a specialist in ancient coins because all he and his colleagues could find were archaeologists specialized in other types of objects, who were not knowledgeable enough about ancient coins to provide an expert report on the material, or dealers and collectors who claimed that country of discovery could never be established for smuggled coins. Therefore, based on my knowledge of numismatic material and the realities of circulation processes, and by looking at the group of earth-encrusted coins as a sort of archaeological assemblage, I developed my own methodology for identifying country of discovery for looted and smuggled coins to aid this federal investigator and others since then from Customs and Border Protection, Homeland Security Investigations, and the Federal Bureau of Investigation. I outline this methodology here so that it might be of use to other academics and archaeologists who aid in investigations and to law enforcers who may not know how to approach cases involving looted and smuggled ancient coins.

Looted and Smuggled Ancient Coins Merit Attention

While lobbies, such as the Ancient Coin Collectors Guild (ACCG) and the International Association of Professional Numismatists (IAPN), advocate against legislative measures and international agreements in order to promote an unregulated trade in fresh supplies of ancient coins (from the ground to the buyer), it is clear that the ancient coin market is an integral part of the antiquities trade, and is indeed the largest part of it in terms of volume (on this subject, see Elkins 2008; 2012). Those who loot ancient coins damage archaeological sites and also loot other objects (see Brodie, Chapter 1, on "The Looting and Trafficking of Syrian Antiquities Since 2011"). Millions of ancient coins, the vast majority without recorded collecting histories, are sold openly on the North American antiquities market each year, which

180 *Nathan T. Elkins*

significantly eclipses what has been recovered in more than a century of scientific archaeology and what is held in public collections. On eBay and other venues, recently looted coins are sold in volume so that buyers can conduct 'archaeology' at home to clean and identify coins (on eBay and ancient coins, see, for example, Elkins 2008; 2012: 97–99; Wartenberg and Dmitričenko, Chapter 7 on "Plenitudinous: An Analysis of Ancient Coin Sales on eBay") in this volume.

In addition to the evident intellectual cause for concern wrought by the market's sourcing practices, law enforcement and government should attend to the trade in antiquities and ancient coins, as smugglers often use the antiquities trade to launder money from other illicit activities in which they are involved (e.g., Center for the Study of Democracy 2007: 177–197). The smugglers of the Elmali Hoard, looted in 1984, had links to organized crime and drug trafficking (e.g., Acar and Kaylan 1988; Fielder 1993; Acar 2001). From my own work with federal law enforcement, I can attest that investigators have found that some smugglers and dealers of ancient coins have been involved with the unauthorized export of military technology, human trafficking, and international mob activity. These smugglers also typically evade taxes.

The Myth That All Ancient Coins Circulated Widely

The first point that must be made about making a case on smuggled ancient coins is that the claim that all coins circulated broadly and, thus, no country of discovery can be reasonably established is incorrect and untheorized (see Gerstenblith 2020 on the government's burden of proof to the probable cause standard regarding seizures and forfeitures). Representatives of the ACCG and IAPN continuously argue this point through written submissions to the Cultural Property Advisory Committee (CPAC) at the U.S. Department of State, and at its public hearings, in an attempt to stall international agreements that restrict the import of ancient coins and antiquities that do not have export licenses or verifiable collecting histories before the implementation of an agreement.

Unable to convince, and in an effort to have the courts strike down import on restrictions on coins from various countries, in 2009 the ACCG staged the import and seizure of 23 coins of ancient Cypriot and Chinese origin (Ancient Coin Collectors Guild 2009). Cyprus and China were chosen because the United States had bilateral agreements with these nations that specifically restricted the import of ancient coins from these countries. These were also the first restrictions on the importation of ancient coins through the Cultural Property Implementation Act (see Gerstenblith on "Hobby Lobby, the Museum of the Bible, and the Law: A Case Study of the Looting of Archaeological Artifacts from Iraq" in Chapter 2 in this volume on the legal framework regarding importation of antiquities into the United States). The Federal District Court of Maryland dismissed the case on the government's motion in 2011 and in 2012 the United States Court of Appeals for the Fourth Circuit upheld the decision (U.S. Federal District Court of Maryland 2011; U.S. Court of Appeals for the Fourth Circuit of Maryland 2012). In 2013, the Supreme Court elected not to hear the ACCG's case (U.S. Supreme Court 2013). Following the failure of its 'test case,' the ACCG attempted to relitigate the case by challenging the forfeiture of the coins, which was ultimately unsuccessful; the Cypriot coins were repatriated in 2020 and the long saga of the 'test case' came to an end (U.S. Customs and Border Protection 2020).

Through the course of the ACCG's 'test case' and in halls of the U.S. Department of State, the lobbyist for the ACCG and IAPN, has relied on the unsubstantiated declaration that coins circulated widely and that country of discovery cannot be reasonably established. Reliance on that claim is not based on the research of academic numismatists or archaeologists who actively study coin finds, but on the writings of the attorneys Urice and Adler (2010: 33–34; 2011: 154–159), who followed the lobbyist's own unresearched claims that ancient coins circulated very widely (see Tompa and Brose 2005: 205, 214).[2] Indeed, to the contrary, numismatists and archaeologists have long been aware that certain types of coins circulated locally and regionally, making it apparent that certain types of coins are more likely to come from specific regions or countries, and often very near to the place they were minted (for a rebuttal to the lobbyist's claims to the U.S. Department of State and in the 'test case' regarding coin circulation, see Elkins 2015a with reference to studies of coin circulation; Gerstenblith 2020 summarizes from a legal perspective many aspects of the 'test case,' its outcome, as well as the evidentiary standard). Types of coins that circulated more regionally or locally include most Greek silver and bronze coins and Roman provincial coins (Roman provincial coins were struck for local use at various mints across the Roman Empire and are distinct from the Roman republican or imperial coinage, which was struck primarily at the central mints of Rome and Lugdunum [Lyons]).

Identifying the Country of Discovery

In 2009, when I began working with Homeland Security Investigations and the Department of Justice, the first case on which I was consulted involved a well-known and major supplier of ancient coins who was a Bulgarian national living and working in the United States. His family business involved arranging for the mass looting of ancient coins in Bulgaria that were then shipped to him in the United States where they were sold to other dealers and directly to collectors. I was charged with the examination and analysis of approximately 150lbs (68kg) of material, which amounted to between 20,000 and 25,000 coins, seized from his domicile during a raid conducted by Homeland Security Investigations and the Federal Bureau of Investigation, and asked to make a determination as to country of origin (in

182   *Nathan T. Elkins*

the case of archaeological artifacts, the country of origin is defined as the country of discovery, i.e., the modern country within whose boundaries the object was discovered; on such terminology and its application to the importation of ancient objects, see Gerstenblith 2020).

Photographs from the seizure showed the coins in bags, pegged to cork boards, and lying in piles on tables in various stages of cleaning the dirt and encrustation from them. Most of the coins seemed to have been sorted by size, metal, and condition. Records and invoices seized from the residence clearly indicated that he had consigned rare and high-quality coins to prominent auction houses specialized in ancient coinage. He sold more common, but desirable, coins to individual mid-range dealerships, while even more common and less collectible coins were sold directly to customers on eBay, often in bulk and with the dirt still on them. When the material was seized, some individual coins or groups of coins had already been set aside and marked to send to specific dealers. Some officers and financial backers had been supplied by this importer, according to invoices and eBay feedback records. The importer's feedback rating on eBay among his known accounts was around 10,000; as the feedback rating only counts unique buyers, he had sold material directly to at least this number of different individuals, in addition to other dealers and to auction houses. It is also important to remember that a single transaction could contain multiple objects, especially in the seller's bulk offerings.

While the lobby often insists that fresh supplies of ancient coins on the market do not come from sites of archaeological interest but instead from hoards (i.e., groups of coins deliberately hidden or buried in antiquity) devoid of other contexts, this case boldly illustrated the contrary. The assemblage contained coins ranging from the sixth-century BCE through the Middle Ages and early modern periods – over two millennia; the group also contained what appeared to be hoards of Greek silver coins and late Roman bronze coins, owing to the close chronological and typological associations. Mixed in with everything were also ancient figurines, engraved gemstones, gold and bronze jewelry, Byzantine crosses, bronze arrowheads, and other metal objects. This was clearly not a hoard, but an amalgamated group of individual coin finds, coin hoards, and other objects systematically looted from multiple occupational layers at hundreds of archaeological sites – ancient settlements and graves – with the aid of metal detectors. Most of the coins were bronze, although there was also a substantial number of silver coins and some gold coins. The vast majority of coins came from the ancient Greek, Roman, and Byzantine worlds, while the medieval and early modern material amounted to no more than 20 pieces.

When I began analyzing the group, I focused on legible coins that tended to have more regionalized or localized circulation patterns in antiquity: Greek silver and bronze coins, Roman provincial coins, and the late Roman bronze coins. There were a number of Roman republican and early Roman imperial silver coins, typically struck at the mints of Rome or Lugdunum, but these coins generally had a wider range of circulation across the Roman world. There were also many early Roman imperial bronze coins struck at the mint of Rome that were also used in multiple regions; these sorts of coins on their own do not easily point to a country of discovery.

Although there was a mass quantity of material to evaluate in this case, I handled every coin that appeared to be diagnostic and identifiable and recorded its place of minting. In my evidence report, I referred to what I called "regionally diagnostic" and "locally diagnostic" coin types to determine the probable country from which the material was looted and smuggled. By "regionally diagnostic" coin types, I meant types of coins expected to be found in a relatively broad region that might not on their own identify the specific country in which they were removed. For instance, Macedonian bronze coins were struck in ancient Macedonia and circulated in the Balkan Peninsula. Their remarkable presence (over 500 coins) in this seized assemblage of coins suggested to me that they were found in a country that formed part of, or was very near to, the ancient Kingdom of Macedonia, but they alone could not be indicative of a more specific country of origin. Their abundance also negated a find spot farther west of the Balkan Peninsula or much farther to the east. The large numbers of Byzantine coins and Bulgarian "cup coins" also suggested a find spot in the Balkans, rather than some region farther to the west.

Another regional indicator was the large number of late Roman bronze coins. In the later Roman Empire, Roman authorities closed the provincial mints and decentralized the imperial mint, which means that coins were then produced only at certain branches of the imperial mints throughout the Roman Empire. Examples of such mints include London, Lugdunum, Trier, Arles, Ticinum, Rome, Aquilea, Siscia, Sirmium, Serdica, Thessalonica, Heraclea, Constantinople, Nicomedia, Cyzicus, Antioch, and Alexandria. Although these coins did travel, and a single coin on its own does not point to a country of discovery, late Roman coins from individual sites to tend to come from the most proximate late imperial mints. This was evident to me, for example, in my study of the excavation coins from the Roman fort at Yotvata, Israel, where the most represented mints among the fourth-century CE coins were Antioch and Alexandria (Elkins 2015b: 173–174). And, in modern Germany, where I worked for the Fundmünzen der Antike Projekt in 2008–2009, late Roman coin finds are primarily from the mint at Trier (see *FMRD* 1960–). Therefore, a large group of legible late Roman bronze coins can point to a general region from which they were looted and smuggled.

Most late Roman bronze coins from this seizure were struck at Constantinople and Nicomedia (Table 6.1). Constantinople corresponds with modern Istanbul, Turkey. It was in the ancient region of Thrace and is very near to modern Bulgaria. Nicomedia is in northwestern Turkey and also would have had economic relationships with Thrace. Thessalonica, which was in ancient Macedonia, was also near to Thrace and a number of coins in the group bore that city's mintmark. Coins from Cyzicus, also in

184 _Nathan T. Elkins_

northwestern Turkey, too were abundant in the group. Siscia, which is modern Sisek in Croatia, lies in the western part of the Balkan Peninsula. By far, these five mints were the most prevalent among the legible late Roman bronze coins. The eastern mints of Antioch and Alexandria and the western mints of Rome and Trier are underrepresented by comparison, which suggested that the find spots for this group of coins would have been in an area in Balkan Peninsula or northwestern Turkey. Like the late Roman bronze coins, the Byzantine coins are good regional indicators, but are often not as informative on account of the smaller number of mints. The most prevalent mint for the Byzantine coins from the seizure was Constantinople (Table 6.2), followed by Nicomedia, Cyzicus, and Thessalonica, suggesting an origin for the coins in northwestern Turkey or the Balkan Peninsula, as eastern mints were less common in the group.

When examining a group of coins such as this, it is also worth noting what is _not_ present. There were no Ptolemaic coins from Egypt, which told me they did not come from that region, and there were only two Seleucid bronze coins, which indicated that the country of discovery was not in the Levant.

Table 6.1 Legible late Roman bronze coins from the seizure

Quantity	Ancient City/Region	Modern City/Country
124	Constantinople, Thrace	Istanbul, NW Turkey
153	Nicomedia, Bithynia	NW Turkey
114	Thessalonica, Macedonia	Thessaloniki, N Greece
114	Cyzicus, Mysia	NW Turkey
108	Siscia, Pannonia Superior	Sisek, Croatia
19	Antioch, Syria	Antakya, Turkey
7	Trier, Germania	Trier, Germany
6	Rome, Italia	Rome, Italy
3	Heraclea, Pontus	N Turkey
1	Sirmium, Pannonia Inferior	Sremska Mitrovica, Serbia
1	Alexandria, Egypt	Alexandria, Egypt

Table 6.2 Legible Byzantine coins from the seizure

Quantity	Ancient City/Region	Modern City/Country
180	Constantinople, Thrace	Istanbul, NW Turkey
12	Nicomedia, Bithynia	NW Turkey
8	Cyzicus, Mysia	NW Turkey
8	Thessalonica, Macedonia	Thessaloniki, N Greece
4	Antioch, Syria	Antakya, Turkey

And, although there were a number of Greek silver coins in this group, most of the Greek material came from the mints north of Greece, in the central Balkan Peninsula, with the conspicuous absence of coins from important cities further to the south in mainland Greece, such as Athens and Corinth.

Coins that represent a more localized circulation pool and, therefore, the probable source country in concert with the "regionally diagnostic" types, are what I referred to as the "locally diagnostic" types. These are primarily Greek silver and bronze coins and Roman provincial bronze coins. The addition of some medieval and modern coins was also indicative of the specific source country.

The Greek world was not unified and there was no central mint for precious-metal coins like there would be when Roman rule spread to these areas. City-states struck coins for their own uses. Thus, Greek silver coins, although mobile and used for interstate transactions, can be used as an indicator of the probable find spot in a tighter geographical region. Roman provincial coins are silver or base-metal coins that were produced locally at cities that were granted special status to produce a subsidiary coinage for local use. These coins would have circulated locally and are excellent indicators for a probable country of discovery.

While the regionally diagnostic coins suggested a find spot for the material in the central Balkan Peninsula (north of Greece), or perhaps even north-western Turkey according to the late Roman bronzes, the locally diagnostic types indicated that the most probable origin for the coins is the modern nation of Bulgaria. In addition to the hundreds of Macedonian bronze coins that pointed to an origin in the Balkan Peninsula, many other Greek coins were produced by colonies in or near to what is now the modern nation of Bulgaria (Table 6.3). There were 277 silver coins from Apollonia Pontica, Thrace, which corresponds with the modern city of Sozopol, Bulgaria. These appeared to be the contents of a hoard. After Macedonian bronze coins and the silver coins from Apollonia Pontica, silver coins from Histiaea in Euboea formed the third-largest group with 106 coins; I had seen large groups of these coins in Bulgarian assemblages before. The seizure also produced 43 coins from the Thracian Chersonese, which is the modern Gallipoli Peninsula in Turkey, near modern Istanbul and very near the border of modern Bulgaria. Many other Greek coins in the group were produced at cities north of Greece or in northwestern Asia Minor, all within the economic sphere of ancient Thrace (modern Bulgaria).

The best indicators for the probable country where the coins were looted were the bronze Roman provincial coins, which quite clearly showed a Bulgarian origin (Table 6.4). There were 57 coins from Marcianopolis (modern Devnya, Bulgaria) and 46 from Nicopolis ad Istrum (Nikyup, Bulgaria). While these were the most common provincial mints represented in the group, other Roman provincial mints present in the seized assemblage were Deultum (Burgas, Bulgaria – 9 specimens), Odessus (Varna, Bulgaria – 3 specimens), Philippopolis (Plovdiv, Bulgaria – 1 specimen), and Serdica (Sofia, Bulgaria – 1 specimen). Other provincial coins were struck in northern Greece (i.e., Thessalonica – 9

186   *Nathan T. Elkins*

Table 6.3 Legible Greek coins from the seizure

Quantity	Ancient City/Region	Modern City/Country
c. 515	Macedonian bronze coins	Macedonia, Bulgaria, Serbia, etc.
277	Apollonia Pontica, Thrace	Sozopol, Bulgaria
106	Histiaea, Euboea	NW Euboea (Island), Greece
43	Thracian Chersonese, Thrace	Gallipoli Peninsula, NW Turkey
42	Mysia	NW Turkey
11	Maroneia, Thrace	Maroneia, N Greece
9	Philippi, Macedonia	Filippoi, N Greece
4	Thrace	Bulgaria, N Greece, NW Turkey
4	Halicarnassus, Caria	Bodrum, SW Turkey
3	Caria	SW Turkey
3	Ephesus, Ionia	W Turkey
3	Thasos	N Aegean Greek Island
3	Parion, Mysia	NW Turkey
3	Moesia	Macedonia, Bulgaria, Serbia, etc.
2	Cyzicus, Mysia	NW Turkey
2	Istros, Thrace	Istria, Romania
2	Ionia	W Turkey
2	Rhodes	Greek Island, SE Aegean
2	Antioch, Syria (Seleucid coins)	Antakya, Turkey
1	Smyrna, Ionia	Izmir, W Turkey
1	Colophon, Lydia	W Turkey
1	Skepsis, Troas	NW Turkey
1	Proconesus, Island of Mysia	NW Turkey
1	Mesembria, Thrace	Nesebar, Bulgaria

specimens) or in northwestern Turkey, near modern Bulgaria. The lack of any Roman provincial coins from the southern part of the Balkan Peninsula or from eastern or southern Turkey was conspicuous.

In addition to the ancient coins, there were also some medieval and modern coins present in the group. There were 12 coins from medieval or modern Bulgaria (Table 6.5). There were also some coins from nearby countries: two coins from Austria and one from medieval Hungary. There was one gold coin from Venice.

Curiously, there were also some modern forgeries of ancient coins mixed in with the coins that were looted and smuggled into the United States from Bulgaria. Most of these forgeries were of collectible Roman silver coin types. These particular types of forgeries are well known, published, and come from Bulgarian forgers' workshops. These were, therefore, even further evidence that the coins were looted in modern Bulgaria, where the forgeries were mixed in with authentic coins prior to shipping them to the United States.

Table 6.4 Legible Roman provincial coins from the seizure

Quantity	Ancient City/Region	Modern City/Country
57	Marcianopolis, Thrace	Devnya, Bulgaria
46	Nicopolis ad Istrum, Thrace	Nikyup, Bulgaria
14	Viminacium, Moesia	Kostolac, Serbia
9	Thessalonica, Macedonia	Thessaloniki, N Greece
9	Deultum, Thrace	Burgas, Bulgaria
3	Odessus, Moesia	Varna, Bulgaria
1	Philippolis, Thrace	Plovdiv, Bulgaria
1	Cyzicus, Mysia	NW Turkey
1	Maroneia, Thrace	Maroneia, N Greece
1	Perinthus, Thrace	Near Istanbul, Turkey
1	Serdica, Thrace	Sofia, Bulgaria
1	Byzantium, Thrace	Istanbul, Turkey
1	Hadrianopolis, Thrace	Edirne, Turkey, near Istanbul
1	Nicaea, Bithynia	Iznik, NW Turkey

Table 6.5 Legible medieval and modern coins from the seizure

Quantity	Ancient City/Region	Modern City/Country
12	Medieval /modern Bulgarian silver coins	Bulgaria
2	Medieval/modern Austrian coins	Austria
1	Medieval Hungary	Hungary
1	18th Century Venetian gold coin	Venice, Italy

Conclusion

The work summarized here did not result in a successful prosecution. The investigator and I had assembled a strong body of evidence, and so the lack of prosecution on smuggling was not a reflection on the merits of the case itself. A challenge to federal investigators is the lack of knowledge regarding antiquities and laws related to them. When the case was brought to an assistant U.S. attorney, who was unfamiliar with both the material and legal framework, she was uncomfortable prosecuting it under the National Stolen Property Act despite the fact that the material itself pointed to a Bulgarian origin, a Bulgarian national was the importer, and there was a money trail and correspondence going back to Bulgaria. I suspect that lack of knowledge about antiquities and the regulatory framework, as well as a lack of interest informed the assistant U. S. attorney's decision. Instead, the subject under investigation was indicted on tax-evasion charges and forfeited most of the seized objects. From my

188 *Nathan T. Elkins*

experience, and from my conversations with investigators, some federal prosecutors prefer the quick and easy win in such cases, since antiquities smuggling is largely perceived as a victimless crime and they would rather devote their energies to higher profile cases that will better advance their careers. This can lead to the disillusionment of both the investigators and the evidence experts, who devote hundreds of hours to building these cases.

At the time this particular investigation was undertaken, there was no Memorandum of Understanding with Bulgaria; this was no matter, as stolen material from any country is prosecutable under the National Stolen Property Act. The benefit of Memoranda of Understanding is that they more easily allow seizures and call specific attention to at-risk objects from countries that suffer from looting.

For any investigator who deals with cases involving ancient coins, the best thing one can do is to identify a numismatic expert, preferably one with a background in archaeology, as he/she will have knowledge of coin circulation. In the years since I worked on the case that began 2009, I routinely receive emails from various federal investigators asking for assistance on cases with ancient coins and often find myself unable to help or asking for more information, and so I conclude with a few tips that will help material experts on ancient coins. If the seizure contains only one or just a few coins, there is often not much that can be done, unless the type is specifically included in an active Memorandum of Understanding from the U.S. State Department and is subject to import restrictions, appearing on one of the designated lists. In such shipments, often from European auction houses, most importers are, however, including documentation that the coin was in trade prior to the implementation of restrictions, as is required for import into the United States. In larger shipments of coins to the United States that have been intercepted, particularly those appear to have been recently looted (e.g., large groups of dirt-covered coins with other artifacts mixed in), investigators often send me pictures of the gold or silver coins from the group, as these naturally attract attention. It is, however, the bronze coins, like the Roman provincial coins, that are typically more diagnostic to an expert. While many silver coins can be indicative of a country of discovery in a bigger assemblage, there are large classes of coins, such as the Roman republican and early Roman imperial coinage that do not help much on their own. For an expert, it is helpful to have clear photographs of the fronts and backs of as many objects as possible, and oftentimes the less attractive bronze and copper coins are the most helpful in pointing towards to the country from which the material was looted and smuggled.

Notes

1 Associate Professor of Art History (Greek and Roman Art and Archaeology) and Director of the Allbritton Art Institute at Baylor University. I am grateful to Patty Gerstenblith, Ute Wartenberg, and the editors of this volume for comments on drafts of this chapter, and to federal investigators for their important and

underappreciated work on antiquities crimes. I have had the opportunity to work with federal investigators from Homeland Security Investigations and the Federal Bureau of Investigation since 2009. Much of this methodological information was also presented at the international law-enforcement training workshop, "Detecting and Dismantling Antiquities Trafficking Networks: Balkan Regional Workshop," in Sofia, Bulgaria, June 4–6, 2013, organized by the U.S. Embassy in Sofia and the Federal Bureau of Investigation.

2 Urice also has a doctorate in archaeology.

Bibliography

Acar, Özgen. 2001. Will 'Blind Edip' Sing? *Archaeology* 54 (1) (January/February). Electronic document, https://archive.archaeology.org/0101/newsbriefs/edip.html.

Acar, Özgen and Melik Kaylan. 1988. The Hoard of the Century. *Connoisseur* 218: 74–83.

Ancient Coin Collectors Guild. 2009. Coin Collectors to Challenge State Department on Import Restrictions. Electronic document, http://www.accg.us/news/item/coin_collectors_to_challenge_state_department_on_import_restrictions.aspx.

Beckmann, Martin. 1998. Numismatics and the Antiquities Trade. *The Celator* 12 (5) (May): 25–28.

Butcher, Kevin and David W.J. Gill. 1990. Mischievous Pastime or Historical Science? *Antiquity* 64: 946–950.

Center for the Study of Democracy. 2007. Organized Crime in Bulgaria: Markets and Trends. Sofia: Center for the Study of Democracy. Electronic document, https://www.files.ethz.ch/isn/48411/28_organized_crime1.pdf.

Dietrich, Reinhard. 2002. Cultural Property on the Move – Legally, Illegally. *International Journal of Cultural Property* 11 (2): 294–303.

Elkins, Nathan T. 2008. A Survey of the Material and Intellectual Consequences of Trading in Undocumented Ancient Coins: A Case Study on the North American Trade. *Frankfurter elektronische Rundschau zur Altertumskunde* 7: 1–13. Electronic document, http://www.fera-journal.eu.

Elkins, Nathan T. 2009. Treasure Hunting 101 in America's Classrooms. *Journal of Field Archaeology* 34 (4): 482–489.

Elkins, Nathan T. 2012. The Trade in Fresh Supplies of Ancient Coins: Scale, Organization, and Politics. In *All the King's Horses: Essays on the Impact of Looting and the Illicit Antiquities Trade on Our Knowledge of the Past*, edited by Paula K. Lazrus and Alex W. Barker, 91–107. Washington, D.C.: Society for American Archaeology.

Elkins, Nathan T. 2014. Investigating the Crime Scene: Looting and Ancient Coins. *Biblical Archaeology Review* 40 (4) (July/August): 26, 69.

Elkins, Nathan T. 2015a. Ancient Coins, Find Spots, and Import Restrictions: A Critique of Arguments Made in the Ancient Coin Collectors Guild's 'Test Case'. *Journal of Field Archaeology* 40 (2): 236–243.

Elkins, Nathan T. 2015b. The Coins. In *The 2003–2007 Excavations in the Late Roman Fort at Yotvata*, edited by Gwyn Davies and Jodi Magness, 172–199. Winona Lake, IN: Eisenbrauns.

Fielder, Wilfried. 1993. Art Robbery and the Protection of Cultural Property in Public International Law. In *Proceedings of the XIth International Numismatic Congress Organized for the 15th Anniversary of the Société Royale de Numismatique de Belgique, Brussels, September 8th–13th 1991*, edited by Tony Hackens and

190   *Nathan T. Elkins*

Ghislaine Moucharte, 429–433. Louvain-la-Neuve: International Numismatic Commission.

Finley, Moses I. 1975. *The Use and Abuse of History*. New York: Viking Press.

FMRD. 1960–. *Die Fundmünzen der römischen Zeit in Deutschland*. Multiple vols. Berlin and Mainz: Mann and Philip von Zabern.

Gerstenblith, Patty. 2020. Provenience and Provenance Intersecting with International Law in the Market for Antiquities. *North Carolina Journal of International Law* 45 (2): 457–495.

Göbl, Robert. 1987. *Numismatik. Grundriß und wissenschaftliches System*. Munich: Battenberg.

Kersel, Morag M. 2006. From the Ground to the Buyer. In *Archaeology, Cultural Heritage, and the Antiquities Trade*, edited by Neil Brodie, Morag M. Kersel, Christina Luke, and Kathryn Walker Tubb, 188–203. Gainesville: University Press of Florida.

Kraay, Colin M. 1976. *Archaic and Classical Greek Coins*. Los Angeles and Berkeley: University of California Press.

Tompa, Peter K. and Ann Brose. 2005. A Modern Challenge to an Age-Old Pursuit: Can Cultural Patrimony Claims and Coin Collecting Co-Exist? In *Who Owns the Past? Cultural Policy, Cultural Property, and the Law*, edited by Kate Fitz Gibbon, 205–216. New Brunswick: Rutgers University Press/American Council for Cultural Policy.

Urice, Stephen K. and Andrew Adler. 2010. Unveiling the Executive Branch's Extra-legal Cultural Property Policy. *Miami Law Research Paper Series*, Paper No. 20120–20120: 1–44.

Urice, Stephen K. and Andrew Adler. 2011. Resolving the Disjunction between Cultural Property Policy and Law: A Call for Reform. *Rutgers Law Review* 64: 117–163.

U.S. Court of Appeals for the Fourth Circuit of Maryland. 2012. Ancient Coin Collectors Guild v. U.S. Customs and Border Protection, Department of Homeland Security, 801 F. Supp. 2d 382 (D. Md. 2011), aff'd 698 F.3d 171 (4th Circ. 2012).

U.S. Customs and Border Protection. 2020. Baltimore CBP Repatriates Priceless Artifacts to Cyprus Government Officials. Electronic document, https://www.cbp.gov/newsroom/local-media-release/baltimore-cbp-repatriates-priceless-artifacts-cyprus-government.

U.S. Federal District Court of Maryland. 2011. Ancient Coin Collectors Guild v. U.S. Customs and Border Protection, Department of Homeland Security, 801 F. Supp. 2d 382 (D. Md. 2011).

U.S. Supreme Court. 2013. Ancient Coin Collectors Guild v. U.S. Customs and Border Protection, Department of Homeland Security, 801 F. Supp. 2d 382 (D. Md. 2011), aff'd, 698 F. 3d 171 (4th Circ. 2012), cert denied, 133 S. Ct. 1645 (2013).

von Kaenel, Hans-Markus. 1994. Die antike Numismatik und ihr Material. *Schweizer Münzblätter* 44 (173): 1–12.

von Kaenel, Hans-Markus. 1995. La numismatica antica e il suo materiale. *Bollettino di. Numismatica* 13 (1): 213–223.

Walker, Alan S. 1977. The Coin Market Versus the Numismatist, Archaeologist and Art Historian. *Journal of Field Archaeology* 4: 253–258.

Part III

Antiquities Trade in the Cyberworld

7   Plenitudinous

An Analysis of Ancient Coin Sales on eBay

Ute Wartenberg and Barbora Dmitričenko[1]

Art and cultural goods have always been among the more attractive spoils of war. It was, therefore, not surprising to see an increase of looted treasures and antiquities on the market after the war in Syria began in 2011 and then extended into Iraq. Many of the famous sites were systematically ransacked by ISIS such as that of Palmyra in 2015. What should have been a fairly uncontroversial discussion about plundering turned into a battle over whether looting was occurring and if it was, who was looting and benefitting from these activities. Arguably the most important actor in the presumed looting was ISIS (also called Daesh, IS, or ISIL), which was declared a terrorist group by the United States in 2015. A few studies have looked at the extent of looting in Syria and have tried to estimate the impact, both the destruction as well the amount of antiquities sold (Brodie and Sabrine 2018, Al-Azm and Paul 2019). Both authors of this chapter participated in Countering Looting of Antiquities from Syria and Iraq (CLASI), a project organized by the Terrorism, Transnational Crime, and Corruption Center (TraCCC) of George Mason University and funded by the US State Department. Over the course of this project it became rapidly clear that coins were undoubtedly among the most popular archaeological items looted in Syria and Iraq. But exactly how popular was not at all clear. Over the last four years, we began to address this question by examining the coin market, with a focus on eBay in particular, and in this chapter, we are presenting the first set of results of this study. As we shall argue in detail, the market of ancient coins without provenance, offered on eBay, has been growing enormously over the last five years. When this study was finalized, we concluded that the ancient coin market had grown significantly and, by 2020, around 2.5 million ancient coins were being offered on eBay annually, with only a small part having any recorded provenance. These coins were being offered between *c.* \$88–199 million, with actual concluded sales approximating \$26–59 million. This chapter explains the methodology of these results and looks at the background of these sales on eBay, which are far larger than previously imagined. These enormous figures show the need for much tighter regulations of eBay sales, if the numismatic and cultural heritage of the many countries from these coins were looted is to be protected.

DOI: 10.4324/9781003023043-11

194 *Ute Wartenberg and Barbora Dmitričenko*

Coinage in ancient Syria has a long and significant history. First adopted in the fifth century BCE, coinage proliferated in the Hellenistic period (323–31 BCE), and a significant number of mints were established in the region. Excavations at Dura Europos, Al Mina-Tyre, Damascus, Aleppo, Palmyra have produced large numbers of coin finds. This numismatic evidence for such hoards and individual coins of the period before the Romans has been recorded in a detailed study by Frédérique Duyrat, who recorded 360 hoards and additional individual finds from 58 excavated sites (Duyrat 2016). Her work was focused on a slightly larger area than modern Syria and did not take Iraq into account. Nevertheless, it is clear from the data presented in this book that the monetary circulation, reflected by these finds, involved coins from Greece and the entire Mediterranean from the Archaic period (550–480 BCE) onwards. Although coins were minted only in the later Classical period (480–332 BCE) in cities located today in modern Syria, it was clearly a heavily monetized region from the Archaic period onwards. As in other parts of the Achaemenid empire, we find hoards of Athenian tetradrachms, northern-Greek, Cypriote, and many Classical mints, mixed with so-called *Hacksilber* pieces, in this region.[2] During the Hellenistic period, while bronze and other issues are being minted in Syria, many of the coins circulating were from other parts of the Mediterranean. Syria became an important province of the Romans as early as 64 BCE, which was an important border zone against their fight against the Parthians. Roman imperial coinage and provincial issues of the various cities in Syria are extremely common. The evidence for coinage and its circulation in Roman Syria was studied by Kevin Butcher, who emphasized that most hoards contain silver, not bronze coins.[3]

The problem that we face in recognizing coins with a suspected Syrian provenance is that the types of ancient coins are not specific to Syria. Most coins of these series are also circulating in Jordan, Israel, Lebanon, but also Turkey, and even Egypt or other parts of the Mediterranean. There are some series minted in Syria which circulated only in this region, such as for example the very rare coins of Queen Zenobia (born *c.* 240 CE) and her son Vaballathus. These appeared in significant numbers on the coin market after 2010; the same phenomenon is apparent for the group of wreathed silver tetradrachm of various Ionian mints of the second century (Wartenberg Kagan 2015). Brodie also reported on the increased number of provincial silver tetradrachms of Emesa under Caracalla and Marcrinus in the beginning of the third century CE (Brodie 2017).

Evidence for extensive looting in Syria is evident from the photos and firsthand reports from ancient sites, even if we do not know exactly what is being looted or where. Interestingly, Syria was at times given as a provenance for coin hoards from Turkey, since the import of coins from Syria into European countries and the US was generally seen as unproblematic with such a provenance.[4] Here the most famous example is a hoard, supposedly found in the mid-1990s near Karkemish, which contained a number of Athenian decadrachms, which was recorded initially as the "North of Aleppo" find. Technically correct, it was supposed to give the impression that the country of origin was Syria, not Turkey.[5] Nowadays, the focus on Syria and Iraq has, however, diverted the attention from looting activities in other countries such as Egypt or Turkey, for which we have observed a remarkable increase in new, unprovenanced coins. Since many ancient coins were used for long-distance trade or payment of mercenaries, they often circulated far from their place of origin and are found today in areas that can be thousands of miles from their original place of production. This distinguishes them from many other archaeological objects, which often have more specific local characteristics and are more specific to a particular culture or region. Since the country-based approach to coins is somewhat difficult to research, an alternative approach of researching the question of illegally exported coins needs to be developed. While it is hard to know the find context of most coins – and of an individual coin even more so – in order to determine illegal activities and looting of coins in any given country, one would gain a better understanding of the totality of the problem of looted coins today if one could estimate the total number of new ancient coins entering the market. Although ambitious in scope, we decided to try to tackle this question and, as a secondary goal of this chapter, we wanted to test a method of estimating the sales volume of this market, which could be used for similar studies in the future.

Because of its increasing popularity and its open structure, we chose eBay as a basis of our analysis and included relevant examples from Amazon. While we initially researched a wide variety of topics (quantifying the sales volume, networks of sellers; the proportion of uncleaned vs cleaned coins; the US site vs other eBay countries; and counterfeit coins), we soon realized that this project was far too ambitious for this contribution. This chapter, therefore, focuses on quantifying the sale of ancient coins on eBay and initial conclusions based on these figures.[6] Already in 2007, Elkins reported the sale of ancient coins and looked at eBay in a small study, which gave a first overview on this subject (Elkins 2008). In order to better understand the nature of the market, we monitored the extent of the online sales on eBay during a three-week period in March 2016. We recorded all ancient coin sales, with an initial focus on uncleaned coins. The data sets allow us to analyze not only the type of coins sold (cleaned vs. uncleaned; cheap vs. expensive) but also the countries from which various sellers operate. By using open access data provided by eBay or Amazon, for example in reviews of sellers, the motivation of buyers and profit margins of such operations become more transparent. The evidence from such online sales of poorly preserved ancient coins illustrates vividly that material that was once hard to sell now finds a good market and in turn encourages looting on a scale previously unseen. When it comes to global online sales platforms, similar regulation is needed such as those for ivory or other illegal items that are not permitted to be sold there.[7] For antiquities, the situation appears to change, since studies such as that by the Athar Project have been able to highlight how Facebook has enabled the trafficking of illegal antiquities. The executive report of the Athar Project for 2019 sums up concisely the situation: "Today, Facebook offers a veritable digital toolbox for traffickers to utilize, including photo and video uploads, live streaming, disappearing 'Stories,' mechanisms, and encrypted messaging. Facebook is the perfect platform for a one-stop-shop black market."[8] In the summer of 2020, as a result of mounting pressure, Facebook announced that it would prohibit the sale of historical artifacts. Although the definition should include ancient coins, it is not clear how effective and inclusive this new policy will be.

Before the advent of eCommerce, coins were sold in public auctions or directly by dealers. Until the early 1980s, there were a few major auction houses in the US and Europe which organized two or three major auctions a year (to mention just a few: Bank Leu, Münzen und Medaillen, Vinchon, or Sotheby's and Christie's). Smaller businesses existed as well, and were usually run by one or two people attending auctions and finding interesting coins for their clients. Sometimes referred to as "vest pocket dealers", such individuals were often exceptionally well-versed in numismatics and would travel widely to find coins to sell. Before World War II, Rome, Istanbul, and Athens had extensive antiquity dealer networks, whereas by the 1960s, Switzerland, London, and Munich began to develop as major centers of the international antiquities trade, of which ancient coins formed a significant part. In such places, many of the major coin hoards from Italy, Turkey, Greece, and other Mediterranean countries would be brought by a small group of well-connected individuals to dealers in the main centers in Switzerland, Germany, and England. The hoards that provided these coins were supposedly found accidentally during construction or by farmers.[9]

The flow of illegally excavated material was relatively small until the 1970s, when metal detectors, which were used on battlefields for mine detections during World War II, began to be used by treasure hunters and looters. Metal detecting became increasingly popular in countries such as the UK, where it has been legal as long as finds were reported; this is true for other European countries but a variety of rules apply for licenses and other permits. It is noticeable that by the 1980s many more ancient coins without prior provenance entered the market than previously. Many of these coins were known to have come from hoards, and occasionally they were recorded by numismatists to preserve a record.[10] Of course, parcels of single finds, accumulated over some time and different places, became also much more common. Although almost all countries in the Mediterranean and elsewhere have had legislation in place for decades to prevent the export of any such cultural material, there were few cases in which governments actively pursued the return of coins.[11] On the whole, numismatic auctions throughout the twentieth century featured largely expensive coins for wealthy collectors. It was a rarefied field. There are no precise estimates of the total number of ancient Greek coins known before 2000 when coinarchives.com began to record numismatic auction sales, but resources such as the card files of ancient coins at the American Numismatic Society in New York and at the Institute of Numismatics in Vienna allow an estimate of at least 650,000 coins that were published in printed auctions before then.[12] Roman coins are undoubtedly much more numerous and exist in the millions. Projects such as *Die Fundmünzen der römischen Zeit in Deutschland*, in which excavation coins of the Roman period are published, lists over 300,000 pieces; similar numbers of Roman coins are found and published in Britain, where hoards of thousands of coins are not unusual.[13] The recent online publication of Richard Schaefer's Roman Republican coinage project has *c.* 150,000 coins.[14] In short, there are undoubtedly millions of ancient coins preserved today.

All this is not to say that there was not always a market for small, inexpensive coins. Coins such as silver fractions and bronzes, or simply poorly preserved coins, were – and are – not worth adding to a printed catalogue and were sold in coin shops or offered at coin fairs. The change that came with the introduction of digital imaging, the Internet, and the establishment of online sales platforms such as eBay was dramatic for the field of numismatics. Suddenly, it offered easy market access for a much wider spectrum of customers across the globe. Online transactions became a cheaper and faster option for buyers, although initially only inexpensive coins were sold in various online auctions. Even more significantly, the online market became flooded with coins that, due to their small size, can be easily delivered by mail or courier to virtually any international destination. The popularity of online sales has been growing, and recent technological advancements such as digital communication and social media continue to refashion the trade even more.

Arguably the largest and most diverse platform for the sale of ancient coins is eBay. In September 1995, in the early days of the Internet, a project called AuctionWeb was founded by Pierre Omidyar. In the following few years, he and his first full-time employee Jeffrey Skoll developed this startup initiative into a successful online marketplace that is today known as eBay.[15] At the time eBay went public in 1998, it mainly served as an auction site with a focus on collectibles. Since its launch, the biggest strength of the site has been its global reach: objects from all over the world can be purchased as long as both the buyer and the seller have Internet access and funds. Online payments were facilitated by PayPal, which was founded in 1998 as well and owned by eBay from 2002–2015. Today, eBay has grown into an emporium of 1.5 billion listed objects and a GMV (Gross Merchandise Volume) of US $27.1B in the second quarter of 2020.[16] The popular sale strategy for the seemingly infinite assortment of goods gradually shifted from auctions towards an easier and speedier "Buy Now" option. This, in turn, led to the development that, as of 2020, second quarter, over 81% of items sold are now brand-new.

One of eBay's strategies allows buyers to use the site free of charge, whereas sellers are charged a variety of small fees – 10% of a purchase price on average – once an item is sold. In terms of collectibles, this fee compares very favourably to almost any other auction, whether run by traditional auction houses or other online sites. eBay's business model thus encourages the collecting of low-end items, which are typically of no significant interest in a conventional market. The eBay policy for collectibles lists some very general rules intending to prevent the sale of counterfeits or wrongly described material, but actual sales are predominantly regulated through buyer-seller relationships.[17] Reviews, through which buyers and sellers openly express their satisfaction or complaints, hold this system in place. In theory, only the top-rated sellers survive and the "bad apples" are discarded. Selling art and coins usually rely on the expertise of the seller, but eBay has turned this relationship around. When buying on eBay, the principle of *caveat emptor* rules: i.e., the recipient needs to be expert enough to judge their purchases. Although eBay specifically states that selling counterfeits is illegal, the problem of counterfeit coins, so-called museum imitation coins, or other replicas for sale on eBay is evident to any specialist. Here, it is often a fine line how coins are described, and coins described like genuine coins are obvious counterfeits. For this chapter, it was not possible to consider this problem in any detail, although it is undoubtedly true that counterfeiting and smuggling coins often go hand in hand.[18]

The substantial increase of online transactions on eBay resulted in a shift towards massive sales of large quantities of low-end items. An important aspect to ancient coins, which is often neglected, is that these represent archaeological objects recovered through excavations from the ground or the seabed. Authorized archaeological operations, official declarations of recovered objects, conservation procedures, as well as the exportation and collecting of this type of material are increasingly coordinated by sets of national and international laws in most countries. Unauthorized excavations, handling, and export of archaeological finds are considered criminal activities not only in regions of the former Roman Empire but in most countries of the world. Despite heavy export limitations, some countries (for example Israel, UK, and Italy) issue export permits for ancient artifacts of a lesser importance. In terms of global movement of antiquities, in the US, for instance, various countries have entered Memoranda of Understanding (MOUs) with the United States government to control the import of such objects. Despite these rules, the market in the United States and elsewhere appears to be growing, and this chapter shows the extent and mechanisms of the continuous growth by analyzing sales on eBay.

Remarkably, not much recent data regarding the size, scope, and nature of the coin market has been published, which prevents us from mapping and, ultimately, targeting illegal and unethical activities in this sphere.[19] As mentioned above, Elkins undertook an important study of the size of the ancient coin market in 2007, in which he analyzed data from eBay and Vcoins (Elkins 2008: 2–4). For Vcoins, he reported 73,000 lots offered at $14.5 million; on eBay 5,000 to 5,300 lots of ancient coins sold per week. Elkins estimated that *c.* 260,000–280,000 ancient coins were offered per year and concluded that, "the trafficking in undocumented coins is clearly a multi-million-dollar industry in the U.S. and Canada alone" (Elkins 2008: 4). Today one of the problems that those interested in cultural property issues face is the lack of properly documented figures about the size of the illegal antiquities market overall. This problem of the size of the antiquities market has been highlighted in a report by the RAND Corporation published in 2020. It points out that the figures of billions of dollars of sales of illegal antiquities, which are commonly found in the press and on blogs cannot be easily substantiated.[20] As a result of an extensive study, in which various aspects of the market were analyzed, the authors of the RAND Report provide two different estimates for the market of antiquities in their study: on p. 88, in the summary of their key findings, one reads of a market of "tens of millions of US dollars per year" for the market of illicit antiquities, whereas p. 84 states that, "our aggregate data suggest that the market for all antiquities, both licit and illicit, is on the order of, at most, a few hundred million dollars annually rather than the billions of dollars claimed in some other estimates." It is clear that a distinction is made between the illicit and the legal trade, but how these figures are computed is not as clear as one would wish. For the subject of our chapter, the size of the coin market on eBay, the question whether coins were included in the figures presented in the RAND report, is obviously of significance. When reading the report, one gains the distinct impression that coins were treated as antiquities and thus included, since coin dealers and their operations were clearly analyzed and are discussed frequently. Even at a first glance, the numbers for so-called illicit material (i.e. with no earlier provenance) appears curiously low if ancient coins were included in this number. Hence, we approached James Marrone, one of the authors of the report, and we are most grateful to him and the other authors for clarifying that coins are not included in the overall quantitative analysis. In an email, he responded:

> First, the RAND estimate of the aggregate antiquities market does not include coins, but this was not made clear in the report. We offer a very broad definition of antiquities on Page 2, footnote 5, which conceivably could include coins. The fact that we did not include the coin market – which is clearly much larger and more dynamic – in our systematic aggregation of total market size was never made explicit. And because we included images and references to illicit coin sales throughout, it certainly became ambiguous whether coins were included in our aggregate estimates. [... .] In the end, we agree that the numismatic market appears to be much larger and more active than the art and artifacts market that we studied, but we did not have the appropriate data to allow us to estimate its size. We should have been more clear that our number on page 88 excludes coins, especially since we do use coins throughout the rest of the report as case studies, in our dark web search terms, and anecdotally with reference to smuggling.[21]

The RAND report makes it clear that a full analysis of the market of ancient coins should be undertaken. As Brodie has also shown in Chapter 1, an assessment of the overall coin market would be valuable since there is clear evidence for the sale of looted coins from Syria, but too few random examples to allow researchers to construct a wider picture.

Methodology

Because of the exceptionally large volume of ancient coins being offered for sale and its open access, eBay offers an ideal setting for this type of study. The methodology applied for this chapter was simple. The US version of the site was strategically monitored and recorded for a period of three weeks in March 2016. The data was collected manually between 6–24 March 2016 four times a day (12 AM, 9 AM, 2 PM, 7 PM); no data was collected on 7 March at 2 PM; on 16 March at 9 AM; on 19 March at 2 PM and 7 PM; on 21 March at 2 PM; and at 23 March at 9 AM. On 2 June 2020, just before the completion of this chapter, a set of current data was collected for some categories in order to assess the change over the four-year period. The data was recorded in spreadsheets. These sheets were organized for categories such as uncleaned coins, lots, coin series, coins sorted by different metal as well as price categories. In July 2020, we noticed that eBay greatly improved its search functions for ancient coins, which allowed for a much more accurate search result for ancient coins, even within various categories. We recorded a set of data for late July as well, which is discussed below. Additionally, Amazon, which offers genuine ancient coins for sale, was used to assess the motivations of buyers of such uncleaned coins through their feedback, sometimes in extensive comments.

To obtain the widest possible scope of data within the limited period of time, the monitoring of eBay coin sales and auctions has been approached from two angles.

First, numbers for all coins, ancient coins, and lots were recorded. Ancient Greek and Roman coins were recorded respectively. Monitored subsets of these two major categories can be viewed by lots, uncleaned coins, type of material, and pricing ranges. These categories were accessed on eBay by manually recording the data into spreadsheets. Since the various categories on eBay are often based on sellers entering the relevant details (metal or type of coinage), the overall figures for total ancient coins on sale are not always entirely consistent as the tables below illustrate. This is partially because certain information categories are left blank by sellers. To put it differently, some coins are listed simply as ancient coins, but no further definitions, which results in much higher overall numbers than all subcategories being totalled.

As a secondary subset of our study, we observed closely 818 individual sales and auctions, which we document in two spreadsheets as well as pdfs of each transaction. Our main aim was to document details on such transactions and obverse patterns, but most importantly see how many sales were actually concluded in the mass of coins on offer. Since eBay does not post results or archive any sales, one has to rely on estimates, and we opted for an actual observation of a variety of different sellers and auctions.

Findings

Table 7.1 shows readings for a total number of coins that reached a maximum of 1,016,877 listings during the period of monitoring in 2016, with an average of 996,996 coins (this figure is based on the search entry "coins" under the category of "coins and paper money"). Under this group "coins", one finds mainly coins, in lots, but also occasionally related objects. Over the last years, we regularly checked the figures and in June 2020, when we recorded another set for comparison, this figure was 1,073,571 coins (2 June 2020), which did not represent a significant increase overall. The figure was at times much higher, reaching close to 1.7 million in October 2017. While the fluctuations of these numbers are of interest, it needs to be kept in mind that the listings include large quantities of modern collectible and bullion coins, which are beyond the scope of this study. The category of *coin lots* are discussed below in more detail.

The dataset of ancient coins presented below is divided into Roman Republican, Roman Imperial, and Greek Coins. Within the ancient coins listing, Roman coins are the largest group. This is hardly surprising since in sheer mintage figures, Roman coinage is among the largest in world history. Just for the imperial period (27 BCE–476 CE) 42,750 types are known, many of which were produced in multiple styles and die-pairs; even a conservative estimate would indicate that well over 100 million coins, but probably many more, were minted, of which easily several million Roman coins survive today. A project collecting known and recorded hoards of the period has identified over 7,400 hoards, with over 2.5 million coins.[23]

During the three weeks of monitoring, the number of single Roman coins grew slightly by 563 coins to a total of 15,944 coins, and the number of Roman lots increased by 38 listings to 701. While monitoring the lots, we noticed more fluctuation in the listing of Roman lots than in other categories.

Table 7.1 Overall coins and lots[22]

	All coins	Coin lots	Greek	Greek lot	Roman	Roman lot
June 2020	1,073,571	62,488	25,254	501	15,798	860
Average March 2016	996,996	42,837	14,648	167	15,571	657
Maximum March 2016	1,016,877	43,777	14,534	162	15,940	707
Final count 24 March	1,016,877	43,153	14,477	157	15,944	701

202   Ute Wartenberg and Barbora Dmitričenko

It is hard to determine whether this is due to sales of lots being replenished by new lots. It is also noteworthy that the number of individual Roman coin listings for 2020 was actually lower than in 2016 (15,798 coins offered). When narrowing down into series within the Roman group, the following tables show the distribution by metal within the two main series (Tables 7.2–7.3 for Roman Republic and Roman Imperial coins by metal). The identification of the metal is not always consistently marked, which has to be kept in mind when assessing these figures. On the Roman end, there is nothing surprising: the majority of coins are base metal (bronze or copper, billon), but silver is also common. Gold is rare, in fact much more so than in printed auction catalogues.

The availability of less valuable items confirms the role of eBay as a seller of low-end items in 2016. Looking at the most recent 2020 figures in the Roman imperial series, it is obvious that all categories have grown significantly, just as in the Greek series (Table 7.4). For that category, the highest number recorded for the 19 days in 2016 were 14,784 coins and 201 lots respectively. The low volume of listings as well as the steady decline points towards much less activity than in the Roman areas. In 2020, the number of Greek coins listings had increased significantly, including coins of much higher value. We will return to this issue below, when we discuss value and pricing. Overall, the figures show an upward trend of ancient coins offered on eBay across all categories in ancient coinage.

Table 7.2 Republican coins by metal

	Bronze	*Copper*	*Gold*	*Silver*	*Unspecified*	*TOTAL*
March 2016	98	–	4	566	–	668
2 June 2020	151	9	5	879	301	1,345

Table 7.3 Roman imperial coins by metal

	Billon	*Bronze*	*Copper*	*Gold*	*Silver*	*Silvered Bronze*	*Unspecified*	*TOTAL*
March 2016	540	4,471	745	69	3,464	42	–	**9,331**
2 June 2020	2,756	6,210	2,843	152	4,832	138	7337	**26,686**

Table 7.4 Greek coins by metals

	Bronze	*Copper*	*Electrum*	*Gold*	*Silver*	*Unspecified*	*TOTAL*
March 2016	876	76	16	35	1,466	–	2,469
2 June 2020	2,629	188	63	88	2,815	6,244	12,027

Analysis of Ancient Coin Sales on eBay 203

The data on uncleaned coins and lots collected for 2016 and 2020 suggests an enormous increase over the last four years (Table 7.5). Although it is possible that there are some differences in the eBay classification by buyers, we observed over the years a marked increase in coins that have not been cleaned or which are deliberately left encrusted.

Under the term "uncleaned coins" hides a peculiar group, which is unusual for the numismatic market. In principle, these are coins, looted in source countries, of insignificant monetary value, which have not been cleaned to any extent; silver or gold coins appear rarely under this category. Such encrusted, low-value coins are often sold directly in large quantities from countries where they were found, being smuggled or directly shipped to the US or elsewhere. In a 2012 article, Elkins reported the case of a Bulgarian dealer living in New Jersey, who was selling ancient lots, largely uncleaned, as a wholesale operation. One of the shipments to him was seized and contained over 60 kg of uncleaned coins (Elkins 2012: 99–100).

Uncleaned coins sold in large lots at competitive prices are a relatively new phenomenon on the coin market. Before the internet, such coins, largely worn Roman coins of the third and fourth centuries, were mainly offered at coin shows. The idea behind selling those uncleaned coins is clearly one of treasure hunting, since below the encrustation, which is supposed to come off with acid and other chemicals sold as well, a rarity might surface. Their condition is of secondary importance to the buyers, who purchase them

Table 7.5 Uncleaned ancient coins and lots

	All uncleaned coins	All uncleaned lots	Uncleaned Greek	Uncleaned Greek lot	Uncleaned Roman	Uncleaned Roman lot
Average March 2016	105	127	21	<1	98	89
July 2020	1,047	292	340	42	879	196

Figure 7.1 Sale of uncleaned ancient coin on Amazon.com

either as educational gifts for children or because they enjoy cleaning the coins themselves. Oddly, these Roman coins often have a high lead content – up to 30% in some series – which should be a warning to anyone marketing to children under a certain age. However, neither eBay nor Amazon seems to be concerned by liabilities in this area. In fact, such Roman coins are treated like a modern toy, categorized as "discontinued by manufacturer" and with manufacturer recommended age as "12 months and up" despite the obvious choking hazard and dangerous metal content.

The coins in Figure 7.1 appear clearly freshly excavated, and some sellers such as Ancient Coin House (via Amazon) advertises this fact: "The coins are straight from the excavators", and the photo of a pile of Roman coins states in red letters "freshly dug." The fact that these coins are newly discovered, not sorted by experts, but fresh out of the ground is part of their appeal for their customer base. Legal issues seem of no concern, but a few sellers emphasize that their coins are legally exported, such as a certain eBay vendor who sells "uncleaned and unsorted coins from Israel"; a copy of an export permit from the Israel Antiquities Authority is shown with some coins (Figures 7.2–7.3). A number of sellers are based directly in source countries, in particular in Israel, Austria, and around the Balkans, where the export of such objects is in all likelihood illegal.

Because of the system of extensive written reviews and answers on Amazon, which does not exist on eBay, we can occasionally gain some insight into the expectations of buyers or their knowledge about these coins. On Amazon (listing accessed on 2 June 2020), the question "Hello, where are the coins from?" posed on October 13, 2017, received the following answer from an Amazon buyer: "Either this is the stupidest question I've ever heard or the coins are obviously from somewhere else. Read the title it says ancient Roman coins!" What is a perfectly legitimate question receives a somewhat

Figure 7.2 Uncleaned ancient coins from Israel on eBay

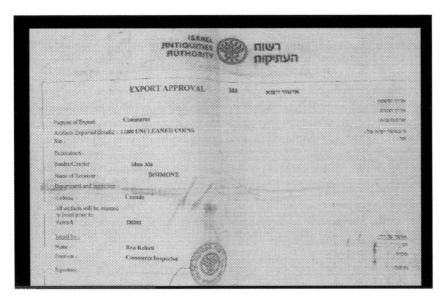

Figure 7.3 Export license accompanying uncleaned ancient coins

arrogant answer which ignores the issue. Whether this is done deliberately in order to deter further enquiries about provenance or whether this is simply sheer ignorance is difficult to determine. In a different January 22, 2013 review posted by the same buyer his one-star rating was accompanied with the following text:

> I bought 2 uncleaned Ancient Roman Coins at $1.90 a piece and it was a waste of money. The shipping made it worse, I have spent at least 8 hours scrubbing these coins and they are unsalvagable [sic]. If these coins were under a dollar or I got 20 coins for what I paid it might be worth it.

Other reviews illustrate the operations in place to uncover a coin with a design, but when the coin is worn it results in a poor review for the sellers. While numbers of such sales of uncleaned coins on eBay look modest in comparison to other categories discussed here, they are nevertheless of interest to our study. The fact that even totally worn coins attract buyers, simply as objects to be cleaned, has increased the market significantly. Such amateur archaeology in the US clearly encourages looters in source countries such as Bulgaria and Turkey, as well as Iraq and Syria in their activities since almost any metal object can be sold online in 2020. Overall, it is noteworthy that the vast majority of ancient coins sold on both eBay and Amazon had no known provenance or any indication where they were found.

206   *Ute Wartenberg and Barbora Dmitričenko*

Overall Numbers and Prices

One of the more intriguing questions of our study was to understand how much money the sale of ancient coins produces on an annual basis. This question turns out to be more difficult to answer than it initially appeared. We used two sets of data based on slightly varying searches carried out in 2016 and 2020. When conducting the 2020 check, we realized that our data from 2016 only captured individual, properly catalogued coins, which underestimated the number of ancient coins on eBay.

Dataset 1: 2016

In order to calculate the overall Greek and Roman coin numbers based on our 2016 dataset (see Tables 7.6–7.7), we used pre-set eBay price ranges from $0–$20, $20–$100, $100–$500, $500–$1,000, and over $1,000 to analyze the categories of Roman Republican (300 BCE–27 CE), Roman Imperial (27 BCE–476 CE), Roman Provincial (100 CE–400 CE), and ancient Greek coins. In Table 7.6, the average number of coins based on the number over the monitored period is used; in Table 7.7, we calculated the overall amount per category as well as the total number of coin sales.

Not surprisingly, coins selling for $20–$500 dominate all categories; however, a healthy number of coins listed for less than $20. This is hardly surprising since traditionally more expensive items are sold through established

Table 7.6 Number of ancient coins per series and per price category (March 2016)

	<$20	>$20	>$100	>$500	>$1,000	Total number of coins
Roman Republic	115	232	466	80	41	934
Roman Imperial	4,116	8,085	4,080	311	155	16,747
Roman Provincial	295	1,398	1,001	65	23	2,782
Ancient Greek	670	3,677	2,566	465	355	7,733
Total number per category	**5,196**	**13,392**	**8,113**	**921**	**574**	**28,196**

Table 7.7 Dollar amount of ancient coins per series and price category (March 2016)

	<$20	>$20	>$100	>$500	>$1000	Total
Roman Republic	$2,300	$4,640	$46,600	$40,000	$41,000	$134,540
Roman Imperial	$82,320	$161,700	$408,000	$155,500	$155,000	$962,520
Roman Provincial	$5,900	$27,960	$100,100	$32,500	$23,000	$189,460
Ancient Greek	$13,400	$73,540	$256,600	$232,500	$355,000	$931,040
Total	$103,920	$267,840	$811,300	$460,500	$574,000	$2,217,560

Analysis of Ancient Coin Sales on eBay   207

auction houses. Within individual categories, we see that Greek coins had the largest number of expensive coins over $1,000. In this category, a few dealers offered expensive, often wildly overpriced Greek silver or gold coins. Often such coins were available for months after they were posted. These were, however, exceptions and the overall picture that we saw from the pricing of ancient coins is that eBay offered cheap coins in large numbers.

The overall volume of coins for sale by dollar amount for the period of almost three weeks was estimated, based on the total sale of individual coins in all four categories at $2,217,560. A closer look at the data in Table 7.7 shows that Greek and the Roman imperial coins represented over 85% of the total, with each category over $900,000. Within the Greek coins, some 355 coins dominate the picture, and here, we observed a few high-end coins, some with old provenances, at very high prices. It is not clear if these coins ever sold. In the Roman imperial section, coins between $100–$500 represent the largest group overall.

In order to assess the volume of sale of coin lots (Table 7.1), we have used figures of an average number of 167 Greek and 657 Roman lots, which we multiplied by a low average of $50 per lot ($41,200 for both ancient lots), although we saw many lots for sale as $100 or more. However, the term "lot" was not always consistently applied to a larger group of coins, and even individual coins were offered as a "lot." How the figure of "uncleaned coin lots" fits into these numbers was even more difficult to determine, since these uncleaned coins are potentially counted under Greek or Roman as well. We have left the category of uncleaned lots out altogether in order to avoid double counting material.

Using the numbers provided in Table 7.1, which lists a total of 40,000 individual coins and *c.* 1,350 lots for the month period monitored from 6–24 March 2016, ancient coins totalling at least $2,258,760 were offered. It should be kept in mind that this estimate is based on data collected in just under three weeks within a single month.

We further wanted to assess how many coins actually sold of these groups and for how much. This problem is much more difficult to determine. Initially, we decided to narrow down to a specific group of sales and auctions in order to document seller and buyer behaviour. As mentioned above in the discussion of our methodology, in the course of this participant observation we documented 818 sales and auctions in more detail. During the period of 19 days, 39.7% (325) of all ancient items were successfully sold. The Roman section has a higher sale rate with 41.2 % (301) of sales; only 27.5% (24) of Greek items sold. 400 items (313 lots and 87 single coins), went for sale as uncleaned, of which a total of 190 (170 lots and 20 single) were successful. This represents a total of 47.5% successfully closed sales. These numbers confirm in principle the picture of eBay as a place to sell unprovenanced or uncleaned coins, where the predominance of Roman coins is hardly surprising. It is also clear that many of the high-end items offered in the Greek series are perhaps more for show. If we look at calculating overall sales for

208   *Ute Wartenberg and Barbora Dmitričenko*

ancient coins based on the subset in Table 7.1, we will assume that only 20% of Greek coins offered sell. For the Roman section 40% of all listings sold. The formula applied does not take into account that coins continue to be added on a continuous basis but assumes, for a simpler calculation, that coins sell after three weeks and are then replaced by an identical number. This underestimates in all probability that actual number of sales.

Based on these figures, Table 7.8 represents the estimates for 2016.

While harvesting data through pre-set eBay categories in 2016, we realized that the numbers of coins and sale numbers for 2016 clearly underrepresent the picture of ancient coins on eBay. As Table 7.1 shows, both Roman and Greek coins make up almost 40,000, whereas the numbers provided by the subcategories only add up to 28,000 coins. As noted earlier, not all sellers properly categorize their coins, perhaps because they are not knowledgeable or simply do not care. We also left out the uncleaned coins, which are offered in very large numbers. Overall, the main issue was how to capture this huge mass of coins that was not well organized. When searching "ancient coins" alone, other objects would show up, which led us to our very conservative approach where we were sure that we only used actual Greek and Roman coins as listed in the subcategories.

Dataset 2: July 2020

When reviewing the figures of 2016 in the final stages of writing this chapter, we became aware that the number of all categories within "ancient coins" had grown very significantly (Tables 7.2–7.6). Whether this was a result of the searches operating differently on eBay or an actual growth was hard to determine at first, although looking at the actual coins for sale, we noted a much higher number of expensive coins. In order to set our figures of coins and sales of 2016 in an updated context, we decided to run a different search for ancient coins in July 2020, when a variety of new search functions became available on eBay (such as sorting by emperors, denominations, or date ranges). Under the general search of "ancient coins", we found on a regular

Table 7.8 Estimate of number of Greek and Roman coins sold on eBay (March 2016)

Number of ancient Greek and Roman coins on offer in 19 days	*28,196 coins*
Number of ancient Greek and Roman coins on offer over one year	535,724 coins
Amount of ancient Greek and Roman coins on offer in 19 days	$2,217,560
Ancient Greek and Roman coins offered annually	$42,133,640
Ancient Greek and Roman coins sold in 19 days	$700,816
Ancient Greek and Roman coins sold annually	$13,315,504

Analysis of Ancient Coin Sales on eBay   209

basis over 130,000 coins on offer at any given moment (Table 7.9). It should be noted that this group included Byzantine and so-called "other ancient" coins, which appeared to include all sorts of coins, including yet more Roman coins.

In 2020 sellers are able to categorize their coins in much more detail. I t was also noteworthy that both in the Roman Imperial and in the Greek sections, almost 50 coins in each section on offer were over $10,000. Pre-set prizing categories used in this analysis were also different from 2016. The trend towards higher priced coins, many of them without any prior provenance was evident; many of the coins were also on offer from various foreign countries such as Spain, Latvia, and in particular France.[24] We used the pre-set eBay division for pricing of $13 or less; $13–50; and over $15 to calculate the overall sales on eBay for this grouping of ancient coins. It should be

Table 7.9 Number of ancient coins, with subdivisions provided by eBay, accessed on 30 July 2020

Type	Number of Coins Total
Ancient coins (total)	134,27
Divided into:	
Roman imperial	56,650
Greek coins	25,506
Byzantine	10,402
Roman provincial	9,580
Roman republic	4,563
Other ancient	6,387

Table 7.10 Estimate of number of ancient coins sold on eBay (based on figures accessed on 30 July 2020)*

	Number of Coins	Total of Low-end ($)	Total of High-end ($)
Ancient coins over $50	81,552	$4,077,600	$8,155,200
Ancient coins $13–50	45,058	$585,754	$2,207,842
Ancient coins under $13	9976	$9,976	$119,712
Total number and dollar value range	**136,586**	**$4,673,330**	**$10,482,754**

* Prices for low- and high-end are calculated by using the following numbers: coins over $50 use an average of $50 (low) and $100 (high); coins $13–$50 use $13 (low) and $49 (high); coins under $12 use $1 (low) and $12 (high). Note that some coins might be counted in two categories, which would explain the discrepancy between all coins added up (136,586) and the search for ancient coins alone (134,273).

210   *Ute Wartenberg and Barbora Dmitričenko*

noted that the total number given was smaller than what was added up in the three categories. We applied the same formula to this number as for the 2016 dataset, but adjusted to an overall sale percentage of 30%. The results of coins on offer and coins sold are listed in Table 7.11.

The overall sales figures in these two datasets (2016 and 2020) differ dramatically. The explanation lies in the two different search methodologies applied. While in 2016 we were concerned to capture ancient coins within the identified groups in order not to count non-numismatic materials, we were unaware that we underreported the actual number of ancient coins sold on eBay. By 2020 eBay improved its search categories, which now allows for the capture of all ancient coins and separation into Greek, Roman, Byzantine, other ancients, including lots and uncleaned coins. As mentioned, the improved search functions now allow the identification of groups of coins with a simple click for very specific categories: for example, Roman imperial coins can be searched by emperor and by year which allows a very targeted search for people interested in specific items. Here eBay provides an impressive functionality that is not known for other, more specialized online platforms such as Sixbid or Vcoins. Although this system depends on an informed seller (who knows their coins and describes them correctly), it appears from a casual inspection that this is the case for a remarkable number of coins. A second reason for the much higher number is simply that much more coins are on offer than in 2016. This is particularly noteworthy in the areas of more expensive coins (over $500), which are often certified by Numismatic Guaranty Corporation, a grading service.

For the whole of 2020, we estimate that around 2.5 million ancient coins might be offered on eBay (data collection ended in July 2020). The sale of ancient coins on offer for that year can be estimated to fall between $88 million and $199 million; the actual concluded sales (named GMV by eBay for growth merchandise value) of $26 million to $59 million is not as surprising as it would initially appear.

In comparison to other antiquities, largely illicit or fake, sold on eBay, the figures for ancient coins show the strength of this segment of the market.

Table 7.11 Based on Dataset 2: July 2020

Number of ancient coins on offer in July 2020 – high figure	$10,492,710
Number of ancient coins on offer in July 2020 – low figure	$4,673,330
Number of ancient coins over one year – high figure	$199,361,490
Number of ancient coins over one year – low figure	$88,793,270
Number of ancient coins sold in July 2020 – high figure @ 30%	$3,147,813
Number of ancient coins sold in July 2020 – low figure @ 30%	$1,401,999
Number of ancient coins sold one year – high figure	$59,808,447
Number of ancient coins sold one year – low figure	$26,637,981

When contrasted with antiquities, similar numbers can be found on eBay, although from our observation of such pieces, the number of fake objects appears much higher than in the coin section. The authors of the RAND Report investigated the sale of Roman antiquities on eBay in some detail. For July 2018, some 916 sellers offered 11,896 items, with annualized sale value of $3,564,068. Interestingly, the average sale per transaction was $48, with a median figure of $25 (Sargent et al. 2020: 79). Although only Roman antiquities are covered, this group is among the larger ones, but if compared to the numbers provided in Tables 7.6 and 7.7 (for 2016) and Table 7.9 (2020), it is clear how relatively weak the antiquities market is comparison to the Roman coins market. Set against other, non-archaeological items, ancient coins appear to be a surprisingly strong category. Other popular American collectibles, however, such as baseball cards, comic books, dolls, and toys (for example American girl dolls have over 85,000 entries alone) have much higher number than the current figure of ancient coins, a fact that needs to be kept in mind in the eBay context. It is also likely that due to the COVID-19 pandemic, a few more people are selling their coins online. For eBay as a whole this strong upward trend in sales was noted, with a reported increase for the second quarter of 2020 of its total, worldwide GMV, to $27.1B, a growth rate of 26% from the previous quarter.[25]

One can set these numbers from eBay against those of one of the bigger auction houses specializing in ancient and medieval coins: Classical Numismatic Group, one of the leading firms in the US and Europe, stated in a press release from 2015 that it had sold more than $200 million at auction in a span of ten years, with annual sales of about 20,000 coins.[26] In July 2020, CNG advertised on its website that it sold 341,434 items for a total of $341,415,265.[27] Some of the items sold were coins that are not ancient, since medals, medieval coins, small antiquities, and books are also auctioned. However, the lion's share are probably ancient coins, and CNG's sale of ancient coins over the period of almost 20 years is probably over $250 million. Looking at the CNG auctions, it is obvious that the larger feature auctions contain more expensive and provenanced coins. What is significant about the numbers that the eBay study provides are the enormous numbers of unprovenanced, recently looted coins that enter the market via this platform. Furthermore, it is clear that the numbers of such illegally excavated coins are growing fast, not only on eBay, but also on other platforms such as eBay in other countries, Etsy, Vcoins, Facebook and other websites. How widespread and clearly profitable the business of selling uncleaned coins has become shows that there are companies exclusively dedicated to selling only uncleaned coins and artifacts. When we look at the eBay figures of 2016 and 2020, there is little doubt that the amount of illegally excavated ancient coins grows annually by perhaps a 1 million coins, perhaps much more. Among the estimated 2.5 million coins offered on eBay, there are undoubtedly a certain number of coins with a prior provenance, although this number is unlikely to be higher than about one third of the total. Provenance here would mean that the coin has

212 *Ute Wartenberg and Barbora Dmitričenko*

sold somewhere before, even if this is only a month earlier. Coins with older provenance might exist, but most sellers do not bother to state any provenances. So, it might be possible that over 1.5 million (or more) coins are freshly looted. This figure is particularly revealing when we look at Elkins' estimate of *c.* 260,000–280,000 ancient coins sold on eBay in 2007: effectively, the number of ancient coins has grown massively over the last 13 years.

This increase is visible across other sales platforms such as Etsy, Vcoins, Heritage Auctions, or Classical Numismatic Group, to name just the major players in the US market. Even though many dealers advertise across more than one site (for example many dealers are present simultaneously on eBay and Vcoins), the numbers of ancient coins are augmenting continuously: as mentioned above, Elkins gave a number of 73,000 ancient coins across Vcoins for 2007; this number is over 95,000 for July 2020. Although this chapter is dedicated to eBay and does not attempt to estimate a full assessment of the ancient coin market, the figures for eBay alone in all countries and the major coin auction houses in the US and Europe must lie annually well $100–$150 million in sales. How high the illicit part is, i.e., coins which left the country illegally, is hard to estimate without a further detailed study. If one applies the 1970 UNESCO convention date to the coins sold, perhaps 10% of the sales volume fall into this group. These figures for ancient coins are of significance in the debate about the size of the entire antiquities market, in which coins clearly fall. Here the figure of a few hundred million dollars, cited in the RAND Report, with illicit antiquities in the tens of millions of dollars, only makes sense, if the numismatic portion is not included here.

Conclusions

As an online sales platform for ancient coins, eBay has grown massively over the last two decades. The expansion is largely fuelled by coins without any prior provenance, many of which were illegally excavated. The figures of ancient coin sales for 2016 and 2020 presented above speak for themselves but they do not give the full picture of the growing popularity of eBay for ancient coins.

Number of Ancient Coins and Sales on eBay

To summarize, around 2.5 million coins are offered on eBay per year, worth more than $200 million, of which perhaps 30% or more are sold annually. Figures attained in 2016 showed a lower number – just over 500,000 – but this figure was limited to Greek and Roman coins alone and was undoubtedly a conservative estimate. Sales figures are difficult to attain since eBay does not archive them and only individual monitoring would allow a precise figure, but our estimates show a robust market of ancient coins sold. It should be kept in mind that this analysis only covered the US eBay site, and that the many other platforms and sites all offer ancient coins as well.

Size of Overall Ancient Coin Market

While this chapter does not attempt to assess the market for other illicit antiquities, it would appear that the annual market of illicit and provenance ancient coins alone is over $100 million or more in a normal year. The antiquities market as a whole is unlikely be in the billions of dollars in sales as sometimes postulated, but it appears that a number of $300–$500 million per year is likely. The numbers of a few hundred million dollars for the entire market, quoted in the RAND Report, are therefore not dramatically different. Based on the numismatic evidence, one would probably think that the number of illicitly traded antiquities is higher than in the tens of millions. In any case, it should be stated that this figure is too low to include ancient coins, as we have shown above. Some advocates of the dealer community have greeted this lower number with enthusiasm, which is hard to understand if one reads the whole RAND Report.

Total Number of Coins for Sale and Widespread Looting

Leaving aside whether the dollar numbers are low or high, there is simply no question that the number of coins sold on eBay without any provenance and mainly looted in the last few years is staggering. The number of illegal excavations and large-scale destruction of cultural property is clearly on the rise. The role eBay plays is that of a facilitator: looters or middlemen in countries have a perfect platform to sell anything that is not high in value and therefore marketed through the markets in Munich, Brussels, London, and elsewhere. The fact that more expensive coins, many from recent hoards, are now on sale on eBay shows that this platform allows a much wider reach than most conventional auction houses.

Increased Online Resources and Coin Sales

The sellers on eBay US are from many countries, often from the Mediterranean or greater Europe, which sell coins directly into the US market. Currently, finders sell to small eBay stores, who can market coins directly to collectors or dealers in the US. Thanks to the academic online catalogues for most coin series, most coins can be correctly identified by dealers without libraries or traditional research facilities.[28] With much more specific categories, such as for Roman emperors, buyers searching for specific categories, such as a specific Roman emperor and denomination, can now find such coins more easily since thousands of coins are catalogued properly.

eBay Fee Structure and World-wide Marketing

Another observation coming from this study is that thanks to its attractive fee structure and worldwide range of hundreds of millions of users, eBay can be

214   *Ute Wartenberg and Barbora Dmitričenko*

used to sell literally any coin, however insignificant it may be. By combining multiple, uncleaned coins in a lot, which would not have found a buyer some twenty years ago, sellers have developed a market for low-end coins, which goes well beyond the regular coin collector. Marketing such coins to the amateur archaeologist for cleaning has created an entire market segment. Here it is not so much acquiring an interesting coin or a variety, but the thrill of cleaning and discovering something in the process of cleaning. The archaeological context, which might provide a historical setting to such objects, is destroyed, ironically for people who often profess a deep love of archaeology and history. At this point, any coin is worth digging up, since money can be made by selling such minor objects through eBay in quantities that only a global enterprise such as eBay can facilitate. The effect on archaeological sites and regions rich in coins is devastating, since metal detectorists reach ever more-remote regions where coins are looted (note, however, that some metal detecting is legal; make sure you note the difference). One has to keep in mind that such ancient coins and other objects in the ground are ultimately limited to a finite number and that with every looted coin, archaeological and historical research and knowledge is lost forever.

Due Diligence and Legality of Coins Imported into the United States

eBay as a company has apparently no obligation to ensure the legality of the sales on its platform, which allows a no-questions-asked operation for any dealer, where due diligence is not required. The principle applied to the sale of illegal coins is that the lack of evidence for looting is sufficient for a "legal" sale on eBay. Many coins available on the eBay US are in violation of current MOU rules, which are in place with a variety of countries and should not be imported into the US. Although eBay officials have been quoted as saying that eBay has "zero tolerance" when it comes to the sale of illicit antiquities, there is little evidence that this statement is true.[29] Unlike most regular US-based numismatic auction houses, which are bound by US legislation for its imports, eBay is able to take advantage of various legal frameworks, which regulate each seller or buyer, who is in turn is responsible to obey the relevant legislations of their country. Here eBay has created a perfect system where individuals smuggling objects can hide as being part of the huge network. Of course, the concept of due diligence is very hard to apply to less inexpensive coins, which are often sold without a provenance, even when one exists and is simply lost. Here extensive sales archives such as coinarchives.com, acsearch.net, sixbid.com as well as individual auction companies (Classical Numismatic Group, Heritage Auctions, etc.) have created a much more transparent market by listing their sales results, usually fully illustrated. eBay could do a huge service to collectors easily by archiving or at least facilitating the setup of a database that records their sales of ancient coins and archaeological objects, which would allow proper due diligence.

Based on these conclusions, we argue that eBay, a company of global reach, needs to consider implementing the following recommendations:

a   Ensure that sellers do not break antiquities and cultural property laws and enforce such rules on its site;

b   Ancient coin sales should fall under eBay's *Artifacts and cave formations policy*. [30] These rules should be strictly enforced for coins;

c   Stop the sale of uncleaned and clearly obviously looted coins;

d   Create a group of experts monitoring the sale of coins to prevent looted and looted coins as well as replica.

Notes

1 We are most grateful to Louise Shelley and Layla Hashemi for inviting them to contribute to this volume and for their helpful comments on an earlier draft. The eBay project presented in this chapter was not part of the CLASI project. It began in 2016 as part of bigger study of the ancient coin market and its size. We would like to thank Austin Andrews, Nathan Elkins, Layla Hashemi, Andrew Reinhard, and Louise Shelley for commenting on various drafts of this chapter.

2 Duyrat 2016: 30–41 for a discussion of various hoards of the Late Archaic and Classical periods.

3 Butcher 2004: 180–95; 185 for the predominance of silver coins in hoard finds.

4 Brodie (Chapter 1, this volume) makes the same comment about antiquities with a Syrian provenance prior to 2011.

5 Meadows and Wartenberg (forthcoming).

6 For an overview of the online market in antiquities, see Brodie 2018; for the trend of increasing democratization of the market see Hashemi and Waddell (Chapter 8, this volume).

7 Although eBay has a policy about not selling unprovenanced antiquities, it is not clear how this is being enforced. Coins do not seem to fall under the category of antiquities.

8 ATHAR Project, http://atharproject.org/report2019.

9 Many examples could be cited, but see for example Price and Waggoner 1975: 9: "In the spring or summer of 1969, Egyptian workmen came by chance upon a hoard of about silver coins."

10 For compilations of Greek hoards see IGCH 1975, Coin Hoards 1970, and recent decades in the *Numismatic Chronicle*.

11 See Gerstenblith 2020 for an overview of legislation.

12 De Callataÿ 2000: 75 for a similar estimate of coins.

13 See https://finds.org.uk.

14 Available on http://numismatics.org/archives.

15 For a brief of overview of the history of eBay see https://www.ebayinc.com/company/our-history.

16 Figures retrieved in July 2020 from https://investors.ebayinc.com.

17 For the general policy about counterfeit items in 2020 see https://www.ebay.com/help/policies/prohibited-restricted-items/counterfeit-item-policy?id=4276&st=12&pos=1&query=Counterfeit%20item%20policy&intent=counterfeit; for replica coins and currency policy see https://www.ebay.com/help/policies/prohibited-restricted-items/replica-coins-currency-policy?id=5042&st=12&pos=3&query=Replica%20coins%20and%20currency%20policy&intent=counterfeit.

216 *Ute Wartenberg and Barbora Dmitričenko*

18 For the issue of counterfeit antiquities, see Fay 2011.
19 See Topçuoğlu and Vorderstrasse 2019 for a study of online sales of coins and cylinder seals.
20 Sargent et al. 2020, 10–12, cite various sources for such statements; see Faucon, Kantchev, and MacDonald 2017 for a highly publicized example.
21 Email correspondence, from James Marrone to Ute Wartenberg, 9 September 2020.
22 See Appendix for links used to find coins.
23 *Coins Hoards of the Roman Empire* at http://chre.ashmus.ox.ac.uk.
24 It should be noted that some of the high-priced coins had provenances and were from prior auctions or other dealers. Such provenances were always noted, and prices were high for such coins. For example, one person advertised a Greek coin from the J.P. Morgan collection, with a long history attached.
25 Accessed at https://investors.ebayinc.com on 30 July 2020.
26 See CNG 2015.
27 https://www.cngcoins.com/Coins_sold.aspx in July 2020. Although it is not clear which period this CNG figure captures, it appears that the earliest sale is 2002.
28 Site such as http://numismatics.org/ocre/, which presents a complete, fully illustrated online catalogue of Roman imperial coins, provides through Google analytics a good idea that users in countries such as Ukraine, Bulgaria, and Turkey are among the main users in the world.
29 See Kantchev 2017: "We have zero tolerance for illicit items like looted antiquities," said Wolfgang Weber, global head of regulatory policy at eBay.
30 Details on eBay's Artifact and cave formations policy: https://www.ebay.com/help/policies/prohibited-restricted-items/artefacts-cultural-heritage-graverelated-items-policy?id=4282.

References

Al-Azm, A., and K. A. Paul. 2019. Facebook's Black Market in Antiquities: Trafficking, Terrorism, and War Crimes. Athar Project. http://atharproject.org/wp-content/uploads/2019/06/ATHAR-FB-Report-June-2019-final.pdf.
Brodie, Neil. 2017. "Virtually gone! The Internet market in antiquities", in *Proceedings of the 6th International Conference of Experts on the Return of Cultural Property*. Seoul: Overseas Korean Cultural Heritage Foundation, 190–204.
Brodie, Neil, and Isber Sabrine. 2018. "The Illegal Excavation and Trade of Syrian Cultural Objects: A View from the Ground." *Journal of Field Archaeology* 43(1): 74–84.
Butcher, Kevin. 2004. *Coinage in Roman Syria: Northern Syria, 64 BC–AD 253*. London: Royal Numismatic Society.
Coin Hoards. 1970. *Coin Hoards, Volumes I–X*. Edited by Price, M.J., McGregor, K., Meadows, A.R., and Wartenberg, U.Royal Numismatic Society.
Coins Hoards of the Roman Empire. Online at http://chre.ashmus.ox.ac.uk/.
CNG. 2015. "A Brief History of Classical Numismatic Group, Inc. On the Occasion of CNG's Auction 100", *The E-Sylum*, vol. 18, no. 37, September 13, 2015, article 10, accessed July 2020 online https://www.coinbooks.org/esylum_v18n37a10.html.
Duyrat, Frédérique. 2016. *Wealth and Warfare: The Archaeology of money in ancient Syria*. New York: The American Numismatic Society.
de Callataÿ, Frédérique. 2000. "Le taux de survie des émissions monétaires antiques, médiévales et modernes, essai de mise en perspective et conséquences quant à la productivité des coins dans l'Antiquité", *Revue Numismatique* 155, 87–109.

Elkins, Nathan. 2008. "A Survey of the Material and Intellectual Consequences of Trading in Undocumented Ancient Coins: A Case Study on the North American Trade," *Frankfurter elektronische Rundschau zur Altertumskunde* 7, 1–13.

Elkins, Nathan. 2012. "The Trade in Fresh Supplies of Ancient Coins: Scale, Organization, and Politics," in P.K. Lazrus and A.W. Barker (eds.), *All the King's Horses: Essays on the Impact of Looting and the Illicit Antiquities Trade on Our Knowledge of the Past*, 91–107. Washington: The Society for American Archaeology Press.

Fay, Emily. 2011. "Virtual Artifacts: eBay, Antiquities, and Authenticity," *Journal of Contemporary Criminal Justice*, Vol. 27, No. 4, September 2011.

Faucon, Benoit, Georgi Kantchev and Alistair MacDonald. 2017. "Antiquities: The Men Who Trade ISIS Loot – The Middlemen Who Buy and Sell Antiquities Looted by ISIS from Syria and Iraq Explain How the Smuggling Supply Chain Works," *The Wall Street Journal*, August 7.

Gerstenblith, Patty. 2020. "Provenience and Provenance Intersecting with International Law in the Market for Antiquities," *North Carolina Journal of International Law* 45.

IGCH: 1973. *An Inventory of Greek Coin Hoards.* Thompson, M., Noe, S.P., Kraay, C. M., and Mørkholm, O., Published for the International Numismatic Commission by the American Numismatic Society. New York: American Numismatic Society.

Kantchev, Georgi. 2017. "Buyer Beware. Looted Antiquities Flood Online Sites like Amazon, Facebook," *The Wall Street Journal*, 1 November.

Meadows, Andrew and Ute Wartenberg. Forthcoming. "Two Fifth-century Hoards? The So-called Karkemish Hoard".

Price, Martin and Nancy Waggoner. 1975. *Archaic Greek Silver Coinage: The "Asyut" Hoard.* London: V.C. Vecchi and Sons.

Sargent, Matthew, James V. Marrone, Alexandra T. Evans, Bilyana Lilly, Erik Nemeth, and Stephen Dalzell. 2020. Tracking and Disrupting the Illicit Antiquities Trade with Open Source Data. RAND Corporation.

Topçuoğlu, Oya and Tasha Vorderstrasse. 2019. "Small Finds, Big Values: Cylinder Seals and Coins from Iraq and Syria on the Online Market," *International Journal of Cultural Property*: 239–263.

Wartenberg, Ute. 2015. "Collecting Coins and the Conflict in Syria," *ANS Magazine* .

Appendix

Links for the searches used to find coins.

All coins: http://www.ebay.com/sch/i.html?_odkw=Greek+coins+lot&_osacat=0&_from=R40&_trksid=m570.l1313&_nkw=coins&_sacat=0.

Coin lots: http://www.ebay.com/sch/i.html?_odkw=coin+lots&_osacat=0&_from=R40&_trksid=m570.l1313&_nkw=coin+lot&_sacat=0.

Greek coins: http://www.ebay.com/sch/i.html?_odkw=coin+lot&_osacat=0&_from=R40&_trksid=m570.l1313&_nkw=ancient+greek+coins&_sacat=0.

Greek lot: http://www.ebay.com/sch/i.html?_odkw=ancient+greek+coins&_osacat=0&_from=R40&_trksid=m570.l1313&_nkw=ancient+greek+coin+lot&_sacat=0.

Roman coins: http://www.ebay.com/sch/i.html?_odkw=greek+coin+lot&_osacat=0&_from=R40&_trksid=m570.l1313&_nkw=Roman+coin&_sacat=0.

Roman coin lot: http://www.ebay.com/sch/i.html?_odkw=Roman+coin&_osacat=0&_from=R40&_trksid=m570.l1313&_nkw=Roman+coin+lot&_sacat=0.

8 Investigating the Online Trade of Illicit Antiquities

Layla Hashemi and Abi Waddell

Democratization of the Antiquities Trade

The internet has democratized the antiquities trade in a way that was unimaginable in the 20th century. Online platforms and payment systems have developed in recent decades and reshaped how global commerce takes place in many markets, cultural artifacts included. While it is difficult to assess the overall value of the antiquities trade, the democratization caused by digital technology brought with it a distinct shift from low volumes of high value objects to a flooding of online platforms with a plethora of often small, low value items such as ancient coins. This shift in trade brings new possibilities but also new challenges for tracking and monitoring sales and the movement of goods. Collecting artifacts using digital channels affords anonymity, convenience and the ability to locate hard-to-find objects. This chapter seeks to provide a generalizable model for investigating online activities related to antiquities trafficking and other forms of illicit trade. By developing new tools for online monitoring and investigations, the authors seek to improve upon existing methods and approaches employed to combat illicit trade and transnational crime.

The internet and other digital technology have transformed international trade. Specific to antiquities, development of software, tools and other technological innovations have led to a democratization of the market, allowing any individual with an interest in antiquities to obtain information on the topic. With the establishment of online payment systems, hobbyists are not only able to obtain information on antiquities but can also bid on and purchase the objects themselves. As this chapter explains, the democratization of the antiquities market benefits some actors and provides various market advantages, but it has also led to an increasingly criminalized market flooded with looted, smuggled, and counterfeit goods.

Monitoring Methodology

Online monitoring for the Countering the Looting of Antiquities in Syria and Iraq (CLASI) project took place over the course of approximately 14

DOI: 10.4324/9781003023043-12

months between September 2017 and November 2018. The CLASI project was run by the Terrorism, Transnational Crime and Corruption Center (TraCCC) at George Mason University and was funded by the United States Department of State, Bureau of Counterterrorism. Searches were conducted in seven languages: English, Arabic, Kurdish, Farsi/Persian, Italian, German and French. The online monitoring team initially examined over 120 sites on the open and dark web in North America and Europe for coins and cuneiform objects (Table 8.1).

The process for conducting regular monitoring of sites offering cuneiform and numismatic objects for sale involved using search terms such as 'coins' or 'cuneiform' within the sites of interest and recording the monitoring information in Table 8.1 where possible.

The 'dark web' is so called because it consists of sites which are not indexed by the usual search engines such as Google and are only accessible via anonymizing software such as The Onion Router (TOR). They are expected to be used by those who want to hide their identity for benign or nefarious purposes and, as such, can be fruitful venues to check for evidence of criminal activity. Because the dark web masks the personal identifying information of the user, dark web marketplaces have become key venues to conduct illicit activities such as drug sales or human trafficking. Despite the

Table 8.1 Monitoring overview

Site Type	Examples
General auction sites	eBay
Antique auction sites	Sixbid, Trocadero, Liveauctioneers
Physical and online antiquities stores	Barakat Gallery
General shopping platforms and marketplaces	Amazon, Alibaba
For sale listings by individuals type sites	Craigslist, Gumtree
Social media sites	Facebook, Twitter, Instagram, Youtube
Darknet markets	Dream Market, Hansa, White Shadow auctions, Silk Road 3, Tochka, WallStreet Market, AlphaBay, Crypto Market, Valhalla

Monitoring Information
Website (URL/hyperlink)
Auction or sales ID/number
Seller ID
Seller contact details
Geographical location
Advert description
Start price
Sold price
Date discovered
Images of interest
Stated artifact provenance

shutdown of several dark web markets such as Silk Road, new markets are quickly established to replace deactivated markets, allowing dealers to continue conducting business (Popper 2019). Because the dark web is known to have illicit activity, researchers monitored several dark web marketplaces for signs of looted or illicit antiquities trade. The dark web markets examined included Dream Market, Hansa, White Shadow auctions, Silk Road 3, Tochka, WallStreet Market, AlphaBay, Crypto Market and Valhalla. Further forensic investigation of sellers and sites on these market platforms did not take place during the project as no antiquities were found to be for sale.

Dark web monitoring was conducted through both manual and automated searches. The analyses used alternative search engines, as the indexing of these marketplaces are limited to the website hosting the content and are not indexed like open websites are by Google. Various software programs were used, including Butler[1] (a prototype application developed by Jataware Corp under DARPA's Memex program) and ShadowDragon's OI Monitor.[2] These tools allowed for the establishment of specific, regularized and iterated queries for terms such as antiquities, ancient coins, cuneiform, Syria, Iraq and other key terms of interest. What was useful about software such as OI Monitor is that it made it easier for the end user to obtain a general overview of darknet activity related to antiquities without having to directly access to the darknet via onion router browsers. Manual dark web searches took the form of visiting various directories of popular onion markets and using these to springboard to those darknet markets that were live and working at the time. During the research period, not all of these market sites were available because of network and site issues. The main focus of the online monitoring were online stores and marketplaces which had previously advertised coins and cuneiform with a higher frequency. Table 8.2 provides an overview of the websites and marketplaces monitored.

Table 8.2 Online sales monitoring list

Multi-seller Platforms	Social Media	Galleries and Auctions	Dark Web Marketplaces
Ebay (US, Canada, UK)	Facebook	http://www.ancientresource.com	Dream Market
LiveAuctioneers	Instagram	http://www.sadighgallery.com	Hansa
Catawiki	Twitter	https://www.sandsoftimedc.com	White Shadow
rocadero		http://www.apoloniagallery.com	Auctions
Sixbid		http://www.ancient-art.co.uk	Silk Road 3
VCoins		http://www.charlesede.com	Tochka
		https://timelineauctions.com	WallStreet Market
		http://antiquities.co.uk	AlphaBay
		http://www.artancient.com	Crypto Market
		http://www.pegasusgallery.co.uk	Valhalla
		http://www.medusa-art.com	
		http://www.griffingallery.net	
		http://www.barakatgallery.com	
		http://baidun.com	
		https://www.aphroditeancientart.com	
		https://nyshowplace.com	
		http://www.palmyraheritagegallery.com	
		https://phoenixancientart.com	

It should be noted that of the listed social media platforms, only Facebook was monitored heavily, with the other sites given more cursory attention. As explained in the following section, collected monitoring data was entered into spreadsheets which were then analyzed for suspicious or illicit activity by subject matter experts. Store websites such as the above did not normally show a high rate of sales advertisements, so it was common to find that a long time (many weeks or months) elapsed before a new artifact was advertised on their website. As noted in Chapter 7, there were also difficulties determining which objects had actually been sold. It is extremely difficult to determine the overall value of the antiquities market, but analysis of specific artifact values helps to get a partial understanding of the potential value. Through the monitoring of listings data, we were able to evaluate the average advertised price for cuneiform artifacts and coins. Our monitoring provided very different values for the antiquities market than other sources that omit the sale of ancient coins, which represent a large share of the market.

Marketplace Data Collection

The monitoring of sites was conducted first by manually collecting data from several prominent online sales platforms on the worldwide web (Ebay, Sixbid, VCoins, etc.). This method proved inefficient and time consuming, motivating researchers to shift to using web scrapers to quickly and efficiently collect listings data for analysis by subject matter experts (SMEs). Web scraping (sometimes called web harvesting, web spidering or web crawling) is a technique employed to extract large amounts of data from websites. The data can then be saved to a file or to a database in table or spreadsheet format. The use of web scrapers allowed researchers to focus resources where needed and to automate aspects of the online marketplace monitoring that did not require human analysis or processing. For example, web scrapers were used to collect basic listing information including but not limited to object ID, listing price, description and number of bids.[3]

Tools capable of scraping deep web social media sites such as Twitter and Facebook were evaluated in the hopes that there could be an automated (and therefore more efficient) equivalent of the manual checks of these sites that were conducted. At the time, none of these tools were found to meet the project's purposes, mainly because of their limited feature sets and in some cases because of the high cost of purchasing a license. Palantir and Datawalk were two such tools falling into the latter category. Shadow Dragon, Analyst Notebook (with the SMC4 plugin), Butler, Tableau Web Connector and Maltego did not offer the ability to scrape Facebook user profiles. Some of the software and tools offered useful visual insights into user connections, allowing for analysis of trade networks through social media data.[4] Because no single tool met the project's research needs, the team began developing its own specialized online investigation tool. This custom tool for Facebook and open source intelligence (OSINT) investigations is explained later in the chapter.

Social Media and Online Forums

Through primary investigation of online discussions related to antiquities sales, it was discovered that several online forums, such as Yahoo Groups, were used by members of the antiquities community. These fora were used to post questions and discuss object identification, appraisal and sales. While the final point of sale often occurred outside of or separate from these venues through private person-to-person encrypted messaging, these fora provide valuable information about antiquities sales and the actors involved in the trade. Likewise, social media platforms such as Facebook and Instagram also facilitate a similar method of buying and selling of objects, where the public can see a post about an object for sale and then communicate privately with the seller to complete the transaction. As explained in this chapter, developments in communication technology have facilitated information sharing and bolstered connectivity among members of transnational antiquities networks, allowing looters in source countries quick and easy access to interested buyers in destination countries.

Blended Sites – Combining Features of Social Media and Listings Websites

Blended websites and online marketplaces such as eBay provide particular market advantages for both buyers and sellers. These platforms often have extremely low barriers to entry, allowing nearly anyone to create an account capable of purchasing or selling antiquities. Any user with a valid email address and the other minimal required credentials is able to make an account and bid on a platform like eBay. This is in stark contrast to larger auction sites where a vendor must be vetted by the host or domain administrator before being able to sell. This democratization of the market has led to increased turn-over and a shift from trade in high-value large objects to low-value smaller items such as coins, which are easier to conceal and transport. The shift to online markets also demonstrates the tremendous adaptability of sellers. If a vendor is banned or removed from a particular platform, they can quickly create a different account on the same platform or move to another venue to re-establish their business and continue sales.

Buyer feedback on sites allows for the vetting of sellers and provides quick access to a seller score or other measurement of individual seller reliability. User feedback on these websites provides valuable data to understand the structure of the market. Users often examine previous feedback when making decisions and these reviews can change purchasing behavior. Buyer feedback sections with ranking systems provide detailed information about the reliability of sellers and facilitate a buyer's vetting of individual vendors. eBay even offers a star rating for vendors, providing a quick visual representation of each individual seller's reputation. At the same time, sellers are known for falsely inflating their online reputations through fabricated positive reviews, a problem that exists in many online markets and is not confined to the antiquities trade. There is evidence of some sellers creating intentionally false positive feedback on their pages. This can occur because feedback fora are open response, so they are often not an actual indicator of the vendors' reputation or integrity. Various fora publicly publish lists of 'bad' vendors known for conducting suspicious transactions. Several online fora have compiled lists of suspicious or fake antiquities dealers (Augustus Coins 2020; Coin Talk 2016; Forum Ancient Coins 2005). User feedback also provides an advantage for researchers, allowing them to conduct online ethnography and monitoring.

What makes popular sales websites like eBay and Etsy unique is that they combine features and characteristics of more traditional gallery or auction sales platforms and social media sites intended for networking. Platforms commonly used for the sale and purchase of hobby or craft goods, such as Etsy, have been used to trade antiquities that could be counterfeits or have questionable provenance. As noted in Chapter 7, illicit antiquities advertised on these sites are often misrepresented as craft materials or falsely described in order to avoid detection. Objects are often cross listed on various websites, some of which are not traditionally used for antiquities sales, making these sales difficult to monitor. This decentralized and small-scale antiquities market also reflects the democratization of the trade.

The monitoring of online marketplaces comes with several limitations. Content on social media sites is often entirely user generated, which means there is a possibility that information is false or misleading. Given the commercial nature of social media sites, it is also possible that content might be automatically (or bot) generated. Researchers are often unable to safely and ethically access private groups on Facebook and other platforms which have been proven to facilitate illicit antiquities sales (Al-Azm and Paul 2018). Finally, though critical to contemporary investigations, the value of social media as data for investigations should not be overemphasized. While social media investigations are helpful, online behavior represents only a part of the supply chain and OSINT findings should be used along with other investigative methods.[5] As regulations are passed to prevent the sale of illicit antiquities on open web platforms such as Facebook, special attention must be paid to record retention and sharing as the data from these online transactions are critical for criminal and financial investigations. Additionally, as policies are established to combat this trade, dealers may shift to tactics and venues more commonly used by other criminal networks, such as the dark web.

Tools for Online Investigations of Trafficking Networks

Various tools mentioned above were used during online monitoring including social network analysis (SNA) and other investigative software. Generally, the tools mine data from open sources using a visual interface to facilitate the analysis of connections among different entities and provide leads to

224   *Layla Hashemi and Abi Waddell*

potential suspects based on the relationships, locations and other key features. During the monitoring period, the research team made extensive use of software including Butler and a variety of tools available from Shadow Dragon. Butler is a Know Your Customer (KYM) tool developed by Jataware and funded by DARPA's Memex. The tool allowed the monitoring team to investigate individuals of interest by name, phone number, or other identifying information and provided a concise dossier of the individuals affiliations, businesses and other data. One major advantage of Butler was that it allowed researchers to investigate the activity and associations of individuals of interest on both the surface and the dark web without the need to use anonymizing applications such as The Onion Router (TOR). The use of sophisticated software allowed researchers to automate the slow process of manually searching for individual vendors on the dark web.

Other tools used for monitoring both the open and dark web for antiquities activity included Maltego by Paterva and OI Monitor and SocialNet by ShadowDragon. OI Monitor customizes and automates intelligence gathering across multiple sources in the open and dark net, allowing researchers to conduct targeted investigations based on the specific research parameters of the project's research. SocialNet is a Maltego (Maltego XL, Maltego Classic) commercial transform package that can be integrated into other platforms using Rest API. The tools mine data from open sources using a visual interface to facilitate the analysis of connections between different entities. The software captures the social media and digital tracks of individuals of interest and maps the aliases and connections of entities in near real time, allowing for a network investigation of criminal and illicit trade supply chains. While many of these tools were useful and helped guide the research, no single tool was able to achieve the full spectrum of tasks required for our project's purposes. As a result, developers from the team began to develop a custom-designed software intended to detect and monitor illicit activity and behavior.

Dark Web Monitoring

The presence of much illicit online activity on the darknet motivated examination of darknet marketplaces for illicit antiquities sales. Darknet market sites are not as easily accessible to most customers compared to websites on the open web. Dark web transactions are based on trust, which takes time to build. It appears that now, as was the case many years before, that dark net markets are where popular but illegal commodities and services such as drugs are traded. In 2017 approximately 80 percent of annual darknet sales revenues came from drugs (Denton 2017). Illegal here appears to mean anything that is not considered the worst on the scale of terrible crimes. Most markets do not appear to offer goods and services that would attract the most animosity - even from other criminals. Wildlife trafficking (including trade in ivory) and child pornography (including child abuse) are widely advertised on both the open and dark web by taking advantage of bullet-proof hosting, a service that allows customers considerable leniency in the kinds of material they upload and distribute, allowing users to bypass internet regulations and terms of service (Noroozian et al. 2019). Many of the most popular bulletproof hosts and payment processors are located in China and Russia and tailor their services to protect their merchants and prevent them from being discovered (Tian et al. 2018, Krebs 2019).

Antiquities and counterfeit goods are considered victimless crimes and, along with even some wildlife products such as ivory, can be legitimate. For instance, an ancient cylinder seal which was bought before the 1970s and has proper provenance information can be legitimately traded on eBay and other markets (Paul 2018). An additional obstacle of dark web trade is the level of technical skill needed to access and enter these closed communities where the illicit trade occurs (Shelley 2018: 141–142). Because they are used for illicit activity, these marketplaces often go offline either temporarily or permanently, and because they are not indexed in the same way as open web search engines, once the website or its content is taken down, it is often difficult to retrieve retroactively. Despite these limitations, attempts have been made to index the dark web for analysis. Darknet Market Archives (2013–2015) is a project that scraped historic data from approximately 90 Tor-Bitcoin darknet markets and forums and related material from 2011–2015. "This uniquely comprehensive collection is now publicly released as a 50GB (~1.6TB uncompressed) collection covering 89 DNMs and 37+ related forums, representing <4,438 mirrors, and is available for any research." (Branwen 2013). A similar study examined the content of nearly 3,000 dark web sites and found that 57% hosted illicit content such as drugs or child pornography (Whitwam 2016). As noted earlier, in 2017 approximately 80 percent of annual darknet sales revenues came from drugs (Denton 2017), showing a marked increase in the use of darknet marketplaces for conducting illicit trade.

During June 2019, approximately 20 of the main dark net markets plus additional darknet fora were analyzed with the goal of finding illicit antiquities and other contraband for sale. Various sites' listing categories were browsed and key word searches established. Without exception, the vast majority of goods for sale on these markets were drugs. In one forum a user advertised the sourcing of rhino horn, ivory and exotic pets. There was no evidence of illicit antiquities trade on the dark web.

There are a variety of possible reasons for the lack of evidence of ancient cuneiform and coin sales on the dark web. First, antiquities collecting is largely seen as a legal activity. Most such goods can be easily advertised and purchased on the open web with little risk to buyers or sellers. In contrast, darknet markets usually advertise explicitly illegal items such as weapons, narcotics and child pornography (Sullivan and Satter 2019; Whitehouse 2019). As previously mentioned, not all collectors have the necessary technical knowledge to access darknet markets. Buyers expect higher value items to be associated with a brick and mortar store and are reluctant to purchase these items online. The anonymity of

226   *Layla Hashemi and Abi Waddell*

darknet purchasing methods may not inspire buyer confidence. Finally, antiquities vendors want to reach the largest possible audience which is why they often use the open web rather than the dark web.

Many of the dark web marketplaces had various counterfeit goods on offer. Counterfeit clothing, jewelry and other high-end luxury goods such as Apple products comprised the highest proportion of advertisements. Other popular counterfeit good included false documents such as fake driving licenses or passports (McCoy 2018). The project also investigated the use of cryptocurrencies, another element often associated with illicit trade, for completing antiquities transactions. While many online marketplaces and dealers monitored typically accepted traditional payment methods (bank transfer, credit card, etc.), there were some platforms that accepted Bitcoin and other cryptocurrency as a form of payment. It is likely that dealers and buyers use the electronic payment methods readily available on platforms such as Facebook or cash transfer apps like Venmo and Paypal to complete transactions. Similar to the lack of a need to sell on the dark web, the grey antiquities market does not require the anonymity of cryptocurrencies. As financial investigations continue, the anonymity provided by cryptocurrencies may be used by antiquities smugglers and looters as they are by other criminal networks in order to avoid detection. Major measures were adopted by the US Congress in late 2020 as part of the National Defense Authorization Act expanding the Bank Secrecy Act to introduce financial transparency measures to the arts and antiquities market (Small 2021). As additional regulations are developed to prohibit and prevent the sale of illicit antiquities on the open web, some dealers will likely shift to using cryptocurrencies and other encrypted and anonymous communication and payment processes, including the use of bulletproof hosting and dark web marketplaces.

Explaining the Average Antiquities Sale

The supply chains for antiquities are comprised of several stages. While the most visible stage often resembles the supply chains of legal commodities, the stages close to the source are much more clandestine and mimic the trading practices of illicit commodities. Once an item is looted or trafficked, advertisement of the object typically begins with a public post, often on a social media or blended site as discussed earlier, in order to reach the widest possible audience. After initial marketing, dealers will often invite only those individuals interested in making a purchase to private groups or encrypted communication channels. The actors will then continue to negotiate and complete the transaction using private person-to-person encrypted messaging such as Telegram or Whatsapp. Shipping is often fulfilled by third parties including international carriers that deliver the item to destination countries via land, air or maritime routes. The documents accompanying the artifact (e.g., provenance, authenticity, etc.) are often falsified or strategically misrepresent the contents of the package in order to avoid detection by law enforcement and customs officials (Halperin 2017, Gerstenblith 2019, Pryor 2020).

The Online Trade in Illicit Antiquities 227

As seen from the steps involved in a typical sale, despite beginning on public platforms, the trade quickly shifts to private and encrypted messaging after initial contact. In a similar way, sellers constantly modify their behavior and practices in order to avoid detection, strategically offering false or misrepresented descriptions of objects (ex. being careful not to label something as explicitly 'Syrian' or 'Iraqi'). These findings led to shifting the monitoring research to a focus on individuals of interest rather than an examination of general online activity on fora and social media content of antiquities networks. With a goal of tracking trade from source to transit and ultimately destination countries, the team partnered with Sayari[6], a global corporate data provider and commercial intelligence platform, other data analysts and subject matter experts to map the networks involved in the antiquities trade. A summary of the findings regarding the countries involved in the trade is presented in Table 8.3.

Results From Antiquities Monitoring on eBay – 2014–2017

Over a three-year period from mid-2014 to mid-2017, listings of antiquities on eBay that mentioned 'cuneiform' were recorded. Artifacts bearing cuneiform inscriptions were chosen to be monitored because ancient writing is harder to falsify, making it easier to determine whether a particular object was genuine. Additionally, most cuneiform-bearing objects come from MENA countries which have been the site of war, looting and internal conflict. And lastly, if the object was found the be genuine, then the presence of writing could place the source location and date of creation of the object with greater accuracy. In Q3 and Q4 of 2014 there were 30 relevant auction listings with the highest number of listings in June and July. In 2015, there were 85 relevant auction listings, with the highest numbers occurring in February and April. In 2016 there were 13 relevant auctions, of which most were in September and October. Finally, in Q1, Q2 and Q3 of 2017 there were 13 relevant auctions, of which most occurred in January, July and October. The average price of these listings was $605. Some of the cuneiform artifact auction listings did not specifically use the word 'cuneiform' in the description, which meant that the listing was not flagged. Additionally, some listings were relisted objects. While the monitoring of cuneiform fluctuated during this period, the volume of low-value items such as coins has seen a dramatic rise with the democratization of the market resulting from the shift

Table 8.3 Marketplace countries

Source	*Transit*	*Destination*
Iraq	Turkey	US
Syria	Iran	Western Europe (UK,
Other conflict/crisis countries	Free trade zones	Germany, Italy) Canada

228 *Layla Hashemi and Abi Waddell*

to online marketplaces. Similar to the CLASI monitoring, the data outlined in Table 8.2 on objects bearing cuneiform were recorded, both to give a snapshot of results and to refine monitoring going forward.

Most of the items for sale had no stated, or very vague, provenance. This did not necessarily mean that the item was fake or stolen. If provenance evidence was mentioned in the sale advertisement, this was often in the form of a letter or email, a certificate of authenticity or purchase receipts. Some advertisements had vague references to either unnamed or named private collections and acquisition dates. The artifacts of interest were mostly tablets, seals and cones made from clay, followed by limestone, hematite, bronze, chalcedony and stone. These advertisements generally claimed a date for the object offered for sale between 2500 to 1500 BC and had an average price range of $150–$900.

The greatest activity was seen on eBay (UK, US and Canada) and Timeline Auctions. Between February to March 2018, the highest value item was $40,000, followed by $25,000 – all from USA-based stores. All these stores had an online presence and some, but not all, had physical brick and mortar stores. From March to April 2018 the highest value item was $17,000 (Timeline Auctions), followed by $4,000 on eBay USA. The top sale locations were found to be the USA (California, New York, Washington DC, Colorado and Arizona), UK (London, Essex and Surrey), then Germany, Denmark, France and Israel. The majority of the cuneiform items for sale were advertised by a store based in Los Angeles, one of the largest cuneiform dealers, and were found to be genuine. Conversely, a high proportion of the artifacts on sale with another major dealer based in New York were found to be fake by consulting the subject matter experts involved in the project. Fakes can usually be discerned from inaccuracies with the cuneiform symbols, poor quality artwork (both two- and three-dimensional), evidence of modern tools used to manufacture the object and inconsistencies with the date and place the object is purported to be from with what the object looks like. Additionally, the likelihood that a particular seller is offering fake goods for sale is increased by analysing feedback from previous sales, price and frequency that the same item is being offered for sale (which is indicative of mass production). Lastly, it was found that some dealers owned homes of high value ($750,000 to $1.5 million), which suggests that they are gaining financially from the antiquities trade. Dealer home value was obtained from publicly available property prices and sales data.[7] Many of these high-end dealers were found to have direct and indirect connections to individuals in source countries.

Using Data to Detect Online Illicit Trade Networks

The above section demonstrated the importance and relevance of public data and OSINT to track illicit trade. Another promising route is to monitor and investigate the broader networks that move objects transnationally from source to destination countries. Mapping of social media networks of top dealers allows for important insights into the connections between dealers and their networks and provides important data for financial and criminal investigations. Social network analysis (SNA) is a useful methodology for examining group interactions and relationships. SNA characterizes network structures in terms of nodes (individual actors or entities) and the ties, edges or links (relationships or interactions) that connect them. An example network might consist of individual Facebook users as nodes and the links or edges between users could be following relationships (friends) or interactions (comments, likes, etc.). Another possible link between users could be that they are members of the same Facebook group or like the same page. Because SNA considers the relationship between users, it is able to provide a holistic perspective that allows for deeper analysis that goes beyond listings monitoring by analyzing the relationship among network actors. Using this method, it is easier to follow flows of information, goods and finances. The use of SNA software such as SocialNet (ShadowDragon) and Gephi (Open Source) allow for the mapping of the social network connections of users, allowing for an analysis of the affiliations of entities of interest. Through the analysis of affiliates and other connections, the team was able to map both the physical and online networks of dealers and other actors associated with the antiquities trade. Using this method, it was possible to track the location of individuals of interest and hypothesize possible routes for transporting cultural artifacts through online sales and to triangulate this data with findings on the use of various trade routes as presented by Dr. Mahmut Cengiz in Chapter 4 of this volume.

Filling the Gap Through Application Development: The Facebook Profile Intel Tool

The future of investigating the trafficking of antiquities requires approaches that take into consideration the creativity and innovation involved in online illicit trade. Computer-assisted automated approaches facilitate sifting through the vast amount of information currently available. Through a blended approach, the proposed software permits investigators to scrape and analyze the profiles of individuals of interest, combining features of computer programming with the subject matter expertise of law enforcement, archeologists and other researchers. This multidisciplinary approach allows for efficient use of subject matter expertise while processing large amounts of data and providing insights that would likely be overlooked by siloed investigations.

Because no existing software met the CLASI team's research needs, members created a customized OSINT tool specific to tracking and disrupting illicit supply chains that is currently in development. The Facebook Profile Intel Tool (FPIT) is a program that automates scraping a user's profile to allow an at-a-glance view of the profile's contacts, likes, interests, images, videos etc. The tool facilitates collecting intelligence on suspects who may be engaged in illegal activities such as illicit trade, terrorism, money laundering and fraud. FPIT allows for the investigation of existing suspects and the identification of new leads in an efficient and automated fashion. The program can be configured to adjust the parameters in a profile that should be scraped (ex. photos, videos, timeline comments, etc.), the number of friends to scrape and the timing of tool actions. When the program has finished running, a folder is created with the name of the target profile. The folder contains hypertext markup language (.html), the standard language for creating web pages, files containing the results which enable easy visual analysis and key word searches. The target profile results file contains thumbnail images of profile photos and likes. The user name of anyone who has made a comment, reaction and likes is recorded. Another results file outputs thumbnail images and requested content from the target's profile and that of their friends. Future versions of the tool seek to improve speed and offer enhancements such as automatic language translation, quantifying how many times a particular profile has been added as a friend, image recognition and mapping the location of the contacts scraped. The example scenarios below demonstrate how such social media and network analysis can greatly assist in the investigation of the illicit antiquities trade.

Mapping and Visualizing Networks

Once social networks involved in the online trade have been detected, they are mapped to show the network structure of groups involved. Research was conducted to investigate the Facebook connections of the high-end coin and cuneiform dealers and explore their direct and indirect connections to individuals in source countries both manually and using the software mentioned above. Geospatial mapping allowed for a visual analysis of galleries and individuals of interest along with their network ties. Most dealers based in the west have direct and indirect connections to multiple individuals based in the Middle East who are connected to the antiquities trade, including archaeologists, archaeological site workers, metal detecting enthusiasts, coin collectors, antiquities dealers, grave and other site diggers and local law enforcement officials.

During the monitoring period, the Facebook contacts of known dealers (normally based in Europe or North America) were analyzed and the chain of contacts was followed to profiles based in the Middle East. A representative supply chain might include the following example: Lenny has an antiques store in the USA but is it suspected that he obtains artifacts from the Middle East. Lenny has a contact on Facebook, Maria Bloggs, who runs a shipping and storage company in France. Although we cannot see who Lenny's Facebook contacts are, Maria was identified via a comment on one of Lenny's photos. A key word search on Maria's Facebook profile shows that she has a connection to a Zaf Bloggs who lives in Turkey. There are many antiquities and metal detecting equipment images on Zaf's profile. This points to the theory that Lenny buys artifacts from Zaf via Maria.

Contacts of interest could be obtained from the friends list by looking at the profile photo and other user information. This was the best way of finding useful leads owing to the limited resources and time available as it could afford a relatively quick surface analysis. This automated approach provided valuable data for investigation and proved to be less time consuming. Investigating social media connections and network activity has proven useful in discovering the potential path of object source to the final sales destination and tracking those who may be responsible for illegally obtaining objects of interest and their potential links with terrorist activity. As noted earlier, social media and open source investigations only provide partial information about illicit networks and should be used in conjunction with traditional investigative methods.

Investigative Tools: Limits and Possibilities

Links between antiquities trafficking and terrorist activity can be established through the investigation of the online profiles of dealers, purchasers and others involved in the trade. The scenarios below explain how the Facebook tool would facilitate investigation of criminal networks involved in antiquities trafficking.

Scenario 1

- Mike Doe is suspected of receiving stolen antiquities to sell on to customers via his high-end antique shop in New York.
- Mike Doe's name is searched using either manual or automated methods and his 1st, 2nd and 3rd level friends are selected as part of this search.
- A map view of results shows that Mike has many 3rd level friends based in Turkey and Egypt.
- It is found that there is a Bob Smith based in Rome who has been added as a friend more times than any other name within the results.
- A search of Bob Smith along with a key-word search of 'statue' and 'coin' reveal that he has many 1st level friends who are based in two particular towns in Turkey. Further searches of the Facebook comments of these friends reveal that they are offering antiquities for sale.

Scenario 2

- Janet Doe lives in Egypt as an archaeologist and it is suspected that she may have links with middle-man traders of stolen antiquities. Her Facebook settings have been configured to prevent her non-friends from viewing her friends list.
- A search of her name produces a list of 30 Facebook names who have made comments on her Facebook profile.

232 Layla Hashemi and Abi Waddell

- A further search of these comments reveals that there is a user, Jerry Green based in Munich who owns a freight and storage company.
- A search of Jerry shows that he has many 1st and 2nd level friends who are antiquities dealers based in Europe.

Investigation of these scenarios through analysis of social media data can reveal the supply chain from where an artifact is removed from the original site (museum, archaeological site, collection, etc.) to the final end-user customer who is normally based in Europe or North America, showing the connections along key trade routes. In addition to increasing our understanding of the key players in this market and their methods, this data can also provide leads to potential suspects of other criminal activity which may occur alongside other illicit activity such as the trafficking in weapons, humans or narcotics.

Establishing Links to Terrorist Financing

To establish links between online sales and terrorist activity, researchers examined user profiles, timelines and photographs for suspicious activity related to terrorist funding (e.g., jihadist imagery, violence, armed weapons, etc.). Various social media accounts reviewed during the monitoring project showed photographs and videos of kidnappings, violent killings and weapons, along with discussions of glorifying the murder of key political figures. Whilst information on those accounts showing evidence of extremist propaganda would be of interest to specific law enforcement departments, it is relevant that these accounts had connections to antiquities collectors and dealers in the Middle East, and in turn to connections to the high-end dealers in the west.

Reports reveal that these organized crime networks are more sophisticated and strategic than previously assumed. For example, while ISIS militants posted videos of their destruction of statues and idols in Iraq's Mosul Museum and other sites, Westcott reveals that these viral videos might have served as part of the terrorist group's social media smokescreen for terrorist financing. While some artifacts and sites were indeed destroyed, ISIS members also demonstrate sophisticated knowledge about specific artifacts and archeological equipment as they carefully and strategically removed high value objects behind the camera while displaying an outward appearance of knowing little about these objects and claiming that they simply want to destroy them (Westcott, 2020).

This pattern of publicized destruction while strategically preserving certain items to place for sale did not continue. According to an account from a knowledgeable source within Hayat Tahrir al-Sham (HTS),

> ...no Salafist or Islamist group in the region has officially called for the destruction of certain types of pre-Islamic artifact or monuments, at

least not in the very public way that IS did at the zenith of its power in 2015.

(Moos 2020: 6)

These studies reveal that antiquities trafficking by terrorists and other organized criminal groups is often strategic and carried out by sophisticated transnational networks that now use communication technology such as Facebook, WhatsApp and Telegram to conduct their illicit activities. There is evidence of terrorist groups "looting to order" – where buyers will post requests for objects they are interested in purchasing and connect with looters on the ground willing to find the requested object (Kantchev 2017) though some have disputed these claims, pointing out that there is no evidence of these loot to order transactions being fulfilled (Sargent et al. 2020). These links to terrorist financing and the funding of violence and conflict demonstrate the need to prevent the looting and trafficking of antiquities rather than focusing on the return of artifacts to their country of origin.

The Antiquities Trafficking and Heritage Anthropology Research (ATHAR) Project is an investigative group led by a collection of anthropologists and heritage experts who examine transnational trafficking, terrorism financing, and organized crime online. According to the organization's 2019 report, "Facebook's Black Market in Antiquities: Trafficking, Terrorism, and War Crimes," "Violent extremists currently include individuals associated with Syrian-based groups like Hay'at Tahrir Al Sham (HTS), Hurras Al-Din, the Zinki Brigade and other non-Syrian based Al-Qaeda or Islamic State in Iraq and Syria (ISIS) affiliates. All of these groups are using Facebook as a platform for antiquities trafficking, whether through direct interaction with buyers and sellers or through the use of middlemen who facilitate transactions between the general public and terrorist groups." The report also reveals how private Facebook groups are being used to share information on how to loot antiquities, posting instructions in Arabic on how to extract artifacts from the ground (Al-Azm and Paul 2019: 3).

In reaction to reports by ATHAR, CLASI and others which exposed the widespread illicit antiquities trade occurring on the platform, in June 2020 Facebook announced an update to its community standards to add the category of historical artifacts to its list of prohibited goods. While this ban is an important first step to regulating the online antiquities trade on social media platforms, Facebook has released very few details about the updated Community Standards, leaving several concerns about proper implementation of the new policy which will require extensive resources of Facebook and the input of subject matter experts. Detecting and disrupting online antiquities networks requires subject matter and language expertise. While Facebook released a vague report outlining how the platform would partner with academics and NGOs to implement its historical artifacts policy, it provides no details on how it intends to implement these plans, nor does it seem to have key personnel assigned to this effort.

234   *Layla Hashemi and Abi Waddell*

Despite this announcement, Facebook's current Community Standards also fail to provide the means to report and remove pages that engage in the trafficking of cultural property that may be thought to be illegal. This problem also exists for other prohibited goods on Facebook, such as endangered wildlife as determined by the Convention on International Trade in Endangered Species (CITES). Buyers and sellers can flout this ban on Facebook via the use of public and private groups. As a result, terrorist and extremist groups are able to profit from the sale of trafficking goods on Facebook with impunity (Fernholz 2019). Studies of wildlife trade on Facebook in specific countries showed that lions, chimpanzees, bears, cheetahs, elephants and other international wildlife prohibited red-list creatures were advertised for sale in Facebook groups. A 2019 study conducted by one of the authors of the illicit wildlife trade in Jordan also led to information about sales of CITES-prohibited wildlife in other countries. Given that Facebook is not properly enforcing CITES standards as illicit wildlife trafficking persists on the platform despite a ban, it is unlikely that they will be able to properly enforce similar regulations for antiquities (Aung 2020, Ebersole 2020).

Like other forms of transnational crime and illicit activity, antiquities sales will likely continue, but simply no longer on Facebook. Now that the sale and advertisement of historical artifacts is banned on the platform, sellers will likely move their business to other venues, perhaps using encrypted channels or even shifting to the dark web or websites hosted in other countries that are not so vigilant in policing and regulating content, such as has occurred with the online sex trade. Criminals are experts at exploiting loopholes and finding work arounds (Europol 2015). Dealers are incredibly adaptable and due to the illicit nature of their activity, they are prepared to pack up shop quickly if necessary. Thus, while the new policy may result in a decrease of antiquities sales on Facebook, it is ultimately unlikely to disrupt the trade long term.

Perhaps the most pressing concern is that it seems the ban entails Facebook deleting or filtering content related to antiquities. The negative consequences of this data deletion cannot be overstated. Social media data related to online antiquities sales are extremely valuable and should be provided to financial and legal investigators to document and analyze this conflict-driven criminal activity. Assuming that dealers will remain active on the platform but simply move to private or encrypted channels, flagged content should be preserved and archived for evaluation by law enforcement and researchers, not deleted or kept for sole use by Facebook (Swann 2019, Hekking 2020).

Conclusions for the Investigation of the Illicit Antiquities Trade

The trade in looted and counterfeit artifacts appears to be of a lower volume than originally predicted (see Brodie Chapter 1). It is critical to consider the overlaps and differences in physical and online markets.

It is quite likely that items which were advertised for sale in brick-and-mortar stores were also being advertised online. Many items were sourced months or years in the past and stored in warehouses before being sold, which suggests that there is a low turnover of such artifacts. Artifacts available in brick and mortar stores are often of higher value than items advertised on social media or online platforms such as eBay, where, whilst artifacts are lower in value, there is a higher turnover.

Key traders involved in marketing directly to consumers (mostly in the US, Europe and the West) appear to be well connected to individuals involved in obtaining artifacts in source countries, either directly or indirectly. This reflects the importance of monitoring social media connections and trade networks to understand the flow of goods. Tracking the flow of artifacts from source through transition and finally to destination countries reveals that illicit antiquities are often sold along the same trade routes used for other forms of illicit trade such as human or drug trafficking, though studies show little explicit evidence of this connection (Yates 2014). In Chapter 4, Mahmut Cengiz provides a detailed discussion addressing recent shifts in trade routes following the decreased presence of ISIS in the region. It is useful to have SMEs to verify, where possible, the authenticity of artifacts offered for sale online, although it should be remembered that even if fake artifacts are marketed as genuine, this is a crime in itself. These SMEs should have the necessary languages skills, cultural understanding and archeological expertise to conduct analysis in the regions of interest.

The most effective method of conducting social media research involves a mixture of both passive and active reconnaissance, ideally using a temporary account that does not have any connections to law enforcement agencies or research organizations. Passive research involves very low risk and allows for greater visibility of a wider scope of activity. Active research takes the form of having some interaction with suspects, usually with fake profiles. This affords greater insight into illicit activities at the cost of a higher risk to the investigator. Both methods, though, offer the chance to map the flow of illicit trade from source to destination countries whilst understanding socio-economic and cultural dynamics. Likewise, both automated and manual methods have their benefits. Blending of automated and manual methods allows for effective use of time and resources. Finally, such social media research helps illuminate other potential criminal activities which appear to be associated with the illicit antiquities trade such as the dissemination of extremist propaganda activities or exhibiting destruction and violence.

The antiquities trade is global, dynamic and diverse, making assessment or investigation of the overall market difficult. Consequently, the search criteria for future monitoring of online sales should be narrow, focusing attention only on specific dealers and marketplaces of interest. Otherwise, a great deal of time could be spent monitoring dealers and sites which do not produce any results or leads. The CLASI monitoring process conducted general initial investigations and then narrowed the monitoring scope to target specific individuals and networks of interest. Future research should also solicit the knowledge and experience of subject matter experts when developing methodology. Gallery, auction and dealer listing monitoring using both automated and manual methods should be supplemented by social media investigations. Only a multidisciplinary and multipronged approach will allow for successful disruption of these elusive transnational supply chains.

Although open web markets and platforms remain popular and the predominant trade venues for certain illicit commodities such as antiquities, dark web markets should continue to be monitored. As discussed in this chapter, the absence of antiquities activity on the dark web can likely be explained by the fact that the sale of artifacts is not often seen as explicitly illegal, especially when the illegality of the object is obscured by false documentation and provenance. Therefore, there is no need for antiquities dealers to advertise on the darknet which is comprised of a much smaller customer base compared to the open web where they can currently conduct their business with impunity. However, as regulations and policies are developed and implemented to prevent and combat this type of trade, dealers may feel the pressure to move to tactics and venues more commonly used by other criminal networks, such as the dark web. Therefore, continued monitoring of the dark web for activity related to the illicit antiquities trade is critical. The monitoring of dark web marketplaces for illicit antiquities trade is even more pressing given that the recent banning of historical artifact sales on Facebook and Instagram may result in a shift of the trade to dark web marketplaces.

This chapter sought to provide a standardized and replicable model for investigating the online sale of antiquities. The authors hope that future studies will continue to build upon these OSINT methodologies and develop tools to successfully detect and disrupt illicit supply chains. Future studies must consider the tremendous adaptability and creativity of cybercriminals and use innovative and multidisciplinary approaches to collect and analyze empirical evidence on the trade. These cutting-edge approaches will facilitate efforts of law enforcement, policy makers, and investigators to prevent the looting and trafficking of cultural heritage from not only countries in crisis, but also to protect the multitude of historical artifacts which represent and provide knowledge of our common history and culture.

Notes

1 The Defense Advanced Research Projects Agency (DARPA) is a research and development agency of the United States Department of Defense responsible for the development of emerging technologies for use by the military. DARPA's MEMEX program used state of the art content indexing and web searching on the Internet to help law enforcement officers and others perform online investigations to hunt down human traffickers. Butler is a web-based Know Your Customer (KYC) application meant to assist in slot-filling an entity profile via human-in-the-loop feedback and a simple search query capable of hitting the open and dark web as well as enterprise search repositories. More information on Jataware Corp's Butler can be found at https://github.com/jgawrilo/butler_install.

The Online Trade in Illicit Antiquities 237

2 For more on OI Monitor by ShadowDragon, see https://shadowdragon.io/oimonitor.
3 Through the use of web scrapers, large amounts of data related to online listings were populated into comma separated value spreadsheet files (with a.csv file extension) which could be easily analyzed by subject matter experts. This method allowed for efficient use of the time and expertise of SMEs and sped up the overall monitoring process.
4 Various software allows researchers to conduct visual and quantitative analysis of user connections and network relationships. For example, social network analysis (SNA) provides various centrality measures which allow for analysis of influence and importance of nodes within the network.
5 It should also be noted that there are several instances where antiquities are looted, trafficked and sold entirely offline through private and closed networks of collectors. This type of trade had been the precedent in previous decades and remains strong today. In these cases, OSINT investigations might produce few results.
6 For more on Sayari visit https://sayari.com/.
7 If a user's address is known, one can find how much they bought their house for and/or the current estimated value. One such site that does this: https://www.melissa.com.

References

Al-Azm, Amr, and Katie A. Paul. 2018. "How Facebook Made It Easier Than Ever to Traffic Middle Eastern Antiquities." August 14, 2018. https://www.worldpoliticsreview.com/insights/25532/how-facebook-made-it-easier-than-ever-to-traffic-middle-eastern-antiquities.

Al-Azm, A., and K.A. Paul. 2019. *Facebook's Black Market in Antiquities: Trafficking*, Terrorism, and War Crimes. Athar Project. http://atharproject.org/wp-content/uploads/2019/06/ATHAR-FB-Report-June-2019-final.pdf.

Augustus Coins. 2020. "eBay Fakesellers of Ancient Coins." *Augustus Coins*. July 1, 2020. http://augustuscoins.com/ed/fakesellers.html.

Aung, Thu Thu. 2020. "Facebook Purges Ads for Illegal Wildlife in Southeast Asia as Online Trade Surges." *Reuters*, August 6, 2020. https://www.reuters.com/article/us-myanmar-wildlife-idUSKCN2520C3.

Branwen, Gwern. 2013. "Darknet Market Archives (2013–2015)." https://www.gwern.net/DNM-archives.

Coin Talk. 2016. "Master List of eBay Sellers to Avoid." *Coin Talk*. August 23, 2016. https://www.cointalk.com/threads/master-list-of-ebay-sellers-to-avoid.282864/.

Denton, David L. 2017. "Annual Sales Estimation of a Darknet Market." May 25, 2017. https://rstudio-pubs-static.s3.amazonaws.com/279562_48fcbe87ec814596944fb8bb59b10ae3.html.

Ebersole, Rene. 2020. "The Black-market Trade in Wildlife Has Moved Online, and the Deluge Is 'Dizzying.'" *Animals*. December 18, 2020. https://www.nationalgeographic.com/animals/2020/12/how-internet-fuels-illegal-wildlife-trade.

Europol. 2015. *Exploring Tomorrow's Organised Crime*. Luxembourg: Publications Office. http://bookshop.europa.eu/uri?target=EUB:NOTICE:QL0514126:EN:HTML.

Fernholz, Tim. 2019. "Terrorists Are Trafficking Looted Antiquities with Impunity on Facebook." *Quartz*. July 3, 2019. https://finance.yahoo.com/news/terrorists-trafficking-looted-antiquities-impunity-080045960.html.

Forum Ancient Coins. 2005. "Forum Ancient Coins." *Forum Ancient Coins*. April 17, 2005. https://www.forumancientcoins.com/board.

Gerstenblith, Patty. 2019. "Provenances: Real, Fake, and Questionable." *International Journal of Cultural Property* 26 (3): 285–304. https://doi.org/10.1017/S0940739119000171.

Halperin, Julia. 2017. "The Vast Majority of Antiquities Sold Online Are Probably Looted or Fake, a New Report Says." *Artnet News.* November 1, 2017. https://news.artnet.com/art-world/antiquities-sold-online-fake-1135832.

Hekking, Morgan. 2020. "Looting Concerns Prompt Facebook to Ban Historical Artifact Sales." *Morocco World News* (blog). June 25, 2020. https://www.moroccoworldnews.com/2020/06/306840/looting-concerns-prompt-facebook-to-ban-historical-artifact-sales.

Kantchev, Georgi. 2017. "Buyer Beware: Looted Antiquities Flood Online Sites Like Amazon, Facebook." *The Wall Street Journal.* November 1, 2017. https://www.wsj.com/articles/the-online-bazaar-for-looted-antiquities-1509466087.

Krebs, Brian. 2019. "Meet the World's Biggest 'Bulletproof' Hoster." *Krebs on Security.* July 16, 2019. https://krebsonsecurity.com/2019/07/meet-the-worlds-biggest-bulletproof-hoster.

McCoy, Kevin. 2018. "How Potentially Dangerous Fake Apple Products Reach the US Consumer Market." *USA TODAY.* September 20, 2018. https://www.usatoday.com/story/money/2018/09/20/how-potentially-dangerous-fake-apple-products-reach-you/695596002/.

Moos, Olivier. 2020. "Antiquities Trafficking in Syria: Salafists, Tomb Raiders and 'Buried Treasures'." *Religioscope*, February, 40.

Noroozian, Arman, Jan Koenders, Eelco van Veldhuizen, Carlos Hernandez Gañán, Sumayah A. Alrwais, Damon McCoy and Michel van Eeten. 2019. "Platforms in Everything: Analyzing Ground-Truth Data on the Anatomy and Economics of Bullet-Proof Hosting." *USENIX Security Symposium* (2019).

Paul, Katie. 2018. "Ancient Artifacts vs. Digital Artifacts: New Tools for Unmasking the Sale of Illicit Antiquities on the Dark Web." *Arts* 7 (2): 12. https://doi.org/10.3390/arts7020012.

Popper, Nathaniel. 2019. "Dark Web Drug Sellers Dodge Police Crackdowns (Published 2019)." *The New York Times*, June 11, 2019, sec. Technology. https://www.nytimes.com/2019/06/11/technology/online-dark-web-drug-markets.html.

Pryor, Riah. 2020. "The Devil Is in the Paperwork—Don't Be Caught out by Provenance Fraud." *The Art Newspaper.* November 11, 2020. http://www.theartnewspaper.com/news/antiques-dealers-charged-with-fraud-after-allegedly-falsifying-provenance.

Sargent, Matthew, James V. Marrone, Alexandra T. Evans, Bilyana Lilly, Erik Nemeth, and Stephen Dalzell. 2020. *Tracking and Disrupting the Illicit Antiquities Trade with Open Source Data.* RAND Corporation. https://www.rand.org/pubs/research_reports/RR2706.html.

Shelley, Louise I. 2018. *Dark Commerce: How a New Illicit Economy Is Threatening Our Future.* Princeton, NJ: Princeton University Press.

Small, Zachary. 2021. "Congress Poised to Apply Banking Regulations to Antiquities Market." *The New York Times*, January 1, 2021, sec. Arts. https://www.nytimes.com/2021/01/01/arts/design/antiquities-market-regulation.html.

Sullivan, Andy, and Raphael Satter. 2019. "Dark Web Child Porn Bust Leads to 338 Arrests Worldwide." *Reuters*, October 17, 2019. https://www.reuters.com/article/us-usa-crime-exploitation-idUSKBN1WV1WW.

Swann, Steve. 2019. "Antiquities Looted in Syria and Iraq Are Sold on Facebook." *BBC News.* May 2, 2019. https://www.bbc.com/news/world-middle-east-47628369.

The Online Trade in Illicit Antiquities 239

Tian, Hongwei, Stephen M. Gaffigan, D. Sean West, and Damon McCoy. 2018. *"Bullet-Proof Payment Processors."* In *2018 APWG Symposium on Electronic Crime Research (ECrime)*, San Diego, CA: IEEE, 1–11. https://ieeexplore.ieee.org/document/8376208/.

Westcott, Tom. 2020. "DESTRUCTION OR THEFT? Islamic State, Iraqi Antiquities and Organized Crime." *Global Initiative Against Transnational Organized Crime*, March, 50.

Whitehouse, Helen. 2019. "Guns, Drugs and Hitmen Bought with Click of a Mouse on the Dark Web." *Mirror.* August 10, 2019. https://www.mirror.co.uk/news/uk-news/guns-drugs-hitmen-bought-click-18893251.

Whitwam, Ryan. 2016. "Researchers Index Dark Web, Find Most of It Contains Illegal Material – ExtremeTech." *Extreme Tech.* February 1, 2016. https://www.extremetech.com/internet/222245-researchers-index-dark-web-find-most-of-it-contains-ins-illegal-material.

Yates, D. (2014). "Displacement, deforestation, and drugs: antiquities trafficking and the narcotics support economies of Guatemala". In J. Kila and M. Balcells (eds.) *Cultural Property Crimes: an overview and analysis on contemporary perspectives and trends.* Leiden: Brill, 23–36.

Index

Abboud, Nelly 76
Abdulkareem, Inas 24
Abdulrahman, Ammar 23
Aboutaam, Hicham 44
Acar, Ö. and Kaylan, M. 27, 180
Acar, Özgen 180
ACCO (Alliance to Counter Crime Online) 10, 17
Achaemenid empire, hoards from 194
Afeiche, Anne-Marie 21
Affordable Care Act (ACA) in US 59, 83
AFP (Agence France Press) 23, 32, 44
AGI (Il Giornale dell' Arte) 23
Akkadian language, use of 98
Akkadian period seals 123–4
Al-Azm, A., Al-Kuntar, S., and Daniels, B. 39
Al-Azm, A. and Paul, K.A. 8, 10, 17, 165, 193, 223; Syrian antiquities, looting and trafficking of 24, 30, 31, 32, 36, 48n16
Al-Azm, Amr 39
Al-Bayati, Hamid 150
Al-Haj Salih, Yassin 23
Al-Hashimi, Husham 43
Al-Qaeda 165; antiquities trafficking from Syria by Northern Route 150, 154n11; online sale of illicit antiquities 233
Al-Tamimi, Aymenn Jawad 40
Alberge, Dalya 72
Albertson, Lynda 32
Alcharihi, Mohamad Yassin 26, 37
Aleppo Governorate, Afrin district of 24
Alexander the Great 98
Ali, Cheikmous 23, 24
Ali, Zulfiqar 47n3
Alibaba 219
Allred, Lance 89n31

Almalaq, Bandar 6
AlphaBay 219, 220
Alshdaifat, Salem 44
Amazon: eBay, ancient coin sales on 195, 200, 203, 204; online sale of illicit antiquities 219; "where are the coins from" on 204–5
American Association for the Advancement of Science (AAAS) 23, 24
American Journal of Semitic Languages 96
Amineddoleh, Leila 150, 163
Anadolu Ajansi 143
Analyst Notebook media scraper 221
Ancient Coin Collectors Guild (ACCG) 179, 180–81
Ancient Coin House 204
ancient coins: dataset of 201–2; small antiquities and, commercial importance of 46–7; smuggling investigations, lack of specific expertise in 179, 188; without provenance, market for 193
ancient coins, case about looting and smuggling of 15, 178–89; Ancient Coin Collectors Guild (ACCG) 179, 180–81; ancient coins, lack of specific expertise in smuggling investigations 179, 188; antiquities smuggling cases, work on 179; Center for Study of Democracy 178, 180; circulation processes, realities of 179; country of discovery, identification of 179, 181–7; Court of Appeals for the Fourth Circuit of Maryland 181; Cultural Property Implementation Act in United States 180; FBI (Federal Bureau of Investigation) 181–2,

Index 241

188–9n1; Federal District Court of Maryland 181; FMRD (Die Fundmünzen der römischen Zeit in Deutschland) 183, 197; Greek coins, production of 185; indiscriminate trade in ancient coins, looting and 178; International Association of Professional Numismatists (IAPN) 179, 180, 181; looted and smuggled ancient coins, attention to 179–80; Macedonian bronze coins 185; myth that all ancient coins circulated widely 180–81; national and international protections, exemption of ancient coins from 178; numismatic material, knowledge of 179; prosecution, failures of 187–8; Roman mints, examples of 183–4; seizure of looted coins in US 181–7; seizure of looted coins in US, analysis of 182–7; seizure of looted coins in US, Byzantine coins from 183, 184; seizure of looted coins in US, forgeries of ancient coins mixed in 186; seizure of looted coins in US, Greek coins from 185, 186; seizure of looted coins in US, late Roman bronze coins from 183, 184; seizure of looted coins in US, locally diagnostic types 183, 185; seizure of looted coins in US, medieval and modern coins from 186, 187; seizure of looted coins in US, photographs from 182; seizure of looted coins in US, regionally diagnostic types 183, 185; seizure of looted coins in US, Roman provincial coins from 182–3, 185–6, 187; sellers, paid lobbyists for 178; United States, wide circulation of ancient coins in, myth of 180–81; United States State Department 181; US Cultural Property Advisory Committee (CPAC) 180; US Customs and Border Protection 181; US Department of Justice (DOJ) 181; US Homeland Security Investigations (HSI) 181–2, 188–9n1
Ancient Near Eastern Cylinder Seals (Teissier, B.) 125
Anderson, Maxwell Lincoln 9
Andrews, Austin 215n1
ANSA (Armed Non-State Actors) 21–2, 39–41, 45, 46, 47
Anti Money Laundering Act (2020) in US 174–5

antiquities: antiquity dealer networks 196; counterfeit antiquities, filtering through genuine trade of 33; criminal trafficking of 138; democratization of trade in 16–17, 218; investigation of trade in 17–18; market for 7–9; market for, ancient Near East seals on 119–20; sales of, explanation of average sale 226–7; smuggling of, other illicit networks and, similarities between 159–61; smuggling of, work on cases of 179; trade in, changing nature of 29–31; trade in, global and dynamic nature of 235–6; trade in, transnational structure and operation of 25–6; trafficking of, armed violence and 21; trafficking of, Syrian trade before 2011 considered unproblematic 44; trafficking of, value for ISIS of 43
Antiquities Coalition 8
antiquities trafficking from Syria by Northern Route 14, 137–54; Al Qaeda 154n11; Arab Uprisings, regime changes sought by 137; borderland areas, criminal groups in 141; coin smuggling, continuance of 143–4; corrupt officials along Northern Route 146–9; criminal groups as illegal excavators, collectors, and marketers 147; criminals, antiquities trafficking as lucrative source of income for 151–2; criminals, trafficking of antiquities by 138; criminals along Northern Route 146–9; destination countries for Syrian antiquities 140; disguise of purchases by traffickers in Turkey 143; drug trafficking in Syria 139–40; excavations in Syria, control over 146–7; excavators along trafficking routes 152–3; Facebook, sales of purloined antiquities on 140; FSA (Free Syrian Army) 147, 150, 151, 152, 153; geographical factors, smuggling and 141; Global Terrorism Database (GTD) 137; HTS (Hay'at Tahrir al-Sham) 138, 151, 153, 154n11; insurgent and terrorist groups operating in Syria. 150–51; insurgents along Northern Route 149–51; international dealers engaged in antiquities trafficking, linkages and networks of 147–9; ISIS (Islamic State of Iraq and Syria) 137–8, 150–51, 152;

242 Index

JAN (Jabhat al-Nusra) 154n11; local participants along Northern Route 146–9; local smugglers in Turkey, collaboration between 142–3; methodology used in study 138; Northern Route, antiquities traffickers along 144–51; oil smuggling in Syria 139; organized crime groups, post-2000 involvement of 142; police agencies on route, lack of collaboration among 141; SNA (Syrian National Army) 151, 152, 153; Syria, Director of Antiquities in 140; Syria, documented archaeological sites in 140; Syria, illicit economy and antiquities trafficking in 139–40; Syria, local trafficking groups in 153–4n6; Syria, proxy wars and insurgent groups in 137; terrorists, antiquities trafficking as lucrative source of income for 151–2; terrorists, trafficking of antiquities by 138; terrorists along Northern Route 149–51; trafficking routes, changes in preference for 152; Transparency International 2019 Corruption Perceptions Index (CPI) 141; Turkey, Anti-Smuggling and Organized Crime Department (ASOD) in 138, 139–40, 141–2, 143–4, 145–6, 153n4; Turkey, illicit economy and antiquities trafficking in 140–44; Turkish Museums, signs of thefts of antiquities in 142; Turkish provinces with most antiquities seized from traffickers 145; Turkish provinces with most antiquities trafficking investigations 144; UN Office on Drugs and Crime (UNODC) Report (2009) 139; United Nations (UN) Security Council 150; United States, Iraq invasion (2003) by 141, 152

AP (Associated Press) 28

app development, online sales and 229–30

Arab Uprisings, regime changes sought by 137

Arango, T. and Schmitt, E. 28

archaeological site looting (post-2011): preferential targets for 33–4; satellite imagery of 24–5

Archaic period (550–480 BCE), finds from 194

Arraf, Jane 65, 84–5n2

Art Crime Team website in United States 163

artifact smuggling, financial investigations in battle against 14–15, 158–76; Anti Money Laundering Act (2020) in US 174–5; antiquities smuggling and other illicit networks, similarities between 159–61; Art Crime Team website in United States 163; ATHAR (Antiquities Trafficking and Anthropology Research Project) 165; Bank Secrecy Act (BSA) in United States 161; case study, illicit trade in Egyptian antiquity through UAE 168–73; case study, trafficking Italian antiquities 173; CLASI (Countering the Looting of Antiquities from Syria and Iraq) 175n1–3; criminal networks, size and sophistication of 158; criminal supply chain for antiquities 164–8; cultural property crime, law enforcement and 161–4; Egypt, Law on the Protection of Antiquities in (Law 117) 175n13; European Union (EU) 174, 176n22; EUROPOL 173; Facebook, "middlemen" selling artifacts on 165; FATF (Financial Action Task Force) 176n21; FBI (Federal Bureau of Investigation) 163, 175n4; financial crime, shop owners' information and investigation of 159; financial investigation techniques, effective application of 160–61; Global Financial Integrity (GFI) 162; HTS (Hay'at Tahrir al-Sham) 165; illegal antiquities trade, red flags of 166; illicit artifact flow chart 165; illicit supply chain networks 168; Immigration and Customs Enforcement (ICE) in United States 162, 169; international recommendations and laws, recent changes in 174; INTERPOL 163; ISIL (Islamic State of Iraq and the Levant) 160, 165; Italy, Carabinieri Command for the Protection of Cultural Heritage 163, 175n5–7; Justice Department in United States 169; law enforcement, focus of expertise of 164; law enforcement, pressures on 162; looting, frequency and location of 159; NEST (Nafertiti Eastern

Sculptures Trading) 169, 172, 173; Object ID program (International Council of Museums) 163, 175n9; shop owners, role in supply chains 158; smuggling antiquities, illicit networks and 158; sources of looted coins 159; Stolen-Works-of-Art-Database 175n8; supply chain, insurgent and terrorist networks in 160; SWIFT messaging 167; target-rich market 161; TBML (Trade-Based Money Laundering) 166–7; trade-based money laundering, process of 160; United States, art sector regulatory controls in (2020) 174–5; United States Customs and Border Protection Strategy (2020–2025) 162; *United States v Khouli et al* 168–73, 175n10–12, 176n15–20; US Homeland Security Department (DHS) 162–3; US Homeland Security Department (DHS) Cultural Property, Art and Antiquities (CPAA) program 162–3; US Homeland Security Department (DHS) Investigations, Immigration and Customs Enforcement (HSI) 162–3, 172; US Senate Permanent Subcommittee on Investigations 161; value, benefits of following 173–5

Aruz, J., Benzel, K., and Evans, J.M. 130n11

Ashmolean Museum collection in UK 88n28

Ashurbanipal 103, 104, 110

Assad, Hafez 139

ATHAR (Antiquities Trafficking and Anthropology Research Project) 10, 17; artifact smuggling, financial investigations in battle against 165; eBay, ancient coin sales on 195–6, 215n8; online sale of illicit antiquities 233

Athenian decadrachms from Karkemish 194–5

AuctionWeb project 197

Augustus Coins 223

Aung, Thu Thu 234

Bajjaly, Joanne 27, 28, 39

Bakare, Laure 32, 34, 45

Baker, A. and Anjar, M. 27, 32, 39

Bank Secrecy Act (BSA) in United States: artifact smuggling, financial

investigations in battle against 161; online sale of illicit antiquities 226

Banks, Edgar J. 96

Barakat Gallery 219

Barnard, Anne 23

BBC 144; Syrian antiquities, looting and trafficking of 23, 36, 48n24

Beckmann, Martin 178

Bitcoin 167, 225, 226

Black, J.A., Cunningham, G., Robson, E., Zólymoni, G.G. et. al. 129n1–2

Boardman, John 83

Bogdanos, Matthew 21, 142

Bohlen, Celestine 82

Branwen, Gwern 225

bricks (antiquities) 115

Brodie, N. and Sabrine, I. 14; ancient coin sales on eBay, analysis of 193; antiquities trafficking from Syria along Northern Route 140, 143, 145, 146–7; looting and trafficking of Syrian antiquities 28, 32, 35

Brodie, N. and Walker Tubb, K. 9

Brodie, N., Yates, D., Slot, B., Batura, O., et al. 10; Syrian antiquities, looting and trafficking of 31, 32, 42

Brodie, Neil 7, 8, 9, 11, 12, 17, 120, 175n1, 179, 234; ancient coin sales on eBay, analysis of 194, 215n4, 215n6; antiquities trafficking from Syria along Northern Route 140, 146; looting and trafficking since 2011 of Syrian antiquities 21–58; looting of archaeological artifacts from Iraq, study of 65, 74–7, 83–4, 86n8, 86n11, 88n24–7, 89n32

Brodie, N.J. and Kersel, M.M. 74, 88n26

Bulgarian seizure of Syrian artifacts (March 2015) 28

Burke, Jason 24

Burwell v. Hobby Lobby Stores, Inc., 573 U.S. 682 (2014) 59, 85n5

Butcher, K. and Gill, D.W.J. 178

Butcher, Kevin 194, 215n3

Butler app (Jataware Corp) 220, 221, 224, 236n1

Butterfield & Butterfield, San Francisco 64, 65, 68

Butterlin, P. and Mura, M. 24

Caracalla (Marcus Aurelius Antonius) 194

Carroll, Scott 60–61, 79, 82–3, 84n1

244   Index

Casana, J. and Laugier, E.J. 23, 24–5, 89n30

Casana, J. and Panahipour, M. 23

case study: illicit trade in Egyptian antiquity through UAE 168–73; on looting of archaeological artifacts from Iraq, background to 60–68; trafficking Italian antiquities 173

Cassella, Stefan D. 86n9, 87n21

Catanzariti, Antonietta 4, 7, 13, 96–134

CBS News 32

CCP (Cultural Property News) 32, 42

Cengiz, M. and Roth, M.P. 140–41, 147, 150

Cengiz, Mahmut 8, 14, 15; antiquities trafficking from Syria along Northern Route 137–57; looting and trafficking since 2011 of Syrian antiquities 28, 35, 44; online trade of illicit antiquities, investigation of 229, 235

Center for Study of Democracy 178, 180

Chappell, D. and Hufnagel, S. 9

Charbonneau, Louis 41

Charney, Noah 9

Charpin, Dominique 129n5

Chazan, David 34

Cherry, John F. 88n25

Chikar, Nourdine 29

Chivers, C.J. 32

Christie's London 75, 196

Christie's New York 38, 44, 120; looting of archaeological artifacts from Iraq and 64–5, 68, 83, 86n10, 86n12–13, 88n25

Chulov, Martin 41

CITES (Convention on International Trade in Endangered Species) 234

Clark, Justin 23, 27

CLASI (Countering the Looting of Antiquities from Syria and Iraq) 9–10, 16, 17, 47n1; artifact smuggling, financial investigations in battle against 175n1–3; eBay, ancient coin sales on 193, 215n1; online sale of illicit antiquities 218–19, 228, 229, 233, 235; scribes and seal cutters in ancient Near East 129

Classical period (480–332 BCE), finds from 194

clay cones 115

clay tablets: earliest writing inscribed on 98–9; preparation for inscription on 99–101

CNG (Classical Numismatic Group) 211, 212, 216n26–7

CNN (Cable News Network) 24

CNN Turk 145

Cockburn. Patrick 23, 33

Coggins, Clemency C. 69

Coin Talk 223

coins: ancient coin market, size overall of 213; coin smuggling, continuance of 143–4; counterfeit coins 195; Greek coins, production of 185; recognition of coins, problems of 194, 195; sources of looted coins 159; uncleaned coins, data on 203–5. see also ancient coins; ancient coins, case about looting and smuggling of; eBay, ancient coin sales on; seizure of looted coins in US; smuggling of coins

collaboration: local smugglers in Turkey, collaboration between 142–3; police agencies on Northern route, lack of collaboration among 141

Collins, Paul 88n28

Collon, D., Sax, M., and Walker, C.B.F. 121, 124, 125, 131n22

Collon, Dominique 123, 124, 125, 130n21, 131n22

commercial tablets, Neo and Late Babylonian (7th-2nd century B.C.E.) 99

Connally, Bess 75, 86n8

Emperor Constantine the Great 18n1

Convention on Cultural Property Implementation Act (CCPIA) in US 68

corruption 5, 13, 23, 40, 141, 153n4, 176n21; art sector, vulnerability to 161; civil strife and 119; funding of violence and 18; government officials and 14, 24, 35, 41, 44, 138, 146–9, 151; Middle East, corrupt leadership in 17; Northern Route, corrupt officials along 146–9; supply chains and 12; Turkish border guards and 28. see also CLASI project; TraCCC; Transparency International 2019 Corruption Perceptions Index (CPI)

counterfeiting 4, 6, 7, 35, 150, 159, 162, 215n17, 218; counterfeit and suspect seals 125–8; counterfeit antiquities, filtering through genuine trade of 33; counterfeit coins 195; Dark Web, counterfeit goods on 226; faking of

artifacts or provenance 168;
identification of counterfeit items 167;
online markets, proliferation on 8;
sale of counterfeits on eBay,
prevention of 198
country of discovery, identification of
179, 181–7
Court of Appeals for the Fourth Circuit
of Maryland 181
COVID-19 pandemic 211
Cox, Simon 27
Craigslist 219
criminality 3, 12, 27, 31, 59, 82–3, 141,
161, 174, 198, 219; ANSA (Armed
Non-State Actors) and 21–2, 39–41,
45, 46, 47; antiquities trade, criminal
organization of 22; antiquities
trafficking as lucrative source of
income for criminals 151–2;
borderland areas of Syria and Turkey,
criminal groups in 141; "conflict" and
"criminal economies" in Syria 35;
corrupt officials and 146–9; criminal
groups as illegal excavators, collectors,
and marketers 147; criminal liability,
limiting of 26; criminal networks
150–51, 152–3, 158, 166–9, 175, 226,
232–3, 234, 236; criminal networks,
size and sophistication of 158;
criminal organization and operation
of antiquities trade 34–6; criminal
prosecutions in Homeland Security
Investigations (HSI) 179; criminal
prosecutions of dealers 71; criminal
supply chain for antiquities 33, 164–8;
criminal trafficking of antiquities 138;
cybercriminals 236; Dark Web and 11;
dealers or collectors, difficulties of
proving criminal intent by 45;
innovation and flexibility of criminals
17–18; metropolitan cities, criminal
organizations in 142; Northern Route,
criminals along 146–9; organized
crime groups, post-2000 Syrian
involvement of 142; quasi-criminal
action, Hobby Lobby and 86n9;
security vacuums filled by 14–15;
Shabiha criminal gangs 23; specialized
services, organized crime and access
to 35; transnational criminals 5, 16,
142–3, 146, 149, 159–60
Crow, Kelly 89n37
Cryptocurrency 226
Crypto Market 219, 220

cultural property crime, law enforcement
and 161–4
Cultural Property Implementation Act
in United States 180
Cuneiform Digital Library Initiative
(CDLI) 88n28, 89n32
cuneiform tablets, birth of writing on
97–103
Cuneo, A. and Danti, M. 32
Cuneo, A., Penacho, S., Danti, M.,
Gabriel, M., and O'Connell, J. 24
Cunliffe, Emma 23
Cuno, James 138
cyber environment 4, 6, 9, 12, 15, 236
cylinders (antiquities) 115–16

Dandachi, Nidaa 38
Daniels, B. and Hansen, K. 32, 89n34
Daou, Rita 153–4n6
Dark Web: Darknet antiquities trading
31; Darknet Market Archives 225;
markets 219–20; monitoring 220,
224–6; trade 10–11
Darke, Diana 24
DARPA (Defense Advanced Research
Projects Agency) MEMEX program
220, 224, 236n1
Database of Neo-Sumerian Texts
(BDTNS) 89n32
Datawalk media scraper 221
Davis, T. and Mackenzie, S. 21
De Callataÿ, Frédérique 215n12
De Lapérouse, Jean-Francois 129n7
De Sossi, Giovanni 88n28
democratization of antiquities trade
16–17, 218
Denton, David L. 11, 224, 225
DeSilver, Drew 85n5
deterrent effect on looting of
archaeological artifacts 82–3
DGAM (Directorate-General of
Antiquities and Museums) in Syria
23, 24, 32
Diab, Afif 153–4n6
Dietrich, Reinhard 178
digital imaging, eBay sales and 197
Dikov, Ivan 28, 33
diplomatic and military personnel,
exemption from customs inspections
26
Dmitričenko, Barbora 7, 8, 15–16, 33,
180, 193–217
Dream Market 219, 220
drug trafficking in Syria 139–40

246 *Index*

Dupree, Nancy 21
Duyrat, Frédérique 194, 215n2

eBay: activities on 228; antiques monitoring on, results from (2014–2017) 227–8; artifact and cave formations policy 216n30; choice as basis of analysis 195; data sets, analysis of 195–6; Fee Structure and World-wide Marketing 213–14; largest and most diverse platform 197; number of ancient coins and sales on 212; online sale of illicit antiquities 219, 222, 223; principle of *caveat emptor* on 198; recommendations for 215; sale of counterfeits on eBay, prevention of 198; seller of low-end items (2016) 202; strategies of 197–8; substantial increase of online transactions on 198; unprovenanced antiquities, enforcement of policy against sales of 215n7
eBay, ancient coin sales on 15–16, 193–216; Achaemenid empire, hoards from 194; Amazon 195, 200, 203; Amazon, "where are the coins from" on 204–5; American Numismatic Society 197; Ancient Coin House 204; ancient coins, dataset of 201–2; ancient coins, market for coins without provenance 193; ancient coins, size overall of market for 213; antiquity dealer networks 196; Archaic period (550–480 BCE), finds from 194; ATHAR (Antiquities Trafficking and Anthropology Research Project) 195–6, 215n8; Athenian decadrachms from Karkemish 194–5; AuctionWeb project 197; Caracalla (Marcus Aurelius Antonius) 194; CLASI (Countering the Looting of Antiquities from Syria and Iraq) 193, 215n1; Classical period (480–332 BCE), finds from 194; CNG (Classical Numismatic Group) 211, 212, 216n26–7; coinage in ancient Syria, history of 194; coins for sale, widespread looting and 213; data sets, analysis of 195–6; digital imaging 197; Etsy sales platform 211, 212; export limitations 198; findings of study 201–12; findings of study, coin numbers and prices 206–12; findings

of study, dataset (2016) 206–8; findings of study, dataset (2020) 208–12; GMV (Gross Merchandise Volume) 197, 211; *Hacksilber* pieces 194; Hellenistic period (323–31 BCE), proliferation of coinage in 194; Heritage Auctions 212; ICGH (Inventory of Greek Coin Hoards) 215n10; illegally excavated material, flow of 196–7; Institute of Numismatics in Vienna 197; ISIL (Islamic State of Iraq and the Levant) 193; ISIS (Islamic State of Iraq and Syria) 193; Israel Antiquities Authority 204; looted treasures and antiquities, market for 193, 196–7, 198–9; looting in Syria, evidence of 194–5; Macrinus (Marcus Ophilius Macrinus) 194; Memoranda of Understanding (MOUs) with United States 198; methodology for study 200–201; numismatic auctions 196–7; numismatic evidence 194; Numismatic Guaranty Corporation 210; online resources, coin sales and 213; online transactions 197, 212–13; public auctions of coins before eCommerce 196; RAND Corporation Report (2020) 199–200, 211, 212, 213; recognition of coins, problems of 194, 195; Roman Syria, coinage in circulation in 194; Schaefer's Roman Republican coinage project 197; Sixbid sales platform 210; TraCCC (Terrorism, Transnational Crime and Corruption Center) at George Mason University 193; unauthorized excavations 198; uncleaned coins, data on 203–5; UNESCO Convention on Means of Prohibiting and Preventing Illicit Import, Export and Transport of Ownership of Cultural Property (1970) 212; United States, due diligence and legality of coins imported into 214–15; Vaballathus 194; VCcoins sales platform 210, 211, 212; "vest pocket dealers" 196; Queen Zenobia 194
Ebersole, Rene 234
Egypt 4, 59, 84–5n2, 125, 139, 184, 194–5, 231; case study, illicit trade in Egyptian antiquity through UAE 168–73; Egypt Exploration Society 60; Law on the Protection of Antiquities

in (Law 117) 71, 175n13; ownership
law in 78, 89–90n38; scribes in royal
court in (18th dynasty) 99; tomb
paintings from Saqqara in 121
electronic messaging, encrypted means
of 31
Elibol, Kamil 153n1
Elkins, Nathan T. 4, 7, 15, 162; ancient
coin sales on eBay, analysis of 195,
198–9, 203, 212, 215n1; looted and
smuggled ancient coins, expert witness
in case of 178–90
Englund, Robert K. 129n6, 129n8
EPIC Antiquities Act in US 86n16
Estrin, Daniel 79, 86n6
Etsy sales platform: eBay, ancient coin
sales on 211, 212; online sale of illicit
antiquities on 223
European Union (EU) 174, 176n22
EUROPOL: artifact smuggling, financial
investigations in battle against 173;
online sale of illicit antiquities 234
evidence-based analysis 21–2, 42, 46
excavators 146, 147, 148, 150, 151, 160;
along trafficking routes 152–3;
Ancient Coin House (via Amazon)
and 204; illegal excavators, tomb
robbers and 142; in Syria, control over
146–7
export limitations, sales on eBay and 198

Fabrikant, Geraldine 60
Facebook: Black Market in Antiquities:
Trafficking, Terrorism, and War
Crimes (2019 Report) 233;
Community Standards 234; contacts
of known dealers on 230–31; FPIT
(Facebook Profile Intel Tool) 229–30;
group memberships, network analysis
of 36; "middlemen" selling artifacts
on 165; monitoring of 221; online sale
of illicit antiquities 219, 222, 223, 234,
236; sales of purloined antiquities on
140; Syrian antiquities, looting and
trafficking of 31
Facebook Groups 233
Facebook Messenger 31
FATF (Financial Action Task Force)
176n21
Faucon, B., Kantchev, G., and
MacDonald, A. 27, 29, 40, 41, 216n20
Fay, Emily 216n18
FBI (Federal Bureau of Investigation):
ancient coins, case about looting and

smuggling of 181–2, 188–9n1; artifact
smuggling, financial investigations in
battle against 163, 175n4; Syrian
antiquities, looting and trafficking of
26
Federal District Court of Maryland 181
Feingold, Rony 127
Fernholz, Tim 234
Field, L., Gnecco, C., and Watkins, J. 35
Fielder, Wilfried 180
finance: financial crime, shop owners'
information and investigation of 159;
financial investigation techniques,
effective application of 160–61;
financial structure of antiquities trade
36–9. see also artifact smuggling,
financial investigations in battle
against
Finkel, I. and Taylor, J. 129n5, 130n16
Finley, Moses I. 178
First Impressions (Collon, D.) 125
Fisk, Robert 29
FMRD (Die Fundmünzen der
römischen Zeit in Deutschland) 183,
197
forgeries: faking of antiquities, Syrian
conflict and increase in 33; layout of
main differences between genuine
seals and 127; provenances, invention
of 26; scribes and seal cutters in
ancient Near East 117–19
Forum Ancient Coins 223
Fossey, John M. 29–30
Foster, Benjamin 130n12
FPIT (Facebook Profile Intel Tool)
229–30
Frahm, Eckart 75
France 6, 143, 145, 228, 230
free trade zones and duty-free
transhipment 29
Freeman, David John 88n26
FSA (Free Syrian Army): antiquities
trafficking from Syria by Northern
Route 147, 150, 151, 152, 153; Syrian
antiquities, looting and trafficking of
23, 39, 41

Ganor, Amir 5
Gellner, Mark J. 129n9
geographical factors, smuggling and 141
George, Andrew 64, 82, 83, 86n11
Gephi 229
Germany 27–8, 36, 140–141, 143, 145–6,
183–4, 196, 227–8; FMRD (Die

248 Index

Fundmünzen der römischen Zeit in Deutschland) 183, 197
Gerstenblith, Patty 5, 8, 12–13, 130n19, 215n11, 226; looted and smuggled ancient coins, case of 180, 181–2, 188–9n1; looting of archaeological artifacts from Iraq, case study on 59–95
Gesche, Petra D. 130n13
Gibson, McGuire 74, 84n1
Giglio, M. and Al-Awad, M. 31, 32, 33, 34, 35, 37, 40
Giglio, Mike 28
"Gilgamesh Dream Tablet" 59, 64–8, 74–5, 77–8, 79–80, 82, 83, 84, 85n5, 86n11, 87n16
Global Financial Integrity (GFI) 162
Global Terrorism Database (GTD) 137
GMV (Gross Merchandise Volume) 197, 211
Gobat, J. and Kostial, K. 35
Göbl, Robert 178
Goldstein, Caroline 84–5n2
Goodhand, Jonathan 35
Gordley, James 87n20
Gorelick, L. and Gwinnett, A.J. 131n25
Gorelick, Leonard 121, 126, 131n25
Grant, Daniel 86n12
Grantham, David 41
Greek coins, production of 185
Green, David 60
Green, P. and Mackenzie, S.R.M. 9
Green, Steve 59, 60–62, 63, 79, 82–3, 84n1, 86n6
Green family 59, 60, 80, 84, 85n5, 89n35
Greenland, F., Marrone, J., Topçuoğlu, O., and Vorderstrasse, T. 33, 60
Greshko, Michael 60
Guardian 151; Syrian antiquities, looting and trafficking of 41
Gumtree 219

Hackmey, Joseph David 64, 86n10
Hacksilber pieces 194
Hall, John 41
Halperin, Julia 226
Hammade, H. 131n22
Hansa 219, 220
Hanson, Katharyn 84n1
Hardy, Sam 21, 33, 46
Harkin, James 23, 32
Harmonized Tariff Schedule (Harm.TS) 26

Hashemi, Layla 3–20, 30, 31, 84n1, 215n1, 215n6, 218–39
Hekking, Morgan 234
Hellenistic period (323–31 BCE), proliferation of coinage in 194
Herbert, Matt 23, 139, 146, 149
Heritage Auctions 212
Higgins, Charlotte 60
HM Revenue & Customs v. Al Qassas 88n24
Hobby Lobby Stores Inc. 59–60, 61–3, 64–5, 67–8, 72, 81, 82–3, 84n1, 85n5, 89n38; law and 77–80; looting of artifacts from Iraq and 74–7
House of Representatives Committee on Homeland Security (HSC) 41–2
Howard, R.D., Prohov, J., and Elliott, M. 41
HTS (Hay'at Tahrir al-Sham) 14; antiquities trafficking from Syria by Northern Route 138, 151, 153, 154n11; artifact smuggling, financial investigations in battle against 165; online sale of illicit antiquities 232–3; Syrian antiquities, looting and trafficking of 22, 24, 39, 40, 41, 46
Hufnagel, S. and Chappell, D. 9
Hunter, Isabel 44
Hurras Al-Din in Syria 233
Hurriyet Gazetesi 145
Hussein, Saddam 74

ICGH (Inventory of Greek Coin Hoards) 215n10
ICSR (International Centre for the Study of Radicalisation) 39, 47
identification of ancient Near East seals 123–5
Iliad (Homer) 104
illicit antiquities trade 3; ancient coin market and 4; antiquities market and 3–4; cross-border networks and 5; forgeries and 4; history of crime and 4; illegally excavated material, flow of 196–7; illicit artifact flow chart 165; illicit supply chain networks 168; indiscriminate trade in ancient coins, looting and 178; international dealers engaged in antiquities trafficking, linkages and networks of 147–9; international recommendations and laws, recent changes in 174; Internet sales, continuance of 30–31; investigation of, online sales and

Index 249

234–6; law enforcement and 6–7, 18; looted and smuggled ancient coins, attention to 179–80; looted antiquities, laundering of 5; looted treasures and antiquities, market for 193, 196–7, 198–9; looting, frequency and location of 159; looting in Syria, evidence of 194–5; looting in Syria, recent history of 22–5; market routes, timelines and 80–82; marketplace countries 227; niche market 11; red flags of 166; smuggling and 4–5; tax evasion and 4; trade-based money laundering, process of 160; trade out of Syria 26–9; traded material, changing nature of 31–4; trafficking routes, changes in preference for 152; transit trade, facilitation by ethnic and linguistic continuities 27; victims of 7

Immigration and Customs Enforcement (ICE) in United States 162, 169

importation contrary to law: improper declaration 72–4; stolen property 71–2

Instagram: online sale of illicit antiquities 219, 222, 236; Syrian antiquities, looting and trafficking of 31

Institute of Numismatics in Vienna 197

interdisciplinary analysis 10

International Association of Professional Numismatists (IAPN) 179, 180, 181

international cooperation 6

INTERPOL 163

Iraq, looting of archaeological artifacts from 12–13, 59–90; Affordable Care Act (ACA) in US 59, 83; Ashmolean Museum collection in UK 88n28; *Burwell v. Hobby Lobby Stores, Inc.,* 573 U.S. 682 (2014) 59, 85n5; Butterfield & Butterfield, San Francisco 64, 65, 68; case study background 60–68; Christie's New York 86n10, 86n12–13; Convention on Cultural Property Implementation Act (CCPIA) in US 68, 69–71, 77, 86n16, 87n20–22; Cuneiform Digital Library Initiative (CDLI) 88n28, 89n32; Database of Neo-Sumerian Texts (BDTNS) 89n32; deterrent effect 82–3; EPIC Antiquities Act in US 86n16; forfeiture (2017) 60–63; "Gilgamesh Dream Tablet" 59, 64–8, 74–5, 77–8, 79–80, 82, 83, 84, 85n5, 86n11, 87n16; Green family 59, 60,

80, 84, 85n5, 89n35; HM Revenue & Customs v. Al Qassas 88n24; Hobby Lobby Stores Inc. 59–60, 61–3, 64–5, 67–8, 72, 81, 82–3, 84n1, 85n5, 89n38; Hobby Lobby Stores Inc., law and 77–80; Hobby Lobby Stores Inc., looting of artifacts from Iraq and 74–7; importation contrary to law – improper declaration 72–4; importation contrary to law - stolen property 71–2; Iraq Stabilization and Insurgency Sanctions Regulations in US 86n16; Iri-Sağrig tablets 72, 75–6, 77, 80, 81, 84, 88n28, 89n32–3; ISIL (Islamic State of Iraq and the Levant) 59–60, 74, 77, 89n30; Israel, legal trade in archaeological artifacts from 81; law, Hobby Lobby and the 77–8; legal framework 68–74; lessons learned (and not learned) 80–84; *Lost Heritage: Antiquities Stolen from Iraq's Regional Museums* (Oriental Institute, Chicago University) 88n25; market routes, timelines and 80–82; Museum of the Bible 59, 77, 79–80, 82, 84–5n2, 85n5; National Stolen Property Act (NSPA) on US 71, 87n21–2; Payne-Aldrich Tariff Act (1909) in US 88n23; *Republic of Iran v. The Barakat Galleries Ltd.,* E.W.C. A. Civ. 1374; (2007) 86n18; scholars, role of 83–4; Stipulation Agreement and "missing" artifacts (2017) 79–80; UNESCO Convention on Means of Prohibiting and Preventing Illicit Import, Export and Transport of Ownership of Cultural Property (1970) 68, 81, 86–7n14–15; implementation of 69–71; UNIDROIT Convention on Stolen or Illegally Exported Cultural Objects 86–7n14; UNITAR 89n34; United States, false documentation for Hobby Lobby objects 81; United States, Government Complaint in Hobby Lobby case 59, 60–62, 63, 64–9, 77–8, 79, 82; United States, informal entry process for low-value goods 63; United States, legality of objects in 87n20; *United States. v. McClain* 71, 86n17, 86n19; *United States. v. Schultz* 71, 78, 83, 86n18–19, 89–90n38; United States State Department 81; *United States v.*

250   *Index*

Antique Platter of Gold 88n23; *United States v. One Cuneiform Tablet Known as the Gilgamesh Dream Tablet, Answer of Claimant Hobby Lobby Stores, Inc.,* Civ. No. 20–2222 (E.D.N. Y. 2020) 68; US Immigration and Customs Enforcement (ICE) 88n25

Iri-Sağrig tablets 72, 75–6, 77, 80, 81, 84, 88n28, 89n32–3

ISIL (Islamic State of Iraq and the Levant): artifact smuggling, financial investigations in battle against 160, 165; eBay, ancient coin sales on 193; Iraq, looting of archaeological artifacts from 59–60, 74, 77, 89n30

ISIS (Islamic State of Iraq and Syria) 14; antiquities trafficking from Syria by Northern Route 137–8, 150–51, 152; eBay, ancient coin sales on 193; online sale of illicit antiquities 232, 233, 235; raid by US forces on ISIS Diwan al Rikaz (Ministry of Natural Resources and Minerals) 31, 40, 42; Syrian antiquities, looting and trafficking of 21–2, 23, 24, 28–9, 31, 33, 38, 39–41, 42–3, 45–7

Israel: Israel Antiquities Authority 5, 204; legal trade in archaeological artifacts from 81

Italy 5, 28, 72, 81, 146, 173, 184, 187, 196, 198, 227; Carabinieri Command for the Protection of Cultural Heritage 163, 175n5–7

Jaba, H. and Arbuthnott, G. 23

JAN (Jabhat al-Nusra): antiquities trafficking from Syria by Northern Route 154n11; Syrian antiquities, looting and trafficking of 21–2, 23, 24, 28, 39, 41

Jarus, Owen 76, 84, 89n33

Jataware Corp 220, 221, 224, 236n1

Jenrick, Robert 41

Jordan as transit route for Syrian and Iraqi antiquities 29

Justice Department in United States 5, 169, 181

Justnes, Årstein 85n4

Kadi, Samar 23

Kaercher, K., Penacho, S., Burge, K., O'Connell, J., and Gabriel, M. 23, 24

Kantchev, Georgi 216n29, 233

Kar, Dev 162

Keller, Andrew 31, 40, 150

Kellner, Mark A. 60

Kennedy, Elizabeth 144

Kenoyer, J.M. and Vidale, M. 131n25

Kersel, Morag M. 81, 84n1, 178

Kheldsberg, Ludvik A. 85n4

Khouli, Jack 170

Khouli, Mousa (Morris) 168–73

Kirisci, K. and Ferris, E. 153n4

Klein, Eitan 81

Klengel-Brandt, E. 131n25

Kloha, Jeff 65, 84–5n2

Koch, Ulla. S. 130n14

Koltrowitz, S. and Arnold, P. 7

Kovacs, Renee 64, 83

Kraay, Colin M. 178

Krebs, Brian 225

KYM (Know Your Customer) 224, 236n1

Lahanier, C. 131n25

Lamb, Franklin 24, 44

Lambert, Wilfred G. 130n17, 131n25

Larsen, M.T. 129n4

law: enforcement of, focus of expertise in 164; enforcement of, pressures on 162; Hobby Lobby and the 77–8; legal framework, looting from Iraq and 68–74; prosecution, failures of 187–8

Lebanon 6

Levine, Jane 84n1

Lightfoot, Chris S. 153n5

Limoges, B., Alhawamdeh, A., and Khaled a-Noufal, W. 24, 27, 35, 40, 41

Liveauctioneers 219

local participants along Northern Route 146–9

looting: archaeological site looting (post-2011), preferential targets for 33–4; archaeological site looting (post-2011), satellite imagery of 24–5; case study, looting of archaeological artifacts from Iraq 60–68; coins for sale, widespread looting and 213; deterrent effect on looting of archaeological artifacts 82–3; forfeiture (2017) of looted artifacts from Iraq 60–63; frequency and location of 159; Hobby Lobby Stores Inc. and looting of artifacts from Iraq 74–7; legal framework, looting from

Iraq and 68–74; looted and smuggled ancient coins, attention to 179–80; looted antiquities, laundering of 5; looted treasures and antiquities, market for 193, 196–7, 198–9; market routes, timelines and 80–82; seizure of looted coins in US 182–7; shipwreck off coast of Turkey, looting from 104; sources of looted coins 159; in Syria, evidence of 194–5; in Syria, recent history of 22–5. *see also* ancient coins, case about looting and smuggling of; Iraq, looting of archaeological artifacts from; Syrian antiquities, looting and trafficking of

Lost Heritage: Antiquities Stolen from Iraq's Regional Museums (Oriental Institute, Chicago University) 88n25

Loughnane, Michael 6–7, 8, 14–15, 27, 158–77

Louvre Museum 6

Loveluck, Louisa 41

Luck, Taylor 29, 39

Lufkin, Martha 44

Mabillard, Boris 27

Macedonian bronze coins 185

Machemer, Theresa 173

Mackenzie, S, and Yates, D. 25

Mackenzie, S., Brodie, N., and Yates, D., with Tsirogiannis, C. 25, 30

Mackenzie, Simon 82

Macquisten, Ivan 32

Macrinus (Marcus Ophilius Macrinus) 194

Mahrzahn, J. 131n25

Makarenko, Tamara 40

Maltego media scraper 221, 224

Manishtushu, king of Akkad 117

mapping and visualizing online networks 230–31

Marrone, James 216n21

Martin, Patrick 139

Mashberg, Tom 48n16

McAndrew, James 32, 34, 45, 86n12

McCarthy, Niall 47

McCoy, Kevin 226

Meadows, A.R. and Wartenberg, U. 215n5

Memoranda of Understanding (MOUs) with United States 198

Menegazzi 89n29

Merrillees, R.S. 121

Mesopotamia, administrative devices from south of 98

metal weights 115

methodologies for studies: antiquities trafficking from Syria by Northern Route 138; eBay, ancient coin sales on 200–201

Michelotos, Ioanni 153n2

Mladenov, Andrei 28

Molina, Manuel 75–6, 80, 88n28

Money Laundering 161; antiquities trade, 37, 164; legislation, 174, organized crime, 35

monuments 110–14

Moody, Oliver 41

Moos, Oliver 140, 151, 233; looting and trafficking of Syrian antiquities 23, 24, 27, 28, 31, 33, 35, 37, 40, 41

Morrison, Cecile 37

Moss, C.R. and Baden, J.S. 59, 60, 85n3, 85n5

Mosul Museum in Iraq 232

Museum of the Bible 59, 77, 79–80, 82, 84–5n2, 85n5

Myers, S.L. and Kulish, N. 32, 33

nails (antiquities) 115

Naím, Moisés 36

Nassar, A. and Atieh, N. 24

National Defense Authorization Act in United States 226

National Stolen Property Act (NSPA) in US 71, 87n21–2

Naylor, R.T. 39

NBC 151

Near East: antiquities from, market for 96, 128; conflict in 96. *see also* scribes and seal cutters in ancient Near East

NEST (Nafertiti Eastern Sculptures Trading) 169, 172, 173

Neumann, Peter 46–7

Nicomedia in northwest Turkey 183–4

Noroozian, A., Koenders, J., Van Veldhuizen, E., Hernandez Gañán, C., et al. 225

Nørskov, Vinnie 65

Northern Route, antiquities traffickers along 144–51. *see also* antiquities trafficking from Syria by Northern Route

numismatic auctions 196–7

numismatic evidence 194

Numismatic Guaranty Corporation 210

numismatic material, knowledge of 179

252 *Index*

Object ID program (International Council of Museums) 163, 175n9

O'Keefe, Patrick 69

Old Assyrian period (1970–1700 B.C.E.), case from 96–7

omens 110

Omidyar, Pierre 197

online auction platforms and: scribes and seal cutters in ancient Near East 120, 127, 128–9

online investigations, tools for 223–4

online sale of illicit antiquities 16, 218–37; Al-Qaeda 233; Alibaba 219; AlphaBay 219, 220; Amazon 219; Analyst Notebook media scraper 221; antiques monitoring on eBay, results from (2014–2017) 227–8; antiquities sales, explanation of average sale 226–7; antiquities trade, global and dynamic nature of 235–6; app development, filling gap through 229–30; ATHAR (Antiquities Trafficking and Anthropology Research Project) 233; Augustus Coins 223; Bank Secrecy Act (BSA) in United States 226; Barakat Gallery 219; blended sites (combining features of social media and listings websites) 222–3; Butler app (Jataware Corp) 220, 221, 224, 236n1; buyer feedback on sites 222–3; CITES (Convention on International Trade in Endangered Species) 234; CLASI (Countering the Looting of Antiquities from Syria and Iraq) 218–19, 228, 229, 233, 235; Coin Talk 223; counterfeit goods on Dark Web 226; Craigslist 219; Crypto Market 219, 220; Dark Web markets 219–20; Dark Web monitoring 220, 224–6; Darknet Market Archives 225; DARPA (Defense Advanced Research Projects Agency): MEMEX program 220, 224, 236n1; Datawalk media scraper 221; democratization of antiquities trade 218; Dream Market 219, 220; eBay 219, 222, 223; eBay, activities on 228; eBay, antiques monitoring on, results from (2014–2017) 227–8; Etsy 223; EUROPOL 234; Facebook 219, 222, 223, 234, 236; Facebook, contacts of known dealers on 230–31; Facebook, monitoring of 221; Facebook Black

Market in Antiquities: Trafficking, Terrorism, and War Crimes (2019 Report) 233; Facebook Community Standards 234; Facebook Groups 233; Forum Ancient Coins 223; FPIT (Facebook Profile Intel Tool) 229–30; Gephi 229; Gumtree 219; Hansa 219, 220; HTS (Hay'at Tahrir al-Sham) 232–3; Hurras Al-Din in Syria 233; illicit antiquities trade, investigation of 234–6; Instagram 219, 222, 236; investigative tools, limits and possibilities 231–2; ISIS (Islamic State of Iraq and Syria) 232, 233, 235; Jataware Corp 220, 221, 224, 236n1; KYM (Know Your Customer) 224, 236n1; Liveauctioneers 219; Maltego media scraper 221, 224; mapping and visualizing networks 230–31; marketplace countries 227; marketplace data collection 221; monitoring methodology 218–21; monitoring methodology, monitoring information 219; monitoring methodology, online sales monitoring list 220; monitoring methodology, overview 219; monitoring methodology, search items 219; Mosul Museum in Iraq 232; National Defense Authorization Act in United States 226; online forums 222; online illicit trade networks, use of data to detect 228–9; online sales platforms 10; online transactions on eBay 197, 212–13; open web markets 236; OSINT (open source intelligence) investigations 221, 223, 228–9, 236, 237n5; Palantir media scraper 221; Rest API software tool 224; Sayari (global data provider) 227, 237n6; ShadowDragon media scraper 221; ShadowDragon OI Monitor 220, 224, 237n2; Silk Road 3 219, 220; Sixbid 219; SNA (social network analysis) 223–4, 229, 237n4; social media 222; social media research, effective method 235; SocialNet 224, 229; Tableau Web Connector 221; Telegram 233; terrorist financing, establishment of links to 232–4; Timeline Auctions, activities on 228; Tochka 219, 220; tools for online investigations of trafficking networks 223–4; TOR (The Onion Router) 219,

224; TraCCC (Terrorism, Transnational Crime and Corruption Center) at George Mason University 219; Trocadero 219; Twitter 219; Valhalla 219, 220; victimless crimes, antiquities and counterfeit goods as 225; WallStreet Market 219, 220; web scrapers 221, 237n3; WhatsApp 233; White Shadow auctions 219, 220; Yahoo Groups 222; Youtube 219; Zinki Brigade 233
Orenstein, Karin 63
OSINT (open source intelligence) 16; investigations 221, 223, 228–9, 236, 237n5
Otto, Adelheid 124
Owen, D. and Mayr, R.H. 84
Owen, David 76, 83, 84
Ozaki, Tobru 79, 85n5, 89n31, 89n33

Palantir media scraper 221
Palmyra, looting of (2012) 23
Parapetti, Roberto 89n29
Parkinson, J., Albayrak, A., and Mavin, D. 27, 42
Paul, Katie 225
Payne-Aldrich Tariff Act (1909) in US 88n23
Payraud, Valentin 6
Pike, D.V. and Friedman, L.M. 72
Pittman, Holly. 130n21, 131n22
Polk, M. and Shuster, A.M.H. 142
Pond, Shelly 85n5
Popper, Nathaniel 220
Porada, Edith 130n21, 131n22
Portman, R. and Carper, T. 8, 11, 18, 161
possessions, Sumerian proverb about 96
Press, Michael 32
Price, M. and Waggoner, N. 215n9
prisms (antiquities) 115–16
'project informants' (PIs) on Syrian antiquities 47–8
Pryor, Riah 226
public auctions of coins before eCommerce 196
Pulak, Cemal 130n11

Qardash, Abdul Nasser 43

Radner, K. and Robson, E. 129–30n10, 129n5, 129n7, 130n13–14
Rakic, Yelena Z. 124

RAND Corporation Report (2020) 7, 15–16, 17; ancient coin sales on eBay 199–200, 211, 212, 213
Reinhard, Andrew 215n1
Republic of Iran v. The Barakat Galleries Ltd., E.W.C.A. Civ. 1374; (2007) 86n18
Rest API software tool 224
Reuter, P. and Petrie, C. 139
Revenu, Nathalie 29
Rihani, Ghassan 64, 74
Robertson, Roland 31
Rollston, Christopher 60
Roman mints, examples of 183–4
Roman Republican coinage project (Richard Schaefer) 197
Roman Syria, coinage in circulation in 194
RT News 40
Ruggiero, Vincenzo 40
Ruiz, Christina 33
Russell, John M. 88n25

Sabah Gazetesi 145; Syrian antiquities, looting and trafficking of 28
Sargent, M., Marrone, J.V., Evans, A., Lilly, B., et al. 3, 7, 8, 10, 11, 16, 17, 31, 165; ancient coin sales on eBay, analysis of 211, 216n20; online trade of illicit antiquities 233
Saudi Gazette 6
Sax, M. and Meeks, N.D. 131n25
Sax, M., Collon, D., and Leese, M.N. 131n25
Sax, M., McNabb J. and Meeks, N.D. 131n25
Sax, M., Meeks, N.D., and Collon, D 121, 131n25
Sax, Margaret 131n25
Sayari (global data provider) 227, 237n6
Sayyaf, Abu 31, 32–3, 38, 40, 42
Schaefer, Richard 197
Schneider, F. and Savasan, F. 139
scholarly tablets from first millennium 102–3
scholars, role in looting of archaeological artifacts from Iraq 83–4
schools and scribal art 108–10
Schøyen, Martin 88n26
Schultz, Fred 82
Schuster, Ruth 5
scribes and seal cutters in ancient Near East 13, 96–132; Akkadian language,

254 *Index*

use of 98; Akkadian period seals 123–4; *American Journal of Semitic Languages* 96; *Ancient Near Eastern Cylinder Seals* (Teissier, B.) 125; antiquities market, ancient Near East seals on 119–20; bricks 115; CLASI (Countering the Looting of Antiquities from Syria and Iraq) 129; clay cones 115; clay tablets, earliest writing inscribed on 98–9; clay tablets, preparation for inscription 99–101; commercial tablets, Neo and Late Babylonian (7th-2nd century B.C.E.) 99; conflict in Near East 96; counterfeit and suspect seals 125–8; cuneiform tablets, birth of writing and 97–103; cylinders 115–16; *First Impressions* (Collon, D.) 125; forgeries 117–19; forgeries, layout of main differences between genuine seals and 127; identification of ancient Near East seals 123–5; Mesopotamia, administrative devices from south of 98; metal weights 115; monuments 110–14; nails 115; Near Eastern antiquities, market for 96, 128; Old Assyrian period (1970–1700 B.C.E.), case from 96–7; omens 110; online auction platforms and 120, 127, 128–9; possessions, Sumerian proverb about 96; prisms 115–16; scholarly tablets from first millennium 102–3; schools and scribal art 108–10; seals and sealings from ancient Near East 120–23, 128–9; seals from early 2nd millennium B.C.E. 124–5; sign forms, emergence of 99; smuggling goods in ancient Near East 96–7, 128; stone weights 116; Sumerian language, use of 98; temples, palaces and monuments 110; Ur III (2100–2000 B.C.E.) messenger tablets 99; writing boards 104–8
SCTH (Saudi Commission for Tourism and National Heritage) 6
Seevers, B. and Korhonen, R. 121
Seif, Assad 27–8, 145
seizure of looted coins in US 181–7; analysis of 182–7; Byzantine coins 183, 184; forgeries of ancient coins mixed in 186; Greek coins 185, 186; late Roman bronze coins 183, 184; locally diagnostic types 183, 185; medieval and modern coins 186, 187;

photographs of 182; regionally diagnostic types 183, 185; Roman provincial coins 182–3, 185–6, 187
sellers, paid lobbyists for 178
Sewell, Abby 32
Shabi, Rachel 34
Shabiha criminal gangs 23
ShadowDragon media scraper 221
ShadowDragon OI Monitor 220, 224, 237n2
Shalmaneser III 110
Sharpe, Michael 64, 82, 83
Shelley, F.M. and Metz, R. 12, 140
Shelley, Louise I. 3–20, 31, 36, 40, 84n1, 215n1; antiquities trafficking from Syria along Northern Route 150, 154n7; financial investigations in battle against artifact smuggling 162; online trade in illicit antiquitiesantiquities, investigation of 225
Sherlock, R. and Malouf, C. 139
Shipman, Donald Jonathan 85n5
shop owners, role in supply chains 158
sign forms, emergence of 99
Sigrist, M. and Ozaki, T. 76–7, 79, 85n5
Sigrist, Marcel 84, 89n31
Silk Road 3 219, 220
Simpson, St John 132n26
Singh, M. and Stroul, D. 150
Sixbid sales platform: eBay, ancient coin sales on 210; online sale of illicit antiquities 219
Skoll, Jeffrey 197
Slanski, Kathryb 130n15
Small, Zachary 11, 226
"small dollar terrorism" 46–7
smuggling antiquities: in ancient Near East 96–7, 128; illicit networks and 158; methods for evading inspections 25–6; target-rich market 161
smuggling of coins: circulation processes, realities of 179; coins for sale, widespread looting and 213; continuance of 143–4
Smyth, Phillip 150
SNA (Syrian National Army) 14; antiquities trafficking from Syria by Northern Route 151, 152, 153
social media 222
social media apps, accessibility of 31
social media research, effective method for 235

Index 255

social network analysis (SNA) 223–4, 229, 237n4
SocialNet 224, 229
Soguel, Dominique 23, 28
Sotheby's London 120, 196
Sotheby's New York 29, 75, 86
Spar, I. and Jursa, M. 129n7
Spar, Ira 4, 7, 13, 96–134
Sputnik News 44
St Hilaire, Rick 26, 44, 45, 169
Staley, David 35
Stanyard, J. and Dhaouadi, R. 3, 10
Steinhardt, Michael 72
Stipulation Agreement and "missing" artifacts (2017) 79–80
Stolen-Works-of-Art-Database 175n8
Stone, Elizabeth 74
stone weights 116
Stoughton, India 27, 28
Studevent-Hickman, Benjamin 44
"subsistence digging" 35
Sullivan, A. and Satter, R. 225
Sumerian language, use of 98
supply chains 3, 5, 6, 9, 10, 14, 159, 178, 223, 224, 229, 232; corruption and maintenance of 12; criminal networks and 158; criminal supply chain for antiquities 33, 164–8; detection and disruption of 17–18; example of 230; financial investigation of 174; global supply chains 175; insurgent and terrorist networks in 160; international supply chains 8, 18; key components within, identification of 161; key facilitators 173; shop owners and 158; stages of 226; terrorist groups and 160–61; transnational criminal organizations and 159–60; transnational supply chains, elusive nature of 236
Swann, Steve 140, 234
SWIFT messaging 167
Pope Sylvester I 18n1, 130n18
Syria: Association for the Protection of Syrian Archaeology (APSA) 47n3; borderland areas, criminal groups in 141; coinage in ancient Syria, history of 194; "conflict" and "criminal economies" in 35; destination countries for Syrian antiquities 140; Director of Antiquities in 140; documented archaeological sites in 140; drug trafficking in 139–40; illicit economy and antiquities trafficking in 139–40; insurgent and terrorist groups operating in 150–51; local trafficking groups in 153–4n6; map of 22; oil smuggling in 139; proxy wars and insurgent groups in 137; transit routes out of 26–7. *see also* antiquities trafficking from Syria by Northern Route

Syrian antiquities, looting and trafficking of 12, 21–48; AFP (Agence France Press) 23, 32, 44; AGI (Il Giornale dell' Arte) 23; Aleppo Governorate, Afrin district of 24; American Association for the Advancement of Science (AAAS) 23, 24; American Society of Overseas Research (ASOR) 23, 32; American Society of Overseas Research Cultural Heritage Initiatives (ASOR CHI) 47n3; ancient coins and small antiquities, commercial importance of 46–7; ANSA (Armed Non-State Actors) 21–2, 39–41, 45, 46, 47; antiquities trade, changing nature of 29–31; antiquities trade, transnational structure and operation of 25–6; antiquities trafficking, actual value for ISIS of 43; antiquities trafficking, armed violence and 21; antiquities trafficking, Syrian trade before 2011 considered unproblematic 44; AP (Associated Press) 28; archaeological site looting (post-2011), preferential targets for 33–4; archaeological site looting (post-2011), satellite imagery of 24–5; BBC 23, 36, 48n24; Bulgarian seizure of Syrian artifacts (March 2015) 28; CBS News 32; CCP (Cultural Property News) 32, 42; CNN (Cable News Network) 24; "conflict" and "criminal economies" 35; criminal organization and operation of antiquities trade 34–6; Darknet antiquities trading 31; dealers or collectors, difficulties of proving criminal intent by 45; DGAM (Directorate-General of Antiquities and Museums) in Syria 23, 24, 32; diplomatic and military personnel, exemption from customs inspections 26; electronic messaging, encrypted means of 31; evidence-based analysis 21–2, 42, 46; Facebook 31; Facebook group memberships, network analysis of 36; Facebook Messenger 31; faking of antiquities, Syrian conflict and increase in 33; FBI (Federal Bureau of Investigation) 26; financial structure of antiquities trade 36–9; free trade zones and duty-free transhipment 29; FSA (Free Syrian Army) 23, 39, 41; *Guardian* 41; Harmonized Tariff Schedule (Harm.TS) 26; House of Representatives Committee on Homeland Security (HSC) 41–2; HTS (Hay'at Tahrir al-Sham) 22, 24, 39, 40, 41, 46; ICSR (International Centre for the Study of Radicalisation) 39, 47; Instagram 31; Internet sales, continuance of 30–31; ISIS (Islamic State of Iraq and Syria) 21–2, 23, 24, 28–9, 31, 33, 38, 39–41, 42–3, 45–7; JAN (Jabhat al-Nusra) 21–2, 23, 24, 28, 39, 41; Jordan as transit route for Syrian and Iraqi antiquities 29; looting in Syria, recent history of 22–5; monetary value of ANSA, terrorist profiting and 41–3; Palmyra, looting of (2012) 23; policy failure, questions about 43–5; "project informants" (PIs) 47–8; provenances, invention of 26; raid by US forces on ISIS Diwan al Rikaz (Ministry of Natural Resources and Minerals) 31, 40, 42; RT News 40; *Sabah Gazetesi* 28; "small dollar terrorism" 46–7; smuggling antiquities, methods for evading inspections 25–6; social media apps, accessibility of 31; specialized services, organized crime and access to 35; Sputnik News 44; "subsistence digging" 35; Syria, map of 22; Syria, transit routes out of 26–7; Syrian Late Roman floor mosaics delivered from Lebanon to Montreal (1991–96) 29–30; Syrian mosaics crossing into Lebanon, seizure of (January 2013) 28; Telegram 31; terrorist profiting from antiques trade, ANSA and 39–41; TraCCC (Terrorism, Transnational Crime and Corruption Center) at George Mason University 38, 47n1; trade out of Syria 26–9; traded material, changing nature of 31–4; transit trade, facilitation by ethnic and linguistic continuities: across borders 27; Turkey, major transit country from Syria 28; Turkey,

media reports from south of 33; UNESCO Fighting the Illicit Trafficking of Cultural Property 48n17; United States 21, 23, 25–6, 32; United States, Byzantine mosaic shipped from Turkey to Long Beach 28; United States, documents seized during Abu Sayyaf raid 42; United States, Hellenistic-Roman gold ring sold for $260,000 38; valuable finds, expectations of 33; WhatsApp 31; YPG (Kurdish People's Protection Units) 28, 40

Tableau Web Connector 221
Tanret, M. 129–30n10
Taub, Ben 42
Taylor, Jonathan 72, 129n7
TBML (Trade-Based Money Laundering) 166–7
Teissier, Beatrice 124, 125, 131n22, 131n24
Telegram: online sale of illicit antiquities 233; Syrian antiquities, looting and trafficking of 31
Telegraph 88n24
temples, palaces and monuments 110
terrorists: along Northern Route 149–51; antiquities trafficking as lucrative source of income for 151–2; profiting from antiques trade, ANSA and 39–41; terrorist financing, establishment of links to 232–4; trafficking of antiquities by 138
Thailand 6
Tian, H., Gaffigan, S.M., West, D.S., and McCoy, D. 11, 225
Timeline Auctions, activities on 228
Tochka 219, 220
Todd, I.M. 129n5
Todd, Zoe 153n3
Tompa, P.K. and Brose, A. 181
Topal, Ahmet 28
Topçuoğlu, O. and Vorderstrasse, T. 30, 33, 60, 120, 216n19
TOR (The Onion Router) 219, 224
TraCCC (Terrorism, Transnational Crime and Corruption Center) at George Mason University 9, 10, 17; eBay, ancient coin sales on 193; online sale of illicit antiquities 219; Syrian antiquities, looting and trafficking of 38, 47n1

Index   257

trade-based money laundering 38, 47, process of 160, 167
transit trade, facilitation by ethnic and linguistic continuities 27
Transparency International 2019 Corruption Perceptions Index (CPI) 141
Trocadero 219
Trump, Donald 153
Turkey 5, 6, 8, 14, 23, 25, 28, 36–9, 40–41, 194–6, 205; Anti-Smuggling and Organized Crime Department (ASOD) in 138, 139–40, 141–2, 143–4, 145–6, 153n4; borderland areas, criminal groups in 141; disguise of purchases by traffickers in 143; illicit economy and antiquities trafficking in 140–44; local smugglers in, collaboration between 142–3; major transit country from Syria 28; media reports from south of 33; Museums in, signs of thefts of antiquities in 142; Nicomedia in northwest of 183–4; Northern route from Syria, trafficking through 137, 138–9, 140–46, 147, 149–53; northwestern Turkey, smuggling of coins from 183–7; provinces with most antiquities seized from traffickers 145; provinces with most antiquities trafficking investigations 144; shipwreck off coast of, looting from 104; transit market inside 44
Twitter 94, 219, 220, 221

Ulbricht, Bailey 151
Ulvin, Philippe Bédos 88n26
unauthorized excavations 198
uncleaned coins, data on 203–5
UNESCO Convention on Means of Prohibiting and Preventing Illicit Import, Export and Transport of Ownership of Cultural Property (1970) 6, 13; ancient coin sales on eBay and 212; implementation of 69–71; Iraq, looting of archaeological artifacts from 68
UNESCO Fighting the Illicit Trafficking of Cultural Property 48n17
UNIDROIT Convention on Stolen or Illegally Exported Cultural Objects 86–7n14
UNITAR International University 89n34

United Nations (UN): Office on Drugs and Crime (UNODC) Report (2009) 139; Security Council 150
United States: Affordable Care Act (ACA) in 59, 83; American Association for the Advancement of Science (AAAS) 23, 24; *American Journal of Semitic Languages* 96; American Numismatic Society 197; American Society of Overseas Research (ASOR) 23, 32; American Society of Overseas Research Cultural Heritage Initiatives (ASOR CHI) 47n3; Anti Money Laundering Act (2020) in 174–5; art sector regulatory controls in (2020) 174–5; Bank Secrecy Act (BSA) 11; Byzantine mosaic shipped from Turkey to Long Beach 28; Congress 11; Convention on Cultural Property Implementation Act (CCPIA) in 13, 68; Cultural Property Advisory Committee (CPAC) in 180; Customs and Border Protection in 181; Customs and Border Protection Strategy (2020–2025) 162; Department of Justice (DOJ) in 5, 169, 181; documents seized during Abu Sayyaf raid 42; due diligence and legality of coins imported into 214–15; EPIC Antiquities Act in 86n16; false documentation provided to customs for Hobby Lobby objects 81; FBI (Federal Bureau of Investigation) 26, 163, 175n4, 181–2, 188–9n1; financial system of 11; Hellenistic-Roman gold ring sold for $260,000 in 38; Homeland Security Department (DHS) 162–3; Homeland Security Department (DHS) Cultural Property, Art and Antiquities (CPAA) program 162–3; Homeland Security Department (DHS) Investigations, Immigration and Customs Enforcement (HSI) 162–3, 172; Homeland Security Investigations (HSI) in 181–2, 188–9n1; House of Representatives Committee on Homeland Security (HSC) 41–2; Immigration and Customs Enforcement (ICE) in 88n25; informal entry process for low-value goods in 63; Iraq, looting of archaeological artifacts from 59, 60–62, 63, 64–9,

Index

84n1, 86n8; Iraq invasion (2003) by 141, 152; Iraq Stabilization and Insurgency Sanctions Regulations in 86n16; Justice Department in 5, 169, 181; legality of objects in 87n20; National Defense Authorization Act 11; National Stolen Property Act (NSPA) in 71, 87n21–2; Payne-Aldrich Tariff Act (1909) in 88n23; raid by forces on ISIS Diwan al Rikaz (Ministry of Natural Resources and Minerals) 31, 40, 42; seizure of looted coins in 181–7; Senate Permanent Subcommittee on Investigations in 11, 161; State Department 9, 47n1, 70, 180–81, 188, 193, 219; Syrian antiquities, looting and trafficking of 21, 32; *United States. v. McClain* 71, 86n17, 86n19; *United States. v. Schultz* 71, 78, 83, 86n18–19, 89–90n38; *United States v. Antique Platter of Gold* 88n23; *United States v. One Cuneiform Tablet Known as the Gilgamesh Dream Tablet, Answer of Claimant Hobby Lobby Stores, Inc.,* Civ. No. 20–2222 (E.D.N. Y. 2020) 68; *United States v Khouli et al.* 168–73, 175n10–12, 176n15–20; wide circulation of ancient coins in, myth of 180–81

Ur III (2100–2000 B.C.E.) messenger tablets 99

Urice, S.K. and Adler, A. 181

Urice, Stephen K. 189n2

Vaballathus 194

Valhalla 219, 220

Van Lit, Tim 42

Van Tets, Fernande 39

VCcoins sales platform 210, 211, 212

Veldhuis, Nick 130n13

"vest pocket dealers" on eBay 196

Viano, Maurizio 75, 86n8

victimless crimes, antiquities and counterfeit goods as 225

Villanueva, Raymond 162

Von Kaenel, Hans-Markus 178

Waddell, Abi 6, 8, 9, 16, 30, 31, 215n6, 218–39

Walker, Alan S. 178

Walker, Christopher B.F. 129n5

WallStreet Market 219, 220

Wartenberg, Ute 7, 8, 15–16, 30, 33, 180, 188–9n1, 193–217

web scrapers 221, 237n3

websites: Art Crime Team website in United States 163; blended sites (combining features of social media and listings websites) 222–3; buyer feedback on sites 222–3

Westcott, Tom 3, 14, 232

Westenholz, Aage 83–4

WhatsApp: online sale of illicit antiquities 233; Syrian antiquities, looting and trafficking of 31

White Shadow auctions 219, 220

Whitehouse, Helen 225

Whitwam, Ryan 11, 225

Wilkinson, Alix 121

Williams, Phil 142

Willis, Richard S. 153–4n6

Wiseman, Donald J. 130n11

writing boards 104–8

Yahoo Groups 222

Yamada, S. and Shibata, D. 130n13

Yates, Donna 235

Yoon, Sangwon 32

Youtube 219

YPG (Kurdish People's Protection Units) 28, 40

Zablit, Jocelyne 23

Queen Zenobia 194

Zinki Brigade 233